1993

W9-AER-232

Visualization in Scientific Computing

VISUALIZATION in SCIENTIFIC COMPUTING

Gregory M. Nielson
and Bruce Shriver, Editors

Lawrence J. Rosenblum,
Associate Editor

IEEE COMPUTER SOCIETY PRESS TUTORIAL

Visualization in Scientific Computing

Gregory M. Nielson and Bruce Shriver, Editors

Lawrence J. Rosenblum, Associate Editor

IEEE Computer Society Press
Los Alamitos, California

Washington • Brussels • Tokyo

Library of Congress Cataloging-in-Publication Data

Visualization in scientific computing / edited by Gregory M. Nielson,
   Bruce D. Shriver ; associate editor of a section, Larry Rosenblum.
      p.   cm.
   Includes bibliographical references.
   ISBN 0-8186-8979-X : $74.00. -- ISBN 0-8186-5979-3 (microfiche)
   1. Computer graphics. 2. Visualization--Technique. I. Nielson,
Gregory M. II. Shriver, Bruce D., 1940-   . III. Rosenblum,
Lawrence J.
T385.V59 1990
620'.00285'66--dc20   90-1596
                                                                CIP

Published by

IEEE Computer Society Press
10662 Los Vaqueros Circle
P.O. Box 3014
Los Alamitos, CA 90720-1264

Sponsored by The IEEE Computer Society Technical Committee on Computer Graphics

Copyright – 1990 by the Institute of Electrical and Electronics Engineers, Inc.

Cover layout by Jack I. Ballestero

Upper right hand corner design from GAS (Graphics Animation System)

Center design global climatic effects of increased greenhouse gases. M.W. Washington and T.W. Bettge of NCAR performed the simulation; J.B. Yost of NCSA performed the visualization.

Bottom left hand from **Rhinovirus** – 1988 T.J. O'Donnell. Data courtesy of Dr. Rossmam, Crystallography Group, Purdue University. Image courtesy of the Electronic Visualization Laboratory, University of Illinois at Chicago

Bottom right hand from **Computational fluid dynamics** – 1989 Michael Norman and Donna Cox of NCSA, University of Illinois at Urbana-Champaign, and Jack Burns and Martin Sulkanen of the University of New Mexico.

Printed in United States of America

IEEE Computer Society Press Order Number 1979
Library of Congress Number 90-80532
IEEE Catalog Number EH0307-9
ISBN 0-8186-8979-X (case)
ISBN 0-8186-5979-3 (microfiche)

Additional copies can be ordered from:

IEEE Computer Society Press
Customer Service Center
10662 Los Vaqueros Circle
P.O. Box 3014
Los Alamitos, CA 90720-1264

IEEE Computer Society
13, Avenue de l'Aquilon
B-1200 Brussels
BELGIUM

IEEE Computer Society
Ooshima Building
2-19-1 Minami-Aoyama,
Minato-Ku
Tokyo 107, JAPAN

IEEE Service Center
445 Hoes Lane
P.O. Box 1331
Piscataway, NJ 08855-1331

Preface

Scientific Visualization is a new and emerging area that is having an impact on how computers are used in research. Scientific visualization is concerned with techniques that allow scientists and engineers to extract knowledge form the results of simulations and computations. Advances in scientific computation are allowing mathematical models and simulations to become increasingly complex and detailed. This results in a closer approximation to reality thus enhancing the possibility of acquiring new knowledge and understanding. Tremendously large collections of numerical values, which contain a great deal of information, are being produced and collected. The problem is to convey all of this information to the scientist so that effective use can be made of the human creative and analytic capabilities. This requires a method of communication with a high bandwidth and an effective interface. Computer generated images and human vision mediated by the principles of perceptual psychology are the means used in scientific visualization to achieve this communication. The foundation material for the techniques of scientific visualization are derived from many areas including computer graphics, image processing, computer vision, perceptual psychology, applied mathematics, computer aided design, signal processing, numerical analysis, and so forth.

The purpose of this text is to provide a reference source to scientists, engineers, and students who are new to scientific visualization or who are interested in expanding their knowledge in this subject. If used properly, it can also serve as an introduction and tutorial. The text is not intended to be read from beginning to end. One should first obtain an overview and then return to study those portions of particular interest.

The video, *Scientific Visualization* compiled by G.M. Nielson, is intended to accompany this text. Although they can be purchased separately, the text and the video are intended to form a package. Each complements the other. The book more nearly stands alone, but one will miss a great deal without the benefit of the video to help in understanding the ideas discussed in the papers. The tape definitely is not intended to be used without the book. It is boring and makes little sense without the material from the book. This has the implication that not only should the video not be viewed without the book, but it is necessary to read the material from the book prior to viewing a particular segment.

This text includes the articles from the August 1989 special visualization issue of *Computer* magazine in addition to the best articles that could not be included in the special issue because of space limitations.

The text is divided into five sections. Section 1 serves as an introduction and overview. In addition to some introductory comments, it includes an annotated bibliography and two survey papers. It may be somewhat unusual to put a bibliography into an introductory section, but the reason for this is that since this area is so new, an annotated bibliography makes for an excellent introduction to the subject. To get a quick idea of the essential material of a particular subtopic of interest, one can read in the annotated bibliography about the relevant recent publications. In Section 2, we have a collection of four foundation and technique papers. While the authors have described certain techniques relative to a particular application, for the most part the techniques have a much broader base of application and consequently become part of the foundation material of scientific visualization. Section 3 consists of a selection of application papers. The applications areas are very diverse and these papers represent a good sample of the universe of application areas for scientific visualization. Section 4 describes the activities in scientific visualization at several of the major research laboratories in the United States. The final section is devoted to the video that serves as a companion to this text.

Gregory M. Nielson
Bruce D. Shriver

Acknowledgments

Many people have contributed to this book and its companion video. We wish to thank the members of the Executive Committee of the IEEE Technical Committee on Computer Graphics for all of their help and support. Larry Rosenblum chaired and guided the committee during most of the time that this activity was going on and he deserves special acknowledgment for all of the effort he put forward. Other members of the Executive Committee during this project consisted of Maxine Brown, Michael Danchak, Tom Foley, Arie Kaufman, Gary Laguna, Steve Levine, Arthur Olson, John Sibert and Mark Skall. We would like to thank John Staudhammer for his general support of the TC on Computer Graphics and for his generous help on this particular project. Mike Wozny was very helpful during the early stages of this project.

We want to thank the members of the Computer Aided Geometric Design Group at ASU for their support and help. Bernd Hamann, Randy Heiland, David Lane, Brett Blomquist, and Joe Reuter have made direct contributions to this project for which we are grateful. Especially helpful during the compilation of the video were Ken Sweat and Wayne Woodland. We want to extend a special thanks to Tom Foley, who has been tremendously helpful on a myriad of tasks. We wish to thank Keith Voegele, who has been a great help in many ways, not the least of which has been as a good source of ideas.

We appreciate the support of the Department of Energy under contract DE-FG-02-87ER25041 to Arizona State University. And finally, special thanks to all the authors and referees. We have listed referees below. This not only serves to recognize these contributors, but it also adds to the list of people who have interest and expertise in the area of Scientific Visualization. For this reason, we have included their addresses.

Referees

Demetrio Manuel Aguero
Casilla de Correo 4745
(1000) Correo Central
Buenos Aires
ARGENTINA

Geoffrey C. Ashton
Department of Genetics
Biomed A-110
University of Hawaii
Honolulu, HI 96822

Norm Badler
Computer Information Science
Moore School D2
University of Pennsylvania
Philadelphia, PA 19104

Alan P. Bangs
Asset Consultants
2761 S. Westgate Ave.
Los Angeles, CA 90064

Richard Bartels
Dept. of Computer Science
University of Waterloo
Waterloo, Ontario N2L 3G1
Canada

Stephen Binkley
Combustion Science Dept.
Sandia National Laboratories
Livermore, CA 94550

Jim Blinn
Jet Propulsion Laboratory
4800 Oak Grove Drive
MS 510-113
Pasadena, CA 91109

Robert M. Blonchek
891 Elkridge Landing Road
Suite 310
Linthicum, MD 21090

Wim Boehm
Department of Computer Science
The University of Manchester
Oxford Rd., Manchester
ENGLAND

John Briggs
Evans and Sutherland Computer Corp.
P.O. Box 8700
580 Arapeen Drive
Salt Lake City, UT 84108

Peter L. Briggs
US West Advanced Technologies
Suite 240
6200 South Quebec Street
Englewood, CO 80111

Frederick P. Brooks, Jr.
University of North Carolina
New West Hall 035a
Chapel Hill, NC 27514

Glenn R. Bruns
MCC
3500 West Balcones Center Dr.
Austin, TX 78759]

David K. Campbell
Center for Nonlinear Studies MS B258
Los Alamos National Laboratory
Los Alamos, NM 87545

Mike Caplinger
Department of Geology
Arizona State University
Tempe, Arizona 85287

Loren Carpenter
Pixar
3240 Kerner Blvd.
San Rafael, CA 94901

Richard M. Casey
Alabama Supercomputer Center
686 Discovery Drive
Huntsville, Al 35806

Massimo Casilli
Via Liberta 88
37053 Cerea
ITALY

Hank Christiansen
Bringham Young University
Department of Civil Engineering
368 Clyde Building
Provo, Utah 84602

J. Dean Clamons
Naval Research Lab
Washington, DC 20375

Elaine Cohen
Dept. of Computer Science
3160 Merrill Engineering Bldg.
University of Utah
Salt Lake City, UT 84112

Terry L. Cole
Tensleep Design, Inc.
Suite 110
1112 West Ben White Blvd.
Austin, TX 78704

Robert P. Comer
The Analytic Sciences Corporation
55 Walkers Brook Dr.
Reading, MA 01867

Jim Connant
AT&T Pixel Machine
Crawford Corner Road
Holmdel, NJ 07737

Larry Cook
Medical Center
University of Kansas
Rainbow Blvd at 39th
Kansas City, KS 66103

Jerome R. Cox, Jr.
Department of Computer Science
Washington University
One Brookings Drive
St. Louis, MO 63130

Bjorn Cronhjort
Royal Institute of Technology
Department of Automatic Control
S-10044 Stockholm
SWEDEN

Martha Crosby
Info & Comp Sc, Keller 308
University of Hawaii
Honolulu, HI 96822

Franklin Crow
Xerox Palo Alto Research Center
3333 Coyote Hill Road
Palo Alto, CA 9304

Tony D. DeRose
Computer Science Dept.
University of Washington
Seattle, Washington 98195

John C. Dill
School of Engineering Science
Simon Fraser University
Burnaby, B.C. Canada
V5A 1S6

David P. Dobkin
Computer Science Dept.

Princeton University
Princeton, NJ 08544

David L. Donoho
Department of Statistics
Statistical Laboratory
University of California
Berkeley, CA 94270

Fred K. Duennebier
Hawaii Inst. of Geophys, HIG 262
University of Hawaii
2525 Correa Road
Honolulu, HI 96822

Rae A. Earnshaw
University of Leeds
Centre for Computer Studies
Leeds LS2 9JT
England

W. Van Edmond
University Honors College
Arizona State University
Tempe, AZ 85287-3102

Lionel N. M. Edward
Department of Electrical &
  Electronic Engineering
University of Canerbury
Private Bag
Christchurch
NEW ZEALAND

Rida T. Farouki
IBM Corporation
T. J. Watson Research Center
P. O. Box 218
Yorktown Heights, NY 10598

Thomas A. Foley
Computer Science Dept.
Arizona State University
Tempe, AZ 85287-5406

Alain Fournier
Dept. of Computer Science
University of Toronto
Toronto, Ontario M5S 1A4
Canada

Gerard J. Fryer
Haw Inst of Geopys, HIG 434
University of Hawaii
2525 Correa
Honolulu, HI96822

Dan Gordon
Department of Computer Science
Texas A&M University
College Station, Texas 77843-3112

Steve Goodnick

Electrical Engineering Department
Oregon State University
Corvallis, OR 97331

Ralph R. Grams
Department of Pathology
Division of Medical Systems
University of Florida, Box J-356
Gainsville, FL 32610

Donald Greenberg
Program of Computer Graphics
120 Rand Hall
Cornell University
Ithaca, NY 14853

James C. Greeson, Jr.
IBM H29/061
Box 12195
Research Triangle Park, NC 27709

Hans Hagen
Universitat Kaiserslautern
Graphische DV
  & Computer Geometric Design
Erwin - Schrudinger - Str. 48
6750 Kaiserslautern
West Germany

Bernd Hamann
Computer Science Department
Arizona State Unversity
Tempe, AZ 85287-5406

Lansing Hatfield
P.O. Box 808 L-156
Lawrence Livermore National Laboratory
Livermore, CA 94550

Patrick Heffernan
Hewlett-Packard Laboratories, Bldg. 28C
1651 Page Mill Road
Palo Alto, CA 94303

Randy Heiland
Computer Science Department
Arizona State University
Tempe, Arizona 85287-6405

Charles R. Henderson, Jr.
Cornell National Supercomp. Facility
Cornell University
Ithaca, NY 14853

Karl Hess
Coordinated Sciences Laboratory
University of Illinois
Urbana, IL 61801

Tim Hill
Department of Decision Sciences
University of Hawaii
2404 Maile Way, E-601J

Honolulu, HI 96822

Julia Hodges
Mississippi State University
Drawer CS
Department of Computer Science
Mississippi State, MS 39762-5623

Eric Hoffman
Department of Radiology
University of Pennsylvania
3400 Spruce Street
Philadelphia, PA 19104

H. Kay Howell
Naval Research Lab.
Code 2840
Washington, DC 20375-5000

Joseph E. Hueser
Old Dominion University
183 Revelle Dr.
Newport News, VA 23602

Ben Huey
Computer Science Department
Arizona State University
Tempe, Arizona 85287-5406

Terrance L Huntsberger
Intelligent Systems Laboratory
Department of Computer Science
University of South Carolina
Columbia, SC 29208

James Inglis
AT&T Bell Laboratories
Rm 3E-146
185 Manmouth Parkway
West Long Branch, NC 07764

Stephen Y. Itoga
Department of Information
  and Computer Science
University of Hawaii
Keller 310
Honolulu, HI 96822

James Ellwood Jordan
Rm. 233, Bldg. U-61, NAE
c/o National Research Council (CANADA)
Montreal Road
Ottawa
CANADA K1A 0R6

Jim Kajiya
California Institute of Technology
MS 256-80
Pasadena, CA 91125

Rangachar Kasturi
Department of EE
Pennsylvania State University

University Park, PA 16802

Stephen Keith
424 Custer Road
Hayward, CA 94544

Alex Kelley
AT&T Pixel Machines
Somerset, NJ

Mike Keeler
Stardent
880 West Maude Avenue
Sunnyvale, CA 94086

G. David Kerlick
M. S. 202A-14
NASA Ames Research Center
Moffett Field, CA 94035

Cheol Kim
Evans & Sutherland
580 Arapeen Drive
Salt Lake City, Utah 84108

David R. King
Execucom
9442 Capital of Texas Hwy.
Arboretum Plaza One
Austin, TX 78759

John Kramer
Institute for Defense Analysis
1801 N. Beauregard Street
Alexandria, VA 22311

Gary Laguna
P.O. Box 808, L-125
Lawrence Livermore Nat'l Laboratory
Livermore, CA 94550

William A. Lampe
Department of Mathematics
Physical Sciences 408
University of Hawaii
Honolulu, HI 96822

Thomas Lasinski
NAS Systems Development Branch
MS 258-5
NASA Ames Research Center
Moffet Field, CA 94086

Lawrence Lee
Theory Cntr Prod. Supercomputer Fac.
Cornell University
Ithaca, New York 14853

Haim Levkowitz
Cardiothoracic Imaging Research Center
Department of Radiology
University of Penn.
3400 Spruce Street

Philadelphia, PA 19104

Kin F. Li
Department of Electrical
 and Computer Engineering
University of Victoria
P. O. Box 1700
Victoria, B.C.
CANADA V8W 2Y2

Mark A. Linton
Center for Integrated Studies
CIS Bldg., Room 069
Stanford University
Stanford, CA 94305

Mike Littlejohn
Electrical and Computer Engineering
North Carolina State University
Raleigh, NC 27695

Stephen F. Lundstrom
PARSA
P. O. Box 9535
Stanford, CA 94309

Carl Machover
Machover Associates Corporation
199 Main Street
White Plains, NY 10601

Michael C. Malin
Department of Geology
Arizona State University
Tempe, Arizona 85287

Patrick Mantey
Dept. of Computer Engineering
335A Applied Science
University of California at Santa Cruz
Sana Cruz, CA 95064

Marialusia N. McAllister
Moravian College
Department of Mathematics
Bethlehem, PA 18018

David McAllister
Dept. Computer Science
North Carolina State University
Raleigh, NC

Bruce McCormick
Computer Science Dept.
237A Zachry Engineering Center
Texas A&M University
College Station, Texas 77843-3112

Daniel McShan
University of Michigan Hospital
1405 E. Ann Street
Ann Arbor, MI 48109

Cleve Moler
Stardent
880 West Maude Avenue
Sunnyvale, CA 94086

Lee R. Nackman
IBM Thomas J. Watson Research Center
P. O. Box 218
Yorktown Heights, NY 10598

Larry G. Nelson
Nelson Research
130 School Street
Webster, Massachusetts 01570

Hilarie Nickerson
Aaron Marcus and Associates
1196 Euclid Avenue
Berkeley, CA 94708

Gregory M. Nielson
Computer Science Department
Arizona State University
Tempe, AZ 85287-5406

Art Olsen
Dept. of Molecular Biology MB5
Research Institute of Scripps Clinic
La Jolla, CA 92037

Dan R. Olsen, Jr.
Computer Science Dept.
Bringham Young University
Provo, UT 84602

Susan Owicki
Digital Equipment Systems Research Center
130 Lytton Ave.
Palo Alto, CA 94301

Alan Parker
Georgia Tech
School of EE
Atlanta, GA 30332

Darwyn Peachy
Pixar
P.O. Box 13719
San Rafael, CA 94913-3719

Michael H. Pendley
Scientific Visualization & Network Design
Sandia National Laboratories
Livermore, California 94550

Charles P. Plinta
Software Engineering
Carnegie Mellon University
Pittsburg, PA 15213

Udo W. Pooch
Department of Computer Science
Texas A&M University

College Station, TX 77843

Sudha Ram
Department of Management
    Information Systems
Callege of BPA
University of Arizona
Tucson, AZ 85721

U. Ravaioli
Coordinated Science Lab
University of Illinois
Urbana, IL 61801

Daniel Reed
Digital Computer Lab.
University of Illinous-Urbana
1304 West Springfield Avenue
Urbana, Illinois 61801

Richard A. Riemke
EG&G Idaho
P. O. Box 1625
Idaho Falls, ID 83415

Anthony Reynolds
Dynamic Digital Displays
3508 Market Street
Suite #257
Philadelphia, PA 19104

Richard Robb
Dept. of Physiology and Biophysics
Mayo Foundation
200 First Street S.W.
Rochester, MI 55905

Alyn Rockwood
Silicon Graphics
2011 N. Shorline Blvd.
P.O. 7311
Mountain View, CA 94039-7311

Wolfgang Roesner
IBM Laboratory
Department 3294
Schoenaicher Str. 220
D-7030 Boeblingen
FEDERAL REPUBLIC OF GERMANY

Jack Noel Rose
College of Technology at Delhi
State University of New York
710 Evenden Tower
Delhi, NY 13753-1190

Larry Rosenblum
Code 5170
Naval Research Laboratory
Washington, DC 20375

John A. Roulier
Computer Science and Engineering

U-157
260 Glenbrook Road
University of Connecticut
Storrs, CT 06268

Gregory Russell
IBM Thomas J. Watson Research Center
Room 36-019, Route 134
Yorktown Heights, NY 10598

Clive C. Sanford
Department of Decision Science
University of Hawaii
BusAd E601C
Honolulu, HI 96822

Lori L. Scarlatos
Grumman Data Systems D12-237
1000 Woodbury Rd.
Woodbury, NY 11797

J. A. Schiavone
AT&T Bell Laboratories
Murry Hill, New Jersey 07974

Philippe Siraut
Obere Flurstrasse 3
CH-2540 Grenchen
SWITZERLAND

Alvy Ray Smith
Pixar Inc.
P.O. Box 13719
San Rafael, CA 94913-3719

Thomas Stephenson
The Analytic Sciences Corporation
55 Walkers Brook Dr.
Reading, MA 01867

Maureen Stone
Xerox PARC
3333 Coyote Hill Road
Palo Alto, CA 94304

Benjamin J. Stoppe
Commandant (G-EAE-4)
U. S. Coast Guard HQ
2100 Second St. S. W.
Washington, DC 20593-001

Werner Stuetzle
Department of Statistics, GN-22
University of Washington
Seattle, Washington 98195

Francis Tang
National Semiconductor
2900 Semiconductor Drive
P. O. Box 58090, MS D3645
Santa Clara, CA 95052-8090

Y. J. Tejwani

Department of Electrical, Computer and
            Biomedical Eng.
Marœuette University
Milwaukee, WI 53233

Demetri Terzopoulos
Schlumberger Palo Alto Reserch
3340 Hillview Avenue
Palo Alto, CA 94304

William I. Thacker
Department of Computer Science
Winthrop College
Rock Hill, SC 29733

Jim Thomas
Batelle
Pacific Northwest Laboratories
P.O. Box 999
Batelle Blvd.
Richland, WA 99352

Spencer W. Thomas
EECS Department
University of Michigan
142 Advanced Tech. Lab Bldg
1101 Beal Avenue
Ann Arbor, MI 48109-2110

Allan Tuchman
UIUC -CSRD
305 Talbot Lab
104 S. Wright St.
Urbana, IL 61801

E. R. Tufte
Graphics Press
P.O. Box 430
Cheshire, CT 06410

Lloyd Treinish
Code 634
NASA/GSFC
Greenbelt, MD 29771

Jayaram K. Udupa
Image Processing Group
3701 Chestnut Medical
Hospital of the Univ. Of Pennsylvania
Philadelphia, PA 19104

Craig Upson
920 Hillview Court
Suite 180
Milpitas, CA 95035

Andy VanDam
Computer Science
Box 1910
Brown University
Providence, RI 02912

Daniel A. Walker

Haw Inst of Geophys, HIG 432
University of Hawaii
2525 Correa Road
Honolulu, HI 96822

Richard Weinberg
Computer Graphics and Animation Lab.
School of Cinema & Television
University Park
University of Southern California
Los Angeles, CA 90089-0782

Robert Wilhemlson
NCSA
Unversity of Illinois at Urbana-Champaign
Champaign, IL 61820

James M. Winget
Silicon2011 North Shoreline Blvd.
Mountanin View, CA 94039-7311

Brian Wyvill
Department of Computer Science
University of Calgary

2500 University Drive N. W.
Calgary, Alberta
Canada T2N 1N4

Thomas Zang
NASA Langley Research Center
Hampton, Virginia 23665

Moshe Zviran
Code S4ZV
Department of Administrative Sciences
Naval Postgraduate School
Monterey, CA 93943-5100

Note

Associate Editor Lawrence J. Rosenblum's biography can be found on page 211. Interested readers should refer to this page.

Table of Contents

Section 1: Introduction and Overviews of Scientific Visualization

"The purpose of computing is insight, not numbers."[1]
[Richard Hamming, 1962]

We are all know how a graph can help us understand a relationship. We learn how to make and read graphs very early in our education and we reap the benefits almost continuously in our daily lives. The graph of a function y = f(x) or the bar chart for a table of values (x_i, y_i), i = 1, . . ., n reveals aspects of the relationship that are not easily discerned by the analysis of formulas or the direct perusal of numerical values. An example mentioned by Philip J. Davis[2] [Davis, 1973] points this out:

> Students fooling around with, e. g., orbits in the many-body problem that have been   graphically displayed have found periodic solutions whose existence defies our keenest analytical analysis.

In a very basic way, the exploitation of this extremely effective means of representing and conveying information about relationships is the foundation this volume on Scientific Visualization is built upon. A graph is a visual image created by using **graphics** (the points, lines, etc.) and **geometry** (relative positions of the points, lines, etc.) The combination of these two well developed fields can lead to some very powerful tools that aid scientists and engineers in their research toward a better understanding of the physical world.

The graphs required by the scientists and engineers of today are more complex than a mere curve in an X-Y Cartesian coordinate system. The relationships of interest often involve multidimensional quantities in both the domain and range and "graphing" such relationships presents quite a challenge; but the same basic principals of graphics and geometry used in the creation of simpler graphs can be applied to yield useful scientific visualization techniques.

Many of the techniques that are in use today and many others that are being researched and developed are discussed in the articles of this book. Some are quite natural and obvious due to their appeal to familiar, but subtle, metaphors. For example, temperature distribution in a 3D volume is really invisible, but a color coded volume rendering with blues for low temperatures and reds for high temperatures can convey a great deal to the combustion scientist. Other techniques use interrogation operators to detect interesting and important regions. This permits focusing of rendering efforts and the viewer's attention.

Advances in scientific computation are allowing mathematical models and simulations to become increasingly complex and detailed. This results in a closer approximation to reality which enhances the possibility of acquiring new knowledge and understanding. Tremendously large collections of numerical values, which contain a great deal of information, are being produced and collected. The problem is to convey all of this information to the scientist so that effective use can be made of the human creative and analytic capabilities. This requires a method of communication with a high bandwidth and an effective interface.

Computer generated images and human vision mediated by the principles of perceptual psychology are the means used in scientific visualization to achieve this communication. Images, which utilize color, intensity, transparency, texture and a myriad of other techniques can, if properly prepared and explained, convey a tremendous amount of information in a short period of time.

While images provide a highly leveraged means of communication, sequences of images can yield even more than the sum of their parts. Animation is a very important additional dimension of scientific visualization. The mind is able to glean information from animation which is virtually impossible to obtain by the separate viewing of still images. It is difficult to realize the whole effect of animation through conventional publication media and so, at the suggestion of *Computer* Editor-in-Chief, Bruce Shriver, we have compiled a video to serve as a companion to this text.

While a video is good at illustrating preprogrammed animation, it lacks the ability to convey the impact of interaction, which is another important dimension of scientific visualization. Allowing the researcher to cooperate with the computer by interactively directing the computations increases the chances for inspiration, insight, and understanding.

The potential benefits of graphics and human/computer interaction were recognized over a quarter of a century ago by Professor Steve Coons and his student Ivan Sutherland. In a 1964 video interview [Herr, 1988] Coons describes Sketchpad (Sutherland's thesis topic):[3]

> You will see a designer, effectively solving a problem step-by-step and he will not, at the outset, know precisely what his problem is, nor will he know exactly how to solve it. But little-by-little, he will begin to investigate ideas and the computer and he will be in cooperation, in the fullest cooperation, in this work.

By drawing from many areas, some very old, such as geometry, and some relatively new, such as computer graphics, researchers are developing new and exciting tools that will allow us to more fully cooperate with the computer so that we may gain a better understanding of the world in which we live in.

We begin this overview section of the book with an annotated bibliography of Scientific Visualization compiled by Keith Voegele. This is the first bibliography of this subject and contains over one hundred and fifty entries. It has the added distinct advantage of being annotated. This adds a great deal to the pedagogical aspects of a bibliography particularly when it is on a relatively new subject. By reading about a certain group of papers, one can quickly gain a rough understanding of what type of work and research is being done there. In this way, this bibliography serves as an excellent introduction to the subject.

A more in depth overview of the entire topic can be obtained from the paper by DeFanti, Brown, and McCormick. This overview is in the spirit of the ViSC report[4] and, in fact, one could view this as a modified and updated version. Even though the material of this survey overlaps the ViSC report by about 40%, there is new and important material here that should be studied by those interested in scientific visualization. The second survey of this section, authored by Cunningham, Brown, and McGrath, concentrates on the aspects of scientific visualization as it pertains to pedagogy and to the entire educational process. According to the authors, visualization's goal is to improve the quality of learning by allowing students to develop more depth in scientific studies and thus to grasp more of the growing knowledge base. They also discuss the barriers to using visualization in education.

For those who want to get a quick idea of what this topic of Scientific Visualization is all about, we recommend that they skim through the annotated bibliography, of course, paying more attention to those areas that interest them, and that they then read the sections of the overview by Defanti, Brown, and McCormick. Later, after they have studied some application papers and possibly some technique papers, they can come back and read in more depth.

References

1. R. W. Hamming, *Numerical Methods for Scientists and Engineers*, McGraw-Hill, New York, 1962.

2. P. J. Davis, "Visual Geomtetry, Computer Graphics and Theorems of Perceived Type," presented at the Missoula Conf. on the Influence of Computing on Mathematical Research and Education, August, 1973.

3. S. Coons, video interview at MIT, 1964, in *Visualization: State of the Art*, ed. L. Herr, SIGGRAPH Video Review, Special Issue #30, ACM, New York, 1988. Order no. 915-130 for VHS, 915-030 for 3/4-inch tape.

4. B. H. McCormick, T. A. DeFanti, and M. D. Brown, eds., "Visualization in Scientific Computing," *Computer Graphics*, Vol. 21, No. 6, Nov. 1987.

Annotated Bibliography

Keith Voegele

This bibliography evolved as a network using the papers in this scientific visualization volume as the root nodes. From there, the supplied reference lists were recursively traversed until a closure resulted either from the common links or from the effective grounding by highly technical literature of application specializations. The obvious gaps were then filled in by suggestions from conversations with Greg Nielson and Tom Foley from the CAGD and graphics group at Arizona State University.

As usual, the standard disclaimers apply; so, for example, this collection is hopefully complete (in the sense that subsets of papers form research vectors that span the space of scientific visualization), but obviously not exhaustively comprehensive. Some of the entries are of a general survey nature, while others are quite specific and technical. Pivotal and often quoted works comprise the bulk of the material but works of historical and developmental significance are also included especially where they point to researchers, research centers, and journals where important work has been, and is being, performed and recorded. The annotations accompanying the references tend to be impressionistic and apologies to the authors are hereby noted for those instances where omissions, misunderstandings, and whimsy have resulted in misinterpretations.

Alfeld, P., "Scattered Data Interpolation in Three or More Variables," in *Mathematical Methods in Computer Aided Geometric Design*, Lyche, T. and Schumaker, L., editors, Academic Press, New York, 1989, pp. 1-33.

In this review of general purpose scattered data interpolation techniques consideration is given to such issues as local versus global behavior, degree of precision, degree of smoothness, invariance under affine transformations, and data requirements. It is also assumed that there is no appreciable noise in the data, that a smooth function is an appropriate representation of the problem solution, and that there is no underlying structure to the data that would suggest a more customized method or that would lead to degenerate cases. The author discusses and references point schemes (Shepard's formula, radial interpolants, Hardy's multiquadrics, thin plate splines), natural neighbor interpolation, tetrahedral schemes (polynomial and rational, including Boolean sums and convex combinations), simplicial schemes, and multivariate splines. Some special topics like interpolation over a sphere and k dimensional triangulations are also included.

Andrews, D.F., "Plots of High-Dimensional Data," *Biometrics*, Vol. 28, 1972, pp. 125-136.

The author discusses a method for representing a small number of data points each of multiple dimension by plotting a Fourier-like sequence of orthogonal trigonometric functions with coefficients equal to the data values. A specific example from anthropology on the attributes of teeth from hominids is detailed. Statistical properties of these functions and their interpretation for clustering, significance testing, and linearity are also presented.

Arnheim, R., *Visual Thinking*, University of California Press, Berkeley, Calif., 1969.

With a dialog moving from studies in art to visual perception as a cognitive activity, the author conducts a readable exploration of visual thinking. The intelligence of perception, the shapes of mental images, pictures, signs, and symbols, the world of abstraction, pure shapes, numbers and words, childrens' art, cosmology, and visual education are a few of the topics touched in between. The book also includes a topical bibliography of over 300 entries.

Artzy, E., Frieder, G., and Herman, G.T., "The Theory, Design, Implementation, and Evaluation of a Three-Dimensional Surface Detection Algorithm," *Computer Graphics and Image Processing*, Vol. 15, 1981, pp. 1-24.

The problem of surface detection in 3D voxel data can be shown to be equivalent to the traversal of a directed graph with nodes corresponding to faces of voxels separating the object of interest from its surroundings. Properties of these graphs are derived in the paper to allow efficient implementation of the algorithm (i.e., need to keep the number of marked nodes used to avoid loops to a small fraction of the total visited in the traversal). The authors first begin with an informal description of the algorithm using a 3 voxel object as an example. The theory relevant to the 2D case is presented first to warm up the intuition and to introduce terminology. The 3D theoretical section is followed by a concise statement of the algorithm and an implementation example using CT data.

Asimov, D., "The Grand Tour: A Tool for Viewing Multidimensional Data," *SIAM Journal of Scientific and Statistical Computing*, Vol. 6, No. 1, 1985, pp. 128-143.

Before disappearing in the mathematics, the authors define the grand tour as a sequence of images extracted from the infinite number of orthogonal projections of p-space data onto 2D subspaces. The desired qualities of these sequences are enumerated and three techniques are suggested for their calculation: slices of an N-dimensional torus, at random techniques, and random walk selections. Concluding remarks reveal that extracting meaning from these sequences could require substantial training and that an organizational taxonomy of scatterplots is needed.

Baker, H.H., "Computation and Manipulation of 3D Surfaces from Image Sequences," in *Visualization in Scientific Computing*, Nielson, G.M. and Shriver, B., editors, IEEE Computer Society Press, Los Alamitos, Calif., 1990, pp. 109-127.

Coming from the perspective of computer vision, the author has developed an image analysis algorithm for producing a coherent 3D description of the evolution of a sequence of 2D images. The results have immediate application in medical imaging, while they effectively serve as a platform for further analysis in 3D machine vision and scene reconstruction applications. Surface facets are generated by the "weaving wall" from the convolution of the volume data with a 3D operator (Laplacian of a Gaussian), but unlike other reconstruction techniques (that potentially traverse the entire volume looking for neighbors of the seed voxel) only two slices of the data are processed at a time. Topologically, the 2 by 2 by 2 subvolume can be categorized into a small number of patterns and the algorithm treats these on a case by case basis. The technique is applied to examples from medical data (spines and jaws in stereo, and excising noses), biophysics (electron microscopy of chromosomes) and modeling of material fracture.

Baker, H.H., "Building Surfaces of Evolution: The Weaving Wall," *International Journal of Computer Vision*, Vol. 3, No.1, 1989, pp. 51-71.

The "Weaving Wall" is a method of constructing surfaces from sequential 2D images and is important in that these surfaces are tracked and accumulated as the data becomes available (as opposed to methods that require the entirety of the volume data). The crux of the algorithm involves the case by case treatment of the Laplacian values from each of the 2 by 2 by 2 cubes of voxel data. The technique readily lends itself to ancillary surface computations such as bounding volumes and local topology. The applications of this technique include medical tomographic data, constructing geometry from surfaces, exploring images in Gaussian scale space, and analytic functions (hyperquadrics). The paper is accompanied by a series of anatomical stereo images that demonstrate the construction method.

Bancroft, G.V., Plessel, T., Merritt, F., Walatka, P.P., and Watson, V., "Scientific Visualization in Computational Aerodynamics at NASA Ames Research Center," *Computer*, Vol. 22, No. 8, Aug. 1989, pp. 89-95.

A research overview including: targeting current and future requirements on a per feature basis for visualization workstations; details of an animation recording system to produce video hardcopy from the Cray to Iris connection; and description of various software packages as tools for visualization (Plot3D for general 3D rendering and Surf, a surface modeler that can send their output to the GAS or Graphical Animation System to create "movies"). The RIP or Real-time Interactive Particle tracer from NASA Ames is noteworthy in that it is an example of a distributed graphics tool communicating at the instance of interaction over a high speed network (as opposed to many of the other systems that precompute and then post process for the display).

Barnhill, R.E., Makatura, G.T., and Stead, S.E., "A New Look at Higher Dimensional Surfaces through Computer Graphics," in *Geometric Modeling: Algorithms and New Trends*, Farin, G., editor, SIAM, Philadelphia, Penn., 1987, pp. 123-129.

With the spirit of interpolation and the practice of approximation higher dimensional surfaces can be constructed to aid the understanding of such physical systems as the pressure distribution on an oblique wing or across the surface of the space shuttle. If the data appears in a rectangular grid, tensor product techniques from univariate methodology can be used (being careful of "twist" derivative incompatibilities). For scattered data, two broad classes of interpolants exist: tetrahedral (i.e., define the tetrahedral subdivision of data space in some optimal way, estimate derivative information at the data sites as needed, and evaluate the selected tetrahedral interpolant) and distance weighted (e.g., Shepard's formula or Hardy's multi-quadrics). Multistage methods (interpolation followed by an approximation that can be efficiently evaluated) are used to display the 3D surfaces that represent the contours of the 4D example problems discussed in the paper.

Barnhill, R.E. and Nielson, G.N., editors, *Surfaces*, Special Issue of *The Rocky Mountain Journal of Mathematics*, Vol. 14, No. 1, Winter 1984.

This special issue comprises the refereed proceedings of a symposium on surfaces held at the SIAM meeting at Stanford in 1982. Three-dimensional surface topics included: triangular interpolants (Barnhill and Little, Alfeld and Barnhill, Nielson and Franke, Renka and Cline), pre-processing for triangular interpolants such as triangulation schemes and gradient estimation (Cline and Renka, Akima, Stead), interpolation and approximation over a sphere (Lawson, Wahba), distance weighted interpolants (Foley), geometric design (Jensen, Kochevar), spline blended approximations (Salkauskas), and dimensions of spaces of piecewise polynomials (Schumaker). The four-dimensional research topics included: tetrahedral interpolants (Barnhill and Little, Alfeld), and distance weighted interpolants (Barnhill and Stead).

Barr, A., "Ray Tracing Deformed Solids," SIGGRAPH 86 Conference Proceedings, *Computer Graphics*, Vol. 20, No. 4, Aug. 1986, pp. 287-296.

Parametric surfaces are added to the set of ray traceable objects by solving the equation $f(u,v) = l(t) = at + b$. A smooth parametric surface is considered to be a deformed flat sheet and when it is transformed into this new coordinate system the surface is flat and the rays are bent. The intersections produced are suitable for use in shading and texture mapping. Since the general solution to this problem would involve solving a stiff differential equation for each ray traced point, a closeness criterion is established to enable practical simplifications.

Becker, R.A. and Cleveland, W.S., "Brushing Scatterplots," *Technometrics*, Vol. 29, No. 2, 1987, pp. 127-142.

Brushing is a highly interactive, dynamic method for viewing multidimensional data that can be used in conjunction with scatterplot matrix displays. Using highlights, selective deletions, and labeling, combined with the attributes of brush shape (defines scope) and paint style (defines persistence), the user is able to perform single point and cluster linking of the data across projections. One and two variable conditioning as a means of data subset selection is also possible in the system that the authors describe in this paper.

Bertin, J., *Graphics and Graphic Information Processing*, Berg, W. and Scott, P., translators, Walter de Gruyter, Berlin, West Germany, 1981.

"The efficacy of a graphic construction is revealed by the level of question which receives an immediate response." Interspersed between the profuse examples, the vocabulary and theory of graphic construction is resolved into components such as matrices, ordered tables, and ordered networks. The author's classic semiological approach to graphic communication explores the difference between pictographs and graphics based on the stages of perception needed to understand their meaning. The graphic sign system is defined by eight variables: spatial position, size, value, texture, color, orientation, and shape. A detailed example using the methods of data tables is used to demonstrate that a graphic is an evolving structure, constantly being reconstructed until the pertinent overall patterns are brought into focus.

Bijl, A., "Making Drawings Talk: Pictures in Minds and Machines," *Computer Graphics Forum*, Vol. 6, No. 4, 1987, pp. 289-298.

Coming from the domain of CAD systems, the author stresses the need to consider drawings as a language. The case is augmented with a review of language, a contrast of words and drawings, and a discussion of the components of a natural drawing system (drawing marks, shape descriptions, and the mapping of shape values). Reading meaning from stick figures (alone and in sequence), and iconic shaping by parametrised line transformations are the specific examples used to support the argument for drawings as language.

Blinn, J.F., "Light Reflection Functions for Simulation of Clouds and Dusty Surfaces," *Computer Graphics*, Vol. 16, 1982, pp. 21-29.

Distilling the scattering theory of Chandrasekhar, the author models the interaction of light with a cloud of similar particles to promote more realistic images of objects like clouds, smoke, or the rings of Saturn. The physical model is simplified by small albedo particles (hence single reflection scattering) with appropriate choices of the phase function (seven classes of which are mentioned) that is integrated in the brightness equation. Extensions to the model include the shadowing effect, multiple scattering, and more physically realistic density functions.

Brewster, L.J., Trivedi, S.S., Tuy, H.K., and Udupa, J.K., "Interactive Surgical Planning," *IEEE Computer Graphics and Applications*, Vol. 4, No. 3, 1984, pp. 31-40.

The authors provide an overview of an Interactive Surgical Planning system (ISP). The system can be described as a 5 step feedback loop: generate the display of the organ, inspect the organ and generate a model based on the desired manipulation, orient the model to the organ by using a composite view, create the modified organ after the manipulation, and record the operation information. Specific examples include ankle and skull operations (in a 2D, slice by slice regime) and the interactive manipulation of a 3D image of a pig heart.

Brisson, D.W., editor, *Hypergraphics: Visualizing Complex Relationships in Art, Science, and Technology*, AAAS Selected Symposium 24, Westview Press, Boulder, Colo., 1978.

This series of papers on hypergraphics, a field comprising computer graphics, perceptual psychology, and modern geometry, brings together efforts to understand and communicate complex, multidimensional relationships. The ideas in this book range from geometry in chemistry, Platonic solids as symbols in organic processes, hyperstereograms (like conventional stereoptic renderings but with *two* parallax axes), computer graphics animations of revolving 4D cubes, and investigations of classical optical illusions extended to higher dimensions.

Brooks, F.P., "Grasping Reality through Illusion—Interactive Graphics Serving Science," *Proceedings of Computer Human Interaction*, Washington, D.C., May 1988, pp. 1-11.

A very readable and at times humorous account of the construction of virtual worlds and their interfaces and how these techniques will be applied to scientific computing. Findings, observations, and rules-of-thumb are given on existing virtual world systems (i.e., Pixel-Planes, GROPE, FLASHLIGHT, GRIP, and GRINCH) and interface issues (i.e., depth cues, exploratory viewing, scene navigation, and the two cursor problem). Brooks concludes with a Chapel Hill VIEW (Visualization Impromptu Evaluation Workbench) of the radical CHiC ethic that systems be "so simple full professors can use them, and so fruitful that they will."

Brotman, L.S. and Badler, N.I., "Generating Soft Shadows with a Depth Buffer Algorithm," *IEEE Computer Graphics and Applications*, Vol. 4, No. 10, Oct. 1984, pp. 5-12.

Shadows are very useful in providing a measure of 3D realism in computer graphics renderings but tend to require computationally costly techniques. Previous efforts include Crow's method of adding invisible shadow planes to the object space, and Atherton, Weiler, and Greenberg's hidden surface polygon technique. These techniques produce sharp shadows and the authors work to overcome this unrealistic artifact by modeling distributed light sources as a large number of point light sources that produce soft shadows. The idea is to render objects into the depth buffer and then use the shadow objects to modify the attributes but not the image of the depth buffer. Opaque and transparent objects are then handled separately as a function of these modified attributes. A detailed algorithm, the intensity formulation, and rendered examples are in the paper.

Brunet, P. and Navazo, I., "Geometric Modeling Using Exact Octtree Representation of Polyhedral Objects," *Eurographics 85, Proceedings of the European Graphics Conference and Exhibition at Nice, France*, Vandoni, C.E., editor, North-Holland, Amsterdam, The Netherlands, 1985.

The incorporation of arbitrary surface patches into solid modeling systems requires special 3D representation schemes to promote efficient intersection algorithms. The authors use extended octtrees that provide the spatial classification needed to simplify the surface intersection problem. The technique can also be used with volume information for representation of half spaces defined by the surfaces. Also of particular interest to scientific visualization from this year's proceedings are the works by Ohashi, et al., on "A Three Dimensional Shaded Display Method for Voxel-Based Representation," and by Hersch on "Raster Rotation of Bilevel Bitmap Images."

Butler, D.M. and Pendley, M.H., "The Visualization Management System Approach to Visualization in Scientific Computing," *Technical Report SAND88-8972 UC-13*, Sandia National Laboratories, Albuquerque, N.M., Sept. 1988.

A visualization management system (ViMS), it is argued, must be approached in the larger context of systems for processing scientific data (such as has dominated business data processing strategies). The design goals include application independence, integrated visualization and computation, flexible geometric and graphic representations, flexible distribution, and host independence. The standardization that the ViMS approach provides meets the objective that "...visualization cannot just produce compelling, aesthetically pleasing pictures; it must produce well-defined pictures."

Cabral, B. and Hunter, C.L., "Visualization Tools at Lawrence Livermore National Laboratory," *Computer*, Vol. 22, No. 8, Aug. 1989, pp. 77- 84.

A research overview including: efforts at distributed visualization via the "Magic" implementation involving the path from Cray to Gould to LSI to Tektronix terminals; the Cray to Sun connection via the GWS or graphics workstation project; and theoretical work in the Advanced Visualization Research Project (AVRP) to abstract symbolic and numerical data into a taxonomy suitable for a generalized interface to visualization tools.

Chambers, J.M., Cleveland, W.S., Kleiner, B., and Tukey, P.A., *Graphical Methods for Data Analysis*, Wadsworth International Group, Belmont, Calif., 1983.

Novel and conventional methods for looking at data sets in the broad context of statistics are critiqued in this book written by some of the original proponents for graphical techniques. Chapters include: data set distributions and interset comparisons (quantile, box, stem and leaf, and density trace plots), 2D data (scatterplots, smoothing, cellulation, and sunflowers!), multivariate data (3D plots, and coding schemes like Kleiner-Hartigan trees or star symbols), distribution assumptions (Q-Q plots), and regression modeling (residual plots). The authors conclude with general principles, visual perception, and graphical analysis strategies.

Chang, S., "Visual Language: A Tutorial and Survey," *IEEE Software*, Vol. 4, No. 1, Jan. 1987, pp. 29-39.

Visual languages are an instance of general visualization techniques applied to the tasks of problem solving and computer programming. This review covers iconic design and representative visual language systems such as Programming-by-Rehearsal, Pict/D, Play System, Vicon, and Hi Visual. Four classes of visual languages are identified: languages that support visual interaction, visual programming languages, visual information processing languages, and iconic visual information processing languages.

Chernoff, H., "The Use of Faces to Represent Points in a K-Dimensional Space Graphically," *Journal of the American Statistical Association*, Vol. 68, No. 342, 1973, pp. 361-368.

The classic paper suggesting the use of cartoon faces with variable attributes (such as length of the nose, or curve of the mouth) to graphically represent higher dimensional data. An example using fossil shell data and another using geological core assays provide evidence that these faces can be used for cluster, discriminant, and time-series analyses. Chernoff was aware of the irony of using faces to distinguish among numbers while the A.I. community was using numbers to distinguish among faces. As an historical note: the computational and printing cost of each face was about a quarter in those early days of computing!

Choi, D. and Levit, C., "An Implementation of a Distributed Interactive Graphics System for a Supercomputer Environment," *International Journal of Supercomputer Applications*, Vol. 1, No. 4, 1987, pp. 82-95.

Consider the standard cycle starting with the execution of a computational application, followed by conversion of supercomputer data formats and data transfer, the execution of a display application on a workstation, and then iterating on these steps as the user changes parameters. The authors describe a distributed system that is designed to overcome the inefficiencies inherent in this cycle. The specific system involves connection between the Cray (4 cpu's at 4.1 nanosecond clock cycle, 268 MW memory, and 48 GB disk storage) and an Iris 2500T (68020 32-bit cpu, VLSI geometry engine, for 20K rendered triangles/ second) via the hyperchannel network (50 MHz, CSMA/ CA) using TCP/IP protocols available in each machine's Unix operating systems. Two programs, RIP and PLOT3D, are benchmarked under several configurations that vary the task distribution between the two machines and the results are presented in this paper.

Claerbout, J.F., *Imaging the Earth's Interior*, Blackwell Scientific Publishing, Oxford, England, 1985.

With a wit that belies the dryness of the mathematics of creating images from reflection seismology data, the author weaves the physics of wave equations with practical filtering techniques to produce a host of line plots to be used in learning the craft of wavefield extrapolation. Ratfor algorithms are also provided for most of the mathematical procedures as well as an extensive bibliography of geophysical interest.

Cleveland, W.S. and McGill, M.E., *Dynamic Graphics for Statistics*, Wadsworth and Brooks/Cole, Pacific Grove, Calif., 1988.

Unavailable for annotation.

Cohen, M.F. and Greenberg, D.P., "The Hemi-Cube, A Radiosity Solution for Complex Environments," SIGGRAPH 85 Conference Proceedings, *Computer Graphics*, Vol. 19, No. 3, 1985, pp. 31-40.

Although they are difficult to achieve, global illumination effects enhance the 3D realism of a rendered image. Radiosity techniques utilize the physics of an equilibrium energy balance and work well for diffuse lighting but have no specular highlighting. Their primary advantage is in being independent of the viewing position thereby reducing calculation costs as multiple scenes are imaged. The authors extend the radiosity technique to complex environments that may contain occluded surfaces by treating each object in the scene as a secondary light source. Form factor geometry is a key element in radiosity and the hemicube is an efficient means of providing this information. It is formed by imagining a cube about each patch and projecting the contribution of secondary illumination from every other patch in the scene. The lighting of a furnished virtual room is pictured as an example.

Cox, D., "Using the Supercomputer to Visualize Higher-Dimensions: An Artist's Contribution to Scientific Visualization," *Leonardo: Journal of Art, Science and Technology*, Vol. 21, No. 3, 1988, pp. 233-242.

The author, an artist at NCSA, presents some aspects of her collaboration with scientists at this research center. In a working instance of a "Renaissance team," various psuedo-color mapping techniques are applied to large volumes of data from numerical simulations in astrophysics. Later in the article, a clay figurine of the Etruscan Venus meets the Romboy homotopy from higher dimensional topology.

Crawford, S.L. and Fall, T.C., "Projection Pursuit Techniques for the Visualization of High Dimensional Datasets," in *Visualization in Scientific Computing*, Nielson, G.M. and Shriver, B., editors, IEEE Computer Society Press, Los Alamitos, Calif., 1990, pp. 94-108.

The goal of exploratory data analysis is in finding structure in p dimensional data sets. Conventional 3D scatterplots utilize color, glyphs, perspective, stereo pairs, shading, or motion to aid the visual perceptual system in detecting structure. For higher dimensions, the number of 2D projections of the data set preclude their exhaustive search so "grand tour" and automatic projection pursuit methodology has been proposed to find that subset of views that are in a structural sense most interesting. The Friedman-Tukey and revised Friedman algorithms are presented as means of accomplishing this goal. The authors end with a discussion of the software and hardware requirements of a projection pursuit workstation as well as some concluding remarks on the utility of the technique in the overall context of statistical investigation.

Cunningham, S., Brown, J.R., and McGrath, M., "Visualization in Science and Engineering Education," in *Visualization in Scientific Computing*, Nielson, G.M. and Shriver, B., editors, IEEE Computer Society Press, Los Alamitos, Calif., 1990, pp. 48-57.

As visualization tools become more available and more necessary for the working scientist and engineer, it will be important for the educational system to incorporate these tools in their teaching curriculum. Unfortunately, powerful visualization systems are not yet cost effective and since the requirements of educators are quite different from computing professionals the gap between what should be taught and what can be taught widens. The authors propose an initiative in visualization for science and engineering education. They outline the barriers facing this initiative (understanding visual learning, the state of computing systems, the educational environment, and institutional support) and what steps must be taken to overcome them (promoting visualization among peers, providing rewards for visualization tools, garnering support from the educational institutions, and researching visual learning).

DeFanti, T.A., Brown, M.D., and McCormick, B.H., ''Visualization Expanding Scientific and Engineering Research Opportunities,'' *Computer*, Vol. 22, No. 8, Aug. 1989, pp. 12-25.

This paper serves as a background introduction to visualization in scientific visualization and provides a synopsis of the NSF panel report toward establishing an initiative for ViSC. Besides the colorful examples selected from the scientific and engineering work of researchers using visualization tools (medical imaging, fractals, storms, planets, fluid flows, and finite element analysis), the report outlines the needs of both the tool users and the toolmakers from both short-term and long-term standpoints.

DeFanti, T.A. and Brown, M.D., ''Insight Through Images,'' *Unix Review*, March 1989, pp. 42-50.

This article is essentially a readable condensation of the full report on scientific visualization mentioned below (McCormick, et al.). Emphasis is on the available systems and how they need to be adapted to meet the needs of the visualization community. An inset article by Linnea Cook provides some information on the status of such systems (specifically, the Graphics Workstation Project) at Lawrence Livermore National Laboratory.

Dickinson, R.R., ''A Unified Approach to the Design of Visualization Software for the Analysis of Field Problems,'' in *Three-Dimensional Visualization and Display Technologies, SPIE Proceedings*, SPIE, Bellingham, Wash., Vol. 1083, Jan. 1989.

Unavailable for annotation.

Diede, T., Hagenmaier, C., Miranker, G., Rubenstein, J., and Worley, W., ''The Titan Graphics Supercomputer Architecture,'' *Computer*, Vol. 21, No. 9, Sept. 1988, pp. 13-30.

The Titan graphics machine is a hybrid superminicomputer with high speed and high quality graphics capabilities (6-20 MFlops and 200K polygons/second). This article outlines the high level design of this architecture with details on the integer processing unit, the Titan bus, the memory subsystem, the vector unit, and the graphics subsystem. Example graphics are also depicted.

Drebin, R.A., Carpenter, L., and Hanrahan, P., ''Volume Rendering,'' SIGGRAPH 88 Conference Proceedings, *Computer Graphics*, Vol. 22, No. 4, Aug. 1988, pp. 65-74.

The key technique in this approach to volume rendering is in converting the 3D scalar data into a density volume by assigning material percentages to each data subvolume. In the example from CT scans these assigned percentages are probabilistic values from a maximum likelihood analysis of the known materials (i.e., bone, muscle, or fat). Color and opacity volumes are then computed from the density volume for use in the lighting model. Special matting volumes are also created that enable spatial set operations on the image (such as cut aways). Surface detection is on the basis of a computed volume density gradient. The actual algorithm involves selecting a viewpoint, transforming the data, resampling to reduce aliasing artifacts, and finally applying the lighting model by source-attenuation reprojection of parallel rays from behind the volume element toward the image plane involving the color, opacity, and surface strength computations. Ethereal full body images of a sea otter and a human male illustrate the method.

England, N., ''A Graphics System Architecture for Interactive Application-Specific Display Functions,'' *IEEE Computer Graphics and Applications*, Vol. 6, No. 1, Jan. 1986, pp. 60-70.

In a review of graphics subsystem architectures, the author characterizes limited purpose systems (capable of lines, characters, polygons, and transformations), and general purpose systems (32 bits, FPU, image processing units, frame grabbers, and flexible display controls). These prototypic architectures are related to the demands of such applications as molecular modeling, medical imaging, CAD, seismic data exploration, and numerical simulation research.

Farin, G., ''Smooth Interpolation to Scattered 3D Data,'' in *Surfaces in Computer Aided Geometric Design*, Barnhill, R.E. and Boehm, W., editors, North-Holland, Amsterdam, The Netherlands, 1983, pp. 43-63.

In analogy to piecewise differentiability defined in some domain of the plane, three-dimensional interpolation techniques obtain smoothness by assuring continuous tangent planes at the patch boundary intersections. The author introduces the Bernstein-Bezier representation by reformulating the nine parameter cubic and the Clough-Tocher schemes with these basis functions. The 3D algorithm assumes a triangulation of the data upon which the cubic boundary curves and the nine parameter cubic patches are built. Each patch is then subdivided to provide the extra degrees of freedom needed to match the required smoothness at the patch boundaries and within the subpatches. The proposed interpolant can be used on topologies without boundary points to yield closed surfaces. The book, *Surfaces in CAGD*, contains the proceedings of a conference held at Oberwolfach, West Germany organized by W. Boehm and J. Hoschek.

Foley, J.D. and Van Dam, A., *Fundamentals of Interactive Computer Graphics*, Addison-Wesley, Reading, Mass., 1982.

The first illustration in the book is Mad magazine's Alfred E. Neuman while the last is the ubiquitous mandrill, but in between the content is serious enough to effectively span the important problems and solutions in computer graphics. The chapters include the basics of graphics interaction, hardware and display architecture, geometric and 3D viewing transformations, modeling and representation of 3D shapes, and the quest for realism in images (hidden surface, shading, intensity, and color). Besides the numerous fragments of pseudocode for significant algorithms, the text includes excellent color plates, and over 550 references from the literature of computer graphics.

Foley, T.A., "Interpolation and Approximation of 3-D and 4-D Scattered Data," *Computer and Mathematical Applications*, Vol. 13, 1987, pp. 711- 740.

Using over 30 illustrations surfaces from the scattered data problem, the author describes the options to a set of Fortran routines that perform three- and four-dimensional interpolation and approximation. One set of procedures are for the bivariate and trivariate forms of Hardy's multiquadric interpolant with options for setting the constant "radius" term. The other procedures implement a wide selection of multistage methods. More specifically, the first stage is a local least-squares or Hardy multiquadric method, followed by a piecewise bicubic Hermite interpolant to the stage one gridded data, followed by a modified version of Shepard's method in the optional third stage.

Franke, R., "Scattered Data Interpolation: Tests of Some Methods," *Mathematics of Computation*, Vol. 38, No. 157, Jan. 1982, pp. 181-200.

The problem of scattered data interpolation as discussed in this paper is one of trying to find a smooth (at least first derivative continuous) bivariate function that matches the known, but arbitrarily dispersed data. Various existing interpolation schemes (distance weighted, rectangular and triangular blended, finite element, Foley's multistage, and global basis function methods) were tested and rated with respect to such attributes as accuracy, visual smoothness, parameter sensitivity, timing, storage requirements, and ease of implementation. The paper is a condensed version of the author's more comprehensive work at the Naval Postgraduate School.

Frenkel, K.A., "Volume Rendering," *Communications of the ACM*, Vol. 32, No. 4, April 1989, pp. 426-435.

A readable essay on the emergence and importance of volume visualization methods, this article provides some historical insight on its development driven primarily by medical imaging applications. The laser scan confocal microscope is discussed as another new important source of 3D data in the biological sciences. Some philosophical questions about the direction of volume visualization research (i.e., fast interactive image processing versus static but photorealistic snapshots) are also explored.

Frenkel, K.A., "The Art and Science of Visualizing Data," *Communications of the ACM*, Vol. 31, No. 2, Feb. 1988, pp. 111-121.

Amidst the Bacchanalia, Karen Frenkel documents the emergence of the domain of volume visualization from the ViSCous atmosphere enveloping SIGGRAPH 87. Laced with colorful figures and quotations from other figures just as colorful, the author provides a layperson's view of the dominant issues and future directions of volume visualization.

Frieder, G., Gordon, D., and Reynolds, R.A., "Back-to-Front Display of Voxel-Based Objects," *IEEE Computer Graphics and Applications*, Vol. 5, No. 1, Jan. 1985, pp. 52-59.

The back-to-front (BTF) method of volume rendering has the advantage of requiring little preprocessing of the data, but no actual surfaces are extracted from the data. The voxels are binary thresholded by density and then rendered with a diffuse lighting model. The order is determined by selecting the z slice most distant from the viewpoint, then the y row most distant in that slice, and finally the furthest x column cell in the current row. The roles of z, y, and x are actually interchangeable in this scheme depending upon the location of the origin with respect to the viewpoint. The technique readily lends itself to global clipping schemes since all of the voxels are processed for each image. The system the authors describe also allows for arbitrary rotation of the data volume for some measure of interactivity.

Friedman, J.H. and Stuetzle, W., "Hardware for Kinematic Statistical Graphics," in *Computer Science and Statistics, The Interface*, Gentle, J., editor, North-Holland, Amsterdam, The Netherlands, 1983, pp. 163-169.

The predecessor of kinematic statistical systems was PRIM-9 named for its Projection, Rotation, Isolation, and Marking capabilities. The paper goes on to describe some hardware aspects of the Orion statistical graphics system. [As an aside, the proceedings of this 15th annual symposium were opened with a sardonic keynote address by R.W. Hamming in which he notes with dispair that statistics was moving in the direction of producing masses of results from little data but without any insight. The goal of scientific visualization is to cultivate insight from a few results extracted from masses of data.]

Frome, F.S., Buck, S.L., and Boynton, R.M., "Visibility of Borders: Separate and Combined Effects of Color Differences, Luminance Contrast, and Luminance Level," *Journal of the Optical Society of America*, Vol. 71, No. 2, 1981, pp. 145-150.

The authors report on a series of experiments quantifying the separate and combined contributions of color difference, luminance contrast, and luminance level on the strength of a perceived border. The measured variable is the length of time before the border fades or disappears because of a phenomena known as fixation fading. In general, visibility improves with higher luminance levels, with the log of the luminance contrast, and for chromatic differences with the log of the tritanoptic-purity difference (stimulation of long and middle wavelength cones).

Fuchs, H., Levoy, M., and Pizer, S.M., "Interactive Visualization of 3D Medical Data," *Computer*, Vol. 22, No. 8, Aug. 1989, pp. 46-51.

This quick glance at the work going on at the University of North Carolina at Chapel Hill shows applications from radiologic therapy, CT and MR imaging, and molecular modeling being rendered by using surface-based reconstruction, binary voxel, and volume rendering techniques. Progress in display hardware is also reviewed including stereo viewers, varifocal mirrors, cine sequencers, head mounted displays, and the coveted Pixel-Planes 4, a real-time image generation system.

Fuchs, H., et al., "Pixel-Planes 5: A Heterogeneous Multiprocessor Graphics System Using Processor-Enhanced Memories," SIGGRAPH 89 Conference Proceedings, *Computer Graphics*, Vol. 23, No. 3, July 1989, pp. 79-88.

With a projected one million Phong-shaded triangles rendered each second, the Pixel-Planes graphics architecture is designed to achieve true interactivity with virtual worlds of simulation and scientific visualization. The paper begins with the development and architecture (i.e., Graphics Processors, Renderers, Frame Buffer, Host Interface, and Ring Network) of the Pxpl5, and then covers the system algorithms for Phong shading, shadows, texture mapping, fonts, radiosity, and volumetric rendering (Levoy's method). The paper includes a good list of further references on hardware systems and rendering.

Fuchs, H., Pizer, S.M., Heinz, E.R., Tsai, L.C., and Bloomberg, S.H., "Adding a True 3D Display to a Raster Graphics System," *IEEE Computer Graphics and Applications*, Vol. 2, No. 7, Sept. 1982, pp. 73-78.

Realizing that depth effects (shadowing, motion blur, etc.) rendered in 2D have limited effectiveness because of the lack of head motion parallax, researchers have explored other 3D mechanisms (stereopsis, holography, integrative photography, and vibrating, rotating mirrors). This article describes a low cost, varifocal mirror display that yields a true 3D perception. The essence of the technique involves reflection of the CRT image in a mirrored surface that is vibrating (set in motion by a loud speaker) at a frequency that matches the refresh rate of the display buffer. For example, a rectangle on the screen will appear as a skewed parallelpiped. The device works well with points and lines, but it is less useful for shaded constructions.

Fuchs, H., Kedem, Z.M., and Uselton, S.P., "Optimal Surface Reconstruction from Planar Contours," *Communications of the ACM*, Vol. 20, No. 10, Oct. 1977, pp. 693-702.

From minimum cost cycles in a directed toroidal graph, the authors are able to extract feature surfaces as triangular tiles connecting a set of cross-sectional contours. This early pivotal work builds the mathematical basis of reconstructive medical imaging techniques. The algorithm uses successive subdivision for efficiency in reducing the search space of the graph. The rest of the paper breezes through theorems and lemmas where acceptible subgraphs are weakly connected to Eulerian graphs by arcs of various in and out degrees, all at a minimum cost. As a foreshadowing of volume rendering techniques, the paper mentions an old practice of stacking successively scanned photographs between transparent layers of filler material to give the appearance of a translucent volume object.

Gelberg, L.M. and Stephenson, T.P., "Supercomputing and Graphics in the Earth and Planetary Sciences," *IEEE Computer Graphics and Applications*, Vol. 7, No. 7, July 1987, pp. 26-33.

The authors initially discuss price/performance issues for a variety of commercially available computer architectures (Cray, Alliant, Vax, etc.) and proceed to a discussion of host/display strategies. The article follows up with coverage of several supercomputing and graphics applications at The Analytic Sciences Corporation (TASC) including: numerical weather prediction, a cloud prediction model (SuperSeer), 3D cloud surfaces from infrared satellite data, local terrain variations in the gravitation field strength, landscape simulations, and image processing from satellite data.

Glassner, A.S., editor, *An Introduction to Ray Tracing*, Academic Press, San Diego, Calif., 1989.

This excellent text evolved out of the SIGGRAPH 87 and 88 one day courses on introductory ray tracing. The book begins with an overview by Andrew Glassner that provides the neophyte with enough background (i.e., camera model, ray tracing directions, recursive visibility, and aliasing) to utilize the other chapters. Eric Haines covers the essential ray tracing algorithms including algebraic and geometric implications of ray/sphere, ray/plane, ray/box, and ray/quadric intersections. Pat Hanrahan extends this work to include intersection algorithms for more general surfaces such as implicit surfaces, tensor product surfaces, and blobs! Glassner presents another chapter on the surface physics for ray tracing such as the mechanisms of light transport (specular, diffuse, etc.), and effective shading models. Robert Cook's paper covers stochastic sampling and distributed ray tracing with applications to anti-aliasing, motion blur, and penumbral shading. Efficient or accelerated ray tracing is the concern of authors James Arvo and David Kirk, who discuss hierarchical organization, bounding volumes, spatial subdivision, directional techniques, and coherence. The last chapter contains 'C' code and notes on the software design of a ray tracer by Paul Heckbert. A complete bibliography and an illustrated glossary are appended.

Gonzales, R. and Wintz, P., *Digital Image Processing*, 2nd Ed., Addison-Wesley, Reading, Mass., 1987.

An excellent basic textbook on digital image processing with many figures and examples and a few Fortran algorithms. Topics covered include: digital image fundamentals (visual perception and sampling), image transforms (Fourier, FFT, etc.), image enhancement (smoothing and filtering), image restoration and encoding, and image segmentation and description.

Goodsell, D.S., Mian, I.S., and Olson, A.J., "Rendering Volumetric Data in Molecular Systems," *Journal of Molecular Graphics*, Vol. 7, No. 1, March 1989, pp. 35-36, 41-47.

Electron densities, electrostatic potentials, and regions for active site binding in proteins are molecular properties that can be expressed as a 3D grid of scalar values. These properties can be displayed as colored, translucent clouds around and within the classic van der Waals surfaces that represent the underlying molecular structure. A ray tracing scheme utilizing opacity summation has been integrated with the RMS rendering system (i.e., in which molecules and atoms are depicted as colored spheres) to provide images with realistic shading and shadowing. The authors report on the system in this paper, and they provide relevant algorithms and colored stereo images as examples.

Gordon, R. and Reynolds, R., "Image Space Shading of 3-Dimensional Objects," *Computer Vision, Graphics and Image Processing*, Vol. 29, No. 3, 1985, pp. 361-376.

Shading is used both for providing 3D realism and for simulating object surface characteristics. Shading is conventionally performed in object space where the surface normal vector is used in relationship to the light and viewing vectors to determine the illumination factors. The authors propose an image space (i.e., after projection to the 2D display plane) shading algorithm that works by extracting normals from the gradient of the z-buffer information (or information from distance only shading techniques). Special handling is required for discontinuities in the z-buffer due to hidden surfaces but the authors obtain gradients from a weighted central difference formula. The quality of images is admittedly of lower quality than object space shading but in the limit of a very large number of modeled polygons the speed improvements can be quite significant. Example figures show a sphere and CT data.

Haber, R.B., "Scientific Visualization and the Rivers Project at the National Center for Supercomputing Applications," *Computer*, Vol. 22, No. 8, Aug. 1989, pp. 84-89.

A research overview describing: the establishment of a visualization and media services group to provide animation and visualization services to researchers in diverse fields; a software development group to create and distribute general visualization tools; and the RIVERS (Research on Interactive Visual Environments) project. The main emphasis of this latter project is to abstract visualization into three components: data enrichment and enhancement, a visualization mapping to create an abstract visualization object (AVO), and finally the rendering of this AVO. The software design is layered, interactive, and utilizes distributed execution; while the hardware systems are three tiered allowing for separate communication channels appropriate to massive graphics transport as well as the few character user interaction messages.

Haber, R.B. and McNabb, D.A., "Visualization Idioms: A Conceptual Model for Scientific Visualization Systems," in *Visualization in Scientific Computing*, Nielson, G.M. and Shriver, B., editors, IEEE Computer Society Press, Los Alamitos, Calif., 1990, pp. 74-93.

Visualization emerges from the integration of computer graphics, image processing, computer vision, computer aided design, geometric modeling, approximation theory, perceptual psychology, and user-interface studies, and the authors explore the underlying commonalities by isolating visualization idioms. For example, simulation studies are conceptualized in three phases: the model, the solution, and an interpretation and evaluation of the solution. Analogously, the simulation data undergoes enrichment and enhancement on its way to an abstract visualization object that can be rendered. Specific examples of these idioms are discussed in the paper from computational fluid dynamics, dynamic fracture mechanics, physics of plastic injection molding, and severe storm simulation. The authors conclude with a discussion of the NCSA RIVERS (Research on Interactive Visualization Environments) project with implications for visualization software and hardware.

Haber, R.N. and Wilkinson L., "Perceptual Components of Computer Displays," *IEEE Computer Graphics and Applications*, Vol. 2, No. 3, May 1982, pp. 23-35.

In a primer of perceptual psychology for the computer scientist, the authors present what is known about optimal organization of information for human information processing to improve computer displays for cognitive activities (preception, retention, retrieval, imagination, creation, and decision making). Chunking is discussed (learned entities linked by a rule), as well as the representation of visual structure (spatial attributes, feature extraction, movement, depth perception, and meaning).

Haeberli, P.E., "ConMan: A Visual Programming Language for Interactive Graphics," SIGGRAPH 88 Conference Proceedings, *Computer Graphics*, Vol. 22, Aug. 1988, pp. 103-112.

ConMan, the Connection Manager, is a working example of the type of interface that the scientific visualization workstation will need to have to permit the researcher to customize the graphics pipeline from simulation to interactive display. Using data flow techniques, the interface enables visual pipes (similar to the Unix command line variety) to be created between components of the graphical creation, interaction, and rendering systems (i.e., output from a curve editor can be piped into a surface of revolution module). ConMan is implemented on Silicon Graphics Iris workstations.

Hall, R., "A Characterization of Illumination Models and Shading Techniques," *Visual Computer*, Vol. 2, No. 5, 1986, pp. 268-277.

This work is a survey of illumination models that usefully organizes and spans the literature while providing one common terminology and notational convention. One category uses perspective geometry and empirical lighting models and is associated with the shading techniques of Gouraud and Phong and the pseudo-transparency of Newell. The ray tracing techniques utilize true geometry, utilize theoretical or empirical illumination models, and consider such effects as reflection mapping, texturing, distance attenuation, refraction, and recursive coherent scattering. The last group covers radiosity with its analytic energy equilibrium model and the extensions that permit improved handling of spectral highlights and complex diffuse environments. A series of colored spheres illustrate some of the various techniques.

Hanson, R.K., "Combustion Diagnostics: Planar Imaging Techniques," in *Proceedings of the 21st International Symposium on Combustion*, The Combustion Institute, Pittsburg, Penn., 1986, pp. 1,677-1,699.

This paper provides technical information on experimental techniques that produce a planar array of data such as laser induced fluorescence, and Mie, Rayleigh, and Raman scattering. An island of color in the 2000 page volume, many examples of 2D pseudo-colored images are included. The author uses the visualization technique of interactively selecting a planar slice from a volume of experimental data to be displayed as a contoured image.

Hart, J.C., Sandin, D.J., and Kauffman, L.H., "Ray Tracing Deterministic 3D Fractals," SIGGRAPH 89 Conference Proceedings, *Computer Graphics*, Vol. 23, No. 3, Aug. 1989, pp. 289-296.

The authors use an unusual construction called the unbounding volume (i.e., a volume that does not contain the object) to enable swift ray tracing of deterministic fractal objects. The objective is to use this 3D visualization tool to explore the higher dimensional existence of Julia sets of quadratic functions. The rendered image is also improved by setting the minimum ray increment as a function of distance from the observer that provides more fractal resolution for closer portions of the image.

Head, C.G., "The Map as Natural Language: A Paradigm for Understanding," *Cartographica*, Vol. 21, No. 1, 1984, pp. 1-31.

The phrase "reading a map" suggests that there is a connection between natural language processing and obtaining information from a map. The accepted model of text reading involves the structures of perceptual store (iconic store in the visual system), short-term memory, and long-term memory. These structures are manipulated by the processes of primary recognition for feature extraction, and secondary recognition for perceptual and conceptual encoding. The author extends this model to map reading and, in this framework, describes the map use types of landscape visualization, navigation, and interpretation for place or space (i.e., what is found where). Over 150 references on cartography and natural language processing are included.

Helman, J. and Hesselink, L., "Representation and Display of Vector Field Topology in Fluid Flow Data Sets," *Computer*, Vol. 22, No. 8, Aug. 1989, pp. 27-36.

Visualization is difficult enough for scalar volumes, but, for vector field problems that arise from computational fluid dynamics, the difficulties are compounded ("imagine 800,000 little color coded arrows in space!"). The authors describe an analysis whereby only the critical points (saddle points, attracting and repelling nodes, and foci, etc.) and their principle tangent curves are displayed. The power of this topological visualization is that an observer can visually infer the structure of the entire vector field. The paper discusses the display, interaction, and implementation of their analysis workbench for this research. The colored stereo illustrations are particularly appealing and readily convey the utility of the technique.

Herdeg, W., editor, *Graphis Diagrams: The Graphic Visualization of Abstract Data*, Graphics Press Corporation, Zurich, Switzerland, 1981.

"The optimum synthesis of aesthetics and information value remains the essential objective in every type of diagrammatic presentation..." and Herdeg explores examples from diverse sources to demonstrate effective graphical technique. Of particular interest to current visualization efforts are the artist renderings of translucent colored surfaces over geographic domains to portray meteorological trends.

Herman, G.T. and Liu, H.K., "Three-Dimensional Display of Human Organs from Computer Tomograms," *Computer Graphics and Image Processing*, Vol. 9, No. 1, Jan. 1979, pp. 1-21.

In medical imaging one goes from a real life *organ surface* to a *detected surface* reconstructed from voxel data, to the 2D *displayed surface* shaded by angle and distance of the surface to the light source, to the *smoothed display surface* that has been low pass filtered to remove granularities. In this early paper, the authors concentrate on the latter two steps. The notion of the faces of a "cuberille" (coined from the quadrille rulings of paper) is introduced and theorems on the local ordering of such volumetric structures are also presented.

Herman, G.T. and Udupa, J.K., "Display of 3D Digital Images: Computational Foundations and Medical Applications," *IEEE Computer Graphics and Applications*, Vol. 3, No. 5, Aug. 1983, pp. 39-46.

Given a 3D digital scene the goals are to first identify (thresholding and interactive segmentation), represent (cuberille or directed contours), and manipulate (slice by slice or cut plane dissection of directed contours) scene objects. The next step is to detect, generate (directed graphs and tree traversal techniques), display (depth cues, shading, transparency, and rotation for motion parallax), and manipulate object surfaces. This general algorithm is discussed in the context of examples from bone grafting, joint disease, NMR imaging, radiation therapy, and diagnostic radiology.

Hesselink, L., "Digital Image Processing in Flow Visualization," *Annual Review of Fluid Mechanics, Vol. 20*, Lumley, J.L., Van Dyke, M., and Reed, H., editors, Annual Review Inc., Palo Alto, Calif., 1988, pp. 421-485.

"Flow visualization results from interaction between light and matter." So begins Hesselink in a review that organizes the relevant literature into a flowchart that classifies the domain of flow visualization and simulation research. The author next offers weighty descriptions of such experimental techniques as particle tracing, scattering, laser fluorescence, interferometry, shadowgraphy, and tomography. Two-dimensional imaging techniques for enhancement, segmentation, classification, and decomposition are discussed. Three-dimensional methods include perspective, color depth encoding, stereopsis, reconstruction techniques, and holography (a white light example of a flow visualization is reproduced in the book). After mentioning automated image analysis, Hesselink concludes with a bibliography of over 150 references mentioned in his comprehensive review.

Hibbard, W. and Santek, D., "Visualizing Large Data Sets in the Earth Sciences," *Computer*, Vol. 22, No. 8, Aug. 1989, pp. 53-57.

The McIDAS (Man-computer Interactive Data Access System) developed at the University of Wisconsin provides a unique opportunity for interactive visualization of problems in the earth sciences. The system has excellent data management facilities allowing manipulation of billions of data elements from such sources as satellites and radar systems. Display software and hardware permit up to a 128 frame animation of complex 3D images, stereo viewing, transparent surfaces from volume scalar data draped over topographic renderings of the earth's surface, vector fields of wind velocities, and perspective images of clouds and storm simulations. Mouse-based user interaction governs rotates, zooms, and pans, as well as variable reselection and animation control. The authors also document new features to be added and mention some of the ongoing projects that utilize the McIDAS system.

Hibbard, W., "A Next Generation McIDAS Workstation," in *Proceedings of the Conference on Interactive Information and Processing Systems for Meteorology, Oceanography, and Hydrology*, American Meteorological Society, Boston, Mass., 1988, pp. 57-61.

While it is recognized that more sophisticated graphics systems exist than that of the current implementation of the McIDAS workstation, none have the highly integrated connection to meteorological data and specific applications software. The design of a new system must therefore maintain this integration while adding the tools and hardware for animation of 3D views, increased frame buffer storage and segmentation, more color resolution, and zoom and pan for user interaction. The author proposes the AT&T pixel machine hosted by a Sun workstation as a possible system and offers details on the management of the video memory and video processor necessary to support these design goals.

Hibbard, W., "4D Display of Meteorological Data," in *Proceedings of the Workshop on Interactive 3D Graphics*, ACM, New York, 1986, pp. 26-33.

Within the McIDAS (Man-computer Interactive Data Access System), the author documents software for producing short animation sequences of 3D renderings depicting atmospheric developments over time. Stereo displays incorporating perspective, shading, and hidden surface removal are used to produce clouds and wind speed surfaces defined over topographic renderings of the earth. The intent of interactivity in this situation is primarily to reduce the information content to an apprehensible level and to fortify the illusion of depth in the images. The author also provides a detailed algorithm for converting a GOES (Geostationary Operational Environment Satellite) image into a perspective image.

Hirsh, N. and Brown, B.L., "A Holistic Method for Visualizing Computer Performance Measurements," in *Visualization in Scientific Computing*, Nielson, G.M. and Shriver, B., editors, IEEE Computer Society Press, Los Alamitos, Calif., 1990, pp. 190-208.

The authors describe an experiment analyzing the performance of a network link between an IBM 4381 and a Cray X-MP. The data were initially examined by using a six-way analysis of variance (ANOVA), but the wealth of the results suggested that a multivariable graphical method using principle components might provide a better overall understanding of the network performance. The Multigraf is a specialized graphic for viewing simple effects, interactions, and higher-order effects from a factorial dataset from a reduced multivariate space. A number of these Multigrafs appear as figures in the paper and the authors explain how their perusal led to interesting observations not otherwise apparent from the more conventional statistical analysis.

Hoehne, K.H., Bomans, M., Tiede, U., and Riemer, M., "Display of Multiple 3D-Objects Using the Generalized Voxel Model," *Medical Imaging II, Proceedings of SPIE*, SPIE, Bellingham, Wash., Vol. 914, 1988, pp. 850-854.

Given the complexity of the surface reconstruction problem in medical imaging, it is understood that a single density value per voxel is generally insufficient to perform such interactive tasks as surface dissection that are at the same time faithful to the underlying anatomy. The authors utilize additional information such as the weighted MR data, or subtraction flow compensation data, and perform a spectral decomposition to classify voxels based on known densities of various tissues to improve the separation of the images. Smooth surfaces are then calculated by using the zero crossings of a convolution (Laplacian of a Gaussian) on the data volume.

Hunter, C., "New Graphics for Cray Users," *Proceedings, Cray User Group*, Lawrence Livermore National Laboratory, Livermore, Calif., Spring 1987, pp. 168-171.

This update from Lawrence Livermore National Laboratory chronicles the status of two projects combining high speed networking and graphics capabilities for researchers using the Cray supercomputers. These systems evolved from the requirements and objectives generated by the Graphics Assessment Project. MAGIC (Machine Graphics in Color) is a system that starts at the Cray and passes data across the HYPERchannel to a Gould SEL in route to LSI Decnet notes that terminate in Tektronix graphics displays. GWS (Graphics Workstation) is a more direct interconnection between the Cray and various Sun workstation configurations.

Jackins, C.L. and Tanimoto, S.L., "Oct-Trees and Their Use in Representing 3D Objects," *Computer Graphics and Image Processing*, Vol. 14, No. 3, 1980, pp. 249-270.

Quad-tree representation of planar images is readily extended to 3D volumes as oct-trees where subdivision into eighths is repeatedly performed until an entire subcube has a single attribute (usually binary). Algorithms for union, intersection, complement, condensation, rotation, and translation of oct-tree structures are extended in this work from their respective 2D analogs. A Pascal program is included for exploration of the oct-tree algorithms.

Julesz, B., *Foundations of Cyclopean Perception*, University of Chicago Press, Chicago, Ill., 1971.

"The essence of cyclopean stimulation is this formation of a percept at some central location in the visual system by using stimuli that could not possibly produce that percept at an earlier location." In rather more idiomatic terms, the whole is more, and in fact different, than the sum of the parts (for example in music a counterpoint melody can be heard from two or more different musical themes). For vision, the classic cyclopean stimulus is the random dot stereogram where recognizable shapes suddenly appear when two monocular views (neither of which visually betray the shape) are cross fused. The author illustrates the topics of cyclopean perception, physiological psychology, depth perception, and form recognition with these random dot stereograms. Colored plastic glasses are provided for the reader who prefers anaglyphic stereopsis!

Kajiya, J. and Von Herzen, B., "Ray Tracing Volume Densities," SIGGRAPH 84 Conference Proceedings, *Computer Graphics*, Vol. 18, No. 3, 1984, pp. 165-173.

Ray tracing is proposed for the large class of natural phenomena that can be described as a partial differential equation yielding scalar or vector values defined on a uniform mesh (i.e., clouds). The authors extend Blinn's work to multiple scattering from systems of high albedo particles in a very general system that allows light sources from within the density and interactions with other procedurally defined objects in the scene. In a two-step process, the density is converted to a brightness volume for each light source and then each ray is integrated for absorption and scattering attenuation. A perturbation solution to the full scattering problem is presented replete with spherical harmonics and integrals. Before concluding with a sequence of frames from a cloud formation animation, the authors describe fractal methods and physical models that can be used to generate typical volume densities.

Kaufman, A., editor, *Volume Visualization*, IEEE Computer Society Press, Los Alamitos, Calif., 1991 (in review).

This tutorial collection of over 35 papers includes both recently published work and original material on volume visualization. The book is organized with an introduction by the editor, followed by chapters on volume representation, viewing algorithms, shading algorithms, 3D descrete space, architectures for volume visualization, and applications of volume visualization. A glossary of terms and an annotated bibliography are also included.

Kaufman, A. and Bakalash, R., "Memory and Processing Architecture for 3D Voxel-Based Imagery," *IEEE Computer Graphics and Applications*, Vol. 8, No. 6, Nov. 1988, pp. 10-23.

The Cube architecture is designed for direct volumetric data manipulation and graphical display from the cubical frame buffer of voxel information. After describing similar systems (GODPA, PARCUM, and 3DP), the authors provide an overview of the Cube. The cubic frame buffer (CFB) is the central component that is operated upon by the FBP3 (a 3D bitblit processing engine), the geometry processor (GP3 for reading geometric constructions into the CFB), and the viewing processor (VP3 for producing real-time projections of the CFB), across the VMWB (voxel multiple write bus that can access an entire "beam" of voxels at once). The design is especially useful for superposition of synthetic images onto real data sets (i.e., skulls overlayed with CT data). A 16 by 16 by 16 CFB system has been implemented and is capable of 20K projections per second.

Kaufman, A., "Efficient Algorithms for 3D Scan-Conversion of Parametric Curves, Surfaces, and Volumes," SIGGRAPH 87 Conference Proceedings, *Computer Graphics*, Vol. 21, No. 4, July 1987, pp. 171-179.

With the advent of computer architectures designed for volume rendering (i.e., CUBE, GODPA, PARCUM, and 3DP) it will be necessary to describe standard 3D parametric objects in their descrete voxel map representations. Such objects include cubic parametric space curves, bicubic patches, and tricubic volumes. For each class of object, the author presents a mathematical discussion, a general 3D scan conversion algorithm using third order, forward difference operators, and a variant algorithm customized for efficient scan conversion into a volumetric frame buffer.

Kluksdahl, N.C., Kriman, A.M., and Ferry, D.K., "The Role of Visualization in the Simulation of Quantum Electronic Transport in Semiconductors," *Computer*, Vol. 22, No. 8, Aug. 1989, pp. 60-66.

The authors describe visualization and animation of simulation data to augment their understanding of the behavior of quantum electron transport in semiconductors. Although the paper is quite technical, the visualization processes employed give a very graphic portrayal of the electron tunneling behavior of the quantum mechanical model and therefore of the underlying real semiconductor device. Use of the so called Wigner formulation reduces the multidimensional phase space solution of these systems to one that involves axes of position, momentum, and probability amplitudes of the electron Gaussian wave packets. These three axes are readily graphed by using colored contours with hidden surface elimination.

Kunii, T.L., *Computer Graphics: Visual Technology and Art*, Springer-Verlag, Tokyo, Japan, 1985.

This collection of papers comprises the Proceedings of Computer Graphics, Tokyo, 1985. Sample works span the topics of computational geometry, graphics standardization, CAD/CAM, graphics networks, visual communication and interfaces, computer animation, and computer art. Several papers on medical imaging, featuring interactive creation of the surface contours for organ visualization in CT scans, are also included.

Lathrop, O., chair, *State of the Art in Data Visualization*, ACM SIGGRAPH 89 Course Notes, Course Number 28, Boston, Mass., 1989.

This volume is an assemblage of articles and visual aids that accompanied the technical courses in data visualization. Speakers included: Lloyd Treinish on multidimensional data management and graphics systems at the National Space Science Data Center; Mark Smith on a general data visualization implementation; Val Watson on scientific visualization tools and research at NASA Ames; Steve Legensky on computational hierarchies for visualization; Maxine Brown on the Array Tracer and code for blt-stones; and Tim Van Hook with an illustrated review of volume visualization techniques. A few of the other courses presented at the 1989 SIGGRAPH conference also touch upon subjects closely related to scientific visualization.

Lenz, R., Gudnumdsson, B., Lindskog, B., and Danielsson, P.E., "Display of Density Volumes," *IEEE Computer Graphics and Applications*, Vol. 6, No. 7, July 1986, pp. 20-29.

The authors describe experiments with two techniques for imaging voxel data. The first is a surface projection method with depth or pseudo- color encoding. The color of each pixel is determined by the distance from the image plane to the first point of intersection with the volumetric object. The second technique involves reprojection where the density is summed along the viewpoint ray. The data in this second situation is filtered first to contrast the boundaries and to reduce the density of homogeneous interior regions. The particular system, PICAP II, is described as well as some thoughts on the hardware and parallel architectures required to bring these techniques to interactive speeds.

Levie, W.H. and Lentz, R., "Effects of Text Illustration: A Review of Research," *Educational Communication Technical Journal*, Vol. 30, 1982, pp. 195-232.

An interesting look at the synergy between textual language and visual illustration and how the interplay effects learning in students of all ages is provided in this review of over 50 experiments in education and psychology. The conclusions confirm the use of illustration to attract and direct attention and to facilitate comprehension and retention (as well as just being enjoyable to look at).

Levin, D.N., et al., "Integrated 3D Display of MR, CT, and PET Images of the Brain," in *Proceedings NCGA 89*, National Computer Graphics Association., Fairfax, Va., Vol. I, pp. 179-186.

Unavailable for annotation.

Levoy, M., "Display of Surfaces from Volume Data," *IEEE Computer Graphics and Applications*, Vol. 8, No. 3, May 1988, pp. 29-37.

When you can overcome the visual distraction of the profusion of ghoulish skulls, this paper concisely details the algorithm used by Levoy to produce these volume renderings. After the raw data is corrected for inherent anomalies and contrast enhancement, the density volume is processed along two paths. The first is responsible for shading the voxel by using resampled ray tracing from the assigned color map. The second path concerns the opacity of the voxel that is a classification problem (but with a soft threshold, not a binary one to reduce aliasing) based on the density. This opacity is scaled by the density gradient to suppress the interiors of tissue that effectively highlights tissue boundaries. These two paths are composited to produce the display pixel attributes. The author concludes with some limitations of the technique involving striping and soft tissue shading, which are sensitive to local gradient density and misalignment between slices of data.

Levoy, M., "Efficient Ray Tracing of Volume Data," *Technical Report 88-029*, Computer Science Department, University of North Carolina at Chapel Hill, Chapel Hill, N.C., June 1988.

The author defines volume rendering as a technique for visualizing 3D scalar fields without fitting geometric parameters to the data. Using local operators for color and opacity at each point, a brute force, front to back, ray tracing algorithm is used to create 2D projections of colored semi-transparent volumes. Two enhancements to the basic method are discussed to improve efficiency. The first uses a pyramid representation of binary volumes to encode coherence (i.e., to compute ray intersections and to quickly discard uninteresting voxels of no opacity). The other improvement results from adaptively terminating a ray when the opacity reaches a given threshold. Specific statements of Pascal algorithms are included and efforts to quantify the computation costs and savings of the techniques are made from the example human skull and electron density map data sets.

Levoy, M., "Volume Rendering by Adaptive Refinement," *Technical Report 88-030*, Computer Science Department, University of North Carolina at Chapel Hill, Chapel Hill, N.C., June 1988.

Starting with a brute force, front to back, ray tracing algorithm for a volume rendering with local operators for color and opacity, the author produces a sequence of images of increasing quality. By casting a small number of rays distributed as a function of local image complexity (based on a recursive subdivision of local color differences), the first image is formed by using bilinear interpolation of the resulting non- uniformly spaced pixel colors. As more rays are cast into the image, the previously interpolated pixels are gradually replaced by colors based upon direct calculation. The algorithm meets the adaptive criteria of distributing the work where is is most useful, of basing intermediate images on partial information, and of minimizing the previous work that is discarded as each image is generated. The paper includes a Pascal statement of the solution and reviews implementation results for CT and molecular modeling data sets.

Long, M.B., Lyons, K., and Lam, J.K., "Acquisition and Representation of 2D and 3D Data from Turbulent Flows and Flames," *Computer*, Vol. 22, No. 8, Aug. 1989, pp. 39-45.

A simple turbulence problem fully characterized would require measurements of temperature, pressure, density, concentrations of all species, and a 3D velocity vector at each of perhaps ten million points of the volume. Yet, the authors maintain solutions are possible by combining laser light scattering techniques providing two- and three-dimensional experimental measurements with improved graphical representations for large quantities of data. The paper includes a discussion of a typical experimental configuration and illustrates a variety of visualization techniques including pseudo-color mappings, stacked flow planes, cast shadow 3D surfaces, and gradient colored reconstructed surfaces.

Lorensen, W.E. and Cline, H.E., "Marching Cubes: A High-Resolution 3D Surface Construction Algorithm," SIGGRAPH 87 Conference Proceedings, *Computer Graphics*, Vol. 21, No. 4, July 1987, pp. 163-169.

High resolution images of medical volume data can be rendered with conventional computer graphics systems by constructing triangle models of constant density surfaces. The algorithm the authors describe considers a cube of eight data values from two slices of the volume data. A case table of the 14 possible triangle topologies (reduced from 256 by symmetry) is used to obtain the interslice connectivity and the vertices of the triangles are calculated with linear interpolation. The surface is constructed as this cube is "marched" throughout the data. Another important step is to central difference the density gradient information in the original data to form the normalized surface vectors needed for realistic shading. Enhancements to the basic algorithm include the use of scan line and slice-to-slice coherence and the provision of Boolean solid modeling constructs to permit cutting and clipping of the volume data. Examples are illustrated from CT, MR, and SPECT medical imaging data.

MacEachren, A.M., "The Evolution of Computer Mapping and Its Implications for Geography," *Journal of Geography*, Vol. 86, No. 3, 1987, pp. 100- 108.

Maps are classic visualization tools for exploring spatially correlated data. This paper examines how computer graphics and output technology has changed and augmented map making and map interpretation. Considerations for hardware and software design toward generalizing map data are typified by the problem of efficiently representing and displaying geographic features such as rivers or coastlines. Current research portends the electronic atlas and the intelligent map that provide base-level access to hypertext databases (i.e., interactive queries).

McCormick, B.H., DeFanti, T.A., and Brown, M.D., editors, "Visualization in Scientific Computing," *Computer Graphics*, Vol. 21, No. 6, Nov. 1987.

This special issue of *Computer Graphics* contains the panel report outlining the political, economical, educational, sociological, and technological aspects of Visualization in Scientific Computing as an emerging discipline. The report includes the definition and the domain of visualization problems and examines specific science and engineering applications. Hardware and software visualization environments from both short- and long-term vantages are discussed in the appendices. The panel also compiled a two-hour video tape to graphically augment their findings. The entire report serves as an excellent starting point for understanding the concerns of scientific visualization.

Meyer, G.W. and Greenberg, D.P., "Perceptual Color Spaces for Computer Graphics," SIGGRAPH 80 Conference Proceedings, *Computer Graphics*, Vol. 14, No. 3, 1980, pp. 254-261.

A useful color space for computer graphics is one with equal perceptual distances between colors. After providing background on color science, tristimulus theory, and television colorimetry, the authors describe two uniform color systems in use. The Munsell system is a distorted cylinder of color with a grey scale axis spanned by three variables: hue (red, yellow, blue, etc.), value (light versus dark), and chroma (the strength or intensity of a hue). Another system is the Optical Society of America uniform color scale that uses a statistical perceptual approach to color definition. A given color is defined on a cubo-octahedral structure with each element a member of six linear color scales and seven color planes indexed by lightness, yellowness, and greeness variables. The use of these color spaces for computer science applications is in the display of temperature or stress in simulations, and also for the accurate and efficient storage, transformation, and redisplay of color images.

Morgenthaler, D.G. and Rosenfeld, A., "Surfaces in Three-Dimensional Digital Images," *Information and Computation*, Vol. 51, No. 2, Nov. 1981, pp. 227-247.

This article offers a rigorous exposition of the mathematical theory behind the algorithms that extract surfaces from 3D computed tomographic data. The authors define simple surface points and simple closed surfaces. The connected collection of surface points is shown to be a closed surface that is the 3D analog of the 2D Jordon curve theorem. A chief feature of this development is the construction of surfaces from sets of voxels themselves rather than the common alternate approach that uses the faces of the voxels.

Papathaomas, T.V., Schiavone, J.A., and Julesz, B., "Stereo Animation for Very Large Data Bases: Case Study—Meteorology," *IEEE Computer Graphics and Applications*, Vol. 7, No. 9, Sept. 1987, pp. 18-27.

Combining the techniques of animation and stereopsis, the authors examine large data sets from meteorology generated by LAMPS (Limited Area and Mesoscale Prediction System). The realism of the resulting images is enhanced by a random jittering of the object boundaries that serves to reduce distracting moire patterns. A 3 by 3 dithering scheme supporting 10 levels is superimposed on the displayed object to allow an extra scalar dimension of data to be incorporated in the image. Since the simulation objects are clouds, a particle system rendering is aptly used to achieve efficient scene and motion realism. Algorithms and codes are included for the stereo projection calculations.

Peachey, D.R., "Solid Texturing of Complex Surfaces," SIGGRAPH 85 Conference Proceedings, *Computer Graphics*, Vol. 19, No. 3, July 1985, pp. 279-286.

Texturing is a method of mapping complex detail onto a rendered surface to improve the image realism. Traditionally, the texture is defined on the unit square and then mathematically mapped onto the surface by altering the lighting and shading model at each display point. The author extends texturing a dimension by defining the texture function on the unit cube. The paper provides examples that generate better realism for such objects as stone and wood and indicates how solid textures can be more readily mapped onto complex surfaces (like spheres). Bubble textures, sums of sinusoids, and projection functions such as concentric rings of cylinders are all typical 3D textures.

Peitgen, H.O. and Richter, P.H., editors, *The Beauty of Fractals: Images of Complex Dynamical Systems*, Springer-Verlag, Berlin, 1986.

A colorful and mesmerizing display of computer graphics portraits from the infinite and chaotic world of the complex plane. Accompanying the excellent images are papers exploring the underlying mathematics and essays placing the fractal image in historical and artistic context. Algorithms are listed for reproducing some of the simpler images based upon the Mandlebrot and Julia sets.

Pereyra, V. and Rial, J.A., "Visualizing Wave Phenomenae with Seismic Rays", in *Visualization in Scientific Computing*, Nielson, G.M. and Shriver, B., editors, IEEE Computer Society Press, Los Alamitos, Calif., 1990, pp. 174-189.

Using examples from seismic prospecting and earthquake seismology, the authors demonstrate the usefulness and necessity of both image processing and visualization techniques for significant problems in applied geophysics. In seismic prospecting, the goal is to image the earth's interior based on reflected, elastic wave energies to increase the efficiency of locating oil and gas fields. Typical graphics include pseudo- colored wave energy plots, interactive selection of a contoured slice from a cube of a given field variable, and tracing ray paths on a Coons patch representation of geological surfaces. In earthquake seismology, the goal is to predict strong ground motions produced by waves through the uppermost crustal layers, and especially look for destructive oscillations in such geologic formations as shallow sedimentary basins. Phase space plots, where many rays are traced by using the dynamics of the system, are useful here for understanding the balance between stable and chaotic systems.

Phillips, R.L., "Distributed Visualization at Los Alamos National Laboratory," *Computer*, Vol. 22, No. 8, Aug. 1989, pp. 70-77.

A research overview including: distributed visualization involving supercomputer computation connected via ultra high speed networks to researcher graphics workstations; the concept and implementation of the scientific visualization workbench; the Cray to Sun connection via ethernet and its importance inasmuch as it uses technology already in place (i.e., socket abstraction in TCP/IP networking); and future work involving implementation of high-speed networks such as CP*.

Pickett, R.M. and Grinstein, G.G., "Iconographics Displays for Visualizing Multidimensional Data," *Proceedings of the 1988 IEEE Conference on Systems, Man, and Cybernetics, Vol. I*, Beijing and Shenyang, People's Republic of China, 1988, pp. 514-519.

By drawing stick figures that map several data dimensions into an iconic configuration, regions are readily observed as varying visual textures. The technique is best applied to spatially coherent data such as multispectral imagery, or temporally coherent data as in seismic sensing. The authors define a 12 member family of icons based on a body and four limbs. Raw data is mapped to the angles that the limbs form with the trunk. An example from weather satellite data is illustrated. Future work includes providing the icons with dynamic properties ("dancing and swimming" textures), extending the concept to 3D, and incorporating icon-icon correlative interaction.

Potmesil, M. and Hoffert, E.M., "FRAMES: Software Tools for Modeling, Rendering and Animation of 3D Scenes," SIGGRAPH 87 Conference Proceedings, *Computer Graphics*, Vol. 21, No. 4, July 1987, pp. 85-93.

FRAMES is a set of software tools running under the Unix operating system for image generation and animation of 3D scenes. A command language is invoked by the user to create the graphics "pipes" that connect the components together. The authors first review similar animation systems including those associated with Whitted and Weimer, Crow, Reynolds (ASAS), Blinn, and Duff (Sequin and Unigrafix). The FRAMES system is then discussed with its three main divisions of image rendering, geometric modeling, and animation, and its numerous tools (geometric transformations, clipping, back face culling, triangulation, shading, projection, raster scan conversion, and visible surface determination with antialiasing). Several illustrated examples, complete with the FRAMES scripts, are included in the paper.

Prueitt, M.L., "A Window on Science," *IEEE Computer Graphics and Applications*, Vol. 7, No. 9, Sept. 1987, pp. 4-8.

The author provides a brief and informal, but nonetheless pictorial, glimpse of visualization projects ongoing at Los Alamos National Laboratory. Snapshots include pollution levels over Colorado skies, world population trends, superconductor electron densities, and molecular rotational energy surfaces.

Reeves, W.T., "Particle Systems—A Technique for Modeling a Class of Fuzzy Objects," *ACM Transactions on Graphics*, Vol. 2, No. 2, April 1983, pp. 91-108.

Reeves describes his particle systems as the wall of fire from the Genesis bomb consumes the dead planet, with a few fireworks thrown in for good measure. These systems define volumes and as such cannot be rendered with the conventional graphics primitives. The model describes the stochastic generation of particles, their dynamics, and their extinction. Additional details are provided about the rendering, manipulation, and hierarchial organization of these systems that facilitate their creative use in graphics imagery.

Rogers, D.F. and Earnshaw, R.A., editors, *Techniques for Computer Graphics*, Springer-Verlag, New York, 1987.

The papers in this collection come from an International Summer Institute on the State of the Art in Computer Graphics held in Stirling, Scotland. Many of the key researchers in current visualization areas presented works at this conference. The volume is divided into chapters for design, modeling, workstations, hardware, human-computer interfaces, and graphics and documentation standards.

Rogers, S.E., Buning, P.G., and Merritt, F.J., "Distributed Interactive Graphics Applications in Computational Fluid Dynamics," *International Journal of Supercomputer Applications*, Vol. 1, No. 4, 1987, pp. 96-105.

Two programs from fluid flow applications have been modified to operate under the distributed computer system at NASA/Ames between the Cray and an Iris graphics workstation. RIP (real-time interactive particle tracer) has the Cray perform the massive computations that set up the flow database, and only sends over the graphics primitives to the Iris needed to trace the path of the target particle selected interactively by the user within the workstation application. The connection details involve spawning child processes on the Cray that load in the computed database and passively await trace requests from the Iris. The other application is PLOT3D that is primarily a tool for the postprocessing and display of flow simulations. The examples depicted in the paper detail flows through the space shuttle, around airplane fuselages, and around a flying broomstick (ogive cylinder).

Rosenblum, L.J., "Visualization of Experimental Data at the Naval Research Laboratory," *Computer*, Vol. 22, No. 8, Aug. 1989, pp. 95-101.

A research overview: much of the effort at visualization at the Naval Research Laboratory is directed toward understanding large volumes of experimental data such as that recording the "activity" of ocean processes (i.e., physical variables such as temperature and shear are distilled into pictures that depict "quick looks" at the oceanographic data). This example of "peer graphics" is an important concept in scientific visualization in that some images are intended primarily for preview and discussion with fellow researchers (who have built up similar histories of visual intuition) rather than for formal publication. The article also mentions work in molecular modeling, underwater acoustics, and synthetic radar.

Rosenblum, L.J., "Visualizing Oceanographic Data," *IEEE Computer Graphics and Applications*, Vol. 9, No. 3, May 1989, pp. 14-19.

The author describes three projects utilizing visualization for oceanographic data. The first uses animated sequences to explore temperature and salinity effects on salt fingering convection (warm salty water mixing with a lower layer of cold fresh water). Another project in bathymetric charting uses interactive overlapping of contour diagrams to align swaths of data into "registered" maps. While in fine scale variability studies, displays of multidimensional signal processing output from thermistor sensors are examined. Future work on the complex task of 3D acoustic prediction is forecast in the conclusion.

Russell, G. and Miles, R.B., "Display and Perception of 3-D Space Filling Data," *Applied Optics*, Vol. 26, No. 6, 1987, pp. 973-982.

The authors argue that vision is inherently a 2D process that is time multiplexed (i.e., motion and stereo "doubling" lead to the perception of the third dimension). Using data examples from fluid flow and medical imaging, images are precomputed and then played back in real time on a PC AT system, generally as rotations about the viewer's vertical axis. The images themselves are calculated by using

source-attenuation methods based on optical physics to create the "solidity" depth cuing. The algorithm involves choosing a view, transforming the world data, deciding the scan order, projecting the data onto the view plane, and then adding in the lighting and shading model.

Sabella, P., "A Rendering Algorithm for Visualizing 3D Scalar Fields," SIGGRAPH 88 Conference Proceedings, *Computer Graphics*, Vol. 22, No. 4, Aug. 1988, pp. 51-55.

Previous rendering techniques for 3D scalar fields have either used cross sections and contours or, as in the case of medical imaging, threshold rendering (i.e., front to back, ray tracing and surface reconstruction methods). The author's work employs a scattering model as might be used to render clouds or smoke or some typical particle system that uses the natural translucence of a density object. Basically, a brightness equation is integrated as a ray passes through the volume data undergoing occlusion effects but no shadowing or color scattering. Such an underlying physical model is known as a variable density emitter (DE) object. Further visual information is mapped onto this basic rendering by color mapping into HSV space such variable attributes (parametrized by the ray's path) as maximum density value and the distance at which the peak is encountered. The brightness equation can also be modified as a function of the computed density gradient to intensify the effects of dense areas. An example using subsoil seismic data is illustrated in the paper.

Saltzman, J., "Simple Interface (SI): An Interface between a Cray Supercomputer and Sun Workstation," *LA-UR-88-2171*, Los Alamos National Laboratory, Los Alamos, N.M., June 1988.

Unavailable for annotation.

Samet, H. and Webber, R.E., "Hierarchical Data Structures and Algorithms for Computer Graphics, Part II: Applications," *IEEE Computer Graphics and Applications*, Vol. 8, No. 4, 1988, pp. 59-75.

The emphasis in this paper is on oct-trees and their usefulness in the display of computer graphics images. Specific instances of oct-tree algorithms are described for constructive solid geometry (CSG), for parallel and perspective projections (where they reduce to a display quadtree), for ray tracing (where they speed up the intersection calculations), and for radiosity lighting. The authors also review quadtree algorithms for hidden surface display in the manner of Warnock, and Weiler and Atherton. This review article is augmented with a bibliography of nearly 100 pertinent references.

Schlusselberg, D.S. and Smith, W.K., "Three-Dimensional Display of Medical Image Volumes," in *Proceedings NCGA 86*, National Computer Graphics Association, Fairfax, Va., Vol. III, May 1986, pp. 114-123.

In a review of direct volume and surface extraction medical imaging techniques, the authors explain advantages and disadvantages of existing methods. The problem of soft tissue modeling is especially targeted since thresholding generally provides poor separation and requires major reprocessing when threshold values are modified. The proposed algorithm involves 3D perspective ray traced images where the specific aspects of filtering, transparency, and coloring are all based on a table lookup of the original voxel density values. Normals are calculated only from a 5 by 5 by 5 neighborhood of the first object voxel struck by a given ray. Examples are taken from craniofacial CT and skeletal injury data. The illustrations describing steps in the algorithm are also quite effective.

Seager, M.K., Werner, N.E., Zosel, M.E., and Strout, R.E., "Graphical Analysis of Multi/Micro-Tasking Execution on Cray Multiprocessors," in *Visualization in Scientific Computing*, Nielson, G.M. and Shriver, B., editors, IEEE Computer Society Press, Los Alamitos, Calif., 1990, pp. 160-173.

Beyond the fundamental algorithm, parallel programming places the additional demands of tasking (distributing the computation among the processors), synchronization (how tasks interact), and data scoping (how data is shared by tasks) on the programmer. Stategraph and timeline are two of the Graphical Multiprocessing Analysis Tools (GMAT) that were developed to help programmers visualize these aspects of their parallel codes. Stategraph represents each task as a node in an ancestry tree where nodes change representation as events are processed. Timeline represents each task as a line with nodes posted as the events occur providing a temporal sense of the process. The authors conclude the paper with three trial sessions by using the timeline tool with snapshots of the screen display to accompany the verbal description.

She, Z. and Nicolaenko, B., "Temporal Intermittency and Turbulence Production in the Kolmogorov Flow," in *Proceedings of IUTAM Symposium on Topological Fluid Dynamics*, Moffatt, H.K. and Tsinober, A., editors, Cambridge University Press, Cambridge, England, 1989.

The authors explore temporal intermittent bursting events in flow systems governed by the Navier-Stokes equation by using a dynamical systems approach. The dynamical significance of the symmetry groups in a particular flow system (2D Kolmogorov flow) are discussed as well as the heteroclinic excursions (or turbulent bursting transitions) between the basic states implied by the symmetry. Vorticity snapshots of the burst and basic states are rendered by using 3D perspective, hidden surface elimination, and shading.

Sloan, K.R., Jr. and Hrechanyk, L.M., "Surface Reconstruction from Sparse Data," in *Proceedings of the IEEE Conference on Pattern Recognition and Image Processing*, IEEE Computer Society Press, Los Alamitos, Calif., Aug. 1981, pp. 45-48.

Existing tiling methods for surface reconstruction from cross-sectional contours require dense data (i.e., slowing varying between slices). By casting reconstruction as a shape-matching problem, the authors propose a method that is effective for sparse data. Using the construct of generalized cylinders defined by an axis and a set of nearly parallel cross sections, a sweeping rule is hypothesized to transform a given contour to its match on the next slice. If the contours are nearly matched, a classical tiling is employed, otherwise an intermediate contour is "hallucinated" from the hypothesized sweeping rule and the problem is recursively divided into two subproblems. The sweeping rules are from the set of translations, rotations, scalings, and deformations, and are chosen in this order of increasing complexity.

Smith, A., "Volume Graphics and Volume Visualization, A Tutorial," *Pixar Technical Memo 176*, Pixar, San Rafael, Calif., May 1987.

After describing five visualization tools (rendering, reconstruction or stacking, interactive "slice of a cube" tool, film loops, and classification coloring) the author annotates 13 demonstration examples and how they use these tools. Especially useful are the sections that review the literature and outline the major paths of continued research likely to be fruitful in this emerging discipline (i.e., volume patches, 3D image processing tools, particle systems, texture mapping, file handling, 3D displays and input devices, and volume graphics standards). The article ends with the author's tantalizing but admittedly fanciful volume design workstation.

Smith, E., "The McIDAS System," *IEEE Transactions on Geoscience Electronics*, Vol. GE-13, July 1975, pp. 123-136.

An interesting historical look at the interactive data acquisition and display system from the University of Wisconsin that has since migrated to an IBM mainframe and over a half million lines of Fortran from the original system with 64K words of memory and 15M disk drives! The article introduces the system components including: the operational language, the executive monitor, software modules, graphics displays, and tools for image acquisition and processing.

Staudhammer, J., "Supercomputers and Graphics," *IEEE Computer Graphics and Applications*, July 1987, pp. 24-25.

This article is the guest editor's introduction to a special issue of IEEE CG&A on supercomputers and graphics. After making the point that television is essentially a 30 MB per second communications channel, Staudhammer proceeds to introduce the papers in this volume and how they attempt to achieve the calculation of the data behind the media through supercomputing.

Stettner, A. and Greenberg, D.P., "Computer Graphics Visualization for Acoustic Simulation," SIGGRAPH 89 Conference Proceedings, *Computer Graphics*, Vol. 23, No. 3, July 1989, pp. 195-206.

Using the similarities of light and sound as wave phenomena, the authors employ ray tracing techniques to evaluate the acoustic properties of structures such as a concert hall. Simulation data provide information about such variables as clarity, definition, spatial impression, and strength of sound and various visualization schemes are described to convey this information to the acoustic designer. This work is an example of the combined use of three-dimensional images, color, animation, and abstract representation to promote the comprehension of a complex scientific simulation.

Stuetzle, W., "Plot Windows," *Journal of the American Statistical Association*, Vol. 82, No. 398, 1987, pp. 466-475.

Plot Windows is a statistical software tool implemented on a Symbolics Machine Lisp workstation that places a desktop interface between the user and a data set. In this system, scatterplots are treated as objects that are automatically updated and are subject to a number of interactive operations. Besides rotation of point clouds as depth cuing, the notion of connected scatterplots is made possible by brushing (identifying and highlighting in a scatterplot) and painting (selecting in one scatterplot while painting the corresponding elements in others). These operators have also been extended to manipulate stem and leaf style histograms as connected objects.

Treinish, L.A., "An Interactive, Discipline-Independent Data Visualization System," *Computers in Physics*, Vol. 3, No. 4, July 1989, pp. 55- 64.

A driving force behind the development of generic, discipline independent visualization techniques is the need to support correlative data analyses when the data are collated from a variety of sources. The NGS system at the National Space Science Data Center (NSSDC) is designed for these data management and data display requirements. The author describes the NSSDC common data format and the components of NGS in the context of the total ozone Nimbus 7 satellite data with numerous illustrations. Future work is also outlined in the face of such staggering data sources as the NASA Earth Observing System Satellite (mid-1990s) with its projected terabyte-per-day data transmission rate.

Tufte, E.R., *The Visual Display of Quantitative Information*, Graphics Press, Cheshire, Conn., 1983.

With an illustration on every page, it would be easy to skip the text, but before adopting that good looking style for your next presentation make sure you are not in the chapter on chartjunk! In this book, that looks as if the author has followed his own suggestions for graphical ex-

cellence and integrity, are discussions of data ink, multifunctioning graphical elements, chartjunk (e.g., unintentional optical art, the dreaded grid, and the self-promoting duck), data density and small multiples, and aesthetics and technique.

Upson, C., editor, *Chapel Hill Workshop on Volume Visualization, Conference Proceedings*, Department of Computer Science, University of North Carolina, Chapel Hill, N.C., 1989.

The Chapel Hill visualization workshop was organized into five major sessions that effectively span the efforts of current research in volume visualization. Software toolkits and visualization environments at Sun Microsystems, Stellar Computer, NCSA (University of Illinois at Champaign-Urbana), and the University of North Carolina at Chapel Hill were presented. The session on algorithms included volume rendering and 3D texture maps, image cube visualization, and interactivity. Typical medical imaging applications were described by researchers from the University of Chicago Hospitals and the University Hospital at Eppendorf. Data classification techniques were described by W.F. Kraske, et al., from the University of Southern California, and by J.R. Rossignac from IBM. A final session examined representative visualization system implementations at the University of Alabama, and at the University of North Carolina at Chapel Hill. For a complete list of the participants and the session papers, refer to the appendix on Recent Conferences in Scientific Visualization.

Upson, C. and Fangmeier, S., "The Role of Visualization and Parallelism in a Heterogeneous Supercomputing Environment," in *Parallel Processing for Computer Vision and Display*, Earnshaw, R., editor, Springer-Verlag, New York, 1989.

The authors explore a simulation case study from gas dynamics to assess the demands that interactive "steering" of large-scale simulations will put on supercomputer and graphics environments. Aspects of the study include feature extraction, data filtering, image computation, bandwidth limitations of data transfer, and the necessity of interaction during the simulation. The analysis suggests systems capable of sustained 15 gigaFlop computation with 100 MB/sec communications channels will be required.

Upson, C. and Keeler, M., "VBuffer: Visible Volume Rendering," SIGGRAPH 88 Conference Proceedings, *Computer Graphics*, Vol. 22, No. 4, Aug. 1988, pp. 59-64.

Contrasted to the constant valued voxel cuberille method, the VBuffer technique utilizes computation cells, a trilinearly interpolated volumetric element with data points at each of the eight corners. Two styles of ray tracing can be used: casting rays through the image plane at the object that is more efficient for nearly opaque volumes, and cell by cell processing that affords greater detail, is readily vectorizable, and is more efficient for nearly transparent data sets. The lighting model involves color and opacity transfer functions that can effectively depict small ranges of scalar values as surfaces; and uses atmospheric attenuation and volume texture mapping to augment visual cuing. This resultant intensity equation is integrated by using trapezoidal quadrature over the sub-volume swept by the target pixel in each of the data sub-volumes. An example from a severe storm simulation is illustrated.

Upson, C., "The Visual Simulation of Amorphous Phenomena," *Visual Computer*, Vol. 2, No. 5, 1986, pp. 321-326.

Amorphous phenomena like clouds or smoke can be modeled with a variety of 3D techniques but this paper surveys these methods by using a more ambitious numerical model of the formation of the large-scale structure of the universe. Contour mapping (displaying arbitrary 2D slices of the volume data), the Cuberille method (voxels represented by simple volumetric shapes, usually a cube), particle advection (releasing "smoke" streams in flow simulations), and surface tiling (complex surfaces from unions of polyhedral intersections with the voxel elements) are all discussed in turn.

Van Dyke, M., *An Album of Fluid Motion*, Parabolic Press, Stanford, Calif., 1982.

A photographic examination of almost 300 graphical images researchers obtain from experimental fluid dynamics. The book covers a diverse set of flow situations including laminar, turbulent, free surface, natural convection, subsonic, supersonic, and shock wave flows. Equally diverse are the techniques employed to create the images: glycerin in water, smoke in wind tunnels, spark shadowgraphs, and light emitting laser dyes. These are the types of images computer graphics experts in computed flow dynamics are attempting to recreate and visualize from numerical simulations.

Vannier, M. and Geist, D., "Shading 3-D Reconstructions," *C Users Journal*, Aug. 1989, pp. 71-80.

Starting with an informative introduction on the method of computed tomography and the data it produces, the authors provide detailed flowcharts of the 3D imaging routines from their C implementation on AT compatible microprocessor systems. First the data are thresholded and all object voxels are given a distance value that is saved in a file. Another routine processes this file looking for the first threshold transition per scan line where a surface gradient is calculated for shading purposes. The code supports viewing only from the six orthogonal directions to the data (i.e., from the faces of a cube). Typical processing times were about one minute per slice of 256 by 256 density voxel data.

Wang, P.C.C., editor, *Graphical Representation of Multivariate Data*, Academic Press, New York, 1978.

This collection of papers from a symposium on graphical representation of multidimensional data at the Naval Postgraduate School quite appropriately begins with an introductory essay by H. Chernoff. Some of the following articles detail the application of his classical faces for data in policy sciences, psychiatric diagnosis, and health sciences. Other articles present extensions and alternatives to the original technique. Some experiments on the visual perception (and thereby the efficacy and limitations) of these faces are also presented.

Ware, C., "Color Sequences for Univariate Maps: Theory, Experiments, and Principles," *IEEE Computer Graphics and Applications*, Vol. 8, No. 5, 1988, pp. 41-49.

Use of pseudo-coloring (assigning colors to value ranges of a variable) is a common technique for spatially encoded univariate mappings. The authors describe three experiments devised to determine the effectiveness of different coloring sequences for two classes of data. Form information conveys shape or structure for which grey scales were found to be effective. Metric information is best displayed by using a physical spectrum as is classically used on geographic maps to convey elevation. The experiments covered simultaneous contrast, form perception, and specific color sequences. References are given on further work toward optimal univariate and bivariate color mapping.

Whitted, T., "An Improved Illumination Model for Shaded Display," *Communications of the ACM*, Vol. 23, No. 6, June 1980, pp. 343-349.

Ray tracing comes of age in this classic paper. Building on the lighting model of Phong and Blinn, the author suggests a random perturbation technique to the specular component so reflected highlights can be treated as a nearly distributed light source from within the object scene. Unlike previous ray tracing models, this technique permits global interactions as the rays are recursively traced until extinction outside of the scene. Although back face culling and clipping are no longer allowed, use of bounding volumes and readily accommodated anti-aliasing permit some computational efficiencies.

Winkler, K.H.A. and Norman, M.L., "MUNACOLOR: Understanding High-Resolution Gas Dynamical Simulations Through Color Graphics," in *Astrophysical Radiation Hydrodynamics*, Winkler, K.H.A. and Norman, M.L., editors, D. Reidel Publishing Company, Hingham, Mass., 1986, pp. 223-243.

The MUNACOLOR graphics system points out the advantages of pseudo-color variable mappings coupled with simple contour plots for examining numerical simulations in fluid dynamics. Besides the direct one variable mapping applied to density, pressure, or vorticity, classification caricatures are used to explicitly define regions of interest in the simulation flow by assigning a separate color to the ambient medium, the bow shock disturbed medium, the beam, and the cocoon about the beam, etc. (An information compression technique born of necessity several years back when the authors were working on a Ramtek graphics display device with a 110 baud serial connection!) The authors conclude the paper with a series of speculative calculations that circumscribe a numerical fluid dynamics simulator that is impedence matched to the information bandwidth of the human visual system.

Wolfe, R.H., Jr. and Liu, C.N., "Interactive Visualization of 3D Seismic Data: A Volumetric Method," *IEEE Computer Graphics and Applications*, Vol. 8, No. 4, July 1988, pp. 24-30.

The authors document a graphics tool for providing a synoptic journey through a volume of data from acoustic depth sounding. The raw data are first digitally deconvoluted to remove ringing and migration effects. The volume is then displayed sheet by sheet, each translated a small amount to give the overall impression of a skewed orthographic volume. The data are color coded by amplitude of the seismic reflection and by not rendering cells of low amplitude the interesting internal features are readily observed. The system was implemented on a PC-AT, which the authors note is too slow for interaction but adequate for static display.

Wu, K. and Hesselink, L., "Computer Display of Reconstructed 3D Scalar Data," *Applied Optics*, Vol. 27, No. 2, Jan. 1988, pp. 395-404.

Using data from fluid flow experiments the authors critique three methods of displaying 40 slices of 512 by 512 scalar values. The first method is a "staircase" reconstruction on a plane-by-plane basis using translucence to provide depth cuing. In another technique, contour outlines for each plane are all simultaneously displayed (with each plane a gradually different color) and motion is used to provide the depth discrimination. The final approach produces contour surfaces by performing cubic spline volume interpolation (contrasted with "lofting," surface interpolation on a regular network of curves). These contour surfaces could be interactively "peeled" away from the remaining image in the system used by the authors to greatly enhance the total understanding of the volumetric data.

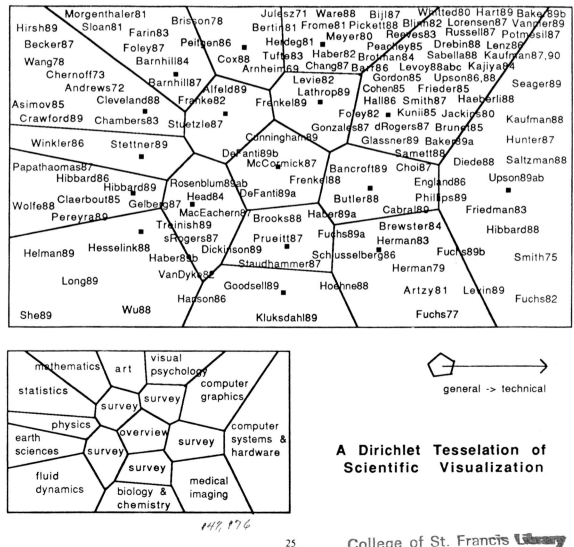

A Dirichlet Tesselation of Scientific Visualization

Recent Conferences and Workshops in Scientific Visualization

First Conference on Visualization in Biomedical Computing, Atlanta, Georgia, May 22-25, 1990, (Hosted by Emory University School of Medicine andGeorgia Institute of Technology).

Technical Committee:
Gabor Herman, Co-Chair, University of Pennsylvania
Ed Catmull, Co-Chair, PIXAR

Executive Committee:
Norberto Ezquerra, Chair, Georgia Institute of Technology
Ernest Garcia, Co-Chair, Emory University School of Medicine
Ronald Arkin, Co-Chair, Georgia Institute of Technology

Topics of Interest:

Theory, Approaches, and Psychological Aspects of Visualization
Models of Visualization
Human-Machine Interaction
Representation of Multidimensional Spaces
Visual Perception
Cognitive Aspects of Visualization
Visual Communications
Psychophysics
Computer Vision and Image Processing in Visualization
Artificial Intelligence in Visualization
Training and Instruction in Visualization
Visualization in Medical Education

Applications, Tools, and Techniques
Diagnostic Radiology
Molecular Biology and Biochemistry
Dentistry, Orthodontics, and Craniofacial Reconstruction
Biomechanics and Prosthetics Development
Modeling and Simulation of Biological Processes
Radiation Treatment Planning
Surgical Planning and Stereotaxy
Neuroanatomical and Neurophysiological Analyses
Hardware and Software Tools for Visualization
Hardware and Software Standards
Interactive Workstations
Acquisition of Data
Visualization Data Bases
Graphics and Display Techniques

Scientific Visualization Workshop at Pasadena, California, January 25-26, 1988, (Sponsored by NASA, JPL, NSF and SDSC).

Participants and Topics Included:

J. Knighton, Scientist's Environment
A. van Dam, Shareable Environments

V. Watson, Representation of Complex Systems
M. Norman, Scientific Opportunities for Scientific Visualization
C. Upson, Issues in Visualization
A. van Dam, Phigs+ Status
apE-Ohio Supercomputer Graphics Project
Dore, Ardent Computer
T. DeFanti and M. Brown, Remote Graphics Facility
L. Treinish, Data Structure and Data Management for Scientific Visualization

The workshop report also lists a database of researchers in the field of Scientific Visualization.

Visualization in Scientific Computing Workshop at Princeton, May 9-10, 1988.

Workshop Sessions and Participants Included:

Session: Present and Future Visualization Technologies
Hisashi Kibayashi, chair (Princeton)
James Clark (Silicon Graphics)
Henry Fuchs (UNC, Chapel Hill)
Alvy Rae Smith (Pixar)

Session: Cultural Roadblocks to Visualization
George Mueller, chair (Princeton)
Judith Brown (University of Iowa)
Robert Cunningham (California State, Stanislaus)
Bruce McCormick (Texas A&M)
Michael McGrath (Colorado School of Mines)

Session: Visual Output Technology
Eric Wood, chair (Princeton)
Frank Dietrich (Silicon Graphics)
Laurin Herr (Pacific Interface)
Robert Sedgewick (Princeton)

Session: Techniques from the Frontiers of Visualization
Douglas Welsh, chair track a (Princeton)
David Laur (Princeton)
Dean Taylor (Cornell)
Jayaram Udupa (University of Pennsylvania)
Michael Zyda (Naval Postgraduate School, Monterey)

Steve Slaby, chair track b (Princeton)
Richard Becker (AT&T Bell Labs)
John Danahy (University of Toronto)
Virginia Hetrick (University of Florida)
Donald Jones (Failure Analysis Associates)

William Thurston, chair track c (Princeton)
Maxine Brown (U of I, Chicago)
Craig Reynolds (Symbolics Inc.)
Nancy St. John (Pacific Data Images)
Gregory Russell (IBM)
Richard Miles (Princeton)

Session: Collaborations in Art and Science
Michael Mahoney, chair (Princeton)
Donna Cox (NCSA)
Vibeke Sorensen (CalTech)

Session: New User-Interface Paradigms and Innovation in

Software Design Strategy
Kirk Alexander, chair (Princeton)
Dana Batali (Pixar)
Eric Brechner (Silicon Graphics)
Richard Feldmann (NIH)
Paul Haeberli (Silicon Graphics)
Randall Smith (Xerox PARC)

Session: Algorithms and Theory
Robert May, chair (Princeton)
Robert Steinberg (NASA/Cleveland)
James Yorke (University of Maryland)

Thomas Lasinski (NASA/Ames)
Michael Wozny (NSF).

Visualization in Scientific Computing Workshop at Naval Research Laboratory, May 12, 1988.

Workshop Sessions and Participants Included:
Larry Rosenblum, Workshop Chairman (NRL)
David Bradley (NRL)
David Salzman (JvNNSC)

Session: Applications of Visualization in Scientific Computing
Azriel Rosenfeld, Chairman (University of Maryland)
Larry Rosenblum, Ocean Sciences (NRL)
Gary Laguna, Engineering Applications (LLNL)
Azriel Rosenfeld, Scene Analysis (University of Maryland)
Arthur Olson, Molecular Modeling (Research Institute of Scripps Clinic)

Session: Emerging Technologies
Craig Upson, Chairman (Stellar Computers)
Hank Dardy, Highly Parallel Processors (NRL)
Craig Upson, Synthesis of Graphics and Large-Scale Computing (Stellar)
Jim Conant, Computers for Graphics/Imaging (AT&T Pixel Machines)
Rober Wolff, Desktop Visualization (JPL)

Maxine Brown (University of Illinois, Chicago)

Workshop on Volume Visualization at Chapel Hill, North Carolina, May 18-19, 1989.

The following information has been abstracted from the conference proceedings as edited by Craig Upson, University of North Carolina at Chapel Hill.

Workshop Sessions and Participants Included:

Session: Software Toolkits and Environments
"Integration of Volume Rendering and Geometric Objects," E. Ruth Johnson and Charles E. Mosher, Sun Microsystems

"Interactive Volume Rendering," Lee Westover, UNC-Chapel Hill
"Volume Visualization at the Center for Supercomputing Research and Development," Peter Shirley and Henry Neeman, NCSA UIUC
"VEX: A Volume Exploratorium," Larry Gelberg, David Kamins and Jeff Vroom, Stellar Computer, Inc.

Session: Algorithms
"Molecular Applications of Volume Rendering and 3-D Texture Maps," David Goodsell and Arthur Olson, Scripps Clinic
"Interactive Image Cube Visualization and Analysis," James M. Torson, U.S. Geological Survey
"Interactivity is the Key," William Hibbard and David Santek, University of Wisconsin

Session: Applications
"Volumetric Rendering of Multimodality, Multivariable Medical Imaging Data," X. Hu, D.N. Levin, S.G. Galhorta, C.A. Pelizzari, G.T.Y. Chen,R.N. Beck, C.T. Chen and M.D. Cooper, University of Chicago Hospitals
"3-D Visualization of Tomographic Volume Data Using the Generalized Voxel-Method," K.H. Hohne, M. Bomans, A. Pommert, M. Riemer, C.Schiers, U. Tiede, and G. Wiebecke, University Hospital Eppendorf

Session: Data Classification
"Morphological Description in 3D Volumetric Biomedical Visualization," Wolfgang F. Kraske, Frederick W. George III, and James M. Halls, University of Southern California
"Considerations on the Interactive Rendering of Four-Dimensional Volumes," Jaroslaw R. Rossignac, IBM, T.J. Watson Research Center

Session: System Implementations
"True Volume Visualization of Medical Data," Steve E. Wixson, University of Alabama, Birmingham
"Design for a Real-Time High-Quality Volume Rendering Workstation," Marc Levoy, UNC-Chapel Hill

Scientific Visualization Videos

Issue 28: Visualization Domain, ACM SIGGRAPH

Contents Include:
L.A.—The Movie, JPL
Instabilities in Supersonic Flows, *Norman, et al.*, NCSA
CalTech Studies in Modeling and Motion, *Barr, et al.*, CalTech
Evolution of Structure in the Universe, *Centrella*, Drexel
Dynamic Crack Propagation with Step-Function Stress Loading, *Haber, et al.*, NCSA
Numerical Simulation of a Thunderstorm Outflow, *Wilhelmson, et al.*, NCSA

Scientific Visualization, Science Data Systems Group, JPL

Poliovirus, *Olson , et al.*, Research Institute of Scripps Clinic

Inertial Confinement Fusion, *Max*, Lawrence Livermore National Lab

RPI Scientific Visualization, RPI/CICG

Rigid Body Dynamics Simulations, *Hahn*, OSU

NASA/CFD Highlights

Computational Fluid Dynamics, *Winkler, et al.*, Los Alamos National Lab

Aerospace Applications of ADAM and Postprocessor, Mechanical Dynamics Inc.

Issue 29: Visualization Systems, ACM SIGGRAPH

Contents Include:

Volume Visualization with the Pixar Image Computer

Connection Machine Applications, Thinking Machines Corporation

Image Processing on PIPE, Kent

Pixel-Planes 4 Demonstration Tape, *Fuchs, et al.*, UNC-Chapel Hill

Rediscover Engineering, Silicon Graphics Inc.

Synthetic Holography, MIT Media Lab

Cartographic Modeling System, *Hanson, et al.*, SRI International

HP9000 SRX, Hewlett-Packard Company

Video Report on the Computer Graphics Industry, *Zaritsky/Herr*, Frost & Sullivan Inc.

Issue 30: Visualization: State of the Art, ACM SIGGRAPH

Over two hours of narrated video coverage of such topics as Interactivity, Workstation Trends, Dynamics: The New Realism, Visualization in Scientific Computing, Medical Imaging and Volumetrics, and future forecasts of the state of the art in hardware and software for computer graphics produced by Laurin Herr and Raul Zaritsky. The video documents candid commentary from the leading experts in the field of visualization:

Alan Barr (CalTech)
Ed Catmull (Pixar)
Tom DeFanti (U of I, Chicago)
Louis Doctor (Raster Technologies)
Jim Dunn (D&D Research Inc.)
Nick England (Sun Microsystems)
Henry Fuchs (UNC, Chapel Hill)
Donald Greenberg (Cornell)
Robert Haber (NCSA)
Bill Kovacs (Wavefront Technologies)
Carl Machover (Machover Associates Corp.)
Eihachiro Nakamae (Hiroshima University)
Koichi Omura (Osaka University)
Jon Peddie (Jon Peddie Associates)
Larry Smarr (NCSA)
Alvy Ray Smith (Pixar)
Turner Whitted (Numerical Design Ltd.)

Contents Include:

Red's Dream, Pixar
Luxo Jr., Pixar
Balloon Guy, Ohio State University
New Threads, AT&T Bell Labs
Fabricated Rhythm, AT&T Bell Labs
Compleat Angler, Turner Whitted
Cornell in Perspective, Cornell University
CG Town, Hiroshima University
Pandora's Chain, CalTech
A-129 Agusta, GE Simulation and Control Systems
TRW Rapid Prototyping, Robert Abel & Associates/Omnibus
Fair Play, Apollo Computer/Midnight Movie Group
Deja Vu, 4D Art & Design
Stanley and Stella: Breaking the Ice, Symbolics Graphics Division & Whitney/Demos
BOIDS, Symbolics Graphics Division
Rigid Body Dynamics Simulations, Ohio State University
Dynamic Simulations of Flexible Objects, Ohio State University
Scientific Simulations, NCSA
Volumetric Imaging, Pixar
Chicago, Roger Abel & Associates
Virtual Workstation Environment, NASA/Ames
L.A.-The Movie, NASA/JPL
Mental Images, Mental Images GmbH
Beating Heart, Mallinckrodt Institute of Radiology
CG Man, Japan Broadcasting Corporation
1987 Demo, Post Perfect
Le Corbusier, Thomson Digital Image

Issue 35: Visualization/State of the Art: Update, ACM SIGGRAPH

This hour long video with over forty examples of state of the art computer graphics examines the areas of High Performance Processors, Advances in Rendering, Color Desktop Pre-Press Systems, Color I/O Peripherals and Video, and Scientific Visualization. Featured on camera are these leading experts in the field:

Richard Beach (Xerox PARC)
James Blinn (CalTech)
Donna Cox (NCSA)
Charles Csuri (Ohio State University)
Henry Fuchs (UNC, Chapel Hill)
Thomas Jermoluk (Silicon Graphics)
Carl Machover (Machover Assoc. Corp.)
Benoit Mandelbrot (IBM)
Joel Orr (Orr Associates, Inc.)
Thomas Porter (Pixar)
Judson Rosebush (Rosebush Visions Corp.)
Daniel Sandin (EVL, U of I, Chicago)
Turner Whitted (Numerical Design, Ltd.)
Dean Winkler (Post Perfect)

Contents Include:
Dinosaur Stuff, Ohio State University/ACCAD
Water Strider, SoftImage
Volume Rendered Female Head, UNC, Chapel Hill
Ray Traced Diamonds, University of Tokyo
A Lilac Twig, University of Regina
A Museum of Constructivist Art, Cornell, Program of Computer Graphics
Muscle Modeling, Ohio State University/ACCAD
Human Dynamics Modeling, Ohio State University/ACCAD
Mathematica-The Theorem of Pythagoras, CalTech
DNA Molecule, du Pont
Scientific Visualization - 1988, NCSA
Fractal Landscapes, IBM
Animation Based on 'The Science of Fractal Images', University of Bremen, UCSC
Constrained Dynamics, CalTech
Anti-Logo, Post Perfect
Hair, AT&T Bell Laboratories
Volume Rendered Cylinder Head, Pixar
3D Terrain Mapping, Pixar
President's Day Storm, University of Wisconsin

Issue 42: Visualization in Scientific Computing—Research ACM SIGGRAPH

Contents Include:
Thinking Machines: Best of Visualization, *Salem*, TMI
Random Dot Motion, *Sandin*, UIC
Spectral Density Functions, *Rogan*, Alcoa
Volume Rendering for Scientific Visualization, *McMillan*, Sun
MATLAB on the Ardent Titan, *Moler*, Ardent
Fractal Transitions, *Norton*, IBM
Dynamics in the Quaternions, *Hart*, UIC
Cubic Polynomial Volume Rendering, *Gunn*, Minnesota Supercomputer Institute
Fluoropolymer Simulations, *Dixon*, du Pont
Molecular Genesis, *Rogers*, du Pont
Imine Ion Interactions in the Gramicidin Channel, *Chen*, Brown Unversity
Tempest in a Teapot, *Desmarais*, Battelle
Rendering of PLIF Flowfield Images, *van Cruyningen*, Stanford

Issue 43: Visualization in Scientific Computing—Research (vol. 2), ACM SIGGRAPH

Contents Include:
BRL Scientific Visualization Highlights, *Muuss*, BRL
Stress Wave Propagation in Graphite/Epoxy Material, *Cardwell*, PVI
SEA Accident Reconstruction, *Leeman*, SEA

Earthquake and Structural Response, *Suzuki*, Shimizu Corporation
Interactive Earth Science Visualization, *Hibbard*, U of Wisconsin
A Little About Bones and Points of Insertion, *Doria*, Swiss Institute for Biomechanics
Visualization of Brain, *Toga*, UCLA Medical School
Volume Microscopy of Biological Structures, *Argiro*, Vital Images
AML Total Hip System and Porocoat, Reed Productions
Ray Tracing of Computed Tomograms, *Meinzer*, Cancer Research Heidelberg
UNC Computer Graphics Sampler '89, *Fuchs*, UNC

Issue 44: Volume Visualization: State of the Art, ACM SIGGRAPH

This hour long video produced and directed by Laurin Herr contains the latest examples of volume visualization from universities, hospitals and research centers in Europe, Japan and America. The following leading experts have been exclusively interviewed for this program:

Vincent Argiro (Vital Images, Inc.)
Frederick Brooks, Jr. (UNC, Chapel Hill)
Thomas DeFanti (EVL, U of I, Chicago)
Nick England (Sun Microsystems)
Henry Fuchs (UNC, Chapel Hill)
Bill Hibbard (SSEC, U. of Wisconsin)
Xioaping Hu (University of Chicago)
Michael Keeler (Ardent Computer)
Marc Levoy (UNC, Chapel Hill)
Arthur Olson (Scripps Clinic)
Stephen Pizar (UNC, Chapel Hill)
Daniel Sandin (EVL, U of I, Chicago)
Alvy Ray Smith (Pixar)
Ulf Tiede (University Hospital, Hamburg)
Craig Upson (Stellar Computer)
Turner Whitted (Numerical Design Ltd.)
James Winget (Silicon Graphics)

Issue 49: Visualization in Scientific Computing— Supercomputers, ACM SIGGRAPH

Contents Include:
Mars: The Movie, *Hall*, JPL
Earth: The Movie, *Hall*, JPL
1988 CFD Highlights, *Watson*, NASA Ames
Visualizing Shuttle Flow Physics and Fluid Dynamics, *Bancroft*, NASA Ames
Self-Portrait, *Goldsmith*, JPL
The Etruscan Venus, *Francis*, UIUC
Numerical Relativity: Black Hole Spacetimes, *Hobill*, NCSA
The Lorentz Attractor, *Hobill*, NCSA

Kodak's Supercomputational Science '88, *Ray*, Kodak

Hydrogen Diffusion on a Platinum Surface, *Ray*, Kodak

Double Diffusive Convection: Saltfingering, *Rosenblum*, NRL

Simulated Treatment of an Ocular Tumor, *Lytie*, CNSF

Issue 50: Visualization in Scientific Computing— Supercomputers (vol. 2), ACM SIGGRAPH

Contents Include:

Pittsburgh Supercomputing Center '89, *Welling*, PSC

Interaction of Cosmic Jets with an Intergalactic Medium, *Elvins*, SDSC

SDSC Scientific Visualization '88, *Sheddon*, SDSC

Monte Carlo Simulation of Excited Electrons in GaAs, *Brady*, NCSA

Molecular Diffusion on Crystal Gold Surface, *Brady*, NCSA

Two-Armed Instability of a Rotating Polytropic Star, *Brady*, NCSA

Large-Scale Structure in the Universe, *Brady*, NCSA

Enzyme Reaction in Triophosphate Isomerase, *Brady*, NCSA

Quantum Molecular Dynamics, *Brady*, NCSA

Cajon Pass Scientific Drilling Project, *Brady*, NCSA

Topology of Coma Supercluster Region, *Brady*, NCSA

VIEW: Ames Virtual Environment Workstation, *Fisher*, NASA Ames

Visualization
Expanding Scientific and Engineering Research Opportunities

Thomas A. DeFanti and Maxine D. Brown, University of Illinois at Chicago

Bruce H. McCormick, Texas A&M University

Visualization
Expanding Scientific and Engineering Research Opportunities

Thomas A. DeFanti and Maxine D. Brown, University of Illinois at Chicago
Bruce H. McCormick, Texas A&M University

Introduction

Computational science and engineering (CS&E) describes a researcher's use of computers to simulate physical processes. CS&E parallels the development of the two other modes of science: theoretical and experimental/observational.

In addition to new methodologies, new technologies or mathematical tools have spurred the scientific revolutions. For example, calculus allowed Newton to codify the laws of nature mathematically and to develop analytic methods for solving simple cases. Similarly, the development of the von Neumann computer architecture gave scientists the ability to solve the discretized laws of nature for general and complex cases.

CS&E now relies heavily on scientific visualization to represent these solutions, enabling scientists to turn mountains of numbers into movies and graphically display measurements of physical variables in space and time. This article explores the convergence of science and visualization, in support of its successful growth and development.

What Is Scientific Visualization?

Computer graphics and image processing are technologies. *Visualization,* a term used in the industry since the 1987 publication of the National Science Foundation report *Visualization in Scientific Computing,*[1] represents much more than that. Visualization is a form of communication that transcends application and technological boundaries.

A tool for discovery and understanding. The deluge of data generated by supercomputers and other high-volume data sources (such as medical imaging systems and satellites) makes it impossible for users to quantitatively examine more than a tiny fraction of a given solution. That is, it is impossible to investigate the qualitative global nature of numerical solutions.

With the advent of raster graphics, researchers can convert entire fields of variables (representing density, pressure, velocity, entropy, and so on) to color images. The information conveyed to the researcher undergoes a qualitative change because it brings the eye-brain system, with its great pattern-recognition capabilities, into play in a way that is impossible with purely numeric data.

For example, an observer instantly sees the vortices, shock systems, and flow patterns in a visualization of a hydrodynamic calculation, while these same patterns are invisible in mere listings of several hundred thousand numbers, each representing field quantities at one moment in time. When computing a space-time solution to the laws of physics, the particular numeric quantities at each event in time-space are not important; rather, what is important is understanding the global structure of the field variables that constitute the solution and the causal interconnections of the various components of that solution.

A tool for communication and teaching. Much of modern science can no longer be communicated in print. DNA sequences, molecular models, medical imaging scans, brain maps, simulated flights through a terrain, simulations of fluid flow, and so on, all need to be expressed and taught visually over time. To understand, discover, or communicate phenomena, scientists want to compute the phenomena over time, to create a series of images that illustrate the interrelationships of various parameters at specific time periods, to download these images to local workstations for analysis, and to record and play back one or more seconds of the animation.

According to the visualization report, "We speak (and hear)—and for 5000 years have preserved our words. But, we cannot share vision. To this oversight of evolution we owe the retardation of visual communication compared to language. Visualization by shared communication would be much easier if each of us had a CRT in the forehead."[1]

Our CRTs, although not implanted in our foreheads, are connected to computers that are nothing more than extensions of our brains. These computers, however, might not be in the same room with us. They could be down the hall, across town, or across the country. Hence, the ability to communicate visually—and remotely—with computers and each other depends on the accessibility, affordability, and performance of computers and computer networks.

The visualization report recommends the development of a federally funded initiative providing immediate and long-term funding of both research and technology developments (see Table 1).[1] Research developments are the responsibility of tool users—experts from engineering and the discipline sciences who depend on computations for their research.

Table 1. Recommendations for a national initiative on visualization in scientific computing.

	Short-term Needs	Long-term Needs
Tool users: Computational scientists and engineers	Funding to incorporate visualization in current research	Funding to use model visualization environments
Toolmakers: Visualization scientists and engineers	No funding necessary	Funding to develop model visualization environments

Technology developments are handled by toolmakers—the visualization researchers who can develop the necessary hardware, software, and systems.

Tool Users' Short-Term Needs

Every researcher requires a personal computer or workstation on his or her desk connected with a remote supercomputer. However, not all scientists require the same level of computing power. Hence, a three-tiered model environment is beginning to emerge that categorizes visualization systems by such factors as power, cost, and software support.

Workstations. Researchers need workstations with access to supercomputers for

- immediate access to local graphics capabilities,
- networked access to supercomputers, and
- hard-copy recording.

Local graphics. Workstations, minicomputers, and image computers are significantly more affordable than supercomputers, and they are more powerful and effective visualization tools. There are already some 20 million personal computers and workstations in the United States, compared with about 200 supercomputers. Workstation users are increasingly treating supercomputers as one of many windows on the screen, and scientists must be able to "cut and paste" between the supercomputer and applications running on their local machines.

Access to supercomputers. Scientists need to transfer data to and from a main computation device, but today's networks are too slow for use in visualization. Some temporary techniques reduce the demand for high bandwidth, such as off-peak image transmission, image compression, image reconstruction from abstract representations, and local image generation. Networking is therefore as critical as computer power in helping scientists.

Hard-copy recording. Whether the visuals are for personal analysis, information sharing among peers, or presentations in formal surroundings, equipment for producing photographs, slides, videotapes, or laser disks needs to be in place and as easy to use as sending text files to a laser printer.

Scientists need the ability to create ad hoc graphics to verify the integrity of their simulations, to gain insights from their analyses, and to communicate their findings to others. Low-cost animation facilities should be connected to every user workstation so researchers can make scientific "home movies" with little effort. High-end visualization capabilities and facilities also should be available at all research centers; high-end graphics become important for presentation and publication of results once researchers conclude their work.

Three-tiered model computational environment. Observations of the way scientists use visualization suggest that a three-tiered model environment is evolving, as defined in Table 2. Each model is distinguished by hardware costs, computing power, bandwidth, location, software support, and administrative considerations.[1]

This model environment assumes that scientists want as direct a visual connection to their computations as possible. While supercomputers (model A) provide scientists with powerful number-crunching tools for generating data, they currently do not produce graphics; they do fill arrays with information that somehow gets piped to display devices. (Table 2 assumes that supercomputers and super image computers have equivalent power. Super image computers, although not commercially available today except in the form of a special-purpose flight simulator, will provide the specialized processing necessary for real-time volume visualization.)

Workstations give scientists more control over their visual output (models B and C). A workstation typically addresses its display memory the same way it addresses regular memory, incurring essentially no hardware overhead to display computed results. (Table 2 also assumes that minisupercomputers and image computers have equivalent power, and that advanced workstations and mini-/micro-image computers have equivalent power.)

Scientists should be able to select either more-expensive workstations with powerful visualization potential (model B) or less expensive ones (model C) while maintaining network connections to larger machines (model A) to do computations when necessary. This interdependency can work quite well. For example, a scientist can calculate 20-60 frames of a simulation sequence on a supercomputer, download the images to a workstation to create a minimovie, and then play back the sequence at any speed under local control.[2,3] (See sidebar, "Low-cost, visualization-compatible workstations and networks.")

Additional models D, E, and F, corresponding to personal computers, alphanumeric CRT terminals, and batch output, respectively, also exist. They do not represent advanced visualization technology, so they are not included in our model environment. Note, however, that model F has been used to produce a great deal of animation for both the scientific and commercial entertainment industries for the past 20 years.

Tool Users' Long-Term Needs

CS&E is emerging as a new marketplace with needs distinct from those of data processing, as shown in Table 3.

Success in the CS&E marketplace of the 1990s will depend on a commitment to standards, ease of use, connectivity, open systems, integrated systems, software portability, multivendor environments, leading-edge technology, and customer service and support.[4]

The list of research opportunities for visualization in scientific computing is long and spans all of contemporary scientific endeavor. The sidebar "Scientific and engineering research opportunities" presents specific examples of advanced scientific and engineering applications to show how visualization tools are helping researchers understand and steer computations. Our examples fall into the following categories:

- Molecular modeling,
- Medical imaging,
- Brain structure and function,
- Mathematics,
- Geosciences (meteorology),
- Space exploration,
- Astrophysics,
- Computational fluid dynamics, and
- Finite element analysis.

Table 2. Visualization facility three-tiered hierarchy.

	Model A	Model B	Model C
Hardware	Supercomputer or super image computer	Minisupercomputer or image computer	Advanced workstations (mini-/micro- image computer
Bandwidth (potential interactive rates, bits/second)	$>10^9$	10^7-10^8	10^3-10^6
Location (where users interact with the display screen)	Machine room (at the center)	Laboratory on a high-speed local area network	Laboratory on a national/ regional network
Software (in addition to discipline-specific data generation and processing)	Commercial packages for output only (no steering). Research required to develop interactive steering capabilities	Commercial packages are are mostly output only. Some interaction is becoming available. Research required to improve discipline-specific interaction	Commercial packages and tools are widely available for both computation and interaction. Research required in languages, operating systems, and networking
Administration Strength:	Support staff	Discipline-specific visualization goals	Decentralization
Weakness:	Centralization	Small support staff	No support staff

Table 3. Total corporate computing needs. (Source: Larry Smarr, NCSA, Sept. 1988.)

	Computational Science and Engineering	Data Processing
Corporate officer responsible	Vice president of research or long-range planning	Vice president of management information systems (MIS)
Tiered architectures	Personal computers and graphics workstations; midrange machines (mainframes/minisupercomputers; supercomputers *Need exists for multivendor, networked, hierarchical computing.*	Personal computers; minicomputers; mainframes *Software portability only partially exists between these levels, and then only within one vendor's product line.*
	Open systems *No vendor has emerged who offers integrated systems and end-to-end solutions. As a result, end users are faced with a confusing set of products from various vendors and nowhere to turn for advice on how to integrate them.*	Closed systems *IBM and Digital Equipment Corporation manufacture all levels of computers and the connections between them.*
Vendors	Fragmented market populated by start-ups and extremely high-growth companies: Workstations (Sun, DEC, Apollo, IBM, Hewlett-Packard, Apple, Silicon Graphics, Ardent, Stellar, AT&T Pixel, etc.); Midrange (DEC, IBM, Alliant, Amdahl, Convex, Scientific Computing Systems, Multiflow, Elxsi); Supercomputers (Cray, IBM).	Mature, slow-growth marketplace dominated by a few giant vendors, such as IBM and DEC.
Operating Systems	Unix	MVS, DOS, VMS (proprietary)
Networking protocols; telecommunications; speeds	Open network standards; Long-haul telecommunications; High speed = 1,000 Mbits/second *Because of the scarcity of $20 million supercomputers, most universities and corporate CS&E users are remote and must gain access to supercomputers over long-haul telecommunication lines.*	SNA, DECnet (proprietary); High speed = 50 Mbits/second *Within a corporation, most networks hook many "dumb terminals" up to a central mainframe where all the computing power resides. PCs are generally used stand-alone; those networked to a mainframe generally use the network to download or upload files, and computing is decoupled.*
Common unit of information	Image (megabyte) *Supercomputer simulations produce such enormous amounts of data that visualization is essential.*	Number (byte)
Common unit for computation speed	Mflops	MIPS

Toolmakers' Short-Term Needs

Commercial industry currently supports visualization hardware and software, as listed below. There is a pressing need to educate the scientific and engineering research communities about the available equipment.

Software. Commercial visualization software exists in the following categories:

Lines. The earliest software for graphics drew lines in three dimensions and projected them onto a two-dimensional plane, offered viewing transformations for looking at the result, and offered transformations (scale, rotate, and translate) for describing the line objects. The theory and practice of drawing lines, expressed in homogeneous coordinates, and the control and display of lines using 4×4 matrices, represented a major development in computer graphics.

A variety of current standards incorporate these basic principles, and the CAD/CAM industry has embraced this level of the art. It is cheap enough to put on every engineer's desk and fast enough for real-time interaction.

Polygonal surfaces. The next level of software—surfaces represented by polygons—has only recently been built into hardware. Polygon filling, or tiling, is commonly available in hardware and software. Hidden surface removal is included, and antialiasing of polygon edges is sometimes provided to remove distracting stair-steps, or jaggies. Light sources can be incorporated into the rendered image, but they are usually point sources at infinity emitting white light.

Patches. The next level of sophistication represents surfaces as curved surface pieces called patches. This is still largely a software domain, although we expect hardware to appear soon. The most advanced software packages handle

---

Low-cost, visualization-compatible workstations and networks

Our ability to communicate visually and remotely with supercomputers and each other depends on

(1) the ease with which we can use our office/home computers to connect with the outside world, receive and transmit visual information, and record this information on videotapes or slides, and
(2) the cost/performance of today's networks.

The Electronic Visualization Laboratory (EVL) at the University of Illinois at Chicago is doing research in both areas. We are designing as our scientific animation workstation a low-cost computer system with a well-integrated visualization programming environment.

Users at the National Center for Supercomputing Applications (NCSA) — or any of the National Science Foundation-funded supercomputer centers, for that matter — cannot do graphics remotely due to slow network speeds, centralized and expensive graphics equipment, lack of graphics software tools, and the need for specialists in film/video production. Our research is motivated by the recent availability of low-cost graphics hardware and a good PC-based visualization toolkit, coupled with a growing awareness that scientists need visualization more for personal/peer analysis than for presentations.

EVL is integrating affordable commercial equipment with specially designed graphics software to make visualization a reality for computational scientists — whether they use their computers on a stand-alone basis or connected to supercomputers over networks. (Regarding affordability, academicians can generally receive $10,000 in equipment monies from their departments or colleges without applying for external grants — our yardstick is that equipment should cost no more than a three-year-old Buick.)

EVL's scientific animation workstation, shown in the accompanying figure, has hard-copy recording capability and an easy-to-use visualization environment to facilitate scientists' needs. The following list corresponds to items 1-6 in the figure.

(1) Supercomputer access. Supercomputers are most ef-

ficiently used to run complex simulation codes, the output of which is numbers. With access to graphics, researchers can convert numbers to pictures to qualitatively examine the global nature of their simulation output. Graphics can be made available on the host machine or, more efficiently, on the local workstation.

(2) Televisualization: graphical networking. As images require more colors, higher resolution, or larger volumes of data, they need more memory and become more impractical to transmit over networks or phone lines, to store on disks, or to convert and display on different frame buffers. EVL's Imcomp compression and conversion software converts images consisting of 24, 16, or 8 bits per pixel to 16 or 8 bits per pixel, then compresses them further to 2 or 3 bits per pixel while maintaining a reasonable full-color representation.[1,2] The program takes only 0.4 seconds to run on the Cray X-MP at NCSA, and it converts and transmits a 512 × 512 × 24-bit image from NCSA to EVL over a 56-kilobyte line within a few seconds.

Moreover, visuals must be transmitted from memory to memory (that is, from supercomputer memory to frame buffer memory in the local computer), not just from file to file as in electronic mail-type networks. NCSA's Telnet communications software has been modified to do this and expanded to include Imcomp routines that automatically compress images.

In addition to compression, value-added nodes speed up graphical transmission by balancing transmission costs with local computing costs. Model data is sent over networks and then rendered or reconstructed at the scientist's end. EVL is currently investigating the use of its AT&T Pixel Machine as a graphics server that would render model data transmitted over the network from the supercomputer and then transmit the resulting images over a local area network to individuals' desktop computers.

(3) Truevision Vista graphics board. Scientists need to be able to preview, record, and play back animations at any speed and in cyclical fashion to examine the dynamics of their data changing over time, to spot anomalies, or to uncover computation errors. The Vista board's large configurable memory allows us to get anywhere from 32 screens at 512 × 512 pixels to 128 a variety of patch types. They also provide very sophisticated lighting models with multiple-colored lights and distributed or point sources located either at infinity or in the scene.

Antialiasing is assumed, and the packages handle optical effects such as transparency, translucency, refraction, and reflection. Research software provides even more features that produce greater realism, such as articulated motion blur, depth of field, follow focus, constructive solid geometry, and radiosity.

The software contains no practical limit on scene complexity (such as the number of allowable polygons), but computation of highly complex scenes on a supercomputer can take anywhere from 0.5 to 1.5 hours per frame.

Image processing. Image processing software has followed a separate path over the last 15 years. The elaborate software packages now available provide functions such as convolution, Fourier transform, histogram, histogram equalization, edge detection, edge enhancement, noise reduction, thresholding, segmentation, bicubic and biquadratic warping, and resampling.

Many of these functions have been hardwired into special boards. General-purpose processors have only recently become powerful enough to make software competitive with hardware while maintaining generality. Image computers can run both computer graphics and image processing software packages.

Animation. In its broadest sense, animation means movement. It frequently connotes the complex motion of many

(Continued on page 43.)

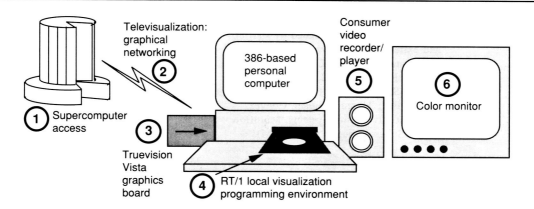

The Electronic Visualization Laboratory's RT/1 graphics language, an 80386-based personal computer, the Truevision Vista board, and consumer video gear comprise a scientific animation production facility that is economical enough to be made available to research scientists and engineers on a broad scale.

screens at 128 × 128 pixels, all at 8 bits per pixel. The board is also video compatible, so images can be recorded directly to videotape.

(4) Real Time/One (RT/1) local visualization programming environment. Scientists need a set of tools for picture composition, picture saving/restoring, fonts and text, resizing, rotation, moving, copying, hand retouching (painting), color manipulation, etc. They also need a local graphics programming environment in which to develop new tools or extend the capabilities of existing ones.

RT/1, an easy-to-use graphics programming language developed by EVL faculty and students, meets the criteria required of a visualization system environment. The language, written in C and running under Unix and MS-DOS, runs on all of EVL's workstations and personal computers. EVL is porting RT/1 to new workstations as they are acquired, extending the capabilities of the language, and developing application programs tailored to the needs of scientists.

(5) Consumer video recorder/player. If it's not recordable, it's not science. Moreover, the equipment for producing videotapes needs to be as easy to use as sending text files to a laser printer. We are integrating low-cost consumer video equipment into the workstation so scientists can quickly and easily preview

and record frames of animation.[3] This equipment also comes with a built-in microphone so scientists can add narration or other sounds to visual recordings.

(6) Color monitor. Today's consumer video systems not only record but also can be attached to any television for immediate viewing of recorded material. Scientists can take a small video unit to a conference and plug it into a television there to share findings with colleagues. Should peers in other towns have similar equipment, colleagues could mail tapes to each other for viewing.

References

1. M.D. Brown and M. Krogh, "Imcomp — An Image Compression and Conversion Algorithm for the Efficient Transmission, Storage, and Display of Color Images," *NCSA Data Link,* Vol. 2, No. 3, National Center for Supercomputing Applications, June 1988, pp. 11-24.

2. G. Campbell et al., "Two-Bit/Pixel Full Color Encoding," *Computer Graphics* (SIGGraph Proc.), Vol. 20, No. 4, Aug. 1986, pp. 215-223.

3. T.A. DeFanti and D.J. Sandin, "The Usable Intersection of PC Graphics and NTSC Video Recording," *IEEE Computer Graphics and Applications,* Oct. 1987, pp. 50-58.

Scientific and engineering research opportunities

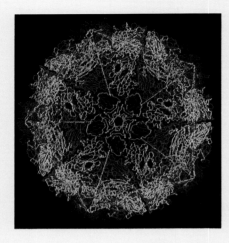

Molecular modeling. The use of interactive computer graphics to gain insight into chemical complexity began in 1964. Interactive graphics is now an integral part of academic and industrial research on molecular structures, and the methodology is being successfully combined with supercomputers to model complex systems. Two types of images can currently be generated: realistic pictures of molecules and 3D line drawings. Raster equipment is used to create realistic representations and animations, while vector hardware, used for real-time display and interaction, creates line drawings.

The image at left is a 3D line drawing of the rhinovirus, the common cold virus, showing its geometric structure and complexity. The image at right is an artistic rendering of the human papilloma virus (HPV). It was done by a group of Chicago-area artists who appreciate the underlying mathematics of nature and the complexity of the inner workings between atoms.[1]

Left-hand © 1988 T.J. O'Donnell. Data courtesy of Dr. Rossman, Crystallography Group, Purdue Univ. Image courtesy of the EVL, Univ. of Illinois at Chicago. Right-hand © 1989 (Art)[n] Laboratory, Illinois Institute of Technology. (Art)[n] artists: Donna Cox, NCSA, Univ. of Illinois at Urbana-Champaign; Stephan Meyers, Dan Sandin, and Tom DeFanti, EVL, Univ. of Illinois at Chicago; Ellen Sandor, (Art)[n] Laboratory, Illinois Institute of Technology.

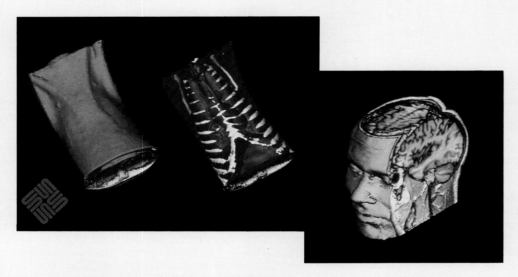

Medical imaging. Scientific computation applied to medical imaging has created opportunities in diagnostic medicine, surgical planning for orthopedic prostheses, and radiation treatment planning. In each case, these opportunities have been brought about by 2D and 3D visualizations of portions of the body previously inaccessible to view.

The above-left image is a shaded surface volume rendering of a 128 × 128 × 197 computerized tomography scan of a tree sloth. The opacity of various structures can be interactively modified to show the skin surface or to reveal internal structures. The bones of the rib cage, shoulder blades, and spine can be seen in the image on the right, as well as the trachea, lungs, heart and diaphragm.

The above-right image is a shaded surface volume rendering of a 256 × 256 × 61 magnetic-resonance imagery (MRI) scan of a human head. The rendering shows a mixture of surface and slice-based techniques, where external structures such as the skin are rendered with surface shading, while slice planes are voxel-mapped to reveal the original MRI data. Physicians can use this technique to relate the position of internal structures such as tumor sites to external landmarks. These images were generated using the Voxvu volume rendering tool on a Sun workstation with the TAAC-1 Application Accelerator.

© 1989 Chuck Mosher and Ruth Johnson, Sun Microsystems. Data for above-left image courtesy of Eric Hoffman, UPA. Data for above-right image courtesy of Jeff Shaw, Vanderbilt Univ.

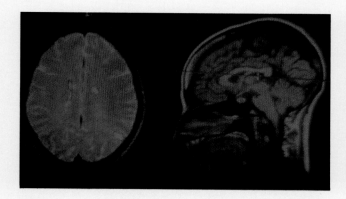 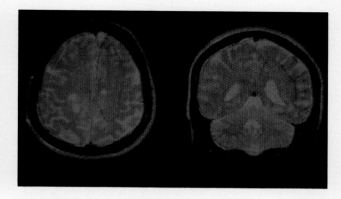

Brain structure and function. Rutgers University is using computer vision and visualization methods to automatically detect white-matter lesions in MRI scans of the human brain.

In the above-left image, low-level vision methods locate the outline of the brain, landmarks such as the interhemispherical fissure plane, and suspected lesions. The system calculates the orientation of the brain and uses the segmentations provided by the low-level methods to fit a deformable model to each patient's brain to determine the position and shape of difficult-to-identify organs or regions of interest. This customized model, shown in the above-right image, is used to obtain information about the anatomical position of the suspected lesions so that the system can reject false positives and determine the affected organs. The system has been tested on more than 1,200 images from 19 patients, producing good results.

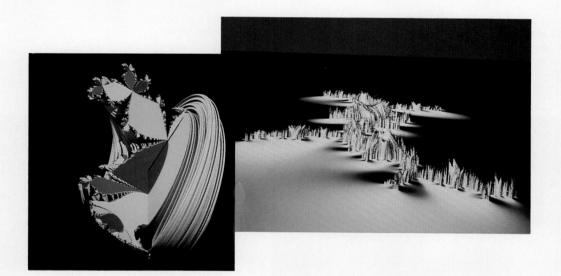

Mathematics. These images illustrate a type of fractal known as the Julia set. A filled-in Julia set is a set of points that do not converge (or diverge) to infinity after repeated applications of a function, such as $f(z) = z^2 + c$. These functions are often investigated in the complex plane, but they also exist in the quaternions, a coordinate system that spans one real and three imaginary axes. Visualization helps mathematicians understand these equations, which are too complex to conceptualize otherwise.[2]

The above-left image is a quaternion filled-in Julia set minus its front-upper-left octant; the inner components of the four-cycle are revealed, defining its basin of attraction. The above-right image is a visualization of a dendritic quaternion Julia set in the complex plane; the unusual lighting uses a 3D gradient in the complex plane.

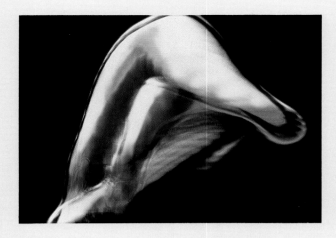

Geosciences: meteorology. The study of severe storms through observation and modeling helps research meteorologists understand the atmospheric conditions that breed large and violent tornadoes and the mechanisms by which tornadoes form and persist.[3] Theoreticians and field workers obtain information on behavior that cannot be safely observed; study the interactions of various environments, characterized by differing vertical wind, temperature, pressure, and moisture structures; and obtain useful guides for future research.

Transparency and volumetric rendering are used to view multiple surfaces; shading is used to display individual solid surfaces.

The above-left image uses voxel (grid cell) data to display rainwater and vertical vorticity information about a storm,[4] providing scientists with more information than if they had observed the storm with their eyes. The fuzzy region indicates low rainwater amounts while the bright white regions indicate large amounts of rainwater within the cloud. The vertical vorticity is texture mapped onto the rainwater with color; purple indicates dominant positive vorticity and blue indicates dominant negative vorticity.

The above-right image is from an animated simulation of a storm over Kansas, in which the rainwater surface was polygonized (tiled) and then rendered. The simulation clearly reveals substantial variations in the structure of the rainwater field not apparent earlier.

Above-left © 1988 Robert Wilhelmson and Craig Upson, NCSA, Univ. of Illinois at Urbana-Champaign. Above-right © 1988 Robert Wilhelmson, Crystal Shaw, Lou Wicker, Stefen Fangmeier, and the NCSA Visualization Production Team, Univ. of Illinois at Urbana-Champaign.

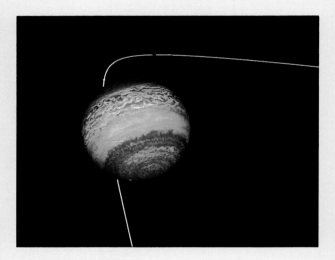

Space exploration. The field of planetary study involves the accumulation of huge volumes of data on the planets in the solar system. Enough data is now available that scientists are beginning to integrate observed phenomena and theory from other fields involved in planetary study: meteorology, geography, planetary physics, astronomy, and astrophysics.

The above-left image is from an animated simulation of the dynamics of Uranus' magnetosphere. The simulation shows that the angle of the dipole axis (purple arrow) is offset from the planet's angle of rotation (aqua arrow). The above-right image is from a simulation of the Voyager 2 Neptune encounter to occur in late summer of 1989. This image illustrates the path of the Voyager 2 as viewed from Earth.

Above-left © 1989 Computer Graphics Group of the Jet Propulsion Laboratory and G. Hannes Voigt of Rice Univ. Above-right © 1989 Computer Graphics Group of the Jet Propulsion Laboratory.

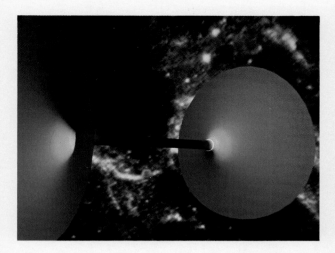

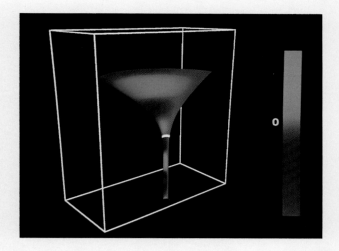

Astrophysics. Computational astrophysicists at the NCSA work with artists in an attempt to see the unseen and create visual paradigms for phenomena that have no known visual representation.

An embedding diagram of a Schwarzschild black hole and the behavior of its gravitational field, illustrated in the above-left image, was obtained from a numerical solution of Einstein's numerical relativity equations. The surface of the diagram measures the curvature of space

due to the presence of the black hole, while the color scale represents the speed at which idealized clocks measure time (with red representing the slowest clocks and blue representing the fastest).

A black hole emits gravitational radiation after it has been struck by an incoming gravity wave. The above-right image is from an animated sequence that shows, for the first time, the influence of the curved space on the propagation of the radiation. Through the use of an iso-

metric embedding diagram, the curvature of the space surrounding the black hole is represented by the surface on which the waves propagate. The white ring locates the surface of the black hole, and the regions above and below represent the exterior and interior of the black hole, respectively.

© 1989 David Hobill, Larry Smarr, David Bernstein, Donna Cox, and Ray Idaszak, NCSA, Univ. of Illinois at Urbana-Champaign.

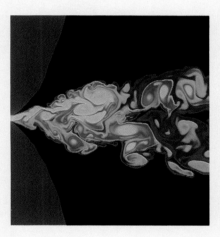

Computational fluid dynamics. Computational astronomers rely on supercomputing and visualization techniques to understand why jets from some galaxies flare dramatically. Magnetohydrodynamics code is used to solve equations that describe the flow of a fluid or gas with magnetic fields using finite differences.

The above image is a visualization of a cosmic jet traveling at Mach 2.5 passing through a shock wave (located at the left of the image). The jet abruptly slows and breaks up into a broadened subsonic

plume whose morphology, or shape, is strikingly similar to that of a radio lobe of a wide-angle tailed galaxy. The morphology of the jet after impact is emphasized through the use of pseudocolor. This research has given astronomers important clues about why jets from some radio galaxies flare into broad plumes while jets from others remain remarkably straight and narrow.[5,6]

© 1989 Michael Norman and Donna Cox of the NCSA, Univ. of Illinois at Urbana-Champaign, and Jack Burns and Martin Sulkanen of the Univ. of New Mexico.

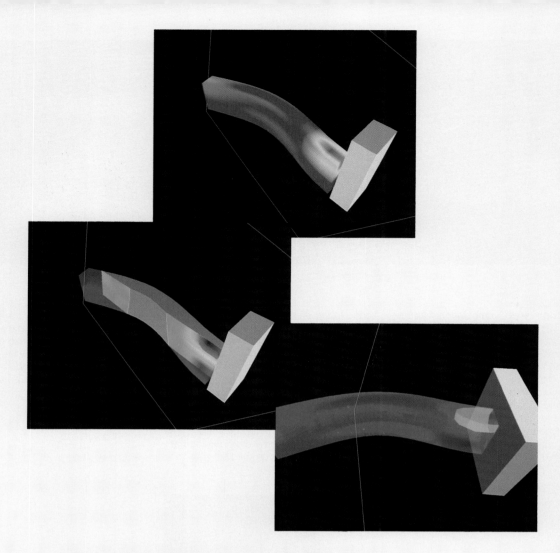

Finite element analysis. Finite element analysis is used in this example to show the stress distribution in a beam at its maximum tip displacement in the third eigenmode. The results were computed using linear elastic elements and a lumped-mass approximation.

The top image uses a conventional approach of displaying the stress values on the outer surface of the deformed shape. The middle image uses a cutting plane to look at the stress values on a cross section of the root of the beam. The bottom image shows a different view of the beam and uses an iso-contour stress surface to convey the three-dimensional nature of the stress concentration at the root of the beam. These images are still frames from fully animated and interactive models. They were computed and rendered on a Silicon Graphics 4D/120 GTX workstation using the SolidView program to perform real-time cutting and iso-contour surface generation.

References

1. R.P. Feynman, *Surely You're Joking, Mr. Feynman! Adventures of a Curious Character*, Bantam Books, 1986, pp. 236-253.

2. J.C. Hart, D.J. Sandin, and L.H. Kauffman, "Ray Tracing Deterministic 3D Fractals," to be published in *SIGGraph 89 Conf. Proc., Computer Graphics*, Vol. 23, No. 4, Aug. 1989.

3. R.B. Wilhelmson, "Numerical Simulations of Severe Storms," *Proc. Fourth Int'l Symp.: Science and Engineering on Cray Supercomputers*, Cray Research, Oct. 1988.

4. C. Upson and M. Keeler, "VBuffer: Visible Volume Rendering," *SIGGraph 88 Conf. Proc., Computer Graphics*, Vol. 22, No. 4, Aug. 1988, pp. 59-64.

5. K.-H.A. Winkler and M.L. Norman, "Munacolor: Understanding High-Resolution Gas Dynamical Simulations Through Color Graphics," *Astrophysical Radiation Hydrodynamics*, D. Reidel Publishing, 1986, pp. 223-243.

6. N.J. Zabusky, "Computational Synergetics," *Physics Today*, July 1984 reprint.

(Continued from page 37.)

objects, possibly articulated, moving simultaneously, and interacting with one another. Animation is desirable for the visualization of dynamic, complex processes. Basic animation control routines should be part of any standard visualization tool kit.

Glue. A class of software appreciated by visualization professionals but not necessarily by scientists is the "glue" used to combine images generated or analyzed by the packages described above. For convenience, a user must have tools for picture composition, picture saving/restoring, fonts and text, resizing, rotation, moving, copying, hand retouching (painting), color manipulation, etc. Together, these functions comprise a visualization environment system, which is to visualization what an operating system is to general computing.

Window systems. Windowing systems are commonplace in black-and-white bit graphics and are being extended to color graphics. Visualization software must incorporate and remain consistent with windowing concepts.

Volume visualization. Volume visualization software is still rudimentary. Algorithms for rendering lines, curves, surfaces, and volumes into volume memories are only now becoming available.[5,6] Hidden volume removal is unknown, the compositing of volumes is yet to be fully addressed, 3D paint programs (sculpting programs) have yet to be written, and general utilities for arbitrary rotation and size change of volumes do not exist. In other words, there is much research to be done in this field.

Hardware. The following are available commercial visualization hardware tools.

Input devices. Current digital input devices include supercomputers, satellites, medical scanners, seismic recorders, and digitizing cameras. The rapidly increasing bandwidth of these devices emphasizes the need for work in volume visualization.

We expect continued improvement in the resolution and bandwidth of input devices. Supercomputers will get faster and the resolution of images from satellites will increase. Real-time video digitizers already exist. Monochrome digital digitizers with 2,048 × 2,048-pixel resolution are becoming quite fast, although they do not yet operate at real-time speeds. Print-quality input scanners are still quite expensive, but we expect the prices to fall as digital technology cheapens and competing scanning technologies mature. CCD (charge-coupled device) array input scanners will improve in resolution and become serious candidates for input devices in high-resolution work.

Interactive input devices are continually improving. Common 2D devices include knobs, switches, pedals, mice, and tablets. Tablets are the most general and also need the most improvement; they need higher resolution, higher speed, and more degrees of freedom.

Six-dimensional interactive devices are also available, providing the usual 3D positional information plus three degrees of orientation information (yaw, pitch, and roll). Higher-dimensional devices, such as the data glove, have begun to appear. These will improve to offer higher resolution, higher speed, and lower cost.

Output devices. Raster displays of 2D frame buffers have improved steadily to offer more colors, higher resolutions, and less flicker. A typical color raster display today offers a 1,280 × 1,024-pixel display at 60 frames per second and 24 bits of color per pixel (16 megacolors).

High-definition television (HDTV)—a proposed standard that will offer larger, brighter, sharper pictures than currently available in video—will affect visualization. Also, video is moving toward an all-digital format, designated 4:2:2, to standardize digital interconnections of diverse video products.

Color raster displays will evolve toward 2,048 × 2,048 pixels in the next several years. The displays themselves already exist in limited quantities, but the computational bandwidth required to feed them is still lacking. Black-and-white 2D raster displays already have resolutions greater than 2,048 × 2,048 pixels with enough bandwidth to feed them. These displays will certainly reach even higher resolutions in the next five years.

Stereo displays are also beginning to appear commercially, and we confidently predict that these will improve in screen size, resolution, brightness, and availability. These displays will be quite helpful in volume visualization.

Other output devices are similarly improving. HDTV will spur the development of compatible recorders. Film recorders will become cheaper as the technology becomes cheaper and the competition matures. Should stereo become a widely accepted mode of presentation for volume visualizations, then stereo film and video standards will have to be developed.

Workstations. Fast vector machines are now common and have extensive use in such areas as CAD/CAM and real-time 3D design. Recently, they have improved to offer color vectors and perfect end-matching. Frame buffers have been added so that surface raster graphics can be combined with vector displays.

Also, fast surface machines are about to arrive. They exist in simplified forms already and in more advanced states as firmware in special machines. Chips are now being built to speed up certain aspects of surface rendering, particularly the tiling of polygons. By 1990, full hardware support of surface graphics will be available, offering rendering features such as texture mapping, bump mapping, antialiasing, reflections, transparency, and shadows.

Vector machines will initially serve as powerful, real-time front ends to surface machines. Eventually, surface machines will be cheap and fast enough to permit scientists to do real-time design using surfaces rather than lines.

Among image processors, fast planar machines have existed for some time. These machines contain special boards for certain aspects of image processing, such as fast Fourier transforms. Faster versions are becoming available that have wider processing capabilities and higher resolutions. In fact, the notion of a general-purpose image processor that can implement any image processing algorithm as a program is becoming common.

Toolmakers' Long-Term Needs

Raw computing power would be more effectively harnessed than it is today if calculations could be understood pictorially and their progress guided dynamically. Modern modes of computing involve interactive, extemporaneous generation of views from masses of data and exploration of model spaces by interactive steering of computations.

A scientist's ability to comprehend the results of his or her computations depends on the effectiveness of available tools. To increase that effectiveness, we need to

- encourage the production of documented, maintained, upward-compatible software and hardware;

- motivate manufacturers to solve network bottleneck problems;

- encourage universities to incorporate CS&E and visualization in computer science, engineering, and discipline-science curricula; and

- guarantee the publication and dissemination of research and results on a variety of media.

Hardware, software, and systems. General visualization issues that need to be supported include:

- Interactive steering of simulations and calculations

- Workstation-driven use of supercomputers

- Graphics-oriented programming environments

- Higher-dimensional visualization of scalar, vector, and tensor fields

- Dynamic visualization of fields and flow

- High-bandwidth picture networks and protocols

- Massive data-set handling, notably for signal and image processing applications

- Vectorized and parallelized algorithms for graphics and image processing

- Specialized architectures for graphics and image processing

- A framework for international visualization hardware and software standards

Networking. The application of networks to visualization, called *televisualization,* encompasses much more than text transfer (such as electronic mail) and gateway protocol decoding. It also involves image transfer, which entails compression, decompression, rendering, recognizing, and interpreting. Televisualization requires a major enhancement over existing network capabilities in the following areas:

Increased data rates. The sheer scale of graphics and imaging data sets challenges the current bandwidth and interactivity of networks. Networks handle screenfuls of textual information well; network nodes are simply gateways that neither add nor detract from the quality of the message. But a 512×512-pixel image with 8 bits per pixel has approximately 100 times more information than a screen of text with 25 rows and 80 characters per row. A $1,024 \times 1,024 \times 1,024$-voxel volume with 48 bits per voxel contains 16,000 times more information than a 512×512-pixel image. Gigabit speeds are sufficient to pass volumes of the current size of $256 \times 256 \times 256$ voxels with 4 bytes per voxel, but this rate will have to be extended within several years to 1-gigabyte/second channels.

Compression/decompression algorithms. Compression improves the speed with which visual data is transmitted. Current schemes for full-color image compression work well,[7] but other forms of compression must be researched, and comprehensive protocols must be developed for managing all these capabilities:

- Transmit the procedures to create the images rather than the images themselves.

- Transmit endpoints of vector images.

- Transmit polygonal, constructive solid geometry, or bicubic patches of surface models.

- Transmit semantic descriptions of the objects.

Value-added processing at nodes. Value-added nodes also speed up graphical transmission. Computers process text and numbers in main memory, occasionally transmitting some of them to peripherals. Images, however, often must be transferred to special memories for rendering, 3D imaging, or viewing. Each instance of transferring and processing an image aims to increase its visualization value to the scientist. The ability to process images at various nodes along a network embraces the central concept of distributed processing.

In distributed computing, transmission costs are balanced with local computing costs. It sometimes makes more sense to send model data over networks and then render or reconstruct the data at the scientist's end. This presumes that there is appropriate equipment at both ends, that the various software modules are compatible with one another, and that the software can run on a variety of equipment types.

A televisualization network for image passing between machines is analogous to the software paradigm of message passing between process layers. This type of networking, combined with interaction, cannot be achieved using conventional Fortran subroutine calls. Significant software development and protocol standardization are necessary to bring televisualization to the discipline sciences.

Interaction capabilities. Interactive visual computing is a process whereby scientists communicate with data by manipulating its visual representation during processing. The more sophisticated process of navigation allows scientists to dynamically modify, or steer, computations while they are occurring. This lets researchers change parameters, resolution, or representation, and then see the effects.

Teaching CS&E and visualization. The principal barrier to growth in the CS&E market is the fact that corporate researchers and managers lack education and training in CS&E technologies and methodologies. Few industrial researchers know how to use distributed CS&E to do their work and, more importantly, they do not know how to think computationally and visually. Other roadblocks include the following:

- The Association for Computing Machinery's approved computer science curriculum lists computer graphics as merely one of many optional topics; image processing is not mentioned at all.
- Engineering accreditors do not require computer graphics or image processing.
- Many engineering school deans are unaware of the importance of visualization or cannot justify the hardware and software expense involved in teaching the subject.
- The number of tenured faculty teaching computer graphics in American universities is about the same today as 15 years ago, and they are roughly the same people.
- Scientists, while educated to read and write, are not taught to produce or communicate with visuals.

Publication and dissemination. Contemporary scientific communications media are predominantly language-oriented. Printed media are coupled weakly, if at all, to the visual world of space-time. By contrast, half the human neocortex is devoted to processing visual information. In other words, current scientific communication leaves out half—the right half—of the brain. An integral part of our visualization task is to facilitate visual communication from

scientist to scientist, engineer to engineer, through visualization-compatible media.

Publication and grants, and therefore tenure, rarely come to researchers whose productivity depends on or produces visualization results. Superiors evaluate scholarly work by counting the number of journal articles published; publications are text, and visual media do not count. Funding itself is based on the careful preparation and evaluation of proposals, which are documents full of words and numbers.

As scientists depend more and more on the electronic network than on the printed page, they will need new technologies to teach, document, and publish their work. Until scientists can build on each other's work, productivity will lag. Publishing (specifically textual materials) has always been a critical part of this building process, and it is one of the primary bottlenecks in CS&E's progress.

Reading and writing were only democratized in the past 100 years. Today, they are the accepted communication tools for scientists and engineers. Table 4 shows that, in time, visualization will also be democratized and embraced by researchers.

Table 4. The evolution of communication tools.

Communications media	Number of years old
Sight	5×10^8
Speech	5×10^5
Writing	5×10^3
Print broadcasting	5×10^2
Visual broadcasting	5×10^1
Visualization	5×10^0

Electronic media, such as videotapes, optical disks, and floppy disks, are now necessary for the publication and dissemination of mathematical models, processing algorithms, computer programs, experimental data, and scientific simulations. The reviewer and the reader need to test models, to evaluate algorithms, and to execute programs themselves, interactively, without an author's assistance. Similarly, scientific publication must extend to use visualization-compatible media.

Conclusion

The use of visualization in scientific computing—in academia, government research laboratories, and industry—will help guarantee

- US preeminence in science and technology,
- a well-educated pool of scientists and engineers with the quality and breadth of experience required to meet the changing needs of science and society, and

• American industries that can successfully compete in the international economic arena.

The information age has yet to deal with information transfer. Visualization technologies can help lead the way to better global understanding and communication.

References

1. B.H. McCormick, T.A. DeFanti, and M.D. Brown, eds., "Visualization in Scientific Computing," *Computer Graphics,* Vol. 21, No. 6, Nov. 1987.

2. T.A. DeFanti and M.D. Brown, "Scientific Animation Workstations: Creating an Environment for Remote Research, Education, and Communication," *Academic Computing,* Feb. 1989, 55-57, pp. 10-12.

3. T.A. DeFanti and M.D. Brown, "Scientific Animation Workstations," *SuperComputing,* Fall 1988, pp. 10-13.

4. T.A. DeFanti and M.D. Brown, "Insight through Images," *Unix Review,* Mar. 1989, pp. 42-50.

5. R.A. Drebin, L. Carpenter, and P. Hanrahan, "Volume Rendering," *Computer Graphics* (SIGGraph Conf. Proc.), Vol. 22, No. 4, Aug. 1988, pp. 65-74.

6. C. Upson and M. Keeler, "VBuffer: Visible Volume Rendering," *Computer Graphics* (SIGGraph Conf. Proc.), Vol. 22, No. 4, Aug. 1988, pp. 59-64.

7. G. Campbell et al., "Two-Bit/Pixel Full Color Encoding," *Computer Graphics* (SIGGraph Conf. Proc.), Vol. 20, No. 4, Aug. 1986, pp. 215-223.

Thomas A. DeFanti is a professor of electrical engineering and computer science and codirector of the Electronic Visualization Laboratory at the University of Illinois at Chicago, and an adjunct professor at the National Center for Supercomputing Applications. He is an international lecturer and author in the computer graphics field, and he has had many interactive computer graphics installations in museums and conferences worldwide. He also serves on the editorial boards of several publications, is past chair of ACM SIGGraph, is editor-in-chief of the SIGGraph Video Review, was recipient of the 1988 ACM Outstanding Contribution Award, and was recently appointed to the Illinois Governor's Science Advisory Committee.

DeFanti was vice chair of the National Science Foundation-sponsored Panel on Graphics, Image Processing, and Workstations and coeditor of its 1987 report Visualization in Scientific Computing. He received his BA in mathematics from Queen's College in New York in 1969 and his PhD in computer science from Ohio State University in 1973.

Acknowledgments

We acknowledge the following individuals for their insightful contributions and comments during the preparation of the NSF report Visualization in Scientific Computing: David Arnett, Gordon Bell, James F. Blinn, Frederick P. Brooks Jr., Mel Ciment, James Clark, John Connolly, Jerome Cox, Martin Fischler, Donald Greenberg, Andrew Hanson, Albert Harvey, Laurin Herr, David Hoffman, Robert Langridge, Thomas Lasinski, Carl Machover, Patrick Mantey, Mike McGrath, Nicholas Negroponte, Arthur J. Olson, Jeff Posdamer, Azriel Rosenfeld, David Salzman, Larry Smarr, Alvy Ray Smith, Barna Szabo, Richard Weinberg, Turner Whitted, Karl-Heinz Winkler.

Maxine D. Brown is associate director of the Electronic Visualization Laboratory at the University of Illinois at Chicago, where she is responsible for funding, documentation, and promotion of its research activities. Brown is an international lecturer and author in the computer graphics field, and she has consulted for a number of companies in the computer graphics industry in the area of professional and technical communications.

Brown is past secretary and vice chair for operations of ACM SIGGraph, is a member of the executive committee of the IEEE Technical Committee on Computer Graphics, and was coeditor of Visualization in Scientific Computing. She received her BA in mathematics from Temple University in 1972 and her MSE in computer science from the University of Pennsylvania in 1976. She is a member of the IEEE Computer Society.

Bruce H. McCormick is professor of computer science and director of the Visualization Laboratory at Texas A&M University. McCormick is an international lecturer and author in the areas of computer vision, computer architecture, and scientific visualization. He has held positions at the University of Illinois at Urbana-Champaign, where he was principal investigator of the Illiac III image-processing computer, and at the University of Illinois at Chicago.

McCormick has served on committees of the National Institutes of Health, participated in the 1981 Fifth-Generation Computer Conference in Japan, and was chair of the NSF-sponsored Panel on Graphics, Image Processing, and Workstations and coeditor of Visualization in Scientific Computing. He received his BS in physics from the Massachusetts Institute of Technology in 1950 and his PhD in physics from Harvard University in 1955. He is a member of the IEEE.

Visualization in Science and Engineering Education

Steve Cunningham, California State University at Stanislaus
Judith R. Brown, University of Iowa
Mike McGrath, Colorado School of Mines

Introduction

Although a significant use of visual technology exists in scientific research, it is at an early stage of development and is primarily used to display information from finished work. The potential for using visualization in research and discovery is vast and almost untapped. The report on visualization in scientific computing (VISC) recognized this and defined visualization as a major new field in terms of the tools it brings to scientific discovery and understanding.[1] Visualization is more than a supporting field: it affects the way the scientist performs research and makes discoveries using intensively interactive graphics tools.

Similarly, educators use such visuals as diagrams and figures in static displays to support scientific learning, but the techniques are manual and primitive. Visualization can significantly affect learning just as it can affect scientific discovery. We define visualization in science and engineering education as using images and graphics, in a highly interactive and dynamic manner to enhance learning and understanding. As such, in education, it is also more than a supporting field, because it affects the quality and amount of learning for each student. Visualization's goal is thus to improve the quality of learning by allowing students to develop more depth in scientific studies and thus grasp more of the growing knowledge base. Realizing visualization's full potential in science education will require major research to discover how learning is accomplished visually, especially with interactive computer graphics, and how to build the tools to support this learning.

The VISC report described not only the development needed for scientific research but also some of the technical and cultural roadblocks as well. Roadblocks also exist for visualization in science and engineering education and are discussed in detail later in this paper.

To accomplish these goals, we propose an initiative on visualization in science and engineering education (VISE[2]) that can emerge as a result of the visualization tools defined by the VISC report and which can also benefit the VISC initiative by providing the visual training of future scientists. The VISE[2] initiative would parallel the developments in visualization for scientific computing while focusing on the unique problems of visual teaching and learning.

What Is Visualization in Education?

The vocabulary for communicating ideas is visual. We say "Let me show you. . . ." and "Can you see that . . . ?" but we often do not know how to create or use images effectively. To become better scientists and engineers, students must learn the skills of thinking and communicating visually. This applies across the entire spectrum of science, including biology, chemistry, engineering, geology, mathematics, and physics.*

Most engineers and scientists use sketches extensively to describe objects under discussion. In a classroom, science educators rarely stand still and talk about concepts. At the very least, they make hand gestures to communicate their thoughts better, adding a visual body language to ordinary spoken language. More commonly, they write or draw on the chalkboard or sketch on an overhead projector. Some use an "electronic blackboard" and run a computer program that provides images they cannot draw, such as those generated by three-dimensional mathematical functions or by an interactive simulation. Yet the use of good computer graphics programs and techniques in science classrooms and laboratories is minimal at best. Why are science educators unable or unwilling to take advantage of this new technology? What capabilities and opportunities could it provide?

We believe that effective use of computer graphics can enhance teaching and learning in science. Just as visualization in scientific computing means using computer graphics to gain more information from research, visualization in science and engineering education means using computer graphics to enable or enhance learning about science. Just as visualization of scientific data can help a researcher make new discoveries, visualization can help a science student make discoveries which, though not new to the world of science, are very new to the student. Computer graphics enable an instructor to create an image, animation sequence, or interactive simulation, thus kindling the student's interest to learn scientific concepts rather than merely memorizing descriptions and processes.**

Our ability to obtain information from images usually exceeds the ability to gain information from words, numbers, and tables. The strength of the visual information

---

*By "science," we mean any or all of these disciplines, including engineering.

**In this, and in the rest of this chapter, we speak of graphics in the broad sense, including the display of scanned images as appropriate for an educational application.

48

channel may be even more pronounced for the current generation of students who grew up in an intensely visual environment. Yet in most classrooms, they must learn from lectures that usually use only simple graphs, charts, and diagrams to supplement primarily symbolic information. These students seem more comfortable with a visual environment, and therefore their scientific learning can be improved through good visual techniques.

Traditional science education has been largely symbolic, rather than visual. Students learn scientific principles by manipulating symbols such as words, numbers, and formulas. But it takes a considerable amount of learning in this mode for most math and science students to understand fully the concept represented by an integral sign or a derivative. Other examples include differential equations, harmonic motion, and the behavior of a multidimensional function based on single-variable traces. But images such as those in *The Mechanical Universe,* about running an equation through the "derivative machine," get a student's attention and provide a visual image for learning abstract concepts and shortening the time to learn.* In return, science students improve their interactive and visual thinking, helping them better steer and interpret scientific experiments as working scientists.

Visualization is important for education. Visualization complements the usual symbolic approach to science education and strengthens both avenues to learning. In some scientific areas, the visualization tools are more obvious than others. Plane geometry, for example, is very symbolic but has obvious visual representations. Group theory for quantum mechanics and atomic orbitals, where a visual understanding of symmetry operations makes groups much more understandable, also has obvious visual representations. Many scientific processes are governed by complex mathematical equations that lend themselves to exploration by animations controlled by varying parameters.

The visual method or tool is not the goal in itself. Visualization in the sciences is a method for getting at the meaning behind the symbols. Visualization techniques enhance traditional learning because of our ability to absorb visual information, but they cannot replace it. The fundamental concepts do not change, and learning is enhanced, not limited, by these techniques. A good foundation in visual thinking during college can give the next generation of scientists and engineers the ability to take advantage of the visualization tools of the early twenty-first century for scientific applications and research.

As an example of the benefits a visual tool can bring to education, consider the work of Mary Ann Lila Smith, a

plant physiologist at the University of Illinois, Urbana-Champaign. Smith uses image analysis to allow students to do exploratory work that would not otherwise be possible. She has adapted a video digitizer and image-analysis software for plant analysis. Stored images of biological phenomena such as cell growth allow an undergraduate to simulate the phonomena interactively with the instructor's guidance. These interactive simulations can fit into a class or lab period, whereas the actual process would not. Her techniques apply not only to any area of plant or animal biology, but to many other natural processes that would take a prohibitive amount of time to complete.

Using video-digitized images also allows us to quantify qualitative information, such as the colors that indicate genetic behavior.[2] Students can learn about plants, both in the laboratory and in the field, without destroying them. Similar nondestructive methods can be used in animal biology.

Visualization cannot be used in a course without careful planning. Science educators must still specify the knowledge desired, the information and experiences to be given to the student to achieve this knowledge, and the way that information is organized into courses. The goal of computer graphics and animation tools is to assist in acquiring this information. Achieving this goal will benefit science in three ways. First, more concepts can be introduced. Second, students will gain deeper understanding of scientific concepts by interacting with and steering scientific simulations—with appropriate guidance from their instructor. Finally, students will learn to think more visually and intuitively about scientific problems, which will help them analyze research or application data.

The state of visualization for education. Visualization is not a new tool for science education. Since ancient Greece, where geometers sketched diagrams in the sand, figures illustrating theory and relations have accompanied science. From the theories of Ptolemy to those of Kepler, scientific knowledge before calculus was based on geometry; Kepler's discoveries, for example, were based on graphic displays of the movement of heavenly bodies.

Historically, textbook use of figures has been consistent and critical. Barbara Saigo, biology consultant and textbook author, notes that if textbooks are to teach, they need significant use of illustrations that have both instructional value and aesthetic appeal.

Computer-based visualization for education goes back well over 15 years to the Plato system,[3] and Bork's[4] work in physics, and others. This early work used time-shared systems with special graphics terminals, making the systems quite expensive and giving them limited application. But they proved that visual methods could improve learning.

The graphics capabilities of personal computers opened the door for the benefits of inexpensive graphics-based educational software. Among the best are those available from Conduit (Iowa City, Ia.) and Kinko's (Kinko's Service Corp., Ventura, Calif.). Figures 1 through 5 show individual

---

* *The Mechanical Universe* is a joint project of the California Institute of Technology and the Annenberg/Corporation for Public Broadcasting. It provides videotapes for public television to support undergraduate instruction in physics. Portions may be seen on *SIGGraph Video Reviews,* Nos. 17, 20, and 25.

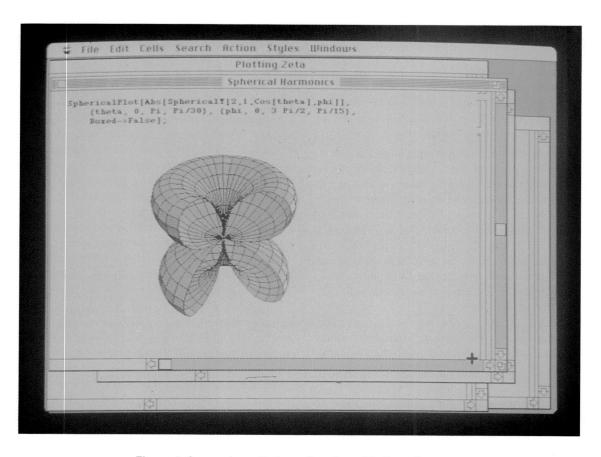

Figure 1. Screen from _Mathematica_. From Wolfram Research.

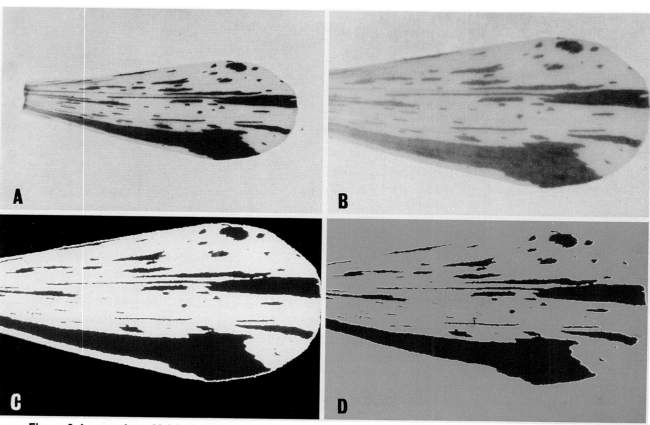

Figure 2: Images from M.A.L. Smith's genetics work: (a) Original photograph of Zinnia petal; (b) Digitized image of (a); (c) Thresholded and colored version of (b); (d) Final version of (b) prepared to quantify the amount of color in the petal.

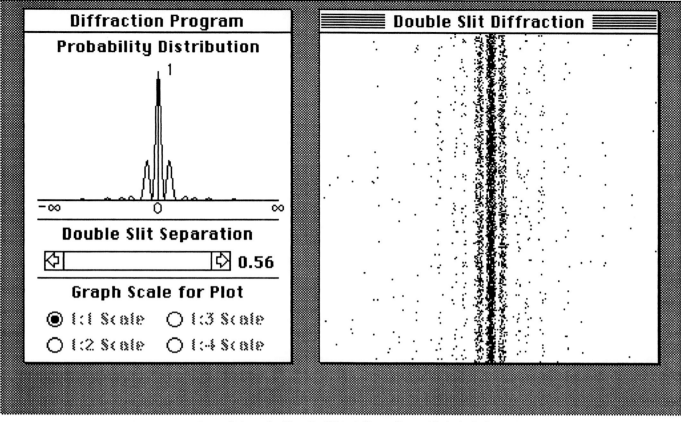

Figure 3. Screen from Cabrera's *Physics Simulations.* From Kinko's Software Exchange.

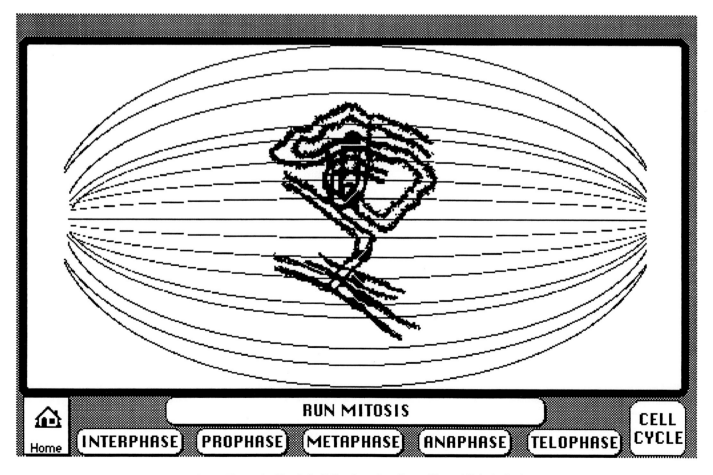

Figure 4. Screen from Matten's *Plant Cell Cycle animations.* From Kinko's Software Exchange.

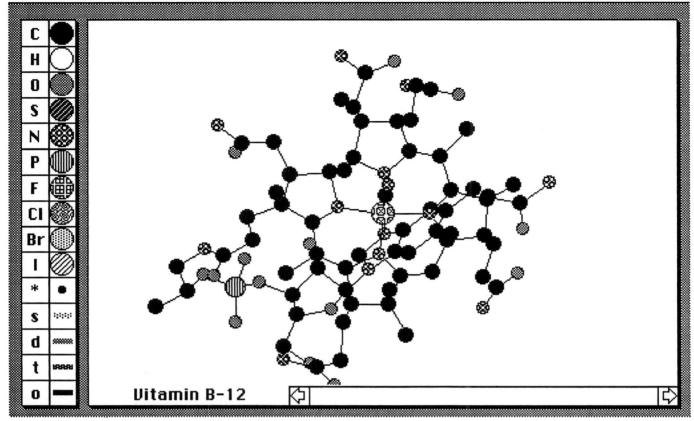

Vitamin B-12

Figure 5. Screen from Smith's *Molecular Editor*. From Kinko's Software Exchange.

examples of quality visualization from Stephen Wolfram's *Mathematica*, M.A.L. Smith's work in biology,[2] Blas Cabrera and the Stanford Faculty Author Program's *Physics Simulations*, Lawrence C. Matten's *Plant Cell Cycle* animation, and Allan L. Smith's *Molecular Editor*, respectively.

Similarly, graphics on personal computers made cost-effective CAD possible. Engineering education has taken advantage of this and has replaced manual drafting with CAD. But this is only a small beginning. Applications such as three-dimensional solid modeling and simulation, including animation of complex systems, are rapidly evolving on workstations and PCs in industry. Much more effective applications of visualization are now possible and important to develop.

Education is moving very slowly toward good visualization use, but effective visual education now depends almost entirely on motivated instructors. There is rarely any depth or continuity to visualization across a curriculum. Only a few departments are systematically integrating symbolic manipulation and visualization in selected courses, much less across a curriculum.

Animation, just now available, is an exciting opportunity for educational visualization. *The Mechanical Universe* included several hours of computer-generated animation that conveyed physics theory to the audience. These physics animations and the mathematics animations in Tom Apostol and Jim Blinn's *Mathematics!*—a California Institute of Technology project of computer-generated videotapes for teaching fundamental mathematics—show that carefully planned animation can be an exciting teaching tool. Wolfram's *Mathematica* also includes animation tools. Many effective animations and interactions need to be developed to demonstrate scientific principles.

Visualization tools for teaching science do not have quite as stringent display, network capability and bandwidth, and processing requirements as do visualization tools for scientific research; but the needs are very similar. At this time, 900 × 1100 resolution in 256 colors, networking, and 2-4 MIPS processing seem quite adequate for a student workstation. Students need to interact with experimental data and simulations, just as a researcher needs to interact with and steer a simulation running on a remote supercomputer. Students need graphic and color capabilities so their computer simulations can provide adequate information for discovery.

Barriers to Visualization in Education

Why is education making so little use of computing, visualization especially, as a teaching tool? Many barriers, both within and outside education, impede educational computing. These barriers fall into four categories: understanding visual learning, computing systems whose price or capability do not fit education, inflexibility in the current educational environment, and lack of institutional support. We will examine each in some detail and suggest ways to lower or remove them.

Understanding visual learning. Current educational computing is based on traditional teaching techniques. Its use of images grew from the textbook and blackboard diagrams instructors saw when they were students. These are limited uses of the graphics capabilities of computers, and there is a potential for much more effective visual learning tools. But this requires an understanding of visual learning unavailable today. This learning is different from traditional symbolic learning in the sciences and needs a new set of communication tools.

Video games are an example of visual learning. People can spend hours engaged in visual experiences that offer intense interaction and control in a simulated environment. They are learning the parameters and behavior of this environment and are paying money to do so. We need to offer learning in similar interactive and stimulating environments where students will acquire not only factual knowledge but a deeper and more fundamental understanding of the processes being simulated.

Mike Keeler of Ardent Computers proposes three levels for visualization: "postprocessing," where knowledge is complete and we are creating a display of the finished product; "tracking," where knowledge is being developed and we are watching it being displayed to see its nature; and "steering," where we are in the processing loop and can interact with and manipulate the simulation as it is underway.

The VISC report emphasized the need to steer calculations for scientific discovery. There are similar levels for visualization in education. A simulation can present static images that report the results of a single computation, dynamic images that illustrate the behavior of a sequence of computations, or a steerable behavior that lets the student manipulate the simulation as it progresses. These visualization levels give a student different levels of learning and understanding of the processes involved and affect the quality of this learning.

The visual and graphic arts can be tapped to understand how to promote creativity in learning with visual tools.

Although most instructors do not understand visual learning, cognitive scientists are working on models of learning and understanding that include visual techniques.[5] Other studies in the use of illustrations in textbooks indicate that they aid learning.[6] Visualization in classrooms and labs would yield additional scientific learning and insights.

Instructors' lack of experience with visual teaching and learning techniques is not surprising given the lack of system tools available to create visual learning experiences for students and, in the process, to learn how students learn visually. Better computer-systems capacity and prices will enable a broad cross-section of instructors to use visual teaching methods and to learn the practical aspects of teaching with graphics.

Computing systems. Hardware and software in affordable computer systems for education are inadequate. Currently affordable computers do not offer enough computational power or adequate displays, and the variations between them—or even between models and options for the same brand—make it difficult to base software on anything but the lowest-denominator machine. Almost all educational software now available is written for the IBM PC and compatibles or for the Macintosh Plus, as we have found by extensive surveys of software catalogs such as those published by Conduit and Kinko's.

What are the real machine needs for science education? These systems must perform complex computations quickly and return results to the students with good graphics. They must support interaction while taking advantage of all possible communication channels. Thus, they must offer multitasking, windowing operations, and high-resolution graphics, preferably with color, while being affordable for teaching. They should include networking for access to large file servers, special high-capacity computing systems, and the more expensive resources such as color printers, film recorders, or video systems. Finally, they must have extensive file storage or fast access to storage to display images. Examples of suitable systems would include a fully configured Macintosh IIcx, a color Sun 3/80, or a NeXT, although these systems' costs are still too high for widespread use, and the NeXT system does not yet have color.

The software environment of current systems presents an even more serious barrier to science education throughout the entire range of computing systems. Educational software must take advantage of windows, sophisticated user interaction, and other current capabilities. The sophistication of the programming environment and inconsistent computing platforms make this difficult. Professional programmers need a year or longer to become proficient on this kind of system.

The software-development problem is much worse for university faculty than it is for programmers. Instructors should not be concerned with the low-level coding required by current software technology. Faculty working on software must now invest a great deal of time and effort, which makes really good software quite expensive. We must reduce this investment and the resultant cost of software. Faculty members have a primary dedication to teaching, not to computing. Taking time to learn computing reduces professional opportunities in their own areas. Faculty need to produce effective software quickly while working at a level that emphasizes scientific thinking. In a recent article,[7] Steve Jobs of NeXT describes a typical academic application by "I need it by next Tuesday and a grad student and I have to do it and we can invest about two days in it." Two days is clearly not enough time to develop an application with current software tools, and some of us, alas, cannot even use graduate students.

These system barriers result in a lack of curriculum-based software that supports learning scientific concepts. Instructors need a range of educational software from which to choose for any topic. Just as it is necessary to have more than one possible text for a course, it is necessary to have more than one software choice for a subject. Moreover, just as texts are sometimes used in ways different from the author's intentions, the range of available software must be able to support a range of different ideas and approaches.

The educational environment. The computer industry is making advances in hardware and software for scientific visualization. Many problems, however, are inherent to the current educational culture, and these may well be the most difficult barriers to visualization in science education.

Education changes slowly and reluctantly. Even though computing and visualization are natural developments in science and some instructors have used them for some time, most courses still follow the traditional model of lecture, text, and laboratory. These leave out some students who might contribute positively to science. Science faculty have a long history of teaching symbolically, but, as we have noted, most are unskilled in developing and using visual presentations. As an example, we need only compare the quality of blackboard sketches used in typical classroom lectures with the professional images in issues of *Science* or *Scientific American*.

Any instructor might do innovative things in a single course. But current curricula do not take advantage of visualization's teaching opportunities. Courses and course sequences as now constituted have little room for new techniques, and changing them risks incompatibility with other courses in the same program or with other programs. Large-scale curriculum developments, such as those proposed by Redish[8] for physics and some of those being developed by the National Science Foundation curriculum program in calculus, will be needed before major effects can be achieved.

Engineering faces an equally difficult curricular problem in dealing with the professional aspects of computing. Most engineering students learn CAD as part of their studies, but more advanced computing tools are now part of every practicing engineer's needs. Engineering curricula must integrate these advanced tools, which require considerable training, while continuing to provide learning in an expanding field of knowledge and practice.

Finally, the conservative attitude of education seems to lead to serious problems with parochialism. Some educators are unwilling to use software for teaching if it is even the least bit different from their own approach to the subject. This attitude approaches inertia for the more traditional disciplines such as mathematics and engineering. Mathematics, for example, historically has taken pride in needing nothing beyond paper and blackboard. Integrating computing into curricula, visualization especially, requires a willingness to use new approaches.

One of the biggest roadblocks to visualization of scientific data is that research scientists have had little visual training and have not learned how to use visual tools to understand scientific principles. Computer graphics simulations and examples in science education will help students to see the value of images to express scientific concepts. Courses in art and color theory would provide students with visual skills, and such studies should probably be part of science curricula.

Institutional support. Educational institutions must support educational visualization. To varying degrees, academic computing centers provide standard centralized time-shared computing, and many also support clusters of personal computers. Fewer support networked departmental systems and provide instructional computing services. Many resources must be provided before visualization is possible in educational institutions. Universities must support the development of visual educational software, including having staff with creative ideas, expertise in current instructional design, and a computer graphics background. Continuing support for software updates is essential, as is support for faculty development. Presently, sufficient funds are not allocated to provide this kind of support, but universities and computer centers must be willing to accept responsibility for these activities.

Tenure is another problem and is even more difficult to solve. Faculty members cannot commit their time to new educational approaches when the promotion and tenure process will punish them for such efforts. Some institutions believe that the business of education is education and back it up by rewarding educational innovators with promotion, tenure, and salary. But most universities do not. Moreover, since the research world does not yet publish papers on educational innovation and is only beginning to publish visualization in any real form, there are few ways for the junior faculty member to fit personal visualization development into a traditional research program that gives publication credits. Refereed visual publications are needed both in scientific research and scientific education. Senior faculty must take the lead in establishing the importance of visual learning and must recognize such efforts among their junior colleagues as worthy of reward.

Overcoming the Barriers

How can we overcome the barriers identified in the previous section? We describe four general approaches and then give some specific recommendations for action.

Consciousness raising. Many educators, especially in smaller schools, are not aware of visualization's potential. We recommend that educators already using visualization make every effort to describe their work to others. This can be done through articles in newsletters and journals, presentations and papers at conferences, organizing workshops or conferences on visualization in particular courses or disciplines, or writing focused reference books on this special method of teaching. The National Science Foundation's Undergraduate Faculty Enhancement Program is a source for support for the workshops or conferences, for example. We especially hope well-known researchers or educators will take an increased interest in the use of visualization for teaching and will draw attention to its possibilities.

Providing rewards. Teaching is all too often taken for granted, so rewards or recognition are important ways to encourage faculty to try new approaches to teaching. Educom, a national organization for educational computing, now gives awards recognizing good educational software, which may or may not include effective graphics. An award that specifically recognizes excellence in scientific visualization tools or applications for education would be valuable. Other recognition could be provided by cooperation between visualization researchers and university educators. There are two ways this might be done by research centers: they could (1) provide on-site workshops for instructors, and (2) actively seek to add undergraduate faculty to National Science Foundation grants through the Research Opportunity Awards program.

Other concrete rewards are needed. Educators do not now get a reasonable return on their time invested in software development, and, of course, they must have the final reward of tenure, promotion, and salary increases for their creative work in teaching with visualization. The recognition we have described should externally validate the value of educational visualization and assist in promotion and tenure.

Support for visualization in education. The computing vendor community, educational community, and educational institutions can support visualization for science education in a number of ways.

Vendors should support education by providing computing capacity, display quality, and software tools at a price that allows the purchase of enough systems to meet the educational demand. This may require some creative ways to support vendors' efforts. Some vendors see the value of education and provide large discounts. The natural decline in prices may also make this less of a problem.

We indicated that educators need standard platforms and tools; we suggest a Unix or Unix-like operating system with a toolkit that includes windows and object-oriented development tools. The toolkits should probably come from the academic community and emphasize flexibility and adaptability, though cooperative development by educators and vendors will provide the best results for both. Educators need to develop flexible, interactive demonstrations or simulations quickly, as opposed to the large, permanent systems produced by commercial developers over multiple person-years.

At this writing, the system cost of a machine that can be used widely in the teaching community is probably about $4,000, including color. This is much less than the cost of any current capable color system. This is one major difference between a visualization workstation for teaching and the research version of the same: by settling for merely good performance, communication, and color, we hope that educational systems can be brought down to an affordable price. We certainly applaud the efforts of computing companies to provide discounts to education, but prices for teaching systems must be lower yet to achieve the wide use necessary to affect all of education. The computing industry could also support teaching by opening their training courses to educators at a reduced price; it might be interesting to set educators' price per training hour at the price a student must pay per hour to attend the instructor's courses!

The educational community can support visualization for education in two ways. Professional societies, college consortia, and individual departments can develop model curricula and courses integrating computing and visualization with teaching. These curricular models must, of course, start with the science itself and use visualization only as an end to the best teaching of the subject. How to do this is a research area we will describe more fully later. These groups can also provide models for using computing tools with individual students or with classes in a number of learning modes so an instructor can build a personal teaching style that includes these tools. This can be supported and forwarded by special funding from national sources, private foundations, and universities. We especially encourage foundations interested in educational reform to consider such programs; visualization promises to improve science education more than any other technique we know.

Individual institutions can best support visualization education by recognizing that this is an important innovation that must be nurtured by faculty development and professional assistance. The faculty development must not stop at increasing computing skills; it must also help faculty learn to communicate visually and dynamically, to steer students' explorations through visualization, and to build an attitude of mutual discovery without generating the grade anxiety that can accompany discovery learning. The institution should provide support services to faculty to assist with software design, implementation, and use. Depending on the needs of the individual instructor, this assistance could be actual coding support by skilled students or staff or help in designing software and displays. This is precisely the support provided by the Socrates Project at Cornell University, a program funded by the US Department of Education's FIPSE (funds for the improvement of postsecondary education) Program and Digital Equipment Corp. This kind of assistance can be given by development centers in a consortium, a computer center, or even a single department.

Research in visualization for education. We must increase our knowledge of visualization, especially as it applies to education, to remove these barriers. More research is necessary.

The problems of developing visual software for education are a special case of the larger problem of developing visualization software for research and science applications. Research is proceeding in window systems, graphics standards, user interfaces, software environments, and graphics hardware. We need to ensure that the resulting products are available for education. An educator must be able to produce a complete educational application quickly without becoming a computer expert. This clearly calls for very flexible toolkits with large numbers of prebuilt functions, probably as object libraries for an object-oriented language. Such toolkits should be designed by educators and should be based on good learning models.

Since visual learning has a much richer meaning with computers than it does merely with textbook figures and blackboard diagrams, we must ask how visual and symbolic learning complement each other. This varies among disciplines, among subjects and courses within a discipline, and even among topics in a course. But it is the fundamental question behind effective visual education.

At the actual course level, there are dual aspects to this problem. First, what material is best introduced visually, and when should this be treated symbolically? What makes the visual treatment eventually inadequate and requires symbols? Is it a need to get more precision or accuracy? To acquire a vocabulary to do work that goes beyond standard images or two or three dimensional displays? To develop treatments that apply broadly to a wide range of topics? The second aspect is the converse of the first. What material is best introduced symbolically, and when (if ever) should this be discussed visually? What value does visualization give these topics? Is it the development of intuition? To understand a complex problem? To see the topic's principles in an application?

We also need to learn what kind of software modules to develop for a course. Is it better to use a single, large program per course or per set of courses, or to have many small programs for separate topics in each course? The former provides a focused course model with a single user interface, but it requires a great deal of development, is expensive, and tends not to be accepted if any one part is weak or does not fit an instructor's approach. The latter allows smaller development projects, is more modular, and will more readily fit a given course. It also avoids the tendency to keep adding new software features that degrade the original design, but it may face the student with a collection of different interfaces. We prefer the small-program approach, which would be even more appealing if publishers or professional organizations would develop consistent user interfaces, toolkits, or even templates for authors.

Specific Recommendations

We can summarize the preceding section with specific recommendations for an initiative in visualization in science and engineering education:

- Develop a mechanism to support visualization in science education. This can involve forming of specific committees within professional organizations or a program within a private foundation or within the National Science Foundation.

- Support focused conferences on visualization in education or special sessions at conferences in various science and science education areas. Instructors must learn how to use dynamic simulations in their disciplines and their teaching.

- Develop cooperation among the computer industry, visualization research, and education to learn how visualization may best be used to understand scientific concepts. Educators skilled in presenting information are critically important in developing visual-presentation concepts.

- Develop funding to support research and applications in visual learning, in software tools for authors and educators, and in comprehensive course and curriculum models.

- Provide faculty development programs to support educators who want to add visual teaching to their set of educational tools.

- Provide awards and other vehicles for publicizing and rewarding good visualization work in teaching.

These recommendations will require support from many sources. ACM SIGGraph is interested in this question and is prepared to take a positive role. The Technical Committee on Computer Graphics of the IEEE Computer Society is also interested. We encourage others to contribute.

Acknowledgments

This chapter is based in part on papers presented at the 1988 Princeton Symposium on Scientific Visualization and work of the ACM SIGGraph Education Committee. We thank the referees for their comments.

References

1. B.H. McCormick, T.A. DeFanti, and M.D. Brown, eds., "Visualization in Scientific Computing," *Computer Graphics,* Vol. 21, No. 6, 1987.

2. M.A.L. Smith, L.H. Spomer, and R.K.D. Cowen, "Image Analysis to Quantify the Expression of an Unstable Allele," *J. Heredity,* 1988, pp. 147-150.

3. S.B. Peterson, T.R. Lemberger, and J.H. Smith, "Phizquiz: A Proficiency Test in Elementary Mechanics," *Proc. Conf. Computers Undergraduate Curricula,* 1974, pp. 347-356.

4. A. Bork, "Current Status of the Physics Computer Development Project," *Proc. Conf. Computers Undergraduate Curricula,* Texas Christian University, Fort Worth, Tex., 1975, pp. 61-67.

5. F.M. Dwyer, *Strategies for Improving Visual Learning,* Learning Services, State College, Penn., 1978.

6. W.H. Levie and R. Lentz, "Effects of Text Illustration: A Review of Research," *Educational Comm. Tech. J.,* Vol. 30, 1982, pp. 195-232.

7. P.J. Denning and K.A. Frenkel, "A Conversation with Steve Jobs," *Comm. ACM,* Vol. 32, 1989, pp. 436-443.

8. E.F. Redish, "Curriculum Reform in Physics: The Computer as a Vehicle," *Educom Rev.,* Vol. 24, 1989, p. 24.

Steve Cunningham is a professor of computer science at California State University, Stanislaus. He has written visualization software for statistics teaching and was software reviews editor for *The College Mathematics Journal* from 1983 to 1988, while early visual-based software for mathematics was being developed. His interests lie in computer graphics and in computer graphics-based educational software.

He received the PhD in mathematics from the University of Oregon in 1969 and the MS in computer science from Oregon State University in 1982, as well as the BA in mathematics from Drury College. He chairs the ACM SIGGraph Education Committee.

Judith R. Brown is a visualization consultant in the Advanced Research Computing Services Division of Weeg Computing Center at The University of Iowa. She has a BA in mathematics and education and an MA in mathematics, both from The University of Iowa, and has been working in the computing industry since 1964. She is Vice-Chair for Operations of ACM SIGGraph.

Mike McGrath is a professor of engineering at the Colorado School of Mines, teaching graphics, CAD, and design. He developed the CAD facilities at CSM and is presently working on a SIGGraph-funded project to design a graphics curriculum for engineering education for the 1990s. McGrath was a member of the NSF-sponsored panel on Graphics, Image Processing, and Workstations that recommended the initiative on visualization in scientific computing.

He received the PhD in applied mechanics from the University of Colorado, Boulder, and the BSME and MS degrees from the University of Notre Dame.

Section 2: Foundations and Techniques of Scientific Visualization

This section covers techniques and foundations. For the most part, the authors discuss their techniques in the context of a particular application, but most of the techniques have a much larger universe of application. For this reason, the techniques discussed here form some of the foundation material for scientific visualization. Another source of material is the forthcoming tutorial entitled *Volume Visualization* edited by Arie Kaufman and published by the IEEE Computer Society Press.

The first paper of this section by James Helman and Lambertus Hesselink of Stanford University describes techniques for automatically analyzing and extracting information from fluid flow data sets. Rather than trying to simply display the data, the idea is to extract certain topological information and to display this. As the authors point out, a jillion little arrows displayed in a cube would not reveal much about a three-dimensional flow. However, detecting vortices and other interesting places and displaying these in an integrated manner is potentially very useful. This general idea is very important in Scientific Visualization. That is, the idea of having some algorithm find interesting things in the data and then of concentrating the viewers attention and the display efforts on these interesting aspects. Helman and Hesselink deal with time dependent two dimensional flows. A challenging research problem is to extend the techniques presented here to three-dimensional flows.

The next paper, "Visualization Idioms: A Conceptual Model for Scientific Visualization Systems," by Haber and McNabb develops foundation material for scientific visualization by establishing a certain type of conceptual model. The authors make use of a visualization idiom that is defined as "any specific sequence of data enrichment and enhancement transformations, visualization mappings, and rendering transformations that produce an abstract display of a scientific data set." Throughout the paper, there is much discussion about abstract visualization objects (AVOs).

The third paper in this section, "Projection Pursuit Techniques for the Visualization of High Dimensional Data Sets," is by Stuart Crawford and Thomas Fall of Advanced Decision Systems of Mountain View, California. The paper surveys the relatively new topic of projection pursuit as a tool for exploratory data analysis. In a nutshell, they are interested in detecting patterns in multidimensional data sets. The human mind does the detecting and the graphics workstation through the use the techniques of this paper tries to present the data in a form conducive to this. Since the user is busy trying to find interesting things in the data, it is important that he not be distracted by having to think a lot about running the controls of the program. It is important to have an interface that is easy for the user to use and the authors have tried to accomplish this.

Harlyn Baker's paper, "Computation and Manipulation of 3D Surfaces from Image Sequences" is concerned with the development of techniques that will capture 3D structure from sequences of 2D images. The paper is divided into two portions. The first dealing with the case where the sequence of images are obtained from a camera moving around in a fixed scene and the second concerned with sequences that are slices of 3D medical data. While Baker's terminology is a little different, the problem addressed here is exactly the same as the surface based methods of Fuchs, Levoy, and Pizer [which is included in Section 3] in that a contour surface for 3D volumetric data is being computed. Not only are the contour surfaces computed, but they are also modeled in the sense that the interconnection topology between surface facets is determined. This is extremely important for any application beyond just viewing the surfaces. An important component of Baker's approach is a process he calls the "weaving wall" which takes contours on 2D images and assembles them into a 3D surface.

Representation and Display of Vector Field Topology in Fluid Flow Data Sets

James Helman and Lambertus Hesselink, Stanford University

Introduction

Visualization of scientific data sets plays an important role in understanding complex phenomena. In fluid mechanics experiments, extensive use of flow visualization has revealed flow structures such as the large-scale eddies in turbulent shear flows discovered by Brown and Roshko[1] in the early 1970s. Their work has had a pronounced influence on fluid mechanics research, because they showed that flow modeling studies could incorporate stable structures in what otherwise appears to be a chaotic flow.

Visualization of physical processes. Traditionally, visualization of complex physical phenomena has been accomplished experimentally as part of the measurement process. For example, extensive studies of fluid flows have relied on seeding the flow with smoke or photographing patterns of oil streaks on the surface of a body in the flow. The resulting data sets, although of very high resolution, are essentially images, well suited to two-dimensional image processing and analysis.

More recently, however, both experiments and numerical simulations have begun to yield high-resolution multivariate data. These incredibly rich and complex data sets consist of several quantities, defined at hundreds of thousands, sometimes millions, of points on a two- or three-dimensional grid. The size of these data sets increases rapidly as the dimensionality grows when the data are dependent on time or on one or more parameters.

For example, a data set with three velocity components, pressure, and density defined on a $100 \times 100 \times 100$ grid defines five quantities at 10^6 points. If sufficient computational power and storage were available, one might want to consider this for 100 time steps and 100 different values of a parameter; the size would jump to 10^{10} points. Even for the more modestly sized two-dimensional data sets we have studied, such as a 60×121 grid at 180 time steps, manipulation and display of the data is computationally very expensive unless some analysis and feature extraction precede the visualization process.

Extensive interaction and feedback between experiment and numerical analysis is necessary both to verify the theoretical models used in the simulations and to tune parameters before embarking on expensive experimental verification of a design. For example, we may wish to improve the efficiency of a physical process, such as combustion. The full characterization of the combustion process requires the measurement of multidimensional data, including density, velocity, and pressure, in a two- or three-dimensional domain. Visualization and interpretation of these data now take on a new aspect, because we want to extract qualitative information and we need to make quantitative comparisons to iteratively optimize the system.

Ideally, an automated process would use this information to vary input parameters to the experiment or simulation to optimize it for the desired behavior. In most cases of practical significance, however, the processes are insufficiently understood or too complex for such automated optimization. Human reasoning is required, but the data necessary to fully characterize such a complicated physical process are too numerous for human understanding. Therefore, the data must be converted into a form in which humans can comprehend the important aspects. Figure 1 shows this process schematically. Because of the large bandwidth of the human visual system and the speed of computers, the visualization of computer-extracted features provides the most efficient way of effecting this interaction.[2]

Our research effort has concentrated on automated analysis of vector field topology in fluid flow data sets, because topology is central to understanding fluid flows.[3,4] Also, the geometric nature of topology makes it possible to visually communicate this rich and fascinating aspect of fluid dynamics.

The visualization process. Visualization of scientific data includes three processes: analysis, display, and interaction. Most large multivariate data sets are not suited to direct display (imagine 800,000 little color-coded arrows in space!), so analysis is almost always required. Unless the display is founded on an analysis or interpretation relevant to the problem, you end up with a pretty picture that has little scientific value.

Analysis. The analyses we can apply to multivariate data range from general purpose techniques, such as contour surface extraction, to highly specific ones, such as shock

Reprinted from *Computer*, August 1989, pages 27-36. Copyright © 1989 by The Institute of Electrical and Electronics Engineers, Inc. All rights reserved.

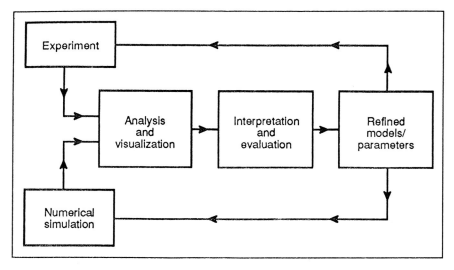

Figure 1. The role of visualization in simulations and experiments.

surface or vortex core extraction in the study of fluid flow data sets. The method described in this article lies between these extremes. One can apply the analysis of critical points and topology to any vector field, but we have adapted the analysis somewhat to situations occurring in fluid flows by including in the analysis walls on which the magnitude of the vector vanishes.

Display. The more complex the data set, the more important it is to maximize the amount of information understandable from the display. This requires tailoring the display to match the capabilities of the human visual system. This tailoring includes the use of colors, surfaces instead of isolated curves, orientation cues such as the lighting and shading of surfaces, depth cues such as stereopsis, and animation.

Interaction. Even with the best display techniques, it is impossible to simultaneously display all of the quantitative information in a large data set in an understandable form. So, when we require more precise information on some element or aspect of the data, we must specify it through user interaction. This interaction can include simple refinement of the color coding of contour levels or complex manipulation of virtual probes that simulate physical behavior or measurements.

Vector field visualization. In the past, several graphics display methods were developed for scalar data sets, but these methods often cannot help us display and understand vector data sets. The difficulty arises from the limitations of our vision and display devices. We cannot directly display vectorial data on a two-dimensional screen, for example as a set of little arrows, and still interpret the result with the same ease as we would a scalar image. Our visual systems simply are not well adapted to interpret large volumes of vectors in this way, whereas we have superb abilities for understanding and interpreting images or depth-cued surface displays.

One method of generating surfaces is to apply a scalar display technique such as isovalue surface extraction to a scalar quantity derived from the vector field. For example, Figure 2 shows an isovalue surface of the velocity magnitude for the experimentally measured two-dimensional flow around a circular cylinder[5] as a function of time. The surface was generated by StanSurfs,[6] which implements a spline interpolation and subdivision technique for extracting contour surfaces.[7] The figure does not show the cylinder, which is located in the foreground. Time increases from top to bottom, and the flow within each time slice is directed into the page. At each instant, each contour line surrounds a vortex, a saddle, or a vortex-saddle pair. You can see the time development of the flow downstream of the cylinder in the separation and merging of the contour surfaces from top to bottom.

Unfortunately, we lose a great deal of information when we reduce a vector quantity to a scalar for visualization. Experimental visualization techniques, such as smoke seeding, often yield information about particle paths or instantaneous streamlines. Thus, for the evaluation of simulations and their verification against experiment, flow visualization packages, such as Plot3D,[8] usually include the ability to visualize tangent curves of velocity and vorticity.

These curves prove extremely valuable in understanding fluid flows, but when we display more than a few well-grouped curves, the display often becomes difficult to understand because the isolated curves are poorly suited to depth cuing and visual interpretation, as shown in Figure 3. Animation reduces the problem by displaying only a small section of the tangent curves at any one time,[9] but there remains the problem of selecting starting points for the curves.

The usual method for determining and visualizing flow topology in a complex flow data set is to choose points at

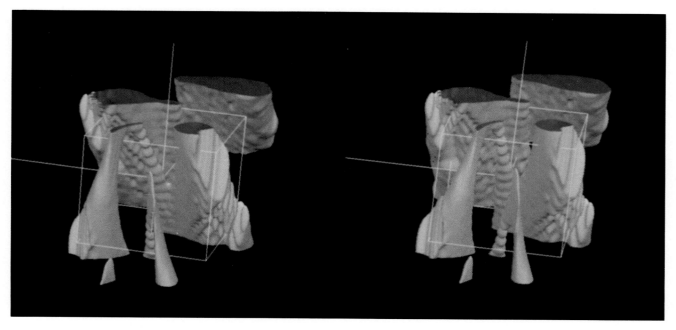

Figure 2. Isosurface of the velocity magnitude in the experimentally measured flow around a circular cylinder (shown as a cross-fusable stereo pair). See the sidebar for viewing instructions.

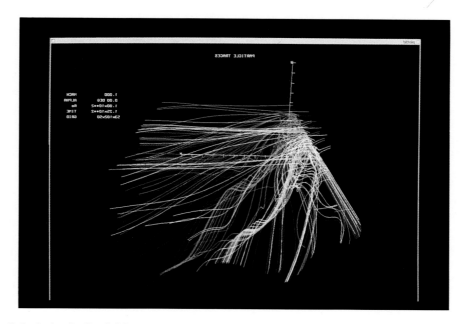

Figure 3. Selected velocity field tangent curves in the computed flow around an airfoil at 90 degrees.

which to start the integration of tangent curves and to interactively refine the starting points until the desired structures are located. The researcher then hand draws surfaces to represent the topology.

We are investigating an alternative approach based on the physics and mathematics underlying the physical phenomenon. In fluid flows, we can determine (assuming a particular frame of reference) critical points in the flow. These are points where the velocity vector vanishes. The critical points, connected by principal lines or planes, determine the topology of the flow.

The decomposition of the flow field into elementary structures provides an effective simplification. Not only have we reduced the complexity of the data set, but we have achieved this without sacrificing the quantitative nature of the data set. The positions of the structures and surfaces are accurately contained in the representation. From this representation, we may directly visualize the topology as surfaces or use the internal graph representation to compare topologies and locate topological transitions.

Analysis

We can think of flow topology in terms of surfaces in three-dimensional flows or curves in two-dimensional flows that divide the flow into separate regions. Two sets of surfaces or curves are of particular interest.[10] The first set consists of those along which the flow close to the wall of a body attaches to or separates from that wall, that is, those tangent curves that actually end on the wall rather than moving along the surface. The second set consists of those surfaces where tangent curves that start arbitrarily close to each other can end up in substantially different regions. This second group of curves relates to critical points. For example, tangent curves starting on either side of a curve that goes directly into a saddle point are diverted by the saddle point to very different regions.

We have developed algorithms for generating representations of the topology for two-dimensional velocity fields. When the two-dimensional field is available for a discretely sampled range of times or parameter values, we link these two-dimensional representations together to form a three-dimensional representation of the flow with time or the parameter as the third dimension.

Tangent curves. A tangent curve of a vector field is a curve for which the tangent vector at any point along the curve is parallel to the vector field at that point. The tangent vector at each point along the curve is the derivative of the position vector along the curve with respect to arc length.

Figure 4 shows several tangent curves in the neighborhood of a saddle point and some of the vectors that generated them. We derive tangent curves by integrating the vector field. Both the magnitude and the direction of the vector field are determined by the tangent curves when the curves are parameterized by the integration parameter instead of arc length.

For a velocity field, the curve parameter is the travel time along the trajectory. If enough tangent curves are known, the entire vector field can be reconstructed from them.

The power of topological visualization is that, given the critical points and their principal tangent curves, an observer can visually infer the shape of other tangent curves and hence the structure of the whole vector field.

Critical points. Critical points are those points at which the magnitude of the vector vanishes. We can characterize these points according to the behavior of nearby tangent curves. If a tangent curve integrates directly into one of these points, the integration must stop, since the tangent is undefined at this point. The tangent curves that end on critical points hold special interest because they define the behavior of the vector field in the neighborhood of the point.

A critical point can be classified to a first-order approximation according to the eigenvalues of the Jacobian matrix of the vector (u,v) with respect to position at the critical point $(x0, y0)$:

$$\frac{\partial(u,v)}{\partial(x,y)}\bigg|_{x0,y0} = \begin{bmatrix} \frac{\partial u}{\partial x} & \frac{\partial u}{\partial y} \\ \frac{\partial v}{\partial x} & \frac{\partial v}{\partial y} \end{bmatrix}\bigg|_{x0,y0}$$

Figure 5 shows how the eigenvalues classify a critical point as an *attracting node*, a *repelling node*, an *attracting*

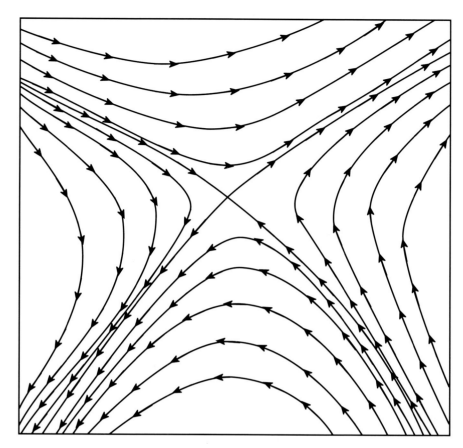

Figure 4. Vector field and tangent curves near a saddle point.

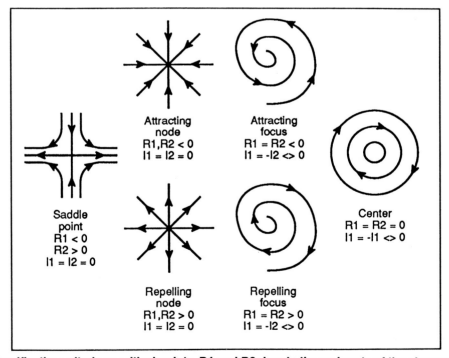

Figure 5. Classification criteria or critical points. R1 and R2 denote the real parts of the eigenvalues of the Jacobian; I1 and I2 denote the imaginary parts.

focus, a *repelling focus,* a *center,* or a *saddle.* We can understand this by observing that a positive or negative real part of an eigenvalue indicates an attracting or repelling nature, respectively. The imaginary part denotes circulation about the point. Among these points, the saddle points are distinct in that only four tangent curves actually end at the point itself. At the saddle point, these curves are tangent to the two eigenvectors of the Jacobian matrix, which are the separatrices of the saddle point. The outgoing and incoming separatrices are parallel to the eigenvectors with positive and negative eigenvalues, respectively.

On walls where the velocity is constrained to be zero, the normal component of the velocity usually vanishes as the square of distance from the wall, and the tangential component vanishes linearly. This causes tangent curves very close to the wall surface to remain close to it. However, there can be singular points at which a tangent curve terminates on the body rather than moving along the surface of it. These points are *attachment nodes and detachment nodes.*

The saddle points and attachment and detachment nodes are the only points where unique tangent curves end on the point itself. Because these points serve as the origin of the tangent curves that characterize the topology, we call them *originators.* All other points are called *terminators.*

Some of the tangent curves end at other critical or wall points. Others may leave the domain of available data. The points at which these tangent curves leave the domain we call *boundary incoming* and *boundary outgoing* points, depending on whether the vector was parallel or anti-parallel to the direction of integration when it left the domain.

Based on this, we classify each point as a saddle point, attracting node/focus, repelling node/focus, center, attachment node, detachment node, boundary incoming, or boundary outgoing. These classifications imply membership in other classes as shown in Figure 6. For simplicity, we excluded centers from the diagram and the subsequent discussion because no tangent curves enter or leave these points. The outer closed tangent curve surrounding a center is

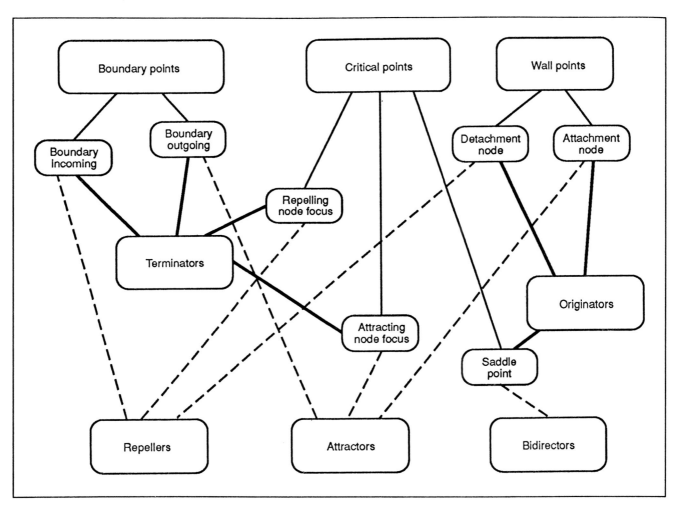

Figure 6. Point classifications. Each point identified by the analysis belongs to one of the classes denoted by the small boxes. For each of these point classes, this implies membership in three superclasses as shown by the connecting lines.

represented by the tangent curves originating from the saddle, which by virtue of continuity and boundary conditions must accompany it. Therefore, this entails no loss of global structural information.

Algorithm for two-dimensional flows. Starting from a two-dimensional vector field defined on a connected grid of points, which is specified by a separate array, we locate and characterize the critical and wall points. Each of these points is represented by a data object that has slots containing intrinsic information about the point, including position, the Jacobian matrix, eigenvalues, and eigenvectors. For each point, these quantities are computed and stored both relative to the grid and relative to physical space. Slots are also provided, as appropriate to the class of the object, to link incoming and outgoing tangent curves.

For those points having principal directions associated with them, namely the *originators,* tangent curves are integrated forward along the outgoing directions and backward along the incoming directions. These tangent curves are used to link the points into a partially connected graph.

Given a two-dimensional vector field, the algorithm is as follows:

(1) Locate, characterize, and classify all critical and wall points.

(2) Integrate tangent curves out of the originators. This generates one curve for each attachment or detachment point and four curves for each saddle point. The beginning of each curve is linked to its originator.

(3) Identify the endpoint of each tangent curve and link the curve to it.

(a) If the curve ends on the boundary, a new boundary is created to represent it, and the curve is linked to it.

(b) If the curve ends at an existing terminator, then the end of the curve is linked to it.

(c) If the endpoint is an originator, then the corresponding tangent curve for that originator is replaced by the new curve. This situation occurs because of integration errors. This algorithm gives preference to the topologically unstable connections between originators.

Figure 7a shows the results of the application of this algorithm to the computed two-dimensional flow around an airfoil at 90 degrees.[11] A saddle point, labeled *sp,* and two foci, labeled *af* and *rf,* behind the airfoil indicate the locations of two vortex cores. These points, as well as the boundary incoming (*bi*) and outgoing (*bo*) points appear in a schematic graph representation in Figure 7b. This format helps us compare topologies because it "unwinds" the curves and unambiguously portrays the topology.

This particular topology is unstable because two originators, a saddle point and a detachment node, labeled *de,* are joined by a tangent curve. Normally, this configuration only exists for one instant in time, but the instant can be spread out slightly by numerical errors. At a slightly later time, the topology has changed to that shown in Figure 8.

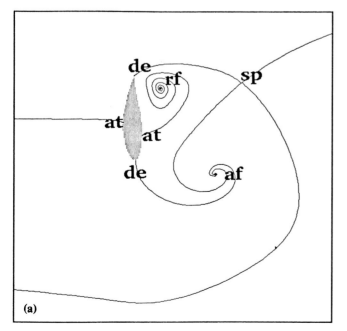

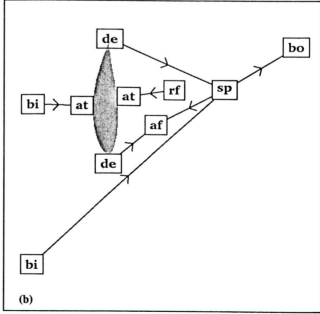

Figure 7. Tangent curves (instantaneous streamlines) and points in the computed low around an airfoil at *t* = 2 (a). Corresponding graph of low topology (b).

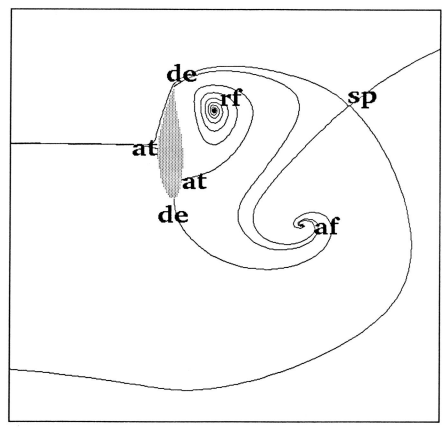

Figure 8. Tangent curves (instantaneous streamlines) and points in the computed low around an airfoil at *t* **= 3.**

Algorithm for two-dimensional parameter-dependent flows. When the two-dimensional vector field depends on some parameter such as time, we can link the representations of instantaneous topologies to form a three-dimensional representation. The order in which we consider points and curves in different slices for linking is important because the distance in the plane between two points of the same class is not sufficient to indicate that they have the same place in the flow topology. This is particularly true of the boundary incoming and boundary outgoing points, which can be very close together both with respect to the grid and in physical space. For this reason, we use the originators as a basis for the linkage. Points connected to corresponding curves from an originator are linked recursively to ensure consistency.

We link slices by applying the following method to the representation for each parameter value:

For each subclass of originators and then for each subclass of terminators, do the following:

(1) Construct the set of all parts consisting of points of that subclass with the first element from the current slice and the second element from the next slice.

(2) Keep only those pairs in which neither of the points is already linked to a point in the other slice and for which the two-dimensional distance separating them is less than a specified tolerance.

(3) Sort these pairs in ascending order according to the separation distance between the points in the pair.

(4) For each pair of points, starting with the ones with the smallest separation:

    (a) Link the points together.

    (b) If there are multiple tangent curves from the point, align them according to direction.

    (c) For each pair of tangent curves, if the points at the other end of the tangent curves satisfy the criteria in (2), link the points together by recursing to (a).

Display

For two-dimensional parameter-dependent vector fields, the representation of the topology can be displayed as a set of surfaces with the third dimension corresponding to the parameter value. The surfaces are created by filling in strips between corresponding tangent curves in each slice of the representation. These strips are drawn only when the starting points and endpoints of the first curves are linked to the starting points and endpoints of the second. When a topological transition occurs, one of the endpoints changes, and no strip is drawn. Figure 9 shows the strips generated by the $t = 3$ and $t = 4$ slices. This corresponds to the topology shown in Figure 7.

In the display of these surfaces, we use several cues to aid visualization. The surfaces are lighted and shaded, and they are colored according to their type. Surfaces corresponding to the attracting direction of a saddle point are colored yellow. Those surfaces corresponding to the repelling direction are colored blue. Surfaces of attachment are colored orange. Surfaces of detachment are colored purple.

To aid in distinguishing the edges of surfaces and to provide more shape cues, we candy-stripe the surfaces paral-

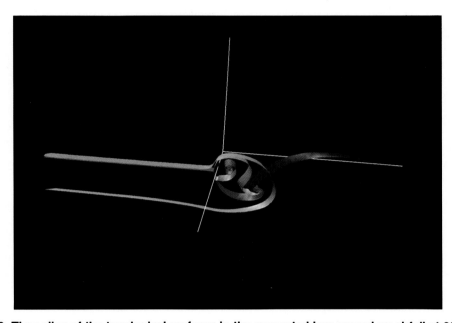

Figure 9. Time slice of the topological surfaces in the computed low around an airfoil at 90 degrees.

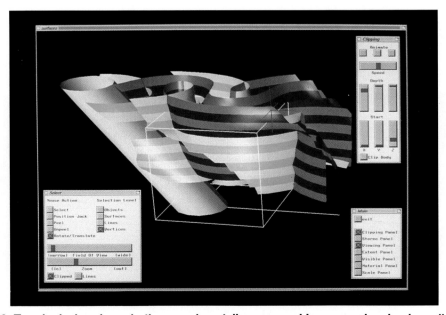

Figure 10. Topological surfaces in the experimentally measured low around a circular cylinder.

lel to the slices. The superimposition of a wireframe cube and stereo viewing provide additional depth cues.

Figure 10 shows the surfaces in the experimentally measured cylinder flow shown in Figure 2. Time increases from bottom to top. Parts of four saddle points are shown: two complete ones in the middle of the flow, one forming at the top of the cylinder, and one in the foreground on the far right. Near the top of the latter, a change in topology is visible as an outgoing (blue) surface from one of the upstream saddles moves out from behind the incoming (yellow) surface of the far right saddle.

Figure 11 shows the surfaces in the airfoil flow for a few cycles of this periodic flow. Time increases from back to front. The orange surface coming in from the left terminates on the body of the airfoil and separates those instantaneous streamlines that go over the top edge of the airfoil from those that pass beneath it. A repelling focus behind the airfoil is wrapping a surface of detachment with the outgoing surface from the saddle point in the lower foreground.

Interaction

When a complex three-dimensional scene is projected on a two-dimensional computer screen, we cannot perceive the complete structure of the scene without some interaction. The manipulations common to most interactive display systems include interactive zoom, rotation, and translation, but these are insufficient for the examination of structures occluded by surfaces on all sides. Some of these hidden structures can be made visible by adding x, y, and z clipping planes in the object frame.

However, these generic methods still don't allow sufficient control of the view. A better technique would take advantage of the natural hierarchy of objects in the display: some objects consist of the set of surfaces attached to a particular stack of originator points; each surface consists of stacks of strips; and strips are made up of a set of quadrilaterals. Given this hierarchy, we have included the capacity to peel structures of any level: objects, surfaces, strips, and quadrilaterals. Peeled structures are made invisible and pushed onto a stack so they can be unpeeled on request.

One problem with graphics displays is the frequent difficulty in getting quantitative information from them. For this reason, we decided to add a visible jack, which can be moved around on the objects and prints out its position on the screen. The jack can be seen near the repelling focus structure in the foreground of Figure 11.

Lighting and shading parameters are also important to viewing. In particular, specular reflections from surfaces give valuable orientation cues, but depend heavily on the position of the light sources. Hence, the positions and colors of the lights, as well as the colors and characteristics of the materials, are under interactive control.

Implementation

As implemented, the software consists of two parts, the analysis package and the display package.

Analysis workbench. The analysis package is written in Common Lisp using the Portable Common Loops (PCL) implementation of the Common Lisp Object System. This

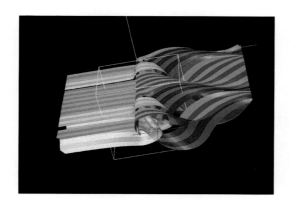 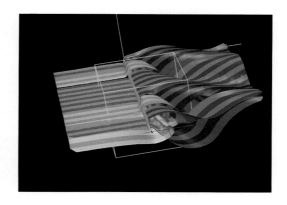

Figure 11. Topological surfaces in the computed low around an airfoil at 90 degrees (shown as a cross-fusable stereo pair). See the sidebar for viewing instructions.

combination has allowed us to develop a workbench on which we can load in various data sets, analyze parts of them, and display the results. Since methods can be interactively applied to the data objects using the interpreter, both the portion of the data under analysis and the algorithms to be applied can be quickly modified and the data reanalyzed without having to reload and restart the analysis from the beginning. For these reasons, LispUs ability to mix interpreted and incrementally compiled code, as well as its garbage collection of discarded objects, greatly facilitated the development of the algorithms.

We accepted some penalty in floating-point performance for using Lisp rather than a compiled and linked language such as C. In spite of the large number of computations required by the analysis, we have found the increased ease of development more than compensates for the somewhat lower performance. For the airfoil flow with a 53×102 grid at 50 time steps, the analysis of this data set takes less than 45 minutes on a Sun-3/260 workstation with 24 megabytes of RAM and a floating-point accelerator board.

One concession to floating-point performance was the use of the tangent curve integration routines from Plot3D. These Fortran routines, called from Lisp via a foreign function interface, allow us to use the floating-point accelerator, which is not directly supported by the Lisp we used.

The analysis package includes a small, object-oriented, two-dimensional graphics system written to display the intermediate two-dimensional results (see Figures 4 and 5). The graphics are created using CLX, the Common Lisp interface to X Windows.

The data sets are read in using the single-grid, three-dimensional data format used by Plot3D. This format defines separate field and grid arrays. Hence, for each grid point five quantities are defined: the x, y, and t coordinates of the grid point and the x and y velocity components. The single-precision data set ($53 \times 102 \times 50$) occupies about 5.5 megabytes of storage.

Display program. The display program is written in C using Silicon Graphics' Graphics Library. Rotation of the objects is accomplished with the mouse by clicking and dragging on an edge of a wireframe cube, which causes the object to rotate around the coordinate axis parallel to the edge so that the edge follows the cursor.[12] Translation is specified by clicking and dragging outside of the cube.

Almost every other aspect of viewing can be controlled by the mouse using buttons and sliders created using the Panel Library.[13] Sliders interactively control zoom, field of view, light positions and colors, material colors and characteristics, stereo spatial and angular separation, and the x, y, and z clipping planes. Other capabilities include using the mouse to select, peel, or unpeel at the four levels of the hierarchy: objects, surfaces, strips, or quadrilaterals. The jack mentioned before can be dragged around on surfaces; it causes the corresponding x, y, and z coordinates to be displayed. Some of the control panels can be seen in Figure 4.

The surfaces are drawn from a triangular mesh using Gouraud shading. The surfaces for the $53 \times 102 \times 50$ airfoil data set are defined by approximately 34,000 vertices, most of which are drawn twice since most curves are the boundaries of two strips. This number is small enough to allow for interactive drawing speeds on the workstation used for the display, a Silicon Graphics Iris-4D/80GT.

Conclusion

Interpretation of large, multidimensional vector fields is a difficult task, and presently available techniques are not adequate. The difficulty stems from the inability of the human visual system to assimilate displays containing a large number of vectors or curves. On the other hand, the visual system is superbly adapted to surface displays.

By reducing the original vector field to a set of critical points and their connections, we have arrived at a representation of the topology of a two-dimensional vector field, which is much smaller than the original data set but retains with full precision the information pertinent to the flow topology. This representation can be displayed as a set of points and tangent curves or as a graph, which is especially useful for comparing data sets and detecting topological transitions. When time defines a third dimension, the representation can be readily displayed as surfaces.

We plan to apply the two-dimensional techniques described in this article to the skin-friction vector field near the surface of a body in a three-dimensional flow. This will provide a valuable basis for comparison of computational results with skin-friction visualizations generated experimentally by photographing oil as it streaks along the surface of a body. Starting from a knowledge of the surface topology, we will then be able to analyze and characterize structures in the three-dimensional volume surrounding the body and generate complete representations of the topology of three-dimensional flows.

Acknowledgments

We wish to thank Brian Cantwell of Stanford University and Stuart Rogers of NASA Ames for providing us with interesting data sets. We also wish to thank Malcolm Slaney for providing evidence that Lisp could be used for number crunching.

Numerous free software packages have greatly aided our work. These include Plot3D from Pieter Buning of NASA Ames, the Panel Library from David Tristram of NASA Ames, PCL from Gregor Kiczales of Xerox PARC, Boxview from Kelvin Thompson of the University of Texas, the

X11 windowing system from MIT, and gnuemacs from the Free Software Foundation.

This work is supported by NASA under contract NAG-2-489-S1, including support from the NASA Ames Numerical Aerodynamics Simulation Program and the NASA Ames Fluid Dynamics Division.

References

1. G.L. Brown and A. Roshko, "On Density Effect and Large Structure in Turbulent Mixing Layers," *J. Fluid Mechanics,* Vol. 64, 1974, pp. 775-816.

2. L. Hesselink, "Digital Image Processing in Flow Visualization," *Ann. Review of Fluid Mechanics,* Vol. 20, 1988, pp. 421-485.

3. M. Tobak and D. Peake, "Topology of Three-Dimensional Separated Flows," *Ann. Review of Fluid Mechanics,* Vol. 14, 1982, pp. 61-85.

4. U. Dallmann, "Topological Structures of Three-Dimensional Flow Separation," *Tech. Rep. DFVLR-IB 221-82 A 07,* Deutsche Forschungs und Versuchsanstalt fur Luft und Raumfahrt, Apr. 1983.

5. B. Cantwell and D. Coles, "An Experimental Study of Entrainment and Transport in the Turbulent Near Wake of a Circular Cylinder," *J. Fluid Mechanics,* Vol. 136, 1983, pp. 321-374.

6. J. Helman et al., "StanSurfs: A Contour Surface Reconstruction and Display Package," Fourier Optics and Optical Diagnostics Laboratory, Durand Building, Stanford University, Stanford, Calif. Copies of the document and software are available from L. Hesselink.

7. K. Wu and L. Hesselink, "Computer Display of Reconstructed 3D Scalar Data," *Applied Optics,* Vol. 27, Jan. 1988, pp. 395-404.

8. P. Buning and J. Steger, "Graphics and Flow Visualization in Computational Fluid Dynamics," in *AIAA 7th Computational Fluid Dynamics Conf.: A Collection of Technical Papers,* American Institute of Aeronautics and Astronautics, June 1985, Paper 85-1507-CP.

9. T. Lasinski et al., "Flow Visualization of cfd Using Graphics Workstations," in *AIAA 8th Computational Fluid Dynamics Conf.: A Collection of Technical Papers,* American Institute of Aeronautics and Astronautics, June 1987, Paper 87-1180, pp. 814-824.

10. J. Helman and L. Hesselink, "Automated Analysis of Fluid Flow Topology," in *Three-Dimensional Visualization and Display Technologies, SPIE Proceedings,* Vol. 1,083, Jan. 1989, Paper 1083-23.

11. S. Rogers and D. Kwak, "An Upwind Differencing Scheme for Time-Accurate Incompressible Navier-Stokes Equations," in *AIAA 6th Applied Aerodynamics Conf.: A Collection of Technical Papers,* American Institute of Aeronautics and Astronautics, June 1988, Paper 88-2583.

12. K. Thompson, "Boxview, an Interactive Graphics Program," University of Texas, posted to Unenet newsgroup comp.sys.sgi, July 1988.

13. D.A. Tristram and P.P. Walatka, "Panel Library: Programmer's Manual, Version 9," *Tech. Report,* NAS Systems Div., NASA Ames Research Center, Moffett Field, Calif., March 1989.

James L. Helman is a research assistant in the Fourier Optics and Optical Diagnostics Laboratory at Stanford University, where he is pursuing a PhD in applied physics. His dissertation work is on the interpretation and visualization of large data sets. Other research interests include computer graphics, dynamical systems, and scientific computing. Before beginning his thesis project, he worked as a consultant writing system-level software for peripheral image and array processors.

Helman received a BA in physics and math from Washington University, St. Louis, in 1982 and an MS in applied physics from Stanford in 1984. He received an A.H. Compton science fellowship from Washington University and a graduate fellowship from the National Science Foundation. He is a student member of the APS, ACM, and IEEE Computer Society.

Lambertus Hesselink holds a joint appointment as associate professor in the Aeronautics and Astronautics Department and the Electrical Engineering Department at Stanford University. His research interests include nonlinear optics, optical phase conjugation, optical signal processing, optical diagnostics, and 3D digital image processing. Before joining the faculty at Stanford, he was an instructor in applied physics at the California Institute of Technology.

Hesselink received a BS in applied mechanics in 1970 and a BS in applied physics in 1971, both from the Twente Institute of Technology in the Netherlands. He received an MS in 1972 and a PhD in 1977 from the California Institute of Technology.

He was awarded the Stheeman prize in 1970, was elected the AIAA teacher of Northern California in 1984, and was a corecipient of the Itek prize in 1985. Hesselink is listed in numerous Who's Who and is a member of the AIAA, APS, OSA, SPIE, and ACM.

Visualization Idioms: A Conceptual Model for Scientific Visualization Systems

Robert B. Haber and David A. McNabb
University of Illinois at Urbana-Champaign

Introduction

The rapid growth of large-scale computing in the basic sciences and the steady accumulation of high-bandwidth data sources (radio telescopes, medical scanners, etc.) are largely responsible for the recent interest in scientific visualization as a computational technology. The origins of the field lie in the applied sciences (engineering). The use of computer visualization in computer-aided design and engineering analysis was the primary force driving the development of computer graphics technology in the late 1970s and early 1980s. The problem of interpreting and understanding large, complex data sets was the same then as it is now. The requirement to deal with realistic complexity in design led engineers to the early use of computer simulations and computer graphics. Early efforts in science applications could also be cited.

Entertainment—movie special effects, computer animations for television advertising, corporate video logos, and the like—became the main focus of computer graphics development during the middle 1980s. The visual vocabulary of computer graphics was extended in breadth and depth to meet the requirements in commercial applications for realism, visual richness, and motion (animation). During this period, significant growth also occurred in the power and sophistication of computer graphics hardware and software systems.

Scientific visualization is now a major focus of computer graphics development. As numerical simulation becomes an accepted tool for research in basic science, scientists must face the problem of understanding complexity in their nunumerical simulations of nature, just as engineers have for some time. Enriched by the advances associated with entertainment, computer graphics technology and visualization have become essential tools in the developing field of computational science and engineering. Computer imaging is not new, but the new term, "scientific visualization," is justified as an indicator of an important new phase of development and a novel alignment of several computational technologies.

Visualization can be defined as the use of computer imaging technology as a tool for comprehending data obtained by simulation or physical measurement. Visualization technology depends on the integration of older technologies, including computer graphics, image processing, computer vision, computer-aided design, geometric modeling, approximation theory, perceptual psychology, and user interface studies. A recent overview of the field is presented in the ACM report "Visualization in Scientific Computing."[1]

The ACM report attributes the quotation, "The purpose of computing is insight, not numbers," to Richard Hamming. This is certainly an overstatement (scientists and engineers need to be concerned with numbers as well as insights in most circumstances). But Hamming's point is an appropriate reaction to the tendency to overemphasize numerical output as the product of computation. Computer visualization methods have emerged as the most effective tool for rapidly communicating large amounts of information to scientists and engineers in a format that enhances comprehension and deepens insight.

This paper presents a model of scientific visualization as a complex of generalized mappings of data obtained from simulation, observation, or experiment. The mappings transform raw data into a geometric abstraction of the scientific information content, which can then be rendered to a displayable image using computer graphics or image processing. Any specific sequence of mappings constitutes a visualization idiom. We review recent work in the development of hardware and software systems for interactive scientific visualization, based on the visualization idiom model in the National Center for Supercomputing Application's (NCSA) RIVERS project.

Visualization Idioms

Visualization in computational science and engineering. In most instances, parallels can be drawn between the various stages of numerical simulation and the corresponding phases in scientific observation or experiment. We divide simulation into three main phases: modeling, solution, and interpretation and evaluation. Multiple steps occur within each phase. We will outline these phases to provide a context and motivation for the use of visualization. It is worth noting that error can arise during each step of each phase, and that the reliability of the information in the final visualization images depends on error control in all earlier stages.

Modeling phase. This phase involves transforming a loosely stated problem, such as "simulate the first microsecond of the universe" or "analyze the crash-worthiness of this automobile frame," into a well-posed mathematical problem. This is one of the most crucial stages in simulation, because the scientist must decide which parts of the physics to include (and exclude) in the simulation model. If we make improper decisions at this stage, the game is lost no matter the quality of the subsequent steps.

The first step in the modeling phase is to develop the physical model. This includes selecting the domain of analysis in space and time and the relevant physical laws to be included and excluded. This step should include a clear statement of the simulation's goals. The next step is to generate a mathematical idealization of the physical model. This might involve forming governing equations, boundary and initial conditions, and a mathematical representation of the domain and the analysis goals. It is only at this stage that the analyst has available a well-posed mathematical problem for solution. Although we can speak of the "exact" solution to this mathematical problem, it is important to recall that it is still an idealization of the real system.

Solution phase. Often, we can calculate only approximate solutions to the mathematical idealization. The solution phase's goal is to generate a reliable approximate solution to the mathematical problem responsive to the mathematical statement of the goals of the analysis. The first step in the solution is to form an approximate mathematical model based on the "exact" mathematical model. For example in continuum models, this might be a finite-difference or finite-element model. The next step involves geometric modeling and geometric discretization of the problem domain (e.g., mesh generation in the finite-element method). We use visualization and graphics input techniques to construct geometry models, to evaluate the results of geometric modeling operations, to detect errors, and to control and monitor mesh generation. Numerical solutions generally involve discrete representations of the field variables and approximate statements of the boundary/initial value problem. The result is that the governing equations and boundary conditions are only approximately satisfied, and another source of error is introduced. Visual displays are important tools for describing and assessing the adequacy of discrete models to the computer.

At this stage, the "exact" mathematical problem has been transformed to an approximate mathematical problem that we can solve on the computer using a numerical method. Solving the approximate problem is often automatic and can proceed without user intervention. In nonlinear or transient solutions, using visualization to monitor the progress of the simulation is still worthwhile. In this way, we can identify and terminate unstable or divergent solutions to avoid unnecessary waste of time and computer resources, or we can adjust solution parameters to maintain accuracy and stability.

The direct product of the numerical solution is a field solution for the primary unknown field quantities. Often, we must compute secondary quantities from the primary solution. We must exercise considerable care to get reliable results in data extraction or postprocessing.[2] The postprocessing calculations' results are essential for interpreting and evaluating the simulation results.

Until recently, the analyst had to determine whether the accuracy of the approximate solution was satisfactory and whether to take corrective action—say, through mesh refinement—to achieve the desired level of accuracy. This process is automated in the latest generation of analysis systems.[3] We should note that the concept of reliability in these systems only limits the discrepancy between the solutions to the "exact" and approximate mathematical models. Errors of idealization and modeling are not addressed. The need to visualize the distribution of error and to monitor the adaptive solution offers opportunities for new applications of visualization.

Interpretation and evaluation phase. Learning occurs in this phase of the simulation. The analyst must interpret the solution (that is, establish an explanation based on causality for the solution results and distill useful conclusions). Often, the analyst will determine that improvements are needed either in the physical model or in the mathematical idealization. In such cases, the overall simulation is repeated, with the appropriate modifications to the model. Visualization plays an important role in interpretation and evaluation. In fact, several open challenges occur in postsolution visualization. For example, the problem of producing graphical abstractions of continuum tensor fields in three dimensions has only recently been investigated. If we use visualization as a primary medium for interpreting scientific simulations, then the same standards of reliability we applied to the modeling and solution phases must also be applied to the visual postprocessing.

Visualization and visualization idioms. The previous discussion is based on a view of computational science and engineering as an extended sequence of abstractions implemented as generalized data transformations. Choosing the abstractions and specifying the transformations can be critical—the care and precision defining them can determine whether the scientific conclusions derived from a given simulation correspond to truth or fiction. Next, we extend this model of sequential abstraction/transformation operations to encompass visualization. Figure 1 shows a conceptual diagram of visualization. We can view visualization as a series of transformations that convert raw simulation data into a displayable image. The goal of these transformations

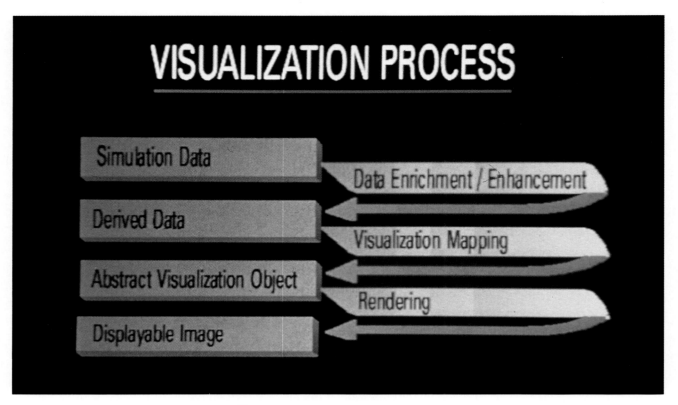

Figure 1. The visualization process.

is to convert the information to a format amenable to understanding by the human perceptual system while maintaining the integrity of the information. Three major transformations occur in most visualization procedures.

Data enrichment and enhancement is the first transformation. It operates on the raw data provided by the simulation and modifies it in one or more ways to derive data for subsequent visualization operations. For example, numerical simulations often provide data values only at certain discrete locations within the domain of a continuum solution. These might not be convenient locations for subsequent operations, or a continuous representation of the field data might be required. We commonly use some form of interpolation between the raw data points to obtain data at the desired locations or an approximate continuous distribution. Various forms of noise might be encountered in the raw data. Often, applying filtering or smoothing operators to produce well-behaved data sets is desirable. Sometimes we need to derive new field quantities from the raw data. For example, the display of a shaded surface representing a potential over a two-dimensional domain requires surface normal-information at each point, in addition to the value of the potential. Calculating the normals is generally based, directly or indirectly, on directional derivatives of the raw data describing the potential function.

The next transformation, visualization mapping, constructs an imaginary object called an "abstract visualization object" (AVO) from the derived data produced by enhancement and enrichment. Typically, this involves mapping the simulation data into the attribute fields that describe the AVO. We can think of an AVO as an imaginary object with some extent in space and time. The attribute fields of an AVO might include geometry, time, color, transparency, luminosity, reflectance, and surface texture. Transfer functions define simple mappings between the simulation data and the AVO fields. The transfer functions can vary widely in complexity. An example of a more general mapping is the extraction of an isopotential surface from a three-dimensional field representation (surface contouring).

The time and geometry fields in the AVO need not correspond to similar quantities in the simulation domain. For example, we can map the simulation z coordinate to time in the AVO model to produce an animation of sequential, horizontal slices through a volumetric domain. Linear mappings are useful for preserving quantitative information (temperature mapped to a perceptually linear color space, for example), but suitable nonlinear mappings can be more effective in revealing subtleties of structure. Histogramming techniques borrowed from image-processing technology,[4] can construct effective transfer functions. No fool-proof method exists to derive effective transfer functions, so interactive systems for real-time modification of the transfer functions are effective tools for exploring computational data sets.[5]

Rendering is the last transformation. Rendering mapping operates on the AVO to produce a displayable image. Rendering can involve familiar operations from computer graphics and image processing but might also involve new algorithms that respond to new requirements of scientific and engineering visualization. Typical rendering operations would include view transformations (rotation, translation, scaling, perspective mapping, and clipping) and optical models (hidden surface removal, shading, shadowing, antialiasing, and so forth). Volumetric rendering is an important new development for visualizing three-dimensional systems.[6-8] Reliability needs to be maintained throughout visualization, so we must balance the accuracy of alternative rendering methods against their other qualities, such as efficiency.

Unlike previous computer graphics applications, accuracy does not necessarily imply photorealism in visualization. It is a crude approximation of real-world optics, but Lambert's cosine law of diffuse reflection can serve perfectly well as the "exact" model for defining a visualization rendering mapping. In fact, such simple models have some appeal in visualization applications because they make it easier to interpret the underlying scientific data and to control accuracy than do more elaborate algorithms, such as radiosity or ray tracing.

Webster's dictionary defines idiom as "an accepted phrase, construction, or expression . . . having a meaning different from the literal." By analogy, we can define a visualization idiom as any specific sequence of data enrichment and enhancement transformations, visualization mappings, and rendering transformations that produce an abstract display of a scientific data set. Just as a listener has difficulty understanding a verbal idiom in a foreign language, a viewer is unable to interpret a visualization display scientifically without an explicit understanding of the steps in the visualization idiom used to generate it. This does not mean that visualization displays should or must be difficult to interpret. But a careful scientist will insist on knowing whether the data is presented in its raw form or is smoothed, whether the data is plotted to a linear or logarithmic scale, what lighting model is used, and so forth. Such information is crucial for an accurate quantitative interpretation. Therefore, proper technical documentation and visual aids—such as on-screen graphical representations of the transfer functions—are important components of scientific and engineering visualization systems.

Yet an effective visualization idiom should not require excessive effort or explanation for qualitative understanding. AVOs should be based on intuitive analogies between familiar objects and the physical abstractions used in the simulation. We should give due regard to the strengths and weaknesses of the human perceptual system. The amount of information displayed at one time for multivariate problems should be carefully controlled to detect meaningful correlations without overloading the viewer's cognition.

Figures 2 through 5 illustrate a hypothetical visualization idiom for representing transient temperature and pressure fields on the nose cone of a rocket. Spline surface patches define the simulation domain, and the solution data include temperature and pressure values at discrete, randomly spaced locations measured at irregular time intervals (Figure 2). In data enrichment and enhancement, we manipulate the geometry and solution data to facilitate subsequent operations. We replace the spline geometry model with a regular grid of polygonal patches, and we interpolate the solution data from the randomly spaced sampling points to the vertices of the polygon grid. The simulation data are also interpolated in time to regular intervals. Figure 3 shows the derived data.

Visualization mapping involves several channels of data. We define the AVO (Figure 4) as a surface characterized by polygonal patches where each polygon vertex has specified three-dimensional coordinates, a normal vector, and a color. We assume specific interpolation functions within each polygonal patch for the vertex data. The three-dimensional surface of the nose cone is mapped to a flat disk in polar coordinates, where the radius on the disk corresponds to the meridional arc length measured from the tip of the nose cone. This provides a map from the three-dimensional coordinates of the polygon vertices in the derived data to the x-y coordinates of the AVO patch vertices, releasing the third dimension to be used for displaying solution data.

In this example, we map the pressure at each vertex of the derived data to the z coordinate of the AVO polygon vertices and map the vertex temperature values to color at the AVO vertices. We can use independent nonlinear transfer functions for the pressure and temperature mappings. We apply an identity mapping between the time intervals of the derived data and the AVO.

The AVO vertex normals play an important role in the subsequent rendering mapping: They control the shading calculations that provide a major perceptual cue for understanding the three-dimensional form of the AVO. Ideally, we should compute the vertex normals from the directional derivatives of the pressure field in the simulation data, modified by the nonlinear transfer function used in the pressure mapping. This would require that secondary derivative information be calculated consistent with the simulation model and be passed along to the derived data set. The derivative information would then be modified by the visualization mapping to determine the AVO normal directions. If the simulation does not provide gradient information,

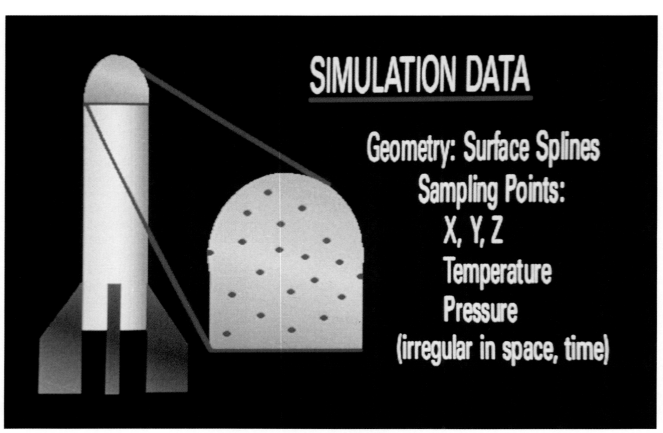

Figure 2. Visualization stages: simulation data.

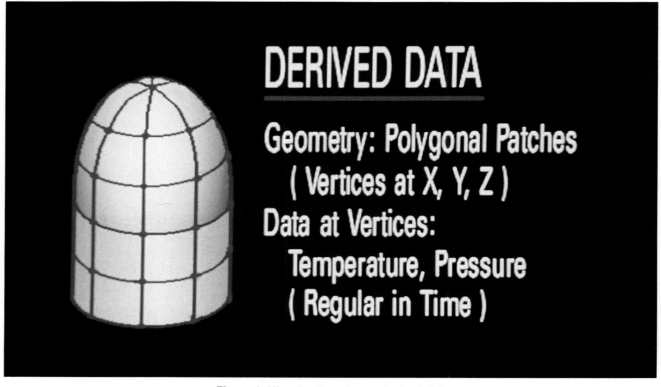

Figure 3. Visualization stages: derived data.

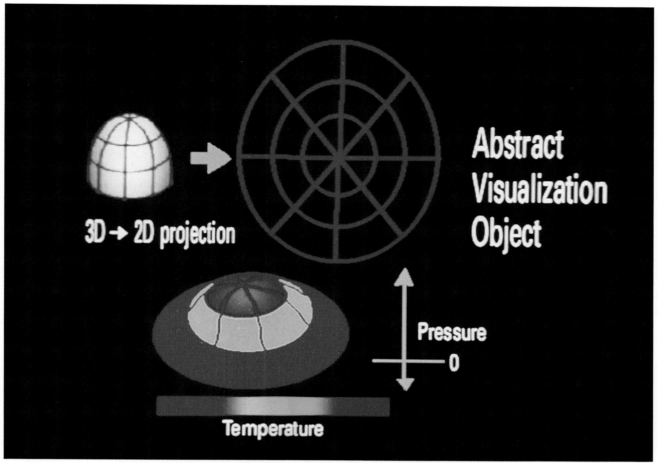

Figure 4. Visualization stages: abstract visualization object.

then we can generate approximate normals as part of the visualization mapping by averaging the normals of the patches adjacent to each vertex in the AVO surface. This operation will produce some error, which might lead to undesirable visible artifacts in the rendered image.

Figure 5 shows the rendering mapping. We generate a mapping between the AVO time and animation time to control the variable speed and direction of the animation. In-between frames are interpolated between the key frames of the AVO data set to match the frame update rate of the animation system. We define a perspective view, model rotations and translations, and a lighting model throughout the rendering interval. Spline techniques, as in computer animation choreography, can specify these parts of the rendering mapping, or they can be generated interactively through a user interface. Algorithms for hidden surface and shading calculations complete the definition of the rendering mapping. Executing the rendering mapping produces a series of displayable images that generates an animation depicting the evolution of the transient pressure and temperature distributions on the nose-cone surface. For efficiency, we can introduce approximations in the rendering mapping. For example, if a Phong shading model defines the "exact" rendering mapping, a Gouraud interpolation would introduce some level of error. The Phong algorithm is an approximate method in realistic rendering, but we can use it as an "exact" model for defining a rendering mapping.

The preceding description might at first seem overly formal. But the authors' experience indicates that this model is useful in defining well-structured software architectures responsive to diverse visualization applications. (We describe one such architecture later in this paper.)

Examples of visualization idioms. We selected examples of visualization idioms from a variety of science and engineering disciplines to indicate how to apply structured visualization and to demonstrate how subtle alterations of the mapping transformations can lead to dramatic changes in the final images.

Figure 6 shows a relatively simple visualization of two-dimensional computational fluid dynamics. It involves kink instabilities in a supersonic jet from astrophysics. We define the simulation domain by a finite-difference grid mapped to an identical grid in the AVO. We map the AVO grid to a rectangular array of pixels in the rendering mapping. The pressure at each numerical grid point is mapped to an eight-bit pseudocolor value in the AVO. In the rendering mapping, we use a look-up table to map the AVO color values to 24-bit red, green, blue (RGB) pixel values. The images are still frames from an animation with constant scaling applied between the time coordinates of the simulation and the AVO.

The image in Figure 6a uses a color mapping consisting of two linear sections. The two-part mapping separates the regions of high and low pressure and reveals the turbulent flow. Figure 6b shows the same frame using a different color mapping suggested by the artist, Donna Cox.[5] The mapping is generated from a set of periodic functions defining the mapping of the AVO eight-bit values into each of the R, G, and B values in the rendering step. This nonlinear mapping reveals more of the shock-wave patterns, demonstrating the sensitivity of visualization idioms to subtle variations in the mappings. We want to have interactive systems for fine-tuning the mappings, because of the difficulty of determining in advance which mappings will best reveal the physics of a given simulation.

Figure 7 shows images from research in computational dynamic fracture mechanics.[9] We performed the simulation with a special two-dimensional moving finite-element code. The mapping of the finite-element grid to the problem domain changes at every time step. The displacement vector field is the primary simulation output data as defined by node values and element interpolation functions. The AVO in this example is a surface tesselated with polygons. At any time step, we map the finite-element mesh and node coordinates to the polygons and x-y vertex coordinates of the AVO. Secondary data fields, computed in a postprocessing step from the displacement data, include strain, stress, strain-energy density, material velocity, and kinetic-energy density.

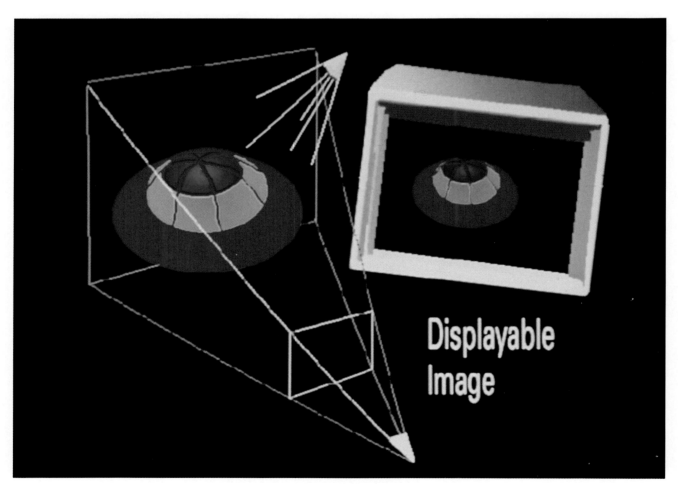

Figure 5. Visualization stages: displayable image.

(a)

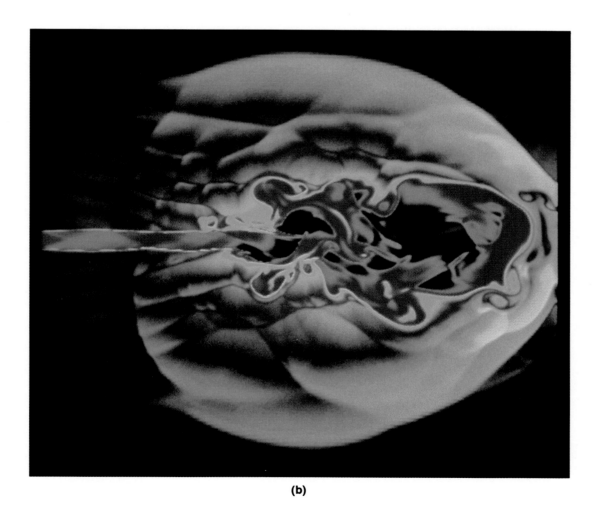

(b)

Figure 6. Kink instability in a supersonic jet: (a) linear map; (b) nonlinear map based on periodic functions.
From Michael Norman, Department of Astronomy, University of Illinois at Urbana-Champaign.

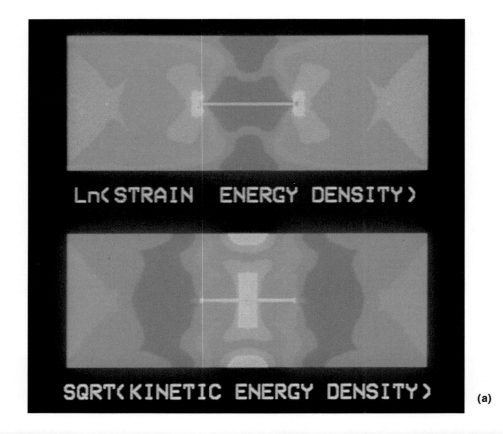

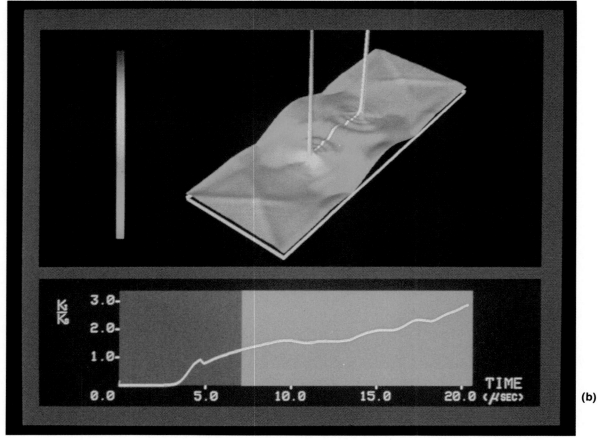

Figure 7. Visualization of elastodynamic fracture mechanics: (a) split-screen, two-dimensional scalar color maps; (b) three-dimensional display of strain-energy density and kinetic-energy density fields. From Hyun Koh, Hae-Sung Lee, and Robert Haber, Departments of Theoretical & Applied Mechanics and Civil Engineering, University of Illinois at Urbana-Champaign.

We compute these quantities at the Gauss integration points of each element. Node values of the kinetic and strain-energy densities are computed by extrapolation of the Gauss point values during the data-enhancement step.

In Figure 7a, the strain-energy density is passed through a logarithmic transfer function to produce an eight-bit color value at each vertex of the AVO. The square root of the kinetic-energy density is mapped to a second eight-bit color at each AVO vertex. We assume a bilinear variation of the color fields within each AVO polygon. In the rendering step, we apply dual two-dimensional scaling and translation transformations to generate a split-screen display of the AVO. In the top image, a step-function color transfer function is applied to the AVO strain-energy color values. The step function emphasizes the shape of isopotential contours in the rendered image. We apply the same transfer function to the kinetic-energy vertex colors in the bottom image. A Gouraud interpolation scheme calculates pixel color values within each polygon. This idiom provides some information about the mechanical behavior of the system but does not reveal the elastic waves that drive the fracture mechanism.

Figure 7b shows a more successful idiom for representing precisely the same information. In this case, we modify the AVO so that the square root of the kinetic-energy density is mapped to the z coordinates of the AVO polygon vertices (instead of to the eight-bit color values). Gradients of the mapped kinetic-energy density field define the surface normal direction at each AVO vertex. The mapping of the strain-energy density field is not modified. We change the rendering mapping to include multiple light sources, general three-dimensional rotations, scalings, translations, and perspective transformations. Z-buffer hidden surface and Gouraud shading algorithms complete the rendering specification and produce the single three-dimensional image (Figure 7b). We have included a plot of the normalized crack-tip stress-intensity factor history at the bottom of the display.

Although Figures 7a and 7b contain the same information, only the idiom in Figure 7b interacts with the human perceptual system to reveal the wave patterns around the moving crack tip. This demonstrates that the perceived information depends strongly on the particular idiom chosen. Scientists should be able to test a variety of idioms rapidly to seek one that best reveals the physics of the problem. In the second idiom (Figure 7b), we want to control the transfer functions used in the mappings for height and color, the time mapping for animation, and the lighting and the perspective view. Only recently have graphics hardware systems achieved the performance needed to support this kind of interactivity.

The scalar strain-energy density field in this example is, in fact, an indirect representation of the second-order tensor strain field. A second-order tensor in three dimensions is generally represented by nine components, arranged in a 3 ×

3 array. An independent array exists at every point in the domain for a tensor field. A double contraction of the strain tensor with the fourth-order elasticity tensor yields the scalar strain-energy density. This mapping is one of the key steps in the data-enhancement stage of the preceding idiom. It reduces the difficult problem of displaying a second-order tensor field to the more familiar problem of displaying a scalar field. But we lose considerable information in the process. The six independent components of the symmetric strain tensor are combined into a single number, eliminating all directional information from the display. Another possibility is to contract a second-order tensor field with a vector field (for example, contract the stress tensor with a normal vector to obtain a surface traction vector) to obtain another vector field. We can then use familiar vector field display methods, such as arrow plots.

We have known about direct graphical representations of second-order tensors, such as the Lame stress ellipsoid and the Cauchy stress quadric, for some time.[10] But they do not appear to be well-suited for computer visualization. Only recently have direct visualization methods for second-order tensor fields appeared.[11]

Figure 8 shows a new direct visualization technique for the symmetric, second-order stress tensor applied to the problem of dynamic-fracture mechanics. We will discuss this idiom in the following section.

In the data-enrichment stage, we compute the stress-tensor components at the centroid of selected finite elements. In each element, we interpolate the nodal displacements from the element node values by using the finite-element interpolation functions. The strain-tensor components are computed at the element (reduced) Gauss integration points from the gradients of the interpolated displacement components. We then compute the stress at each Gauss point by contracting the strain tensor with the material elasticity tensor. Finally, we interpolate the Gauss point stress components to the element centroid. The details of this process are of interest to a numerical analyst, because they are linked with certain accuracy properties of the finite-element solution.

Visualization mapping involves the definition at each sampled location of a geometrical object that encodes the complete information of the stress tensor. We solve an eigen problem to determine the tensor's principal directions and magnitudes. The principal directions are orthogonal, because the stress tensor is symmetric. We construct a cylindrical shaft in the direction of the major principal direction. The color and length of the shaft indicate the sign and magnitude of the stress in this direction. An eliptical disk wraps around the central portion of the shaft. The major and minor axes of the ellipse correspond to the middle and minor principle directions of the stress tensor. The color distribution on the disk indicates the stress magnitude in each direction.

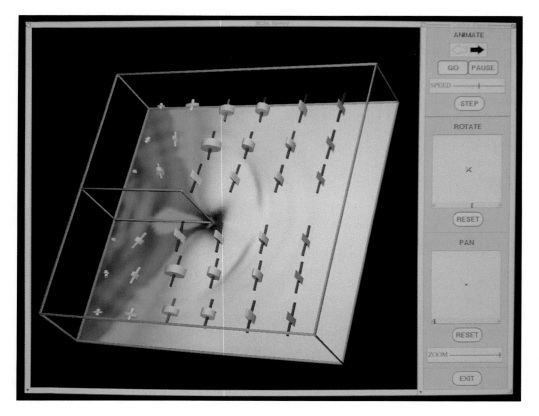

Figure 8. Tensor field visualization using the RIVERS polygon animation tool. From Chen Sheng, Hyun Koh, Hae Sung Lee, Creto Vidal, and Robert Haber, Departments of Theoretical & Applied Mechanics and Civil Engineering, University of Illinois at Urbana-Champaign; and Steve Chall, Ray Idaszak, and Polly Baker, NCSA.

An outline of the structure volume provides a context for the tensor display. Because the tensor display technique can provide only point-wise information, we include a modified version of the idiom for displaying the strain and kinetic energy density fields on the back face of the volume. In this version, we use the kinetic-energy height field to calculate surface normals for shading, but we constrain the polygon vertex coordinates for the display geometry to lie within a plane. This propagates shaded kinetic-energy waves across a flat, colored surface. When this idiom is animated, the tensor display objects reveal the stress content of the elastic waves by rotation and changes in size, shape, and color as each wave passes.

Figure 9 shows an idiom portraying multivariate data arising from a three-dimensional finite-element simulation of plastic injection molding. The mold geometry consists of two joined rectangular cavities of different thicknesses. Heated plastic is injected into the mold under pressure. As the plastic flows to fill the mold, it cools and eventually solidifies. Because the thickness of the mold is small relative to its other dimensions, we assume the pressure to be uniform through the thickness. But temperature variation

through the thickness is modeled by layers of triangle-section, prismatic finite elements. We assume symmetrical response in the mid-surface of the mold.

The solution data includes temperature and velocity fields computed at the element centroids with piece-wise linear interpolation through the depth. We compute pressure as a uniform value within each triangular element. In this case the visualization mapping is not simply a map from one continuum field to another. Instead, geometric "glyphs" communicate the behavior at discrete locations. The height of each glyph corresponds to the half thickness of the mold. The glyphs are seated on a horizontal plane representing the mid-surface of the mold. The glyph's cross-section at any vertical level has the shape of an arrowhead whose length and direction correspond to scaled values of the horizontal component of the fluid velocity vector at that location. No glyphs are drawn in regions where the plastic has not yet penetrated, and we draw the glyphs as cylinders in locations where the flow has ceased because the plastic has solidified.

The temperature through the thickness is represented by color values on the surface of each glyph, and the pressure

Figure 9. Visualization of plastic injection molding. From Rich Elson, Kodak Corp.; and Donna Cox, Department of Art and Design, University of Illinois at Urbana-Champaign; and Ray Idaszak, NCSA.

distribution is represented by a second color scale plotted on the mid-surface plane. We generate a triangular polygon in the mid-surface plane for each finite-element zone with a constant pressure color. We carefully select the two color maps to avoid visual confusion between the two quantitative scales. Finally, the rendering mapping includes a lighting model and three-dimensional transformations. This idiom exemplifies the generality of the concept of visualization mappings beyond the simple case of scalar transfer functions. Although this idiom presents an intuitively comprehensible portrait of the injection flow, it does require some explanation because of its intrinsic complexity.

Figure 10 visualizes a severe storm simulation.[12] The simulation outputs data for each time step at a three-dimensional array of points to describe scalar and vector continuum fields. The visualization idiom involves the extrac-

tion and display of a surface of uniform rain density (a three-dimensional analogue of two-dimensional weather radar images). The rendering operation is performed with the Wavefront Technologies rendering package. The required input to the rendering operation is a polygon surface with coordinate and normal information at each vertex. We have used time in two ways with this AVO. In one instance, we mapped the AVO time directly from the simulation time, so the animation tracks the evolution of the storm surface at a fixed rain density threshold. In another case, we held the simulation time fixed and derived the AVO time from the threshold value defining the isodensity surface. In this case, the animation portrays the surface's motion within the volume of the cloud to reveal its interior morphology. Other visualization idioms for severe storm data are reported in Wilhelmson.[12] Direct volumetric rendering is another al-

Figure 10. Visualization of severe storm simulation. From Robert Wilhelmson, Crystal Shaw, and Lou Wicker, Department of Atmospheric Sciences, University of Illinois at Urbana-Champaign; and Stefen Fangmeier, NCSA.

ternative for visualizing this type of data. This approach has the advantage of using a volumetric AVO, consistent with the form of the original data; no surface construction is needed.

Consistent with the subsequent rendering operation, the AVO in this example consists of a polygon surface with varying geometry and surface normals. A number of algorithmic options exist for generating the coordinates, normals, and connectivity for this tessellated surface. An option in the National Center for Atmospheric Research's graphics package generated the AVO for Figure 10. The "marching cubes" algorithm has also been applied to this data set.[13] Each of these algorithms has implicit assumptions about how the scalar-density field and the vector-normal (or gradient) field vary between the discrete array of data points produced by the simulation. Each algorithm produces different levels of error and consequent visual artifacts in the final image. Because of the importance of shading as a perceptual cue for understanding three-dimensional form,

the accuracy of the gradient information is at least as important as the scalar data itself in this kind of idiom. Figure 10 shows numerical artifacts at the same scale as the simulation numerical grid. We would need a systematic approach to error indication and control, from the simulation through the series of visualization operations, to determine whether these artifacts result from the visualization transformations or from the simulation itself.

Visualization Software Systems

We can identify three visualization modes in computational science, based on current practice and the expressed desires of scientists. Each involves different performance requirements for the computational, graphics, mass storage, and communications system components. The first is post-simulation analysis, wherein we complete the simulation and store the simulation data for later retrieval by the visualization system. This mode is appropriate when the cost in time, effort, or money of repeating the simulation cannot be tolerated and the cost of storing the results is not excessive. This approach supports interactive visualization and real-time animation when the simulation cannot execute at animation rates.

In runtime monitoring, the second mode, the visualization system monitors the simulation's intermediate results while it is in progress. As each step of a transient or iterative simulation algorithm is completed, the output data is passed to the visualization system for immediate viewing. Data histories can be accumulated to permit animation of partial results. This allows the user to monitor progress, study convergence, detect errors, and perhaps determine whether the simulation should be terminated.

The third mode, interactive steering, closes the loop between the simulation and the visualization system. We supplement runtime monitoring of the simulation with interactive tools for modifying the simulation input data or analysis parameters. This provides the analyst immediate visual feedback about the effects of changes in the problem data.

NCSA's RIVERS project investigates and prototypes high-performance hardware and software systems for interactive supercomputing and visualization. ("RIVERS"—short for research on interactive visualization environments—refers to the massive flow of data between the supercomputing and visualization systems in the project.)

High-end hardware performance has improved dramatically, and it is the lack of software systems that can take advantage of these new performance levels that blocks further use of interactive visualization in computational science and engineering. Therefore, software design and development is a major focus in the RIVERS project. Our approach has been first to identify goals and functional requirements based on the visualization idiom model and requests from scientists, and then to identify suitable software strategies. Existing software strategies provide many of the desired qualities and capabilities. But challenging new problems in computer science arise from the need to integrate diverse software concepts into a unified, high-performance system.

Most scientists forego visualization altogether unless provided with high-level tools that keep their energies focused on their science. With few exceptions, scientists and engineers are no more willing to get involved with graphics languages, windowing systems, communications mechanisms, and the like than they are to write low-level device drivers. This indicates a need for carefully layered software systems. Figure 11 shows one such system. Vendors generally provide the three layers immediately above the hardware platform. A scientist or a software vendor provides the top applications layer. The visualization application layer executes the data enrichment and enhancement transformations and the visualization mapping to convert the science data into a renderable object. The rendering mapping is executed with calls to the graphics and window systems layer.

The visualization application layer is the missing link in most existing software environments. We want to apply layering within this level to separate generic, discipline-independent functions from specialized, discipline-specific functions. For example, a generic polygon animation tool (as in Figure 8) can provide rendering and view control for any AVO generated as a polygon list. But the initial transformations that prepare the science output data for visualization mappings tend to be discipline specific. The use of standard graphics languages (such as PHIGS+) and standard window systems (such as X.11) helps ensure the portability of visualization applications with little or no effort on the part of the software developers. If layering is properly

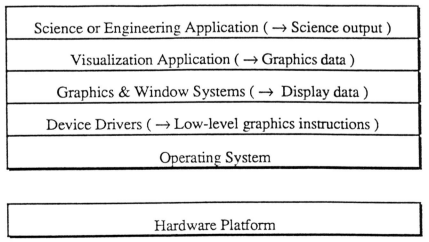

Figure 11. Layered software design.

applied, scientists need not be familiar with the details of graphics languages. Porting a software system to any graphics environment, without altering the internals of the visualization application, should be possible by rewriting the interface between the visualization application and the graphics and window systems layer.

Scientists desire the flexibility to explore visualization idioms without writing new code. In other words, the precise sequence of transformations in the visualization application layer should be "configurable" at run time. This can be done with a data-flow software strategy (Figure 12) with a library of modules to execute a set of mapping transformations. Data-flow models with visual programming interfaces have been used in a variety of computer graphics applications to provide robust capabilities for interactive specification of high-level algorithms.[14] In the present design, the scientist can choose modules at run time and specify how they are connected in the data-flow diagram. In some cases, each module corresponds to an independent process. In others, several modules are grouped hierarchically into a single process.

Once a configuration is established, we should be able to fine-tune the idiom while it is executing. Parameters, which serve as real-time input to the modules to modify their transformation mappings, provide this capability. The parameter data can come from a user interface for interactive applications or from data files for batch execution. Examples of tuning parameters include view control and lighting parameters for a rendering module, function parameters for a nonlinear mathematical mapping, and parameters to control the dimensions and color mapping of an AVO.

A goal of the RIVERS project is to extend visualization from a batch procedure to a real-time interactive process. Therefore, performance is a key concern in hardware and software design. The structure of visualization indicates that we can easily adapt visualization idioms to gain improved performance from pipelined or concurrent execution. The RIVERS software design supports concurrent execution modes on multiprocessor hosts and networks of heterogeneous distributed processors.

Figure 13 shows part of a typical mapping module. The heart of the module is the mapping kernel, which executes the actual transformation—a transfer function, an isopotential surface extraction, data smoothing, rendering, and so forth. We apply the mapping to information received from upstream modules in the pipeline that has been stored in one

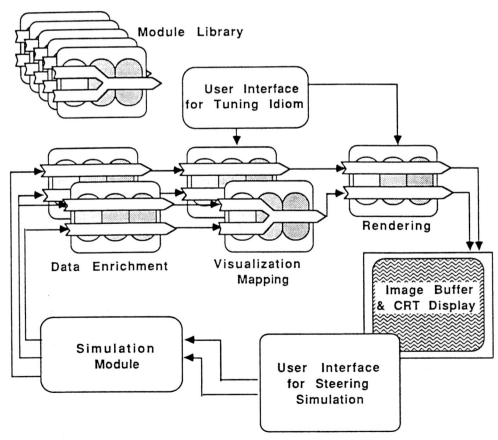

Figure 12. Software architecture for interactive steering and distributed visualization.

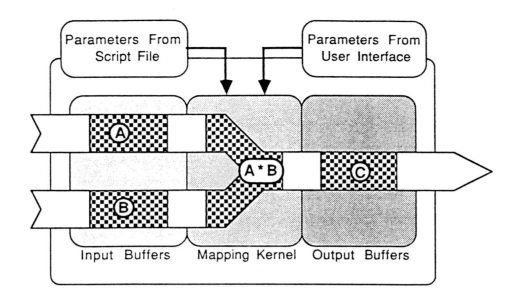

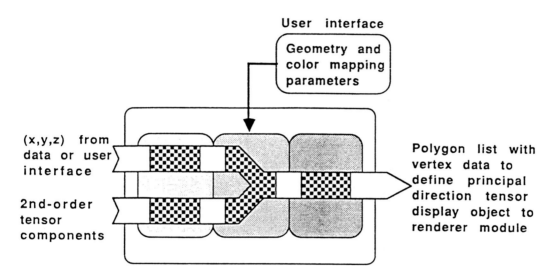

Figure 13. Mapping module architecture: (a) typical mapping module; (b) mapping module for tensor display.

or more input buffers. We store the result of the mapping in output buffers to be transmitted to the next module downstream. We can apply double-buffering techniques to keep the pipeline full. Tuning parameters are received from a user interface or a data file through parameter input ports. Messages for synchronizing, controlling, and passing annotative data between modules in a multiprocessing environment are sent and received through message input/output ports. A specific instance of a mapping module for the tensor display visualization mapping is also shown in Figure 13. Support for communication and synchronization between modules is part of the basic infrastructure of the system design. One of our goals is to make the communications—whether shared

memory, the memory bus of a multiprocessor computer, or a network connection—transparent to the user.

We can extend the system's functionality by adding new modules. For interactive steering, the simulation module must take on an architecture similar to that of a mapping module. The analysis data is accessed through input buffers, and analysis parameters—such as integration step size or convergence tolerance—are received through parameter input ports.

A special type of mapping module, the data accumulator, accumulates and stores frames of data. (A typical mapping module operates on one frame of data at a time, consistent with the data-flow design.) We can insert a data accumulator at any location in the system to archive intermediate results or to accumulate frames for rapid replay when the early stages of the system cannot achieve real-time, interactive performance. Suppose, for example, that the simulation time steps for the system represented in Figure 12 cannot be executed at animation rates. We can insert a data accumulator at the end of the visualization mapping to store the intermediate results of all of the completed simulation time steps. If the system's rendering portion is capable of real-time, interactive animation, then we can view animations of the completed portion of the simulation while the rest of the numerical computation continues.

Visualization Hardware

Commonly, executing a visualization idiom is more data and computation intensive than the original simulation that produced the data. Therefore, the goal of real-time, interactive visualization presents a considerable challenge. Generally, we need specialized hardware to enhance the performance of the most demanding steps in the process. These hardware systems employ pipeline architectures, concurrency, and special-purpose chips to improve price-performance ratios. In general, this leads to a trade-off between performance on one hand and generality or ease of software development on the other.

Balance is the key issue in designing a visualization hardware system. This truism of computer design is especially critical in this context, because visualization idioms naturally have pipeline structures and the worst bottleneck in a pipeline determines the effective performance. In fact, most visualization hardware systems are not well balanced, because improvement has occurred in the price/performance of the underlying hardware technologies: special-purpose graphics hardware, general-purpose processors, communications systems, and mass-storage systems. Although the performance of hardware graphics engines and CPUs have improved dramatically, effective network bandwidths and disk-system transfer rates have not kept up. If one is attempting to animate images in real time, there is no benefit to having a workstation with a graphics engine that can render 100,000 polygons per second if the polygons must be read from a disk or the network at a rate of only 1,000 polygons per second. The recent introduction of networks with effective sustained bandwidths approaching one billion bits per second and of hardware-striped disk-array systems with similar transfer rates offers some hope of improved system balance in visualization hardware environments.

Figure 14 diagrams a distributed hardware system for visualization in a supercomputing environment, now under development within RIVERS and other segments of NCSA. A key theme is the use of dual, three-tier schemes for the computing and network strategies. Personal computers and workstations constitute the lower tier of the computing environment, and true supercomputers comprise the upper tier. High-bandwidth mass storage systems with very large capacity will be available as shared network resources. Middle-tier, near-supercomputer systems provide higher performance capabilities that can be shared by a small group of users without the compromises necessary with the large national user communities associated with true supercomputers. On the other hand, the combination of a very-high-performance graphics engine, a high-bandwidth network connection, and a striped disk array on a multiprocessor host (all useful to achieve a balanced design) is still too expensive to dedicate to a single user.

The supercomputers and middle-tier processors are connected by a very high-speed network (NCSA has installed an UltraNet system with a peak bandwidth of 100 MB/s). This network is optimized for massive data transfers—using large packet sizes and hardware acceleration of protocol processing—to support real-time visualization, distributed processing, and access to the shared high-performance mass storage system. Standards for high-speed channel interfaces (e.g., the HSC specification, designed to operate at 50, 100, or 200 MB/s) appear to be gaining acceptance among computer vendors. This promises to facilitate the integration of the high-performance, multivendor systems needed for real-time interactive visualization.

A middle-tier network forms the backbone for handling messages, smaller data packets, and conventional network traffic between the large machines and the bottom tier networks connecting the workstations. The notion here is to segregate massive data transfers from terminal keystrokes and other smaller messages to optimize efficiency and performance. The FDDI (fiber digital data interface) standard is expected to take on the middle-tier network function during 1989 or 1990.

Conclusions

Visualization's functional requirements appear to demand new advances in several areas of computer science. Subspecialties of distributed processing, network systems, parallel processing, and object-oriented languages seem likely to develop around the problem of visualization. Many existing computer graphics and image-processing technologies are applicable to visualization; but scientific visualization applications have already spurred new developments in such areas as volumetric rendering. Other new classes of rendering algorithms will eventually emerge. Artificial intelligence and computer vision could be introduced to provide tools for computer-aided interpretation of visualization images.

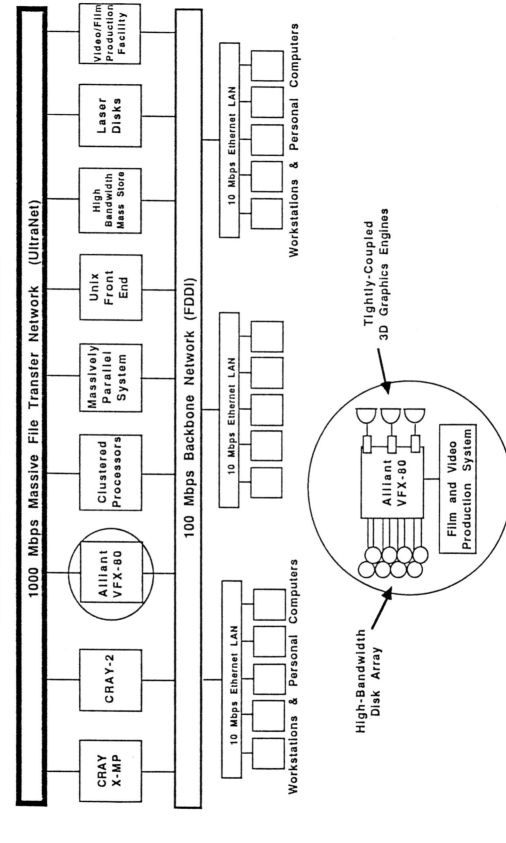

Figure 14. Hardware architecture for distributed simulation and visualization.

Visualization's technical requirements have significant implications for the continued development of the computing infrastructure. First, we need a large-scale software development program to build the high-level tools to make visualization a practical tool in mainstream science and engineering. Second, the high level of system integration required for visualization and the need to share the substantial costs of software development underline the importance of the current trend toward standards and open hardware and software systems.

Finally, the data-intensive nature of visualization supports the need for a national broadband (multigigabit/s) communications capability.

Acknowledgments

The authors wish to thank the scientists and staff of the National Center for Supercomputing Applications, University of Illinois at Urbana-Champaign who contributed to the work described in this chapter. Special thanks are due Chuck Evans, Michael Norman, Donna Cox, Rich Elson, the Software Development Group, the Scientific Media Services team, and the Scientific Visualization group. The National Science Foundation, Apple Computer, Sun Microsystems, and Cray Research supported portions of our work.

References

1. "Visualization in Scientific Computing," A Special Report of ACM SIGGraph, *Computer Graphics,* Vol. 21, App. E, 1987, pp. E1-E7.

2. I. Babuska and A. Miller, "The Post-Processing Approach in the Finite Element Method — Part 1: Calculation of Displacements, Stresses and Other Higher Derivatives of the Displacements," *Int'l. J. Numerical Methods Engineering,* Vol. 20, 1984, pp. 1085-1109.

3. A. Noor and I. Babuska, "Quality Assessment and Control of Finite Element Solutions," *Finite Elements in Analysis and Design,* Vol. 3, 1987, pp. 1-26.

4. R. Gonzales and P. Wintz, *Digital Image Processing,* 2nd Ed., Addison-Wesley, Reading, Mass., 1987.

5. D. Cox, "Using the Supercomputer to Visualize Higher-Dimensions: An Artist's Contribution to Scientific Visualization," *Leonardo,* Vol. 22, 1988, pp. 233-242.

6. R. Drebin, L. Carpenter, and P. Hanrahan, "Volume Rendering," *ACM Computer Graphics,* Vol. 22, August 1988, pp. 65-74.

7. M. Levoy, "Display of Surfaces from Volume Data," *IEEE Computer Graphics and Applications,* Vol. 8, May 1988, pp. 29-37.

8. C. Upson and M. Keeler, "V-BUFFER: Visible Volume Rendering," *ACM Computer Graphics,* Vol. 22, 1988, pp. 59-64.

9. H.M. Koh, H.-S. Lee, and R.B. Haber, "Dynamic Crack Propagation Analysis Using Eulerian-Lagrangian Kinematic Descriptions," *Computational Mechanics,* Vol. 3, 1988, pp. 141-155.

10. Y.C. Fung, *Foundations of Solid Mechanics,* Prentice-Hall, Englewood Cliffs, N.J., 1965.

11. R.R. Dickinson, "Interactive 4D Visualization of Fields," *Tech. Rep. CS-89-15,* Dept. of Computer Science, University of Waterloo, Waterloo, Ontario, Canada, 1989.

12. R.B. Wilhelmson, "Numerical Simulations of Severe Storms," *Proc. Fourth Int'l. Symp. Sci. Engineering on Cray Supercomputers,* Minneapolis, Minn., 1988, pp. 329-345.

13. E. Lorenson and H.E. Cline, "Marching Cubes: A High Resolution 3D Surface Construction Algorithm," *ACM Computer Graphics,* Vol. 21, 1987, pp. 163-169.

14. P.E. Haeberli, "ConMan: A Visual Programming Language for Interactive Graphics," *ACM Computer Graphics,* Vol. 22, Aug. 1988, pp. 65-74.

Robert B. Haber is associate professor of theoretical and applied mechanics and civil engineering at the University of Illinois at Urbana-Champaign. He is also a research scientist at NCSA, where he directs the RIVERS project, a research and development project to prototype hardware and software systems for real time, interactive visualization and distributed supercomputing across gigabit/s networks. He worked in the Cornell University Program for Computer Graphics from 1975 until 1980. His research interests include finite-element methods in computational solid mechanics, computer-assisted design and optimization, and applications of computer graphics visualization to computational science and engineering. Recent research includes moving finite-element techniques for analyzing dynamic crack propagation and new techniques for explicit design sensitivity analysis and shape optimization of structural and mechanical systems. Haber is a member of ASCE, ACM (SIG-Graph), AAM, IACM, AAAS, and Sigma Xi. He is a Cray Research affiliate, a former Beckman associate in the Center for Advanced Studies at the University of Illinois, and past president of ALLUS, the Alliant Users' Society. Haber received the PhD in civil engineering in 1980 and a bachelor of architecture degree in 1977 from Cornell University.

David McNabb is a research programmer and leader of software design and development for the RIVERS project at NCSA. From 1985 through 1988, he was visiting lecturer in the Department of Computer Science at the University of Illinois, where he is finishing a PhD in computer science. His research interests include programming language environments, object-oriented programming languages, distributed computing, and operating systems. He is designing and implementing distributed interactive real-time system support for scientific visualization environments, including dynamic reconfiguration and visual programming interfaces. David McNabb is a member of the ACM (SIGGraph, SIGOPS, SIGPlan) and Sigma Xi. He received the BS in physics and mathematics in 1975 from the University of Illinois at Urbana-Champaign and has done graduate work in computer science at the Chicago-Circle and Urbana-Champaign campuses.

Projection Pursuit Techniques for Visualizing High-Dimensional Data Sets

Stuart L. Crawford and Thomas C. Fall, Advanced Decision Systems

Introduction

Modern data collection is now so efficient that researchers in many fields must analyze very large quantities of highly multivariate data. Census data, for example, consist of many observations, each of which contains a large number of measurements. If we represent each observation as a point in p-dimensional space, the goal of many such analyses is the discovery of structures—clusters, hypersurfaces, and the like—and anomalies among a configuration of the points in p-dimensional space. Because p is often very high, direct visual inspection of the data by traditional means—scatterplots or histograms, for example—is often impossible. In addition, many automated techniques for data analysis rely on interpoint distances to establish structure and, in doing so, fall prey to the fact that very high-dimensional space is inherently empty—the "curse of dimensionality."

Because of the curse of dimensionality, points in high-dimensional space tend to be very nearly equidistant, thus confounding distance-based measures of structure detection. The traditional approach to the problem of analyzing high-dimensional data sets has been to reduce the dimensionality of the data, with a concomitant reduction in the scope of the analysis task. Commonly used dimension-reduction schemes fall into the categories of linear and nonlinear mappings. This chapter reviews projection pursuit techniques, a relatively new class of dimension-reduction techniques.

We can use projection pursuit techniques to examine linear projections of a multivariate point cloud onto subspaces spanned (usually) by one, two, or three display coordinates. These techniques essentially involve selecting directions in the data space, followed by an examination of the data as projected onto these directions. We repeatedly select directions and examine the projected data in the hope that one or more projections will reveal some structure in the data. When we select three directions, powerful graphical workstations allow the analyst to undertake such examinations in real time, manually changing projection directions with a joystick or mouse. As the directions change, the projected point cloud appears to rotate, because parallax provides a powerful illusion of a third dimension. But sheer combinatorics limit the data sets' dimensionality that can be visually explored in this way, and techniques for the automatic pursuit of interesting projections can be used for very high-dimensional data sets.

Manual Projection Pursuit

In data analysis, uncovering structure—clusters, hyperplanes, and the like—embedded in high-dimensional space is at once ubiquitous and difficult. For data in p dimensions, the simplest, yet least-effective, approach is to laboriously construct and examine all $\binom{p}{2}$ pair-wise scatterplots and, in doing so, attempt to reconstruct any underlying structure. Essentially, each scatterplot is an orthogonal projection of the data onto the subspace spanned by the two coordinate axes of choice. Unfortunately, projection is a data-smoothing operation in the sense that information is never gained and often lost. For example, consider the simple two-dimensional scatterplot illustrated in Figure 1. It should be clear that this structure, strikingly clear in two dimensions, is obscured when we project the data orthogonally onto either the x or the y coordinate alone. In a similar manner, the search for three- (or higher) dimensional structure may be fruitless when such structure cannot be revealed by examining the suite of two-dimensional projections.

A more effective technique for uncovering structure is to construct and examine $\binom{p}{2}$ dimensional scatterplots, particularly when the structure we wish to uncover lies across more than two dimensions. When n is three, we must construct three-dimensional scatterplots. But since hardware restricts graphical displays to two spatial dimensions, a third spatial dimension can be accommodated only by illusion. (We describe a variety of techniques for accomplishing this illusion later in this chapter.) When n is greater than three, the additional dimensions may be encompassed by some of the same techniques we describe later. But when n is very large, we must eventually abandon the restriction requiring examination of only those projections determined by data coordinate triplets and, instead, examine projections onto arbitrary subspaces. When approaching the subject of high-dimensional scatterplots, two important issues must be ad-

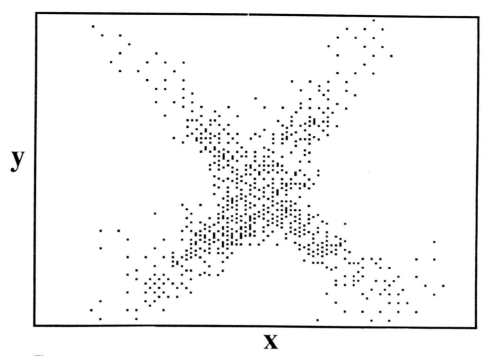

Figure 1. Two-dimensional structure, obscured in one-dimensional projections.

dressed: how the scatterplots are displayed and, more importantly, how we interact with the scatterplots to take full advantage of their high-dimensional structure—issues we discuss later.

A sophisticated software environment for the interactive exploration of high-dimensional scatterplots can reveal tremendous insights into the structure of a data set, and the advent of low-cost, high-powered graphics workstations provides today's data analyst with the potential for building such environments.

Displaying three-dimensional scatterplots. Unfortunately, hardware forces us to represent three-dimensional scatterplots with only two spatial dimensions. The key to creating the illusion of a third spatial dimension is to map that dimension to another that can be effectively perceived. We have a number of choices.

Color. Color intensity provides the illusion of a third dimension, but, unfortunately, differences between similar intensities can be difficult to detect when we use only one pixel per data point. Furthermore, graphics hardware may provide an insufficient range of intensity levels to adequately cover the range of available data values. But when we use several pixels per datum and the graphics hardware is adequate to the task, color intensity can provide a powerful illusion of depth. Some graphics workstations (such as the Silicon Graphics' Iris 4D) allow the software developer to build a ramp of smoothly varying color intensity and provide a depth-cue mode in which the color of an individual datum is determined by simply indexing into this color ramp, with the index determined by the datum's z value.

Glyphs. Although the simplest way to represent a single datum in a scatterplot is to illuminate a pixel, we can use a variety of other techniques. For example, instead of using a featureless pixel illumination, we might display the point by using such features as size, shape, and color. When additional dimensions are so encoded, the data points are known as "glyphs."[1] The use of glyphs as depth cues is typically accomplished by representing each datum as a circle, with the area or radius of the circle made proportional to the value of the datum along the z screen axis. Using size, however, places considerable computational burden on the graphics display device and, more importantly, can be confounded by the use of size for other purposes. For example, when dealing with discrete-valued data, the size of a glyph is often made proportional to the number of data points that lie at a given position in the display space. Using different shapes to provide depth cues suffers from the same problems as using size. In addition, no natural ordering typically occurs for shapes. We can use glyphs effectively, however, when we must encompass more than three dimensions in the display. Common uses of glyphs include "sunflowers," in which each data point becomes an axis radiating lines of different lengths.

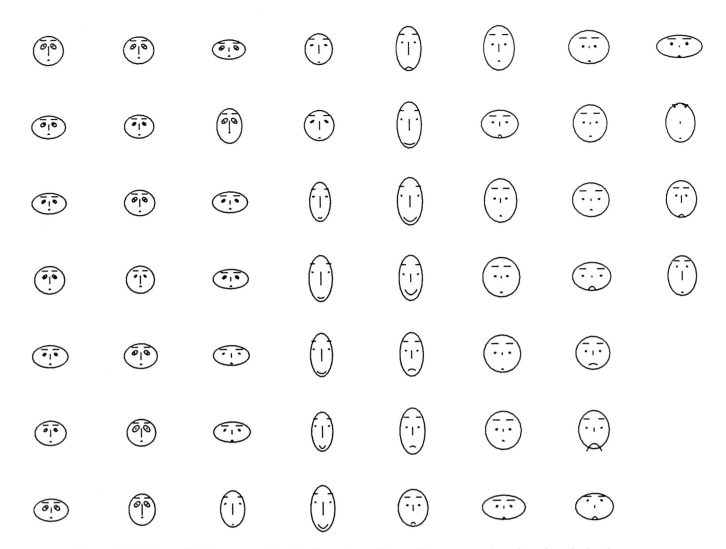

Figure 2. A Chernoff plot representing 12 dimensions. These data represent a mineral analysis of a core sample drilled from a mountain in Colorado. Each of the 53 faces represents 12 variables obtained by sampling sections of the core. Note how clusters and outliers can be readily detected.

In a sunflower plot, each radial line represents an additional variable, and the length of the line indicates the magnitude of that variable. Still more sophisticated is the use of glyphs with more complicated shapes, perhaps the most famous example being the display of "Chernoff's faces."[2] When displaying a scatterplot composed of such faces, each data point is a stylized drawing of a human face, with the size and shape of facial structures—nose, ears, eyes, and so forth—representing variables in the analysis. The human gift for recognizing and integrating features associated with facial structure enables analysts to digest a scatterplot displaying a large number of dimensions. Figure 2 illustrates a Chernoff plot representing 12 dimensions. (For a review of the use of glyphs for scatterplot display, see Tufte.[3])

Perspective. Perspective views provide excellent ways to encode depth into displays of wire-frame or solid-body objects. Typically, however, perspective is of little help for displaying scatterplots unless we superimpose a wire-frame cube representing the coordinate axes upon the point-cloud display.

Stereo Pairs. Stereo scatterplot pairs, when viewed side by side, can sometimes provide a good illusion of three dimensions, particularly when special stereo-pair viewing glasses are used. An alternative approach is to display each data point twice, once in red and once in cyan. For each datum pair, we determine the separation along the x axis by the datum's z value, and we view the scatterplot by wearing glasses with red and cyan lenses. Unfortunately, approximately two percent of the population cannot effectively fuse such pairs into a single image.[4] Furthermore, long-time viewing of such pairs can be rather hard on the eyes.

Shadow. Projecting shadows of each data point on a solid background encompassing the coordinate axes can often provide a good illusion of depth, allowing for the effective display of three-dimensional scatterplots. This approach is typically useful only for relatively sparse scatterplots since, when the data are dense, the shadows tend to obscure one another and we lose the sense of depth.

Motion. Perhaps the most effective means for providing the illusion of a third spatial dimension is to let motion trick the eye by parallax. We can rotate the point cloud separately about either the screen axes or about the coordinate axes. But if the graphics hardware is sufficiently powerful, a very effective approach to interactive point-cloud rotation is to let the analyst manually rotate the data about the screen axes with continuous movement of a mouse or trackball. Rotating points about the screen axes amounts to continuously projecting the data onto a two-dimensional subspace spanned by a pair of orthogonal vectors α and β. The screen location of every datum $\mathbf{x}_i$ is therefore determined as the coordinate pair $(\alpha^T \mathbf{x}_i, \beta^T \mathbf{x}_i)$. Henceforth, we will refer to α and β as the projection axes, or the projection directions.

Despite the illusion of a third spatial dimension, however, the viewer of rotating scatterplots will generally be subject to annoying perceptual "inversions" during the rotation.* Using an additional depth cue will often provide a visual "anchor" that can eliminate this effect. Most useful in this regard is the use of color intensity, since intensities can often be conveniently updated by simply accessing the hardware color map. In this way, a technique for making the color intensity of a point be a function of the z axis value can be easily implemented such that "closer" points have a greater color intensity than more distant points. Another problem with the use of motion is that, quite naturally, the illusion is maintained only when the point cloud is actually moving. When the analyst stops rotation to more closely examine an interesting projection, interpreting the orientation of the point cloud along the z axis can be quite difficult. We can ameliorate this problem by using color intensity, as we have described, or by using point-cloud "rocking." Point-cloud rocking involves repeated random rotations of the cloud in

small increments. Such rotations are small enough to maintain the general orientation of the cloud so that examination is not adversely affected, yet large enough to maintain the illusion of a third spatial dimension while the cloud is being examined.

Software environments for manual projection pursuit have typically relied on motion for displaying three-dimensional scatterplots.

PRIM-9 system. Tukey, Friedman, and Fisherkeller[5] achieved the first significant implementation of a system for manual projection pursuit in the early 1970s. This system enabled the operator to visually inspect data sets of up to nine dimensions. It obtained its name from four basic operations provided to the user: (1) The data could be projected on a two-dimensional subspace spanned by any coordinate pair; (2) the two-dimensional subspace, as projected onto a CRT screen, could be rotated such that parallax deceived the eye into believing that, in fact, a three-dimensional scatterplot was being viewed; (3) when structure was located in a projection, the data points forming the structure could be isolated for subsequent, more detailed, analysis**; and (4) the user could define subregions of the multidimensional space so that, when the point cloud was rotated, points would become masked (extinguished) as they entered and left the subregion.

In addition to simply choosing triplets of variables for rotations, the PRIM-9 system allowed the user to update any given projection with an additional variable to accommodate arbitrary rotations. Given the hardware available at the time, the very fact that the PRIM-9 system allowed the user to rotate points interactively is quite remarkable. Computational requirements exceeded those available on single-user machines, and so one computer (a Varian 620) drove the display device, and another (an IBM 360 mainframe!) rotated the points.

Descendants of PRIM-9. As more powerful hardware became available at lower cost, new systems were developed in the late 1970s. These systems (PRIM-S,[6] PRIM-H,[7] and Orion[8] still essentially followed the PRIM-9 model, but were able to take advantage of special hardware features for processing the point-cloud rotations. The development of the PRIM-H system at Harvard University in 1979[9] was

---

*This phenomenon will be familiar to anyone who has stared long enough at a wire-frame representation of a cube in three dimensions (a Necker cube). Eventually the orientation of the wire frame will appear to invert spontaneously.

**For example, when a pair of clusters were detected in a projection, each cluster could be isolated from the other and then analyzed separately. Proceeding recursively in this manner, a complicated, hierarchical clustering could be detected.

important in that, for the first time, the need to support the analyst with a general-purpose exploratory data analysis package integrated into the PRIM system was recognized. The PRIM-H system made use of ISP (interactive statistical package), an analysis tool that allowed the user of the system to perform data transformations, regressions, and so forth and subsequently use the results of these activities during the PRIM analysis. PRIM systems began to be implemented on low-cost microcomputers in the early 1980s. The first of these, PP,[10] was implemented on a Macintosh computer in 1984, and allowed point-cloud rotation such that the axis of rotation could be any line in the plane of the screen. Mac-Spin,[11] a more sophisticated PRIM system, became commercially available in 1986 but restricted point-cloud rotations to the planes defined by the screen axes.

Limitations of manual projection pursuit. Although the manual exploration of three-dimensional scatterplots by the pursuit of interesting point-cloud projections can often reveal hitherto undetected structure, extending such methods to the exploration of higher dimensional data sets is problematic, because of the "curse of dimensionality." The curse of dimensionality refers to the fact that high-dimensional space is inherently large and, as such, is typically sparsely populated for most data sets. To make this point clear, consider S, a unit p-dimensional hypersphere, and an associated direction, or unit vector α defining a single point on the surface of S. Now the angle between α and any other direction β is defined as the squint angle θ. Finally, all of the directions that come within θ degrees of a constitute a circular cap on S with radius θ degrees. Now, how many directions must we examine to explore the whole hypersurface of S adequately? Table 1 illustrates the fact that the hypersurface area of S grows dramatically with increasing dimension and indicates the difficulty we face when attempting to explore high-dimensional space.

We illustrated the problem of choosing a sufficient number of directions to explore adequately a high-dimensional space in Table 1 in terms of solution vectors. Unfortunately, the problem is much worse when we wish to explore arbitrary projections onto planes spanned by orthogonal directions α and β. For example, for a squint angle of $\theta = 10$ degrees, the number of one-dimensional projections we must view exhaustively to examine a p-dimensional space is approximately 10^{p-1}. But when we wish to exhaustively locate all two-dimensional scatterplots, the number of two-dimensional projections we must explore increases to approximately 10^{2p-4}. Now, assume that the analyst has access to a powerful graphics workstation and examines sequences of two-dimensional scatterplots rapidly enough that the illusion of motion through the p-dimensional space is provided. Given that such an illusion requires that 15-30 scatterplots per second must be displayed, what are the limits imposed by manual projection pursuit? Table 2's left column illustrates approximate time limits for this type of examination. Another approach to manual examination is to select all $\binom{p}{3}$ subspaces spanned by the coordinate triplets, and to carry out an exhaustive exploration, perhaps by using a mouse or trackball to rotate the points, of each subspace in turn. Given such an approach, imposing a cost of 10 seconds for the selection and "digestion" of each subspace, and taking a more relaxed rate of 10 projections per second, what limitations would the curse of dimensionality impose? The right column of Table 2 illustrates time estimates for exhaustive exploration of those subspaces defined by all $\binom{p}{3}$ coordinate triplets.

Table 2 shows that exhaustive exploration of two-dimensional projections is limited to four-dimensional data sets when we desire arbitrary projections. Unfortunately, the estimates in Table 2 are rather optimistic, because they rely on a rather fundamental assumption: Given that the analyst wishes to view a sequence of scatterplots, it is essential that we generate a well-chosen sequence. In other words, if we are to maintain the illusion of motion through the data set, each projection must be close to the projection immediately preceding it in the sequence. Ensuring such smoothness in the sequence of projections can, unfortunately, demand that the analyst actually view some projections more than once. Algorithms for choosing efficient sequences of views are known as "grand tour" algorithms.

Given that, for arbitrary projections, the analyst is limited to exploration of four-dimensional space, the manual exploration of the subspaces defined by the $(p/3)$ three-dimensional coordinate triplets seems much more attractive, as shown in Table 2. Unfortunately, we then risk missing interesting projections of all p dimensions. How then can we hope adequately to explore high-dimensional data?

Table 1. Fraction of S contained within cap covering all directions within θ degrees of α.

	$\theta = 5°$	$\theta = 10°$	$\theta = 15°$	$\theta = 30°$	$\theta = 45°$
$p = 4$	1/526	1/132	1/59	1/15	1/7
$p = 5$	1/92,196	1/5,806	1/1,162	1/78	1/17
$p = 7$	1/14,560,051	1/230,733	1/20,748	1/369	1/40

Source: Tukey and Tukey.[15]

Table 2. Approximate upper limits for exhaustive exploration given θ = 10 degrees.

	Arbitrary Projections	Coordinate Triplets
$p = 3$	3 seconds	10 seconds
$p = 4$	6 minutes	1 minute
$p = 5$	9 hours	3 minutes
$p = 6$	39 days	7 minutes

Note: We assume a projection rate of 30 scatterplots per second for arbitrary projections and a rate of 10 per second for examining the coordinate triplet subspaces.

One obvious approach is somehow to automate the search, letting the computer ascertain whether a given projection would be interesting. Unfortunately, even if we assume that the computer can evaluate as many as 10,000 projections per second, high-dimensional space grows rapidly enough that this approach will still only allow us to explore up to six dimensions.* Since exhaustive search is not feasible for large p, an alternative would be to use heuristic search (we address this topic, automatic projection pursuit, later in the chapter). Other approaches to increasing the dimensionality that manual projection pursuit can address involve initial reduction of dimensionality by encoding data points as glyphs or using color encoding.

Grand-tour techniques. In the last section, we introduced the idea of displaying a p-dimensional data set with a continuous sequence of two-dimensional scatterplots. Presenting such a "movie" requires that each projection must be, in some sense, "close" to its immediate predecessor and successor in the sequence. Asimov (1985) introduced the notion of the grand tour of a data set and formalized these requirements.

The grand tour originated with the Andrews[12] plot and is, in fact, a two-dimensional analog of such plots. Using the terminology introduced earlier, consider a projection direction α and the projection $\alpha^T x$ of a datum onto a line. Depending on the orientation of α, projecting the entire data set in this way may not reveal structure, and so a good strategy for revealing structure is to examine many such directions. One way to achieve this is to use the Fourier series and, for each data point x, plot the curve

$$y = x_1/\sqrt{2} + x_2 \sin t + x_3 \cos t + x_4 \sin 2t + x_5 \cos 2t + \ldots$$

We determine the series' length by the data set's dimensionality and each point on the curve by the value of t. Each point on the curve is essentially a different projection direction, and examining many values of t from $-\pi$ to π can be an effective way of revealing clusters in the data, since points clustering together will tend to have curves that lie close together on the y axis. Although Andrews plots are typically viewed as static y versus t displays, we can envision a dynamic display in which t represents time, and the data points move about on a line as t varies. The grand tour works in just this manner, except that the points are projected on a plane rather than a line.

Several methods can define the route of the grand tour. As we might expect, a trade-off occurs among rapidity, uniformity, and smoothness. One method generating a smooth route is the torus method. The goal of the torus method is to come arbitrarily close to any two-dimensional plane through the origin. The collection of these planes is the Grassman manifold. If we take a plane, then by choosing a rotation from $SO(p)$—the rigid rotations of the unit p-dimensional sphere—we can transform that plane to any other in the manifold. For example, if the Earth plays the role of the unit sphere in 3 space, then $SO(3)$ consists of all rotations of the Earth. If the distinguished plane is the equatorial plane, then we can rotate it to the position of any other plane through the origin.

Given an orthogonal basis for the space, every distinct pair of basis vectors forms a plane, and that plane intersects the unit sphere in a circle (there are $N = 1/(p^2 - p)$ of these). We can obtain any rotation in $SO(p)$ by a sequence of rotations along these circles. That is, there is a surjection from the set of ordered tuplets of rotation angles. The product of circles is a torus, so we have a mapping from the torus to $SO(p)$. Now, using the fact that the line parameterized by $f(t) = (\lambda_1 t, \lambda_2, \ldots, \lambda_N t)$ where the λ_i are linearly independent over the integers** maps to a dense set on the torus, we can find a step size K so that when we move along the line by K, the set of ensuing rotations is sufficiently distributed over $SO(p)$.

Now, in three space, $N = 1/2(3^2 - 3)$, and so on the Earth, for example, we can visualize this toroidal group by the three great circles consisting of the equator, the great circle that includes the prime meridian, and the one through the pole at 90 degrees to it. Actually, we need to look at these as inertial planes; initially, the equatorial plane and the one

---

*Exhaustive search of $p = 6$ would take about three hours, whereas seven dimensions would require about 12 days of computer time.

**The set of λ_N of reals is linearly independent over the integers if the only integer sequence $K_1 \ldots K_N$ that satisfies $(\lambda_1 K_1 + \lambda_2 K_2 + \ldots \lambda_N K_N) = 0$ is the one in which each $K_i = 0$. Effectively, the line does not run through any grid intersection.

rotation plane might be coincident, but eventually the equatorial plane will get rotated around. So, we take the Earth, rotate it $\lambda_1 K$ in the equatorial plane $\lambda_2 K$ in the "prime meridian" plane (the first rotation has already moved the actual prime meridian) and, finally, $\lambda_3 K$ in our final inertial plane. Now, from the viewer's perspective on the Moon, this sequence of rotations amounts to a single rotation along all three planes such that, for example, a fixed spot x once occupied by, say, Des Moines, is now occupied by Chicago. After enough rotations, any point on Earth will come arbitrarily close to x.

This toroidal tour is definitely smooth; one is always moving in the same direction. But it is neither rapid nor uniform. First, the mapping of the torus to $SO(p)$ is not one to one, because a good deal of overlap occurs. A twist from the pole to the equator along the prime meridian followed by a 90 degrees twist along the equator is the same as a single twist from the pole to the 90-degree mark on the equator. Neither is the torus method uniform. For instance, Chicago, on its second pass, might be only 10 miles away from its original position but, it might take until very late in the sequence before it is within a 100 miles of, say, Santa Fe's original position.

Some methods may achieve rapidity or uniformity, but may be less smooth. For instance, Asimov[13] details the "at-random method" and the "smoother random-walk method." The at-random method chooses the next 2 plane in the tour randomly from a distribution uniform on the set of all 2 planes. By construction, this is uniform in a probabilistic sense. Unfortunately, however, it is not smooth and is only about as rapid as the torus method. The random choices can result in the selection of planes much closer to earlier choices than necessary. The smoother random-walk method is more akin to the torus method in that each step is just a small rotation from the previous. But this step is not always in the same direction as for the torus method but is, instead, in a random direction. This method is relatively smooth and is more rapid, though not necessarily uniform.

Automatic Projection Pursuit

Since, even with computer assistance, the exhaustive search of high-dimensional space appears to be feasible only for rather small p, a natural approach is to limit search with an algorithm for heuristic exploration of the multidimensional space. This approach to data visualization is known as automatic projection pursuit, and is characterized as follows:

Formulate an initial model for the structure of the data.

repeat

    1. Locate and save directions indicating departure from current model.

    2. Refine the current model by using structure found in step *1*

until no significant departures from the current model can be found.

Since we can use projection pursuit techniques for a variety of data analysis and interpretation tasks—including density estimation, regression, and classification—the details of the projection pursuit paradigm differ slightly according to task. This chapter focuses largely on the use of projection pursuit for exploratory data analysis, in which the analyst's goal is simply to locate interesting structure within the high-dimensional data space. The basic paradigm for exploratory projection pursuit is

Assume the data is unstructured in p space.

repeat

    1. Locate and save directions indicating the presence of structure.

    2. Return to unstructured assumption by removing structure found in step 1

until no significant structure can be found.

The basic idea of removing structure from an updated model and then reexamining what remains for possible additional structure should be familiar to anyone who has ever carried out an ordinary regression analysis. The standard approach for regression analysis is to fit a model to the data, remove (by subtraction) the fitted model from the data, then examine what remains (the residuals) for departures from Gaussian distribution. In exploratory projection pursuit, this paradigm raises some important questions:

- How can the computer assess whether a given projection shows structure (is "interesting")?

- How can interesting projections be located without exhaustive search?

- How should interesting projections be presented to the analyst?

- How can structure, once found, be removed from the data?

We will answer these questions in the following sections.

Friedman-Tukey algorithm. The original Friedman-Tukey algorithm[14] was developed in an effort to automate the approval to manual projection pursuit elucidated by repeatedly observing the techniques used by operators of the original PRIM-9 system we described earlier (see, also,

Tukey, Friedman, and Fisherkeller[5]). System users typically searched for projections that revealed structures composed of dense clusters of data points, well separated in the projection space. In effect, the human operators were seeking projections that simultaneously maximized the "spread" and the local density of the data points. Projections showing a high degree of "clottedness" in this fashion were typically perceived by the operators of PRIM-9 as interesting, and an attempt was made to define a mathematical measure that captured this notion of data clottedness.

The Projection Index. To keep the notation simple, we first define an index to assess the clottedness of a one-dimensional projection α. Friedman and Tukey defined the clottedness of α as:

$$C(\alpha) = s(\alpha) d(\alpha) \tag{1}$$

In Equation 1, $s(\alpha)$ is a measure of the overall variability of the data as projected onto direction α. Although the simplest way to assess this variability is to compute the ordinary sample standard deviation of the data points along α, this leads to problems of robustness. Simply put, the expressions for both the sample mean and sample standard deviation are quadratic, meaning that we measure the contribution of each datum as a squared distance.* Because of the quadratic nature of these statistics, extreme data exert an undue influence on them, and thus the sample mean and standard deviation are decidedly nonrobust against the influence of outlying observations. Quickly computed robust measures of dispersion and location involve removing the most extreme data points from the computation of the statistics and Friedman and Tukey chose to use $w\%$-trimmed measures of location and dispersion. As such, we compute $s(\alpha)$ as the $w\%$-trimmed standard deviation of the N data points as projected onto α:

$$s(\alpha) = \left(\sum_{i=wN}^{(1-w)N} \frac{(\alpha^T \mathbf{X}_i - \overline{\mathbf{X}}_\alpha)^2}{(1 - 2w)N} \right)^{\frac{1}{2}} \tag{2}$$

where the $\mathbf{X}_i$ are simply the data vectors ordered according to their projections on α. Note that, to reduce the influence of extreme data points on $s(\alpha)$, we introduce a trimming factor w. Using w effectively removes the influence of these extreme data points, thus making $s(\alpha)$ robust against outliers. In Equation 2, the mean of the data points as projected onto α is evaluated as

$$\overline{\mathbf{X}}_\alpha = \sum_{i=wN}^{(1-w)N} \frac{\alpha_T \mathbf{X}_i}{(1 - 2w)N} \tag{3}$$

In Equation 1, $d(\alpha)$ is a measure of local point density, defined as

$$d(\alpha) = \sum_{i=1}^{N} \sum_{j=1}^{N} f(r_{ij}) I_{(R-r_{ij})} \tag{4}$$

In Equation 4, r_{ij} is a measure of the absolute distance between any pair of points as projected onto α, and $f(r_{ij})$ is a kernel function that monotonically decreases for increasing r.**A local cutoff radius R defines the neighborhood within which point density is measured, and an indicator function $I(\eta)$ that evaluates to unity for $\eta > 0$ selects those pairs of points no further apart than R. In words, then, the average nearness of the points along α is computed as the sum of the contributions of all pairs of points no farther apart than R, such that the closer the points, the greater their contribution to the double sum defined in Equation 4. Locating a direction α that maximizes Equation 1 therefore amounts to locating a direction that shows a configuration of well-separated, dense clusters—an "interesting" projection. Extending Equations 2 and 4 to two-dimensional projections is straightforward. We define data variability across the plane defined by (α, β) simply as $s(\alpha)s(\beta)$ and measure point density just as in Equation 4, with r_{ij} defined as the simple Euclidean distance between pairs of points on the projection plane.

Locating interesting projections. Given that we can evaluate any arbitrary projection according to its degree of interest, we must find a mechanism to locate interesting projections efficiently in the p-dimensional data space. If we consider α and β as defining a two-dimensional grid encompassing all possible two-dimensional projections, then the values obtained from the clottedness function $C(\alpha, \beta) = s(\alpha, \beta) d(\alpha, \beta)$ define a third dimension that is a surface over the grid of possible projections. In this context, the search for interesting projections amounts to a search for local maxima along this surface. A standard approach to problems of this sort involves choosing an initial starting point, choosing a "step" size, and then varying α and β by steps until we locate a new point "uphill" of the previous point. Many hill-climbing algorithms are available, but to incorporate such algorithms (as Friedman and Tukey did), the

---

*Although the sample mean $\frac{1}{n} \Sigma x_i$ is not generally thought of as a quadratic estimator, the sample mean is in fact that parameter u for which $\Sigma (x_i - u)^2$ is minimized.

**We indicated earlier that density estimators based on kernel functions can perform poorly for large p. But note that density estimation in Equation 4 is taking place in a strictly univariate setting, and so the curse of dimensionality is not a factor. Friedman and Tukey indicated that the projection pursuit algorithm's performance was relatively insensitive to the exact choice of f.

evaluation function must be smooth. Fortunately $C(\alpha,\beta)$ is very smooth indeed. As is often the case with such hill-climbing approaches, there is a tendency to get trapped in local maxima, and a corresponding variety of heuristics can reduce this tendency (increasing step size, etc.). In projection pursuit, however, many interesting projections of a given space probably exist, and the data analyst will no doubt profit by examining of all of them. In this sense, for projection pursuit, we need not worry unduly about getting trapped in local maxima. A convenient approach to search, suggested by Tukey and Tukey,[15] consists of the following steps.

(1) Choose an initial starting point (perhaps the principal axes or the coordinate axes) and a discounting factor F. Initialize the maximum projection index C_{max} to zero.

(2) Locate, by hill climbing, a point maximizing $C(\alpha,\beta) > C_{max}$, then set C_{max} to $C(\alpha,\beta)$.

(3) Choose a new starting point (α',β') at random. If $C(\alpha',\beta') \geq FC_{max}$, then go to step 2, else choose another starting point. Stop when no new starting points exceed FC_{max}.

Rather than explicitly removing found structure, Friedman and Tukey[14] suggest a number of heuristic approaches. For example, when an interesting projection is found, it is often useful to partition the data based on any clusters made visible in the projection and then recursively apply steps 1-3 on each partition.

Revised Friedman algorithm. Huber[16] points out that, although the concept of what makes a projection "interesting" may be difficult to pin down, the converse notion—what makes a projection uninteresting—is much easier to define. Simply put, Huber suggests that the closer a given projection follows a normal distribution, the less interesting it is. He provides the following arguments in support:

(1) A multivariate distribution is normal if and only if all of its one-dimensional projections are normal. In this way, all projections of a multivariate normal distribution are uninteresting.

(2) As a consequence of step 1, if the least normal projection is close to normal, then all projections are uninteresting.

(3) Most projections of point clouds (even those that contain some striking structure) follow a distribution close to normal.

Friedman[17] also points out that, for fixed variance, the normal distribution contains the least information (in the Shannon entropy sense). In this context, it appears that a good criterion for evaluating the "interestingness" of a given projection is an assessment of how much that projection departs from a normal distribution. In fact, we can interpret the original Friedman-Tukey index, shown as Equation 1, as a measure of nonnormality. The Friedman-Tukey index, however, was developed heuristically and adopted primarily because it made good intuitive sense and performed well in practice. Recognizing that we wish to derive an index explicitly (rather than coincidentally) testing for departures from a Gaussian distribution opens the door for discovering projection indices and optimization techniques more powerful than those proposed by Friedman and Tukey. Friedman proposed a revised version of his original algorithm in this light.

Given that we wish to test for departures from normality in a given projection, we must determine what kind of departures are of most interest. Detecting departures from a Gaussian distribution is, for many data-analysis scenarios, a problem involving the testing for departures in the tails of the empirical density function. In fact, most statistical tests for departures from a Gaussian distribution are most powerful at detecting departures in the tails of the distribution (e.g., departures caused by the presence of outliers). For projection pursuit, however, departures in the central part of the distribution (e.g., the presence of several modes indicating clusters) are typically of greater interest. Recognizing this, Friedman[17] suggests a new projection index, which we will describe next.

Projection index. In data analysis, different variables are often measured on quite different scales. To compare such variables, the analyst typically standardizes the data, often by simply subtracting the sample means and dividing by sample standard deviations. When many variables are correlated, and the analyst is not particularly interested in those simple correlations, an additional standardization measure, called "data sphering," can be employed. Data sphering essentially involves making linear transformations of the raw data such that information about location, scale, and correlation (the obvious structure) is removed, thus allowing the analyst to focus on the less obvious structure. For projection pursuit, data sphering has computational advantages as well, in that the operation occurs only once, at the beginning of the analysis. In this way, we need not compute standard deviations for each projection, as we did in the earlier Friedman-Tukey algorithm (Equation 2). Note that, to facilitate interpreting the found projections, the data are transformed back to their original coordinates before projections are viewed.

Just as we did earlier, we introduce the projection index in terms of one-dimensional projection pursuit. To further simplify notation, we first introduce an abstract version of the index—that is, one that assumes the analyst has a p-dimensional probability density rather than a data sample in p dimensions.

After the raw random variables X have been transformed to the sphered random variables Y, the goal of one-dimensional projection pursuit is to locate a direction α such that the transformed data, as projected onto α, will be highly structured. Bearing in mind that "structure" may be interpreted as "departure from normality in the center of the distribution," it is important to examine the distribution of $\mathbf{Z} = \alpha_T\mathbf{Y}$ for such departures. The first step in this process involves transforming $\mathbf{Z}$ so that subsequent comparisons of structure may be made with respect to a simpler distribution than the standard normal. Friedman[17] suggests performing the transformation $\mathbf{R} = 2\Phi(\mathbf{Z}) - 1$, where $\Phi(\mathbf{Z})$ is the cumulative distribution function (*cdf*) of the standard normal distribution. Transforming in this manner is convenient in that if $\mathbf{Z}$ follows a standard normal distribution, then $\mathbf{R}$ will follow a uniform distribution in the interval $-1 \leq \mathbf{R} \leq 1$. Ascertaining departure from normality in $\mathbf{Z}$ then amounts to assessing departure from uniformity in $\mathbf{R}$, and we measure the extent of that departure simply by computing the integral squared distance between $p_R(\mathbf{R})$, the probability density of $\mathbf{R}$, and the uniform probability density. Since the uniform probability density measure over the interval $-1 \leq \mathbf{R} \leq 1$ is simply $1/1 - (-1) = 1/2$, the integral squared distance measure is simply

$$\int_{-1}^{1} \left[p_R(\mathbf{R}) - \tfrac{1}{2} \right]^2 d\mathbf{R} = \int_{-1}^{1} p_R^2(\mathbf{R}) d\mathbf{R} - \tfrac{1}{2}^2 \qquad (5)$$

We obtain the abstract version of the one-dimensional projection index by approximating $p_R\mathbf{R}$ by the sum of Legendre polynomials, so that

$$\int_{-1}^{1} p_R^2(\mathbf{R}) d\mathbf{R} - \tfrac{1}{2} = \sum_{j=1}^{\infty} (2j + 1) E_R^2[P_j(R)]/2 \qquad (6)$$

Finally, we obtain the sample projection index by computing only the J terms of the sum in Equation 6 and replacing the expected values in Equation 6 with sample means. This yields the following sample index for one-dimensional projection pursuit:

$$I(\alpha) = \tfrac{1}{2} \sum_{j=1}^{J} (2j + 1) \left[\tfrac{1}{N} \sum_{i=1}^{N} P_j(2\Phi(\alpha^T y_i) - 1) \right]^2 \qquad (7)$$

Note that the only user-supplied parameter for the index in Equation 7 is J, the number of terms to be used to approximate $p_R(\mathbf{R})$. Friedman[17] suggests that results are relatively insensitive to the exact choice of J, but recommends a range of $4 \leq J \leq 8$. The costs for increasing J, and thus forming a smoother approximation of $p_R(\mathbf{R})$, grow linearly for one-dimensional projection pursuit and quadratically for two-dimensional projection pursuit. For derivation of the index corresponding to Equation 7 for two-dimensional projection pursuit, the reader is advised to consult Friedman.[17]

Locating interesting projections. Just as for the Friedman-Tukey algorithm, the approach to locating a projection

such that Equation 7 is a maximum involves the techniques of numerical optimization. The smoothness of Equation 7, and the fact that first derivatives are readily obtainable make the application of steepest ascent and quasi-Newton methods practical. Once again, however, we face the danger of getting trapped on local maxima. Friedman[17] suggests a hybrid approach to the optimization problem that involves initially taking large steps to locate the general vicinity of the global maxima and then using one of the finer-grained gradient techniques (such as quasi-Newton) to converge on the global maximum itself. An interesting approach to ensuring that we have located a true global maximum is suggested by Asimov[13] and involves invoking a grand tour algorithm (torus method) with a large step size. Each step in the grand tour becomes a starting direction for two-dimensional projection pursuit, and we obtain the most interesting projection uphill from each starting point. Since, even with the large step size, the grand tour does a good job of sampling the entire space, the analyst can be reasonably certain that the best of these interesting projections is a global maximum.

Removing found structure. We indicated earlier that once an interesting projection has been found, structure should be removed before proceeding to search for additional structure. This approach is analogous to the familiar process of residual analysis in regression procedures. Given that an interesting projection is, by definition, decidedly non-Gaussian, a natural way to remove structure in the projection is to Gaussianize it by transforming the variables in the projection to a standard normal distribution, while leaving all orthogonal projections unchanged. Recall that $\mathbf{Z} = \alpha^T\mathbf{Y}$ is the one-dimensional projection of the sphered data $\mathbf{Y}$ onto the direction α. Defining $F_\alpha(\mathbf{Z})$ as the *cdf* of $\mathbf{Z}$ and Φ^{-1} as the inverse of the *cdf* for the standard normal distribution, then the transformation $\mathbf{Z}' = \Phi^{-1}(F_\alpha(\mathbf{Z}))$ yields a new random variable $\mathbf{Z}'$ with a standard normal distribution. For the sample version of one-dimensional projection pursuit, this transformation amounts to transforming each of the N data points in the projection to their corresponding normal scores. Once again, for derivation of the transformations for two-dimensional projection pursuit, the reader is advised to consult Friedman.[17]

Example. In this section, we provide a simple example (originally appearing in Friedman[17]) of the usefulness of projection pursuit for exploratory data analysis. The data set consists of 506 cases, and each is an observation of a census tract in the Boston Standard Metropolitan Statistical Area. The data, appearing in full in Belsley, Kuh, and Welsch,[18] were collected in 1970 to assess the impact of air pollution on the price of owner-occupied homes in those census tracts. Each observation comprises 13 real-valued variables, described briefly in Table 3.

Table 3. Variables for Boston housing data.

Variable	Definition
x1	Logarithm of the per capita crime rate per town
x2	Proportion of town's residential land zoned for lots $> 25,000$ square feet
x3	Proportion of nonretail business acres per town
x4	Squared nitrogen oxide concentration (ppm)
x5	Squared average number of rooms
x6	Proportion of owner-occupied units built before 1940
x7	Log of weighted distance to five employment centers in Boston region
x8	Log of index of accessibility to radial highways
x9	Full-value property tax rate (per \$10,000)
x10	Pupil-teacher ratio by town
x11	Log $(0.4 - (B - 0.63)^2)$ where B is proportion of blacks in population
x12	Log of proportion of population that is lower status
x13	Log of the median value of owner-occupied homes

Source: Friedman.[17] Reprinted with permission.

It may at first seem that some of the variables are measured in a rather peculiar way—for example, why use the logarithm of per capita crime rate? Since exploratory projection pursuit is intended to discover unknown structure, removing as much as possible of the obvious, known structure prior to beginning analysis makes good sense. Sphering the data helps in this regard, but it is useful to take the additional step of transforming any variables to reduce skewing.

Subsequent to the data sphering and transformation, the projection pursuit algorithm begins. Friedman reports that 10 iterations of exploratory projection pursuit, applied to the Boston data, yielded projection index values of 0.69, 0.51, 0.40, 0.25, 0.34, 0.26, 0.31, 0.20, 0.22, and 0.10. To assess the significance of these numbers, Friedman ran two-dimensional projection pursuit on 20 artificial data sets, each of which was randomly drawn from a 13-dimensional standard normal distribution. The greatest index of interest obtained from these data sets was only 0.063, indicating that all but perhaps the last of the Boston indices indicates significant structure. Table 4 shows the two solution directions associated with the first iteration.

Note that, once a two-dimensional solution has been found, the exact orientation with which the solution points are plotted on the solution plane is arbitrary—rigid rotation about the z axis of the display can reveal no additional structure. Given this, it makes good sense to choose an orientation that yields a large loading to as few variables as possible on either the x or y display axis. Selecting a rotation that maximizes the variance of the variable loadings for one of the solution directions will accomplish this, and rotations of this type (common in such statistical techniques as factor analysis) can greatly facilitate interpreting the solution plot. Friedman rotated the projected data so that the maximum loading variance would appear for the vertical display axis. Note, for example, that the coefficient for the "large plots" variable in the β direction is almost unity, and the remaining loadings are close to zero, allowing the analyst to interpret the vertical axis of the solution plot as the "large lots" variable.

Figure 3 illustrates a scatterplot of the solution directions shown in Table 4, with the data scaled to facilitate interpretation. The striking structure illustrated in Figure 3 indicates that the data fall into two clusters, as determined by

Table 4. Solution directions for first iteration.

Direction	Description
α	0.13, –0.41, –0.50, –0.24, –0.04, –0.02, 0.20, 0.26, 0.24, –0.04, –0.50, 0.14, 0.19
β	0, 0.996, 0.05, –0.02, 0, 0.02, 0.02, 0.04, –0.04, –0.02, 0, 0.01, 0.01

Source: Friedman.[17] Reprinted with permission.

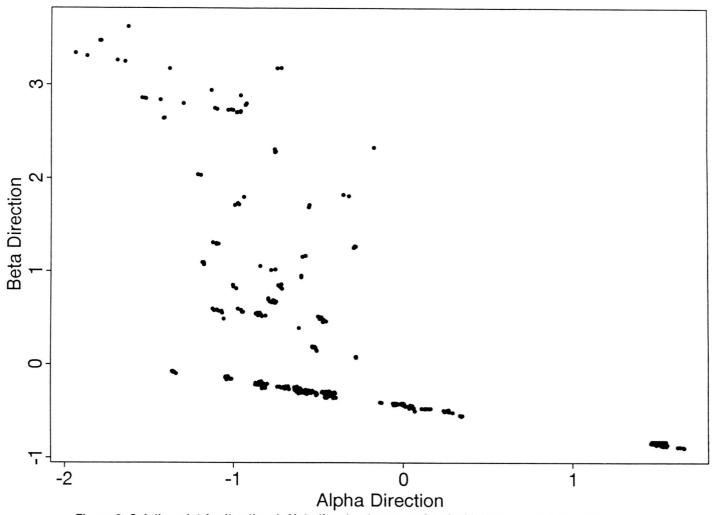

Figure 3. Solution plot for iteration 1. Note the structure associated with the "large-lots" variable.

whether or not the town has any residential land zoned for lots greater than 25,000 square feet. The remaining solutions, not shown here, illustrate additional strong relationships among the thirteen variables. (Refer to Friedman[17] for details.)

Summary. This section provides a nontechnical look at automatic projection pursuit. Readers intending to implement their own versions of the algorithms are invited to consult the referenced materials. The Friedman[17] and Huber[16] papers are particularly recommended.

This article has focused almost exclusively on using projection pursuit methods for exploratory data analysis, partially because it is the authors' main interest, but also because it is perhaps the most easily digested of the various projection pursuit techniques. But we can readily apply projection pursuit in a variety of data-analytic contexts.

Projection pursuit regression[19] locates projections that show interesting associations between a response variable and a suite of predictors. We formulate an initial model, usually suggesting that the relation is a constant, and initiate a search for a projection indicating a departure from that model. For each iteration of projection pursuit regression, we fit a smooth curve to the current projection, remove the structure associated with that smooth function, and begin the search for a new projection of interest. The result is a regression equation consisting of the sum of the initial model and the associated smooth functions. This approach to regression is especially appealing in that it is completely general, freeing the analyst from the often unrealistic assumptions imposed by ordinary least-squares regression analysis.

Projection pursuit density estimation[20] estimates the distribution of a random vector in p space and follows the standard projection pursuit paradigm. We propose an initial density model, perhaps multivariate normal, and initiate a search for projections that suggest departure from that distribution in the marginals. On the basis of the located projections, we update the model and repeat the procedure until no new departures can be found.

We can also use projection pursuit for classification.[19] The simplest approach involves using the paradigm of projection pursuit regression, with the classes in the data set recorded as dummy variables for regression.

Finally, the judicious choice of alternative projection indices can result in a projection pursuit algorithm tuned for a variety of purposes. As a simple illustration, imagine that your data consist of observations drawn from two samples. Choosing the two-sample t statistic as a projection index will locate a projection containing the maximally discriminating hyperplane—a projection pursuit version of classical linear discriminant analysis. More interesting still is the observation that changing the projection index such that robust measures of location and scale are used can conveniently deliver a robust version of discriminant analysis. Huber[16] presents some additional classical multivariate techniques such as principal component analysis and factor analysis from the perspective of projection pursuit.

Requirements for a Projection Pursuit Workstation

Software requirements. In keeping with the paradigm of the original PRIM-9 system, the software must allow the analyst to choose projections, rotate projections, isolate structures, and mask points. Donoho et al.[11] clearly indicate that an interactive statistical package is a crucial component of any environment for projection pursuit. The ability to take static "snapshots" of interesting views so that we may compare different views is quite useful and involves nothing more than using the simple bit-copying procedures offered as primitives by most graphics workstations. Even more useful is a feature enabling the analyst to rotate different views simultaneously (dynamic snapshots). The ability to represent a data set as a hierarchy of graphics objects, offered by workstations such as the Silicon Graphics, allows dynamic snapshots to be readily implemented. Allowing the analyst to display data points in different colors is crucial, particularly when data fall neatly into categories. We can also use color for depth cuing, as we have seen. Allowing the analyst to select or construct glyphs for data display is also useful, because this can be quite helpful for dimensionality reduction. When viewing multiple scatterplots, it is often helpful to associate pixels in one scatterplot with those in another scatterplot representing the same data. We readily accomplish this by the dynamic snapshot approach already described; but this approach imposes significant demands on the workstation, since we must smoothly rotate several scatterplots at once. Other, less computationally demanding approaches, involve scatterplot "brushing," in which the analyst uses the mouse to select and highlight a group of points in one plot and highlights the corresponding points in all of the other plots. Color "MN" plots, in which display data points are mapped to different colors according to which data object they represent, are also useful. When a wide spectrum of colors is available, the analyst can associate displayed data points in different scatterplots by color. Friedman[17] points out that approaches such as these can be extremely useful when the analyst must examine projection solutions delivered by a two-dimensional exploratory projection pursuit algorithm.

Hardware requirements. We discussed some software features that the analyst would require in a useful projection pursuit workstation. The minimal hardware requirement relates to the need to provide the analyst with smooth scatterplot rotation.

McDonald and Pedersen[21] examined this requirement and point out that if we want to rotate 1,000 points about an axis defined by any plane on the screen, the hardware must handle 1.2 Mflops for graphics operations alone. Nine additions, nine multiplications, and two divisions, for a total of 20 arithmetic operations are required per data point. And if the frames are to be displayed at 30 per second, these operations must be done before the refresh cycle; so they must be done within one-sixtieth of a second. The authors implemented a projection pursuit environment on a Silicon Graphics Iris 4D workstation and have smoothly rotated as many as 20,000 points. This is because the Silicon Graphics workstation supplies a "geometry engine"—a specialized array processor for these graphic operations that can run at 10 Mflops. In addition, enough screen memory for double buffering is provided. In double buffering, we display one frame from one set of bit planes while the next is being painted to another set. At the next refresh cycle, the second set is made visible. In this way, we keep the draw-erase cycle separated from the refresh cycle, thus avoiding distracting "beating" or "aliasing" effects. For less-powerful workstations, we can still rotate large numbers of points if we restrict the user to rotations about the display axes. Under such a restriction, the throughput is substantially less: only three multiplies and two adds per point for a total of 50,000 arithmetic operations per second for 1,000 points. Microcomputer implementations of interactive projection pursuit such as MacSpin[6] can successfully rotate as many as 1,000 points in this way.*

---

*On a Macintosh SE. As many as 4,000 points can be managed on a Macintosh II.

Summary

In this paper, we reviewed some very powerful techniques for visualizing high-dimensional data sets. Projection pursuit is a rather large topic and, for space limitations, we focused largely on projection pursuit as an exploratory data analysis tool. Projection pursuit, however, is a technique of sufficient generality that it may be applied to a wide range of analysis techniques. Readers are urged to refer to Huber's[16] excellent treatment for a more detailed look.

Lest the reader be left with the impression that projection pursuit techniques are a cure-all for the problems of multivariate data analysis, it seems prudent to mention a few limitations. Perhaps the most often-heard complaint about such techniques is that the solution directions can be difficult to interpret. Reference to Table 4 illustrates this since, although the β direction can be readily interpreted, the meaning of the α direction is much less clear.* Another drawback relates to the fact that, with the exception of projection pursuit regression, projection pursuit software is generally unavailable commercially. Finally, projection pursuit techniques are limited to being generally exploratory, with little in the way of inference capabilities to support them. For example, how can we ascertain whether found structure is real or only an artifact of our sample? Spurious structure can be rather troublesome, particularly when the data set's dimensionality is rather large relative to the sample size. As an example, Diaconis[22] shows some quite structured solutions obtained from Gaussian samples of 50 points in 10 dimensions. Important new work is, however, addressing the important issue of inference.[23]

Since we dealt separately with manual projection pursuit, the grand tour, and automatic projection pursuit, we have not made the integrated use of these techniques clear. As a simple example, we can define triplets of solutions obtained from one-dimensional automatic projection pursuit as display axes and subsequently rotate them manually in the hope that higher dimensional structure can be elucidated. Similarly, we can rotate any two-dimensional solutions by adding a third screen coordinate. We mentioned briefly that the grand tour can be used in conjunction with automatic projection pursuit techniques to locate a projection of global maximum interest. Similarly, we can use the grand tour in conjunction with manual projection pursuit, because when we locate interesting "frames" in the tour, they can be revisited and, with the addition of a third coordinate, rotated manually with a mouse, trackball, pad, or joystick. Finally, we can use interactive techniques such as scatterplot brushing to great advantage for analyzing solutions obtained from two-dimensional automatic projection pursuit. We should perhaps mention in closing that, although the curse of dimensionality limits the applicability of exhaustive projection pursuit for very high dimensions, it is also one of the reasons that, for many applications involving the analysis of high-dimensional data, projection pursuit algorithms are so much better than other algorithms that do not use projections. Consider, for example, nearest-neighbor or kernel-function classification algorithms. These algorithms classify data by assessing characteristics of the data populating the entire multidimensional space. Unfortunately, the curse of dimensionality tells us that high-dimensional space is inherently sparsely populated. The kernel classifier, then, faces the difficult problem of estimating data densities in a sparsely populated space. Another way of looking at the curse of dimensionality is that, as p increases, points in the space become progressively more equidistant. In this context, for large p, a nearest-neighbor classifier faces the difficult task of ascertaining class membership based on interpoint distances when differences in such distances are rather indistinct. But projection pursuit is not susceptible to such problems, since we carry out all estimation in a low-dimensional (usually univariate or bivariate) setting. An additional advantage of the projection pursuit approach is that a projection pursuit solution involves a small set of parameters (the solution directions in p space), and we can quickly and cheaply apply these solutions to new data sets. Solutions obtained from such techniques as nearest-neighbor analysis, on the other hand, are useful only for the original data set from which interpoint distances were computed. Finally, solutions obtained from kernel-function and nearest-neighbor techniques are essentially uninterpretable "black boxes" compared to the more readily interpretable graphical solutions yielded by projection pursuit techniques.

---

*Although the meaning of the α direction is clearly revealed by interactive color-coding methods, as illustrated in the companion videotape to this paper.

References

1. R. Gnanadesikan, *Methods for Statistical Data Analysis of Multivariate Observations.* John Wiley, New York, 1977.

2. H. Chernoff, "The Use of Faces to Represent Points in k-Dimensional Space Graphically," *J. Am. Statistical Assoc.,* Vol. 68, No. 342, 1973, pp. 361-368.

3. E.R. Tufte, *The Visual Display of Quantitative Information,* Graphics Press, Cheshire, Conn., 1983.

4. B. Julesz, *Foundations of Cyclopean Perception,* University of Chicago Press, Chicago, Ill., 1971.

5. J.W. Tukey, J.H. Friedman, and M.A. Fisherkeller, "Prim-9, an Interactive Multidimensional Data Display and Analysis System," in *Dynamic Graphics for Statistics,* W.S. Cleveland and M.E. McGill, eds., Wadsworth & Brooks/Cole, Belmont, Calif., 1988, pp. 91-110

6. D.L. Donoho, P.J. Huber, and H. Thoma, "The Use of Kinatic Displays to Represent High Dimensional Data," *Proc. 13th Symp. Interface Computer Sci. Statistics,* Springer-Verlag, New York, 1981.

7. D.L. Donoho et al., "Kinatic Display of Multivariate Data," in *Dynamic Graphics for Statistics,* W.S. Cleveland and M.E. McGill, eds., Wadsworth & Brooks/Cole, Belmont, Calif., 1988, pp. 111-120.

8. J.A. McDonald, "Orion I: Interactive Graphics for Data Analysis," in *Dynamic Graphics for Statistics,* W.S. Cleveland and M.E. McGill, eds., Wadsworth & Brooks/Cole, Belmont, Calif., 1988, pp. 179-199.

10. S.L. Crawford, *PP: A Prototype System for Interactive Projection Pursuit on a Microcomputer,* master's thesis, Stanford University, Stanford, Calif., 1984.

11. A.W. Donoho, D.L. Donoho, and M. Gask, "Macspin: Dynamic Graphics on a Desktop Computer," in *Dynamic Graphics for Statistics,* W.S. Cleveland and M.E. McGill, eds., Wadsworth & Brooks/Cole, Belmont, Calif., 1988, pp. 331-352.

12. D.F. Andrews, "Plots of high-dimensional data," Biometrics, Vol 28, 1983, pp. 125-136.

13. D. Asimov, "The Grand Tour: A Tool for Viewing Multidimensional Data," *SIAM J. Sci. Statistical Computing,* Vol. 6, No. 1, 1985, pp. 128-143.

14. J.H. Friedman and J.W. Tukey, "A Projection Pursuit Algorithm for Exploratory Data Analysis," *IEEE Trans. Computers,* Vol. C-23, No. 9, 1974, pp. 881-889.

15. P.A. Tukey and J.W. Tukey, "Data-Driven View Selection; Agglomeration and Sharpening," in *Interpreting Multivariate Data,* V. Barnett, ed., John Wiley, London, 1981, pp. 215-243.

16. P.J. Huber, "Projection Pursuit," *Ann. Statistics,* Vol. 13, No. 2, 1985, pp. 435-475.

17. J.H. Friedman, "Exploratory Projection Pursuit," *J. Amer. Statistical Assoc.,* Vol. 82, No. 397, 1987, pp. 249-266.

18. D.A. Belsley, E. Kuh, and R.E. Welsch, *Regression Diagnostics: Identifying Influential Data and Sources of Collinearity,* John Wiley, New York, 1980.

19. J.H. Friedman and W. Stuetzle, "Projection Pursuit Regression," *J. Amer. Statistical Assoc.,* Vol. 76, No. 376, 1981, pp. 817-823.

20. J.H. Friedman, W. Stuetzle, and A. Schroeder, "Projection Pursuit Density Estimation," *J. Amer. Statistical Assoc.,* Vol. 79, No. 387, 1984, pp. 599-608.

21. J.A. McDonald and J. Pedersen, "Computing Environments for Data Analysis: Part 1: Introduction," Tech. Rep. 24, Laboratory for Computational Statistics, Department of Statistics, Stanford University, Stanford, Calif.

22. P. Diaconis, "Asymptotics of Graphical Projection Pursuit," Project ORION Tech. Rep. 14, Department of Statistics, Stanford University, Stanford, Calif.

23. T. Hastie and R. Tibshirani, "Projection Pursuit," *Ann. Statistics,* Vol. 76, No. 376, 1981, pp. 502-508. [This is a discussion following Huber's (1985) article.]

Stuart Crawford is a senior research scientist and member of the research department at Advanced Decision Systems. His professional interests include knowledge induction, classification, and conceptual clustering, probablilistic approaches to reasoning under uncertainty, the interactive graphical display of high-dimensional data, expert systems for data analysis, data-smoothing, computer-intensive data analysis, and user interface issues. Crawford is working on methods for the induction of Bayesian networks and on a finely grained parallel implementation of the CART classification algorithm. He obtained the BS from the University of British Columbia, Canada, and the MS and PhD from Stanford University.

Thomas Fall is a principal research engineer with Advanced Decision Systems. He has led several projects that have developed systems to aid analysts in situation assessment and event classification. His technical interests lie in data discrimination, information theory, evidential reasoning, and temporal reasoning. Fall has written several papers on temporal reasoning and situation assessment. He is a member of IEEE, AAAI, the American Mathematical Society, and the Mathematical Association of America. He received the BS in chemistry (1966) and the PhD in mathematics (1972) from the University of California, Berkeley.

Computation and Manipulation of Three-Dimensional Surfaces from Image Sequences

H. Harlyn Baker, SRI International

Introduction

This chapter describes the processing of images obtained from television cameras to determine the geometry of a scene—three-dimensional computer vision. This 3D vision by a computer is one of the major challenges in robotics: regardless of the environment in which a robot is to function—a factory, underwater, on land, or in space—it will have to observe in three dimensions, recognize anticipated objects, and build models of the various objects and terrain it encounters. Operating autonomously, with minimal opportunity for manual intervention, a robot will have to carry out these tasks in a manner that leaves little chance for failure—it will need effective, reliable, 3D vision.

3D vision. Providing a robot with such sensing capability has been addressed in the past with approaches varying from the interpretation of single images, to paired-image or stereo analysis, to the use of active ranging devices. Single-image analysis can be of some use in image interpretation—identifying certain known forms from their appearance in two-dimensional images—but is generally inadequate when the objects are three-dimensional. Beyond this inadequacy, we should also note that a single 2D image cannot provide the information necessary for constructing 3D descriptions of a scene or its components. Two views of a scene, however, can provide a 3D perception of this structure, as is readily demonstrated by our human binocular vision. Binocular stereo processing, then, would seem to be a good starting point for a computational study of 3D scene modeling and recognition.

Significant difficulties arise with this approach in computer vision, however, with two major criticisms being that, first, the problem of recovering 3D structure is underdetermined with just two views and, second, even if successful, the information obtained is only a small subset of what is needed to build a truly 3D description of the scene. Furthermore, even the most advanced stereo compilation techniques (see, for example, Barnard)[1] are not as broadly applicable or as robust as required. With the development of special scanners, active sensing has become a more recent pursuit.[2] Yet even this has not achieved robust performance outside of controlled environments.

Image sequences. More recent approaches to 3D vision have addressed the processing of image sequences, where a sequence comprises many views from different positions. This more closely resembles the operation of the human system, where we observe with eyes that are free to move, collecting information from various perspectives. This multiple-view approach could provide considerably more complete descriptions of a scene, revealing, for example, what the back side of an object looks like, and could do so with much less ambiguity. Aside from restricted cases, however, it has proved difficult to exploit this extra data in the coherent manner required. One of the problems lies in organizing and maintaining coherent descriptions of the rather massive amount of data involved—sequences could be hundreds of frames long, or more. As in any experimental study, an important element of vision research involves gaining familiarity with the data, observing patterns or structure, and viewing it in the context of surrounding constraints. The quantity of data considered in sequence analysis has made this difficult. In the case to be discussed here, visualizing the data at the dimension appropriate for its analysis (space and time combined) has led to significant insights and a formulation of the reconstruction problem that gives a robust, precise, 3D vision capability. The mechanism crucial to the process is one that creates 3D descriptions of the evolution of image data over time. The development and use of this data representation is the basis of this chapter.

Sequence Analysis

We mentioned earlier that stereo processing in itself is not adequate for scene modeling. It does, however, share much of the mathematics of sequence analysis. The principal problem in stereo processing is to put into correspondence, accurately and reliably, features that appear in two views of a scene. This correspondence and the relationship between the two imaging sites make it possible to estimate the three-dimensional position of the features viewed. Determining the correspondence, however, is an ill-posed problem: ambiguity, occlusion, image noise, and other influences resulting from the differing appearance of objects in the two views make feature matching difficult. In sequence analysis, where rapid image sampling produces images that change little from one to the next, matching is less problematic. In the approach discussed here, this is taken to an extreme, with sampling sufficiently rapid that images vary smoothly between views. With this temporal continuity, matching features become a simple matter of following contours in time, and the difficult problem plaguing stereo basically goes away. The following sections describe how this temporal continuity has been developed and exploited for robust tracking and estimation of scene features from a moving vehicle.

Epipolar-plane image analysis. One of the main constraints used in stereo reconstruction work is that provided by epipolar geometry. If the cameras are oriented the same and have coplanar imaging surfaces, then a feature in one image will appear just laterally shifted from its appearance in the other image. In Figure 1, a camera is shown at two different positions. At each of the sites, the camera is looking at right angles to the path along which it moved, and it should be clear that a feature such as P, if seen from the two positions, will just be displaced laterally in one view with respect to the other. In fact, it will be displaced in the images along the projection of the plane formed by P and the two camera centers. This plane is termed an "epipolar plane." For a sequence of images collected with this lateral-viewing attitude, the point P will stay on the same image scan line from frame to frame. This means that we can confine all of the processing to deal with locating the position of P in the scene to a single set of scan lines. Figure 2 shows a volume formed by stacking up the data collected in an image sequence (several frames of which are shown in Figure 3) and slicing horizontally to reveal such a set of scan lines. The pattern of streaks in this slice makes the lateral displacement character quite apparent. In fact, for a constant camera velocity, the distance of a feature from the camera is a linear function of the slope of its path in this slice through space-time—near features have low slope, more distant features

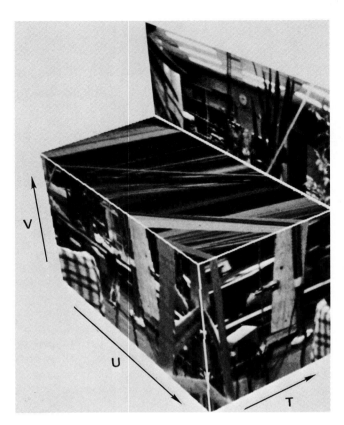

Figure 2. Spatiotemporal volume sliced along a scan line. The sliced image comprises successive scan lines through the volume. With orthogonal viewing, feature paths in the slice are straight lines.

have higher slope (they have less displacement with camera movement). Analysis of these slice images, termed epipolar-plane images (EPIs) after their composition from samples of a single epipolar plane, was the basis of our earliest sequence processing implementation.[3]

In that earlier work, complications arising with geometries other than this simple lateral-viewing one made it difficult to process images acquired with more general viewing attitudes. When the camera looks along its direction of motion, as indicated at V_3 in Figure 4, the corresponding EPIs resemble that of Figure 5. But if the camera changes its attitude as it moves, say from V_1 to V_3, EPIs such as that shown in Figure 6 result. These somewhat arbitrary patterns make a simple linear estimator inappropriate. Another problem of this slice-then-process analysis is that it leads to sliced results—individual planes of points sitting on the epipolar planes of Figure 4. Our results for such an analysis, shown in Figure 7, are as the night sky—a constellation of points, suggestive of but not very representative of the underlying three-dimensional structures in the scene. Scenes are composed of coherent 3D surfaces, not scatterings of points, and this coherence should be captured directly in the analysis. A

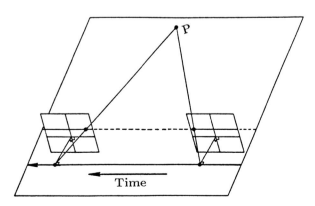

Figure 1. Camera at two imaging sites.

Figure 3. Four frames of image sequence.

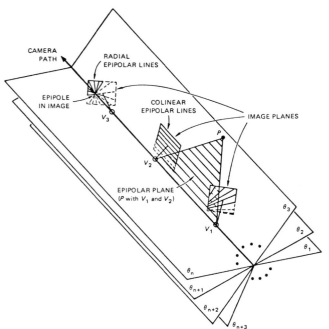

Figure 4. Geometry of camera in linear motion. Camera moves along a straight path, viewing in different directions; the linear path defines a pencil of planes crucial to the analysis. V1, V2, and V3 are camera principal points.

Frame Number (time)

Image Horizontal Position (X)

Figure 5. EPI image for forward viewing. Feature paths are hyperbolic.

Frame Number (time)

Image Horizontal Position (X)

Figure 6. EPI image from varying view direction. Feature paths are arbitrary curves.

final requirement of the analysis is that it should process the images sequentially as the vehicle moves, rather than requiring accumulation of a batch before beginning analysis (as was done in constructing the EPIs of Figures 2, 5, and 6). This is essential for a process that is to work in real time, as one of its principal goals is to provide timely spatial information for a vehicle in motion.

Figure 7. Color-coded depth estimates overlaying image.

As it turned out, all of these characteristics—general viewing attitudes, structural coherence in the results, and image-sequential processing—could be attained if a description of both the temporal (as before) and spatial coherence of the imagery were maintained as the vehicle moves. Achieving this necessitated constructing representations of the 3D evolution of the image data (spatial images changing over time). Where the earlier analysis was based on representing the evolution of individual features over time—forming linear paths in the spacetime EPIs—the new analysis would be based on representing the time evolution of whole spatial contours, and these would sweep out surfaces in spacetime. We searched for existing techniques for building surfaces from image sequences but, finding nothing suitable, designed one to meet the requirements. The resulting surface-building technique is the crucial element in the variety of applications discussed in the following sections.

Building surfaces from image sequences. This surface builder, called the Weaving Wall, operates over images as they are acquired, knitting together a connected representation of the spatial and temporal evolution of a sequence. The process acts as a loom during surface construction, with a wall of accumulators weaving the surface elements together—hence its name. Figure 8 shows stereo views of a surface constructed from a series of coarse images, some of which are shown in Figure 9. Notice the correspondence of the images with the resulting shape.

The principal approach to surface reconstruction from sensed data in the medical imaging field has been that of Artzy, Frieder, and Herman.[4] In that approach, surfaces are built one after another, with each constructed by a sequential

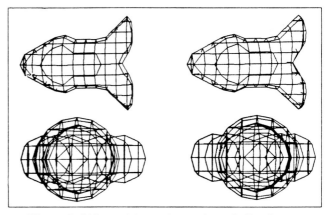

Figure 8. Side and front views of synthetic shape.

process that begins at a selected seed voxel and traverses the isocontour by a connected-component search—for this, all of the data must be available beforehand. Wyvill, McPheeters, and Wyvill[5] improved the search efficiency by characterizing local surface structure but maintained the technique's inherent sequential nature. The process developed in this research, on the other hand, operates incrementally in the third dimension, creating all surfaces simultaneously. The incremental operation was a necessity for the motion-tracking work and is one of the major distinctions of this process.

We determine surface facets by convolving the data with a 3D operator—a Laplacian of a Gaussian. A Laplacian is a second derivative operator. Its zeros (recall from early calculus) are at the extrema of the gradient, the places where the intensity is changing most rapidly. The smoothing Gaussian sets the resolution, and the Laplacian locates "edges" in the data. In 2D images, edges generally coincide with object boundaries (although they can also be texture boundaries or noise or filter artifacts), and the same applies to these 3D facets. By interpolation of the Laplacian values (or intensities, when these are appropriate), we can make surface definition at a considerably higher resolution than the sampling raster. The weaving approach grew out of a two-dimensional contour-finding algorithm.[6] In three dimensions, a binary relation (e.g., inside) is defined over the voxels; this gives rise to 2^8 or 256 voxel combinations in a $2 \times 2 \times 2$ subvolume. These combinations enumerate the various ways the surface (or surfaces) can pass through that subvolume (see Baker[7] for details). A surface-construction algorithm developed independently at GE Laboratories[8] shares many of the characteristics of the Weaving Wall's processing. But, although producing triangular facets for rendering, it does not create coherent surface models, does not distinguish surfaces, and can produce incorrect descriptions (Duerst[9] presents an example of their error, and Baker[7] explains the cause).

Computing on space-time surfaces. Space-time video imagery is considerably more involved than the images in

Figure 9. Figure 10 shows the first and last images obtained from a camera looking forward as it moves through a scene. For simplicity in analysis and display, we will use a reduced-resolution version of this sequence, the first and last images of which are shown in Figure 11. Figure 12 displays the spatiotemporal surfaces produced for the first 10 frames of this sequence. Note in particular the sock-shaped surface at the upper left of Figure 12. Its right is formed by the ladder, its top by the ceiling and lights, and its left by the cabinets against the left wall. These can be seen at the top left of Figures 10 and 11.

Surfaces from this data are unlikely to be intuitively meaningful: the projective sensing and the variable attitude and motion of the camera will make the 3D flow of imagery appear arbitrary and difficult to appreciate. When we know the camera's motion, however, we can use these surfaces to recover the 3D structure of features in the scene; if the motion is unknown, it can be determined using the surfaces and then be used in recovering the scene structure.*

---

*The latter is still an open research topic; this chapter deals only with the former.

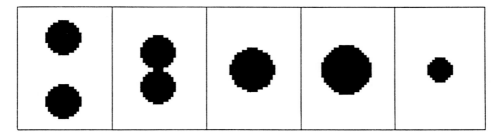

Figure 9. Profile images for synthetic shape.

Figure 10. Forward viewing motion: first and 128th images at full resolution.

Figure 11. Sequence: first and 128th images at reduced resolution.

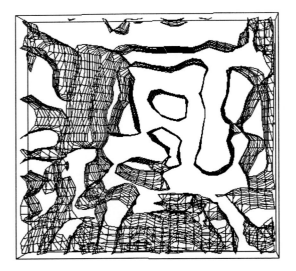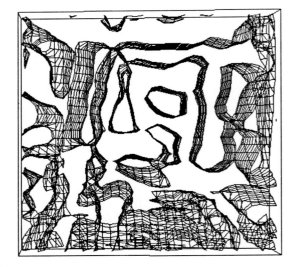

Figure 12. Spatiotemporal-surface representation of image evolution, first 10 frames.

We can apply the constraints derived from the known camera geometry for tracking features on the spatiotemporal surface. These constraints restrict feature movement. Feature trackers on the spatiotemporal surface of Figure 13 (the sock-shaped surface), for example, are restricted to lines as shown in Figure 14. In fact, this figure shows the intersection of the constraint planes of Figure 4 (the thetas) with the spatiotemporal surface of Figure 12. Figure 15 shows seven such constraint planes and their intersections with the spatiotemporal surfaces over the first 30 frames. These planes show exactly the contours we would detect in spatiotemporal intensity images such as depicted in Figure 5. As in Figure 5, the feature paths here are hyperbolic. Figure 16 shows the tracking process operating in the vicinity of the sock-shaped surface. The red wire framing indicates the

spatiotemporal surfaces; the yellow lines show the tracking of features; yellow circles encode the initiation of trackers, and magenta circles indicate a tracker termination. When we have made sufficient observations of some feature, we make an initial estimate of its position and code this in the display by a green circle. As further images are acquired, we update estimates of the feature's position and confidence interval using a least-squares sequential estimator (Baker and Bolles[10] describe the details of this tracking). The tracking described here is a sequential 3D counterpart to the batch detection of straight lines in the 2D data of the EPI in Figure 2 and is computationally quite efficient.

Each path marked in yellow along these surfaces represents a feature in the scene whose position and variance we

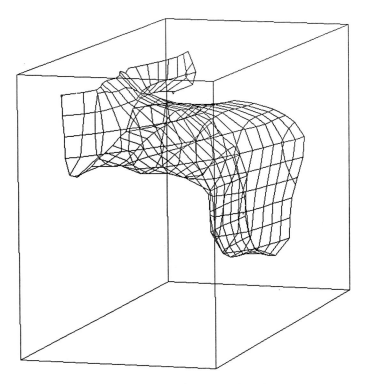

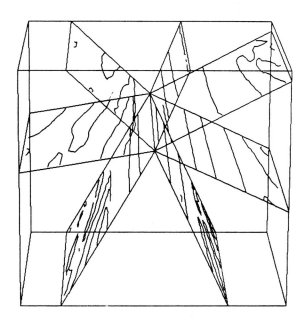

Figure 13. Individual spatiotemporal surface (top left of Figure 11).

Figure 14. Surface structured as epipolar planes.

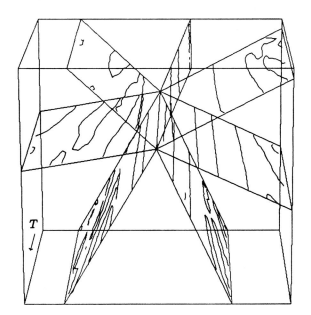

Figure 15. Intersection of seven epipolar planes (as shown in Figure 4) with the spatiotemporal surfaces (taken over 30 frames).

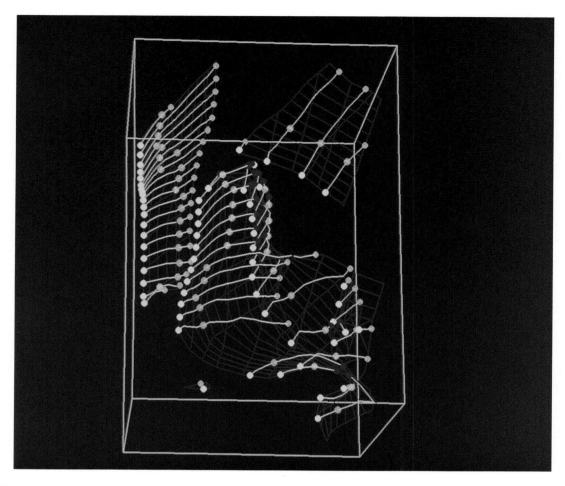

Figure 16. Feature tracking in operation. Spatiotemporal surface is colored red, trackers are yellow, blue circles show initiation of sequential filters, magenta circles are tracker terminations.

are estimating. Figure 17 shows the sequential updating of such a feature estimate at selected frames over the nine in which it is being tracked. The feature is first observed at T_0; at T_4, sufficient observations have been made to enable a reasonable estimate of its position (marked by the cross) and confidence interval (the large ellipse, only part of which fits within the display frame). These estimates are refined as we

observe the feature through frame T_8. The horizontal line at the bottom left of each frame is the camera path. The positional and confidence updating depicted here is occurring along all tracked paths (the yellow lines of Figure 16) simultaneously and, since the surface's 3D connectivity is represented explictly in the description (the red wire frame of Figure 16), this can show the evolution of contours in the

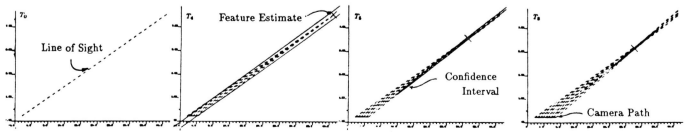

Figure 17. Sequential estimation for one feature through nine images. Vertical axis is radial distance from the camera path; horizontal axis is distance along the camera path from the origin (camera's position at T_0).

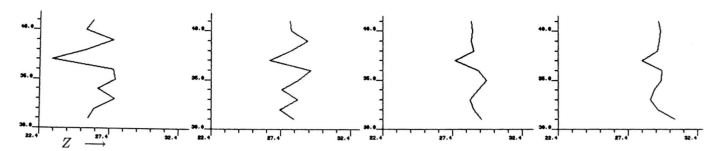

$Z \longrightarrow$

Figure 18. 3D contour evolving over time. Vertical axis is epipolar-plane number; horizontal axis is distance from the origin. The individual estimates and their implied contour refine as time progresses.

scene. Figure 18 shows this for 11 scene features adjacent on a spatiotemporal surface. The left frame shows the first estimate of the contour; the succeeding frames show how this estimate evolves as more images are acquired. Estimates of such contours are being formed and refined over the entire space as the sequence progresses. This means that as a robot enters some environment, its representation of the structures it sees will be initially quite coarse; as it continues moving through the scene, these representations will rapidly improve—within a dozen frames (fractions of a second)—until they accurately describe the scene's contours. We base the current representation of scene structure on these evolving contours. This is a partial solution: planned developments include combining these contours with free-space maps (obtained in our earlier work[3] to build descriptions of scene surfaces rather than contours.

The current implementation, running on a Symbolics 3600, processes the spatiotemporal surfaces at a 1-KHz voxel rate, with the associated intersecting, tracking, and estimation procedures bringing this down to about 150 Hz, 75 percent of which is consumed in the surface intersection (the surface intersection would not be required if a sensor of the appropriate geometry were available). Both the feature tracking and the surface construction computations are well suited to a multiple-instruction, multiple-data (or perhaps a single-instruction, multiple-data) parallel implementation. With these considerations, and the process's inherent precision and robustness, spatiotemporal-surface based epipolar-plane image analysis shows great promise for tasks in real-time autonomous navigation and mapping.

Perhaps the biggest innovations in this tracking work—innovations that may get missed in the geometric mire of the preceding—are the unified treatment of measures taken in space and time, the ability to visualize the data in this space, and to then observe the computations being performed on them. The unified treatment is responsible for the success of the theory, and the visualization explains the success of the implementation.

Images in scale space. An unresolved issue in the motion-sequence analysis work, and in computer vision in general, is

selecting a filter to be the basis for feature detection: in effect, selecting the scale of analysis. If the filter is large, then small features such as blades of grass will be missed. If the filter is small enough to detect grass or wires, it will surely miss large coarse shapes such as clouds. In researching this issue, some limited experimentation has been done with this surface-building process where the third dimension is Gaussian scale (σ). Building a surface of an image's evolution as its resolution varies vividly shows how Witkin's one-dimensional scale-space studies can extend to images.[11] Figure 19 shows a surface constructed at the 3D Laplacian zeros obtained by applying a battery of increasingly larger Gaussians to the image of Figure 20. This sequence comprises eight images, each differing in σ by 0.5 from the one before. Figure 21 shows the zero crossings at the smallest and largest Gaussians. Witkin suggested that an appropriate filter for describing some feature is one for which the feature's position is relatively stable. This stability can be measured by its velocity with respect to $\Delta\sigma$. If the feature moves a lot with a small change in σ, then it is sensitive to and not stable at that σ. The scale-space surface makes this stability explicit, and Figure 22 depicts this stability. It is a stereo display of the scale-space surface color coded by scale velocity over a spectrum from magenta (slow) through red (fast). The stable range of descriptions is in the blue and magenta regions.

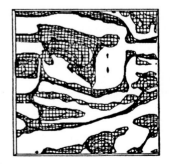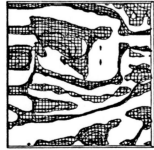

Figure 19. Surfaces defined by the evolution of the image as it blurs: the scale-space surface.

Figure 20. First image in scale-space hierarchy. Box on a table; shirt draped over chair in the foreground.

Developments are underway to enable the Weaving Wall to produce four-dimensional surfaces, where the first three are the spatial and temporal as before, and the fourth is Gaussian scale. The intention is to use the most stable representation of a feature as its instantiation to be tracked. The linear estimators will then use these more appropriate σ values in determining observation weights and in estimating the resulting spatial precisions. Tracking will occur at all scales at once, with the stable observations being the basis for scene reconstruction.

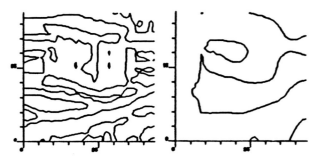

Figure 21. Finest and coarsest Laplacian zeros.

3D Modeling Applications

Designed to satisfy tracking needs where the third dimension is time, surface building has characteristics that make it useful for other applications in which coherent descriptions of nearly continuous 3D data are sought, regardless of what that third dimension represents. Most obvious among these is the construction of surface models from computed tomography (CT) and other medical scanning technologies (i.e., magnetic resonance imaging (MRI), ultrasound, optical-sectioning microscopy, and electron microscopy), and here the third dimension is spatial. The critical element required for applying the algorithm is that the 2D data evolve gradually over the third dimension; this allows that evolution to be tracked and represented as a set of evolving surfaces.

Medical data. Figure 23 shows the evolution of surfaces judged to be "bone" in a 70×30 window of a 52-image CT

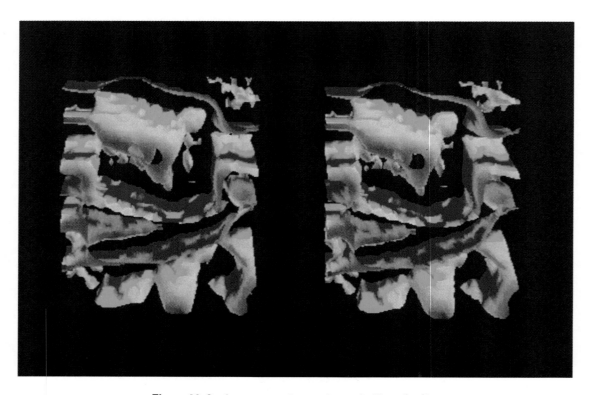

Figure 22. Scale-space surface color coded by velocity.

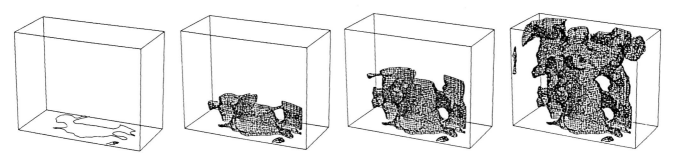

Figure 23. Evolution of spine model from a sequence of CT images.

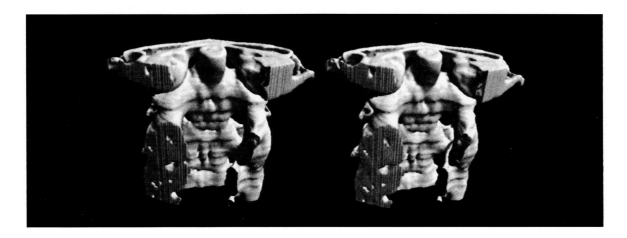

Figure 24. Stereo view of the spine.

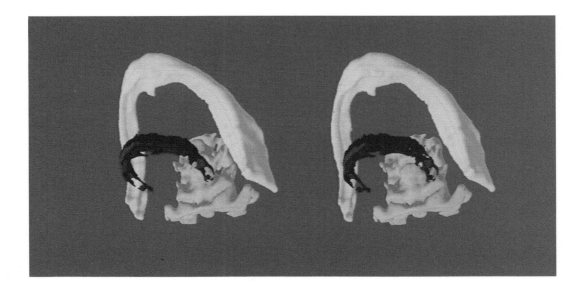

Figure 25. Jaw, upper teeth, and spine.

data set. This shows the incremental nature of the surface development. Figure 24 shows a stereo view of this spine alone, processed at a higher resolution. Figure 25 shows the three major surfaces (jaw, upper teeth, spine) of this data set, individually colored. Since these surfaces are distinct objects, we may manipulate them for whatever purposes we wish— for example, simulation of kinematics and dynamics, as shown in Figure 26, and structural analysis.

Although the surface-display aspects of this technique are quite worthwhile, we should bear in mind that the primary representation is a surface model, with all the connectivity appropriate for full model-based analysis (for example, symmetry mappings, elastic deformati on operations, and computations leading to finite-element analysis). These are geometric models built directly from the data. This is an important distinction to notice in this work. This is not an attempt

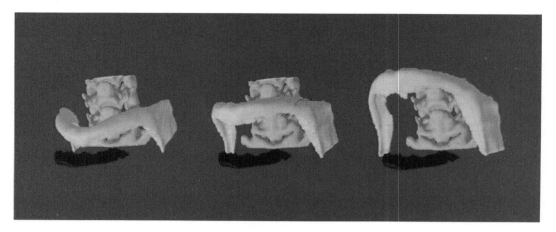

Figure 26. Rough simulation of jaw kinematics.

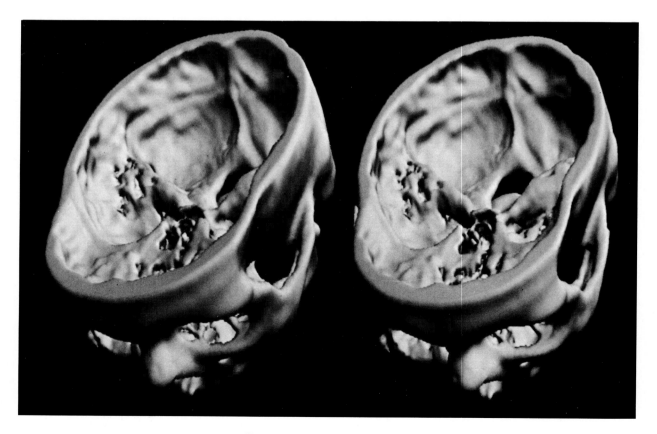

Figure 27. Stereo pair of cranium.

120

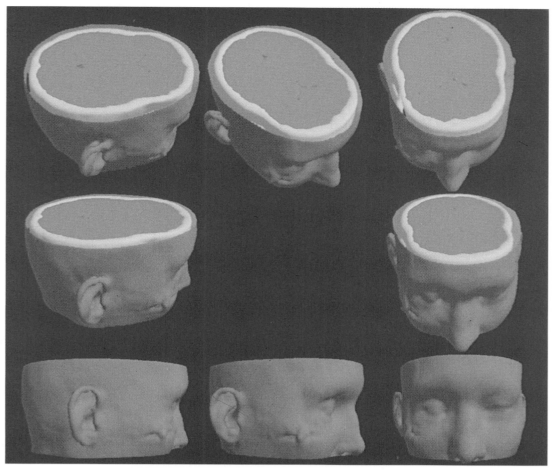

Figure 28. Skin, skull, and brain from CT data set.

to improve on rendering algorithms. What we present is a mechanism and a representation for specifying the geometric structure of tissue from tomographic data. This modeling allows analysis not possible with techniques whose sole purpose is visualization (a topic recently surveyed by Frenkel)[12]. We demonstrate this distinction next.

Figure 27 shows a stereo pair of the cranium from another CT data set, this one of 45 slices and each about 250 pixels square. Figure 28 shows several views of the skin, skull, and brain in place. Figure 29 shows a simulation of a surgical procedure to excise and rotate the nose (rarely a clinically indicated procedure), and Figure 30 displays frames from an interactive operation to cut the flesh and remove it from the skull. In the reverse of this operation, plastic surgeons could visualize the cosmetic results from a reconstruction of the underlying tissue.

Ultrasound data are similarly tomographic, and the Bioengineering Research Laboratory at SRI has been a leader in developing this clinical tool. Figure 31 shows a reconstruction of the bones in a hand from a ten-image ultrasound data set.

We processed the preceding medical data by selecting surfaces on the basis of their sampling measures. This is adequate for some sensing modalities, but not for MRI. Figure 32 shows a reconstruction of a hand from a 125×250 window of a 35-image MRI data set. Here, the surface is defined by the zeros of a Laplacian, as in the motion-tracking work. Because the hand was secured between two foam pads, it suffered some distortion and crinkling. Other blemishes are artifacts of the filter size and the difficulty in distinguishing tissue types in these data. Proper segmentation of MRI data is an open research problem.

Biophysics data. Coupling optical microscopy with image-enhancement techniques, Agard[13] and Sedat and their colleagues at the University of California at San Francisco have investigated cell 3D structure. Their data-collection process—optical-sectioning digital microscopy—enables them to form tomographic images through cell specimens. Figure 33 (top) shows five such images. In a preliminary collaborative study, we used the Weaving Wall to reconstruct the 3D form of chromosomes from their data. Figure

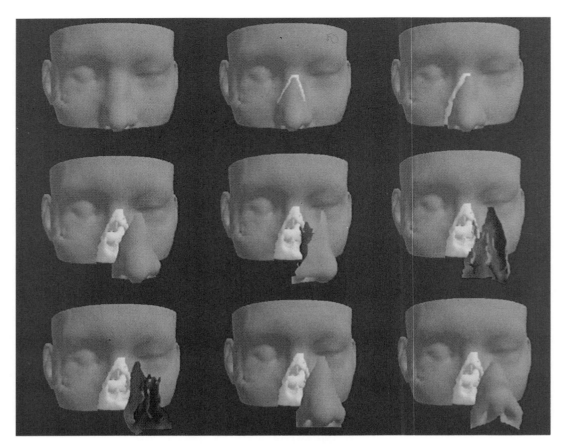

Figure 29. Simulation of nose excision.

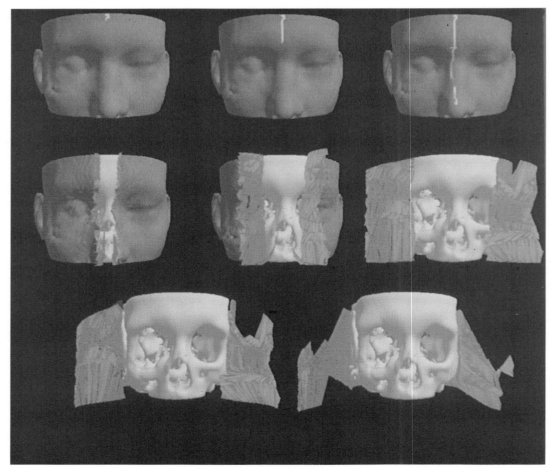

Figure 30. Simulation of skin peeling.

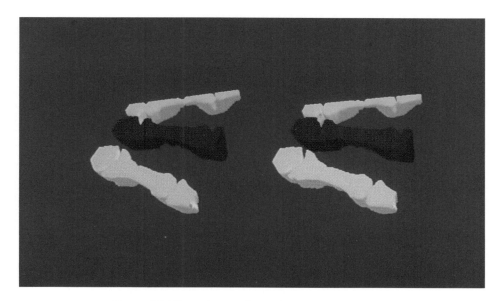

Figure 31. Finger bones from ultrasound data set.

Figure 32. Hand from MRI data set. Surface positioned at Laplacian zeros.

33 (left) shows Drosophila melanogaster chromosomes at prophase, before cell division. Notice the coiling. Figure 33 (right) shows chromosomes at early anaphase while undergoing mitotic division. Figure 34 displays the surfaces color coded by the DNA's marker absorption. Although this is a rough and preliminary display, further development should enable labeling of the chromosomes' gene structure. Tissue-manipulation facilities, such as those demonstrated in Figures 29 and 30, will also be available for structural investigation in molecular biology to cut, unravel, and other-wise manipulate the descriptions. Plans for this development are underway.

Modeling material fracture. Researchers in SRI's Metallurgy and Fracture Mechanics Laboratory study the tensile characteristics and behavior of materials under stress and during fracture. One of their principal observation tools, high-speed photography, records over the period of a few microseconds dozens of images showing the activity on the surface of some sample as it ruptures. Again, these can be

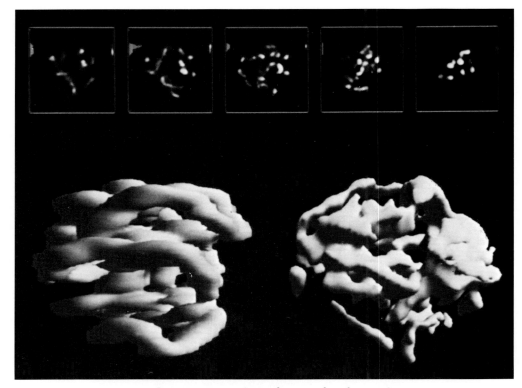

Figure 33. Chromosomes at prophase and early anaphase.

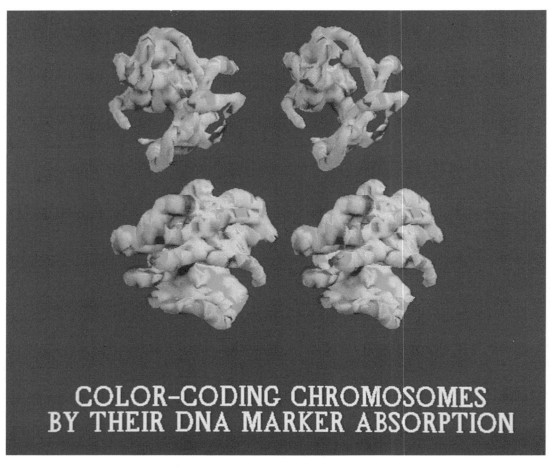

Figure 34. Chromosomes color coded by DNA marker absorption.

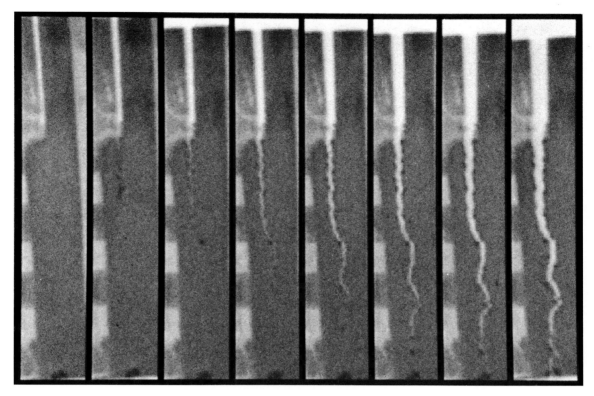

Figure 35. Eight frames of metal fracture.

viewed as time-varying evolutions of 2D patterns, and we can construct surface descriptions of this 3D action. Figure 35 shows a few frames of a growing crack, with Figure 36 showing a surface representing this as a 3D event.* The intention in this area includes providing these researchers with facility for examining and making measurements on this higher-dimension depiction of their data and allowing them editing and manipulation capabilities as employed and to be employed in the medical applications. Future developments in this research should allow the display and analysis of 4D surfaces produced by the interior 3D fracture patterns as they develop during rupture. This latter data will come from 3D plotting of the resulting two halves, followed by time inversion of the fracture process—bringing the two deformed halves back together.

Summary

Developing the Weaving Wall surface-building process was a necessity for further progress in sequence analysis. The structures it produces provide for sequential tracking of features over the full range of possible camera attitudes.

---

*The imaging scatters the photographs in a circular pattern over a sheet of film. The subsequent digitization and registration is close but, as can be seen, not perfectly correct.

These representations also seem to be most appropriate for several other problems that lie ahead, including solving for the camera while in motion and enabling vehicle motion not along a linear path. This unified treatment of the spatial and temporal dimensions and explicit use of its structure may prove to be a significant development for robotic vision. More generally, we can use the surface representation in any application where we desire a description of the evolution of a 2D pattern varying gradually in a third dimension—be that dimension time, space, viewing position, resolution, or any other. As the simulated surgical procedures have indicated, the value of the representations does not end with their visualization. With applications in medical and biomedical imaging and other areas, this surface building should be a powerful tool for many applications in image processing and higher-dimensional data analysis.

Acknowledgments

David Marimont, now with Xerox PARC, has been crucial in this development, providing insights for both the geometry and mathematics of the tracking process, the design of the surface builder, and the approach taken to higher-dimension convolution. The early motion research was instigated by and done in collaboration with Bob Bolles. Lynn Quam provided excellent image manipulation and graphics tools, and, with Alex Pentland, was very helpful in

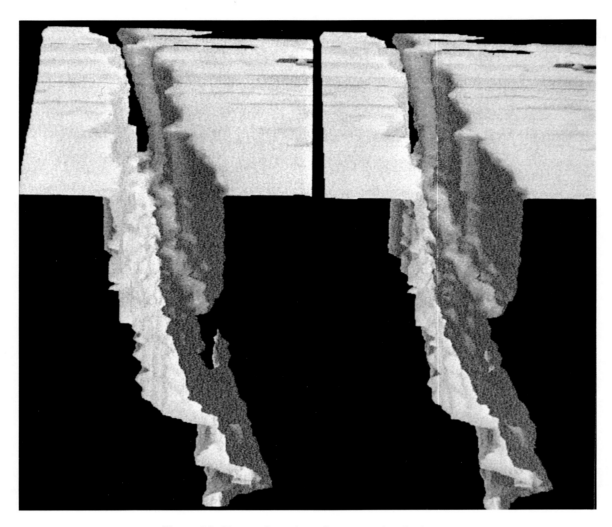

Figure 36. Stereo view of crack progressing in time.

producing the rendered surface displays. The medical CT data are courtesy of Cemax Corporation, Santa Clara, California, and Philips Medical Systems, Shelton, Connecticut; the ultrasound data were courtesy of Philip Green of SRI's Bioengineering Research Laboratory (NIH research grant CA4 2681); the MRI data set was provided by John Drace of Stanford University and the Palo Alto Veterans Administration Medical Center; the electron-microscopy data were supplied by David Agard and John Sedat of the Department of Biochemistry and Biophysics at the University of California, San Francisco; and the fracture data were courtesy of Jacques Giovanola of SRI's Metallurgy and Fracture Mechanics Laboratory (research contract AFOSR/F49620-86-K-0010). This research has been supported by DARPA Contracts MDA 903-86-C-0084 and DACA 76-85-C-0004 and an internal grant from SRI.

References

1. S.T. Barnard, "Stochastic Stereo Matching Over *Int'l. J. Computer Vision,* Vol. 3, No. 1, 1989, pp. 17-32.

2. J. Boyer, C. Jacobus, and F. Pont, "Autonomous Vehicle Guidance Using Laser Range Imagery," *Proc. SPIE,* Vol. 852, 1987, pp. 34-43.

3. R.C. Bolles, H.H. Baker, and D.H. Marimont, "Epipolar-Plane Image Analysis: An Approach to Determining Structure from Motion," *Int'l. J. Computer Vision,* Vol. 1, No. 1, 1987, pp. 7-55.

4. E. Artzy, G. Frieder, and G. T. Herman, "The Theory, Design, Implementation, and Evaluation of a Three-Dimensional Surface Detection Algorithm," *Computer Graphics and Image Processing,* Vol. 15, 1981, pp. 1-24.

5. G. Wyvill, C. McPheeters, and B. Wyvill, "Data Structure for Soft Objects," *Visual Computer,* Vol. 2, 1986, pp. 227-234.

6. D.H. Marimont, "Segmentation in Acronym," *Proc. DARPA Image Understanding Workshop,* Science Applications International Corporation, McLean, Va., 1982, pp. 223-229.

7. H.H. Baker, "Building Surfaces of Evolution: The Weaving Wall," *Int'l. J. Computer Vision,* Vol. 3, No. 1, 1989, pp. 51-72.

8. W.E. Lorensen and H.E. Cline, "Marching Cubes: A High Resolution 3D Surface Construction Algorithm," *Computer Graphics,* Vol. 21, No. 4, 1987, pp. 163-168.

9. M.J. Duerst, "Additional Reference to 'Marching Cubes,'" *Computer Graphics,* Vol. 22, No. 2, 1988, pp. 72-73.

10. H.H. Baker and R.C. Bolles, "Generalizing Epipolar-Plane Image Analysis on the Spatiotemporal Surface," *Int'l. J. Computer Vision,* Vol. 3, No. 1, 1989, pp. 33-50.

11. A.P. Witkin, "Scale Space Filtering," *Proc. Eighth Intl. Conf. Artificial Intelligence,* 1983, pp. 1019-1021.

12. K.A. Frenkel, "Volume Rendering," *Comm. ACM,* Vol. 32, No. 4, 1989, pp. 426-435.

13. D.A. Agard, "Optical Sectioning Microscopy: Cellular Architecture in Three Dimensions," *Ann. Rev. Biophysics Bioengineering,* Vol. 13, 1984, pp. 191-219.

Harlyn Baker is a senior computer scientist in the Artificial Intelligence Center at SRI International in Menlo Park, California, and has been working in computer vision for the past 18 years. He received his BS in computer science from the University of Western Ontario, M. Phil. in machine intelligence from Edinburgh University, and PhD in computer science from the University of Illinois at Urbana-Champaign. From 1974 through 1976 he was a research associate at Edinburgh. From 1978 through 1983 he was a research assistant and then research associate at Stanford and since 1984 has been at SRI. He is a member of the IEEE, committee member of ISPRS Commission II, an associate editor for *Image and Vision Computing,* and a contributing editor to *Robotics Review.*

Section 3: Applications of Scientific Visualization

In this section, we have a selection of papers on applications. Diversity and an overall good sampling were the bases of our selection. The areas that we have represented are quite widespread and include: combution science, medicine, meteorology, semiconductor devices, computer science, and the geosciences.

The first paper, "Acquisition and Representation of Two- and Three-Dimension Data from Turbulent Flows and Flames," by Marshall Long, Kevin Lyon, and Joseph Lam deals somewhat separately with the two aspects of data acquisition and data representation. The data acquisition techniques are new and interesting. Two dimensional data sets obtained on a slice through the flow can be displayed by an image where intensity or color is varying with the quantity that has been measured, or surface contour methods can be used.

The next paper by Henry Fuchs, Marc Levoy, and Stephen Pizer describes work in progress at the University of North Carolina. The paper surveys their research activities in the area of interactive visualization of 3D medical data. In conjunction with other researchers form radiology and biochemistry, they are working on two approaches to rendering 3D volumetric data. The first is what is called surface based techniques and requires the polygonal approximation to a constant contour surface. Once the contour surface is known, present workstations will have no problem with the interactive display of the surface. One drawback to the particular approach described here is that user assistance is required for getting the contours and for providing bifurcation information during the 3D assembly stage. The second area of 3D visualization that is described is volume visualization. Here the idea is to take the entire cubical array of voxel data and to produce a single 2D image. This approach to visualizing 3D medical data was pioneered at PIXAR a few years ago. Most techniques are based upon some type of assignment of opacity to each voxel and then casting rays from the view point through the cube of data and integrating along the rays. While this type of visualization of 3D medical data shows great promise, there are still several drawbacks: It is compute-intensive and this severely limits interaction and interaction is pretty much mandatory for clinical use. A major research goal is to achieve interactive volume rendering; i.e., rates of say 10 to 30 frames per second.

The next paper "Visualization of Large Data Sets in the Earth Sciences" by Bill Hibbard and David Santek describes the functionality of the McIDAS system. This is an acronym for Man Computer Interactive Data Access System. As with several of the application papers, here we have three-dimensional data over a cuberille grid. What is different here is that at each 3D position, there are both scalar values and vector values. For example, a meteorologist may want to display both temperature and wind vector fields in order to learn something about their interplay. Through a very judicious choice of photographs in the paper, we can see the variety of techniques they have used to display this type of three-dimensional data. Two techniques are used for displaying scalar values: contour surfaces and transparent opacity clouds. The first is rendered in traditional computer graphics style as an opaque object with light shinning on it. A transparent opacity cloud can be used to display clouds or other density fields. 3D vector fields are displayed as little arrows of one type or another. Of course, the number of these arrows has to be rather small or the picture is a real mess. At the time the paper was written, the authors were in the process of porting their software to a Stellar (Stardent). The goal here is to get animation and interaction.

The paper by Norman Kluksdahl, Alfred Kriman, and David Ferry describes their use of visualization and animation of simulation data to augment their understanding of the behavior of quantum electron transport in semiconductors. Although the paper is quite technical, the visualization processes employed give a very graphic portrayal of the electron tunneling behavior on the quantum mechanical model and therefore of the underlying real semiconductor device. In a sense, some preprocessing of the simulation data occurs by employing the so called Wigner function. This formulation reduces the multidimensional phase space solution of these systems to one that involves axes of position, momentum, and probability amplitudes of the electron Gaussian wave packets. These three axes are readily graphed by using colored contours with hidden surface elimination. By animating a series of images in the time sequenced simulation, the authors maintain that the real semiconductor device characteristics, such as the observed collective oscillations in the resonant tunneling diode, can be better understood.

The next paper by Mark Seager, Nancy Werner, and Mary Zosel of Lawrence Livermore National Laboratory and Robert Strout of Supercomputer Systems is somewhat different than the other application papers. The goal is to provide visual information to a programmer to aid in the design and debugging of parallel programs. Two portions, "timeline" and "stategroup," of their Graphical Multiprocessing Analysis Tool (GMAT) system are described. In order to appreciate the potential benefits of visual information in this context, it helps to be motivated by some examples. Near the end of the paper in Section 4, there are three example sessions that help in this direction.

The paper by Victor Pereyra and J. A. Rial, "Visualizing Wave Phenomena with Seismic Rays," describes some of their techniques for visualizing data from the geosciences. They use conventional techniques from graphics to show the results of tracking the path of a wave that is generated at the surface and travels down through several layers and is eventually reflected back to the surface. Surface boundaries between the layers are modeled with parametric Coons patches. This is an improvement over previous methods in that folds and other quite natural formations can be modeled.

The final paper of this chapter is by Neale Hirsch of Cray Research and Bruce Brown of BYU. One thing this paper and its companion video illustrate is that the graphics do not have to be fancy or spectacular in order to be useful. The clever use of graphics and geometry can reveal interesting and useful insights into multifaceted phenomena as it does for Hirsch and Brown in their analysis of computer performance measurements. While the particular experiment they discuss in quite interesting, it is not the most important message for those interested in scientific visualization. The way they analyzed the results of their experiment using Principle Component multigrafs is what is of interest.

Reprinted from *Computer*, August 1989, pages 39-45. Copyright
© 1989 by The Institute of Electrical and Electronics Engineers,
Inc. All rights reserved.

Acquisition and Representation of 2D and 3D Data from Turbulent Flows and Flames

Marshall B. Long, Kevin Lyons, and Joseph K. Lam, Yale University

Introduction

Although turbulence has been studied for over 100 years, prediction of many important quantities in turbulent flows is still not possible, leaving turbulence an unsolved problem of classical mechanics. From an engineering standpoint as well, turbulent flows and flames are extremely important. Most naturally occurring flows are turbulent, as are flames in industrial combustors, automobile engines, jet engines, and rockets. A better understanding of this phenomenon would directly impact a broad range of practical devices and aid in the design of more efficient engines, vehicles with reduced drag, and combustors with lower pollution levels.

Part of the difficulty of the turbulence problem lies in the vast amount of information that must be specified. For example, to fully characterize a turbulent flame would require measurements of temperature, pressure, density, concentrations of all species, and all three components of the velocity vector at each point within a volume. Because of the great diversity of length scales present in a turbulent flow, even a relatively simple turbulent flame could require measurements at more than 10^7 points. At each point, all of the quantities mentioned would have to be recorded as functions of time with characteristic time scales on the order of 10 microseconds.

Clearly, the problem is very complex, and the prospect of determining flow quantities with the measure of detail described above remains distant. Significant progress has been made, however, both theoretically and experimentally. We will present laser light-scattering techniques for making two- and three-dimensional measurements in turbulent flows and

flames, along with examples of methods used to represent the large quantities of data obtained. While our work has focused on developing new diagnostic techniques, the methods of data representation and display are topics of immediate importance to scientists hoping to understand the tremendous amount of information their measurements provide. We hope this article will challenge those working in computer processing and graphics by making them more aware of the needs of todays flow and combustion diagnostics community.

Laser Diagnostic Measurement Techniques

In the last decade significant advances in lasers and detector technology, coupled with the advent of laboratory computers to record the data, have prompted development of techniques that have provided a wealth of new data. Rather than relying on disruptive physical probes to make measurements, researchers are making increasing use of the fact that light scattered from the molecules in a flow can reveal a great deal of information. The ability of laser techniques to make nonintrusive, in situ, time-resolved measurements of molecular species, temperatures, velocities, pressures, and densities has been demonstrated.

Figure 1 shows an experimental configuration typical of those used to make two-dimensional measurements in a turbulent flow or flame.[1] The flow used in the examples presented here emerges from a simple round nozzle. Gas issues from the nozzle exit and mixes (and, in some cases, reacts) with the ambient air. To study the turbulent mixing of the gases, a laser beam is formed into a thin sheet that

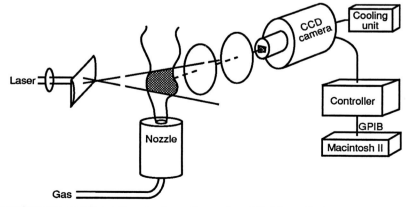

Figure 1. An experimental configuration for two-dimensional light-scattering measurements in turbulent flows and flames. A laser beam is formed into a thin sheet to illuminate the flow. Scattered light is collected and imaged onto a CCD (charge-coupled-device) array detector. The images stored in the computer contain information on temperature, density, or species, depending on the scattering mechanism used.

EH0307-9/90/0000/0132$01.00 © 1989 IEEE

intersects the flow centerline slightly downstream of the nozzle exit. A very small fraction of the laser light is scattered by the flow. This scattered light is collected normal to the illumination sheet by a lens, and an optical filter selects a specific range of wavelengths. The selected wavelength is imaged onto a computer-controlled digital camera, and the intensity distribution is recorded. The particular quantity deduced from the scattered light depends on the specific gases present, the laser power and wavelength, and the detected wavelength. A number of light-scattering mechanisms can be used in this way, including Rayleigh, Lorenz-Mie, fluorescence, and Raman scattering. A recent review article summarized the specifics of these techniques.[2]

Figure 2 shows an example of the data obtained from this type of experiment. In this case the flow is a nonreacting Freon jet mixing with the ambient air. The measurement shows the distribution of Freon within the thin illumination sheet. In the figure a false-color representation is used, with different colors representing different Freon concentrations (that is, mole fractions). Because the dynamic range of the measurement is too great to be easily reproduced by a continuous change in intensity or color, a discontinuous sequence of hues with varying degrees of saturation is used. The color bar shows the mapping of colors to gas concentrations.

As mentioned, many quantities are required to fully characterize a turbulent flame, and current experimental techniques cannot provide them all simultaneously. Some simultaneous measurements can be made, however, by using multiple detectors, with each detector measuring a different quantity by monitoring a different light-scattering mechanism.[3] Figure 3 shows two pairs of concentration and temperature distributions from a turbulent nonpremixed methane-hydrogen flame. The lower part of the figure shows the concentration of methane as determined from Raman scattering, and the upper part shows the corresponding

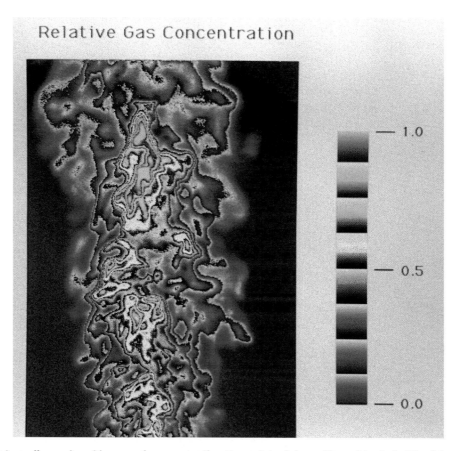

Figure 2. A two-dimensional image of a nonreacting Freon jet mixing with ambient air. The false-color map represents the different Freon concentrations. A discontinuous sequence of hues of varying saturation is used, as the dynamic range of the measurement exceeds the capabilities of easy reproduction by continuous-color variations.

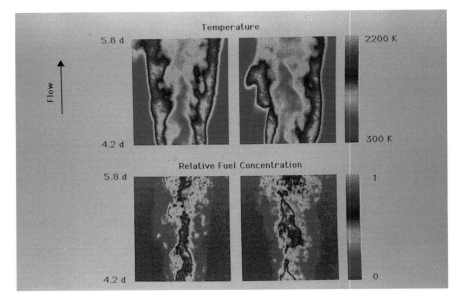

Figure 3. Two pairs of simultaneous temperature and concentration measurements in a turbulent methane-hydrogen flame. The lower part of the figure shows the methane concentration as determined from Raman scattering, while the upper portion shows the corresponding instantaneous temperature distributions as determined from Rayleigh scattering.

temperature distributions as determined by Rayleigh scattering. The correspondence between the two quantities can be seen by noting that regions of high fuel-gas concentration (shown in yellow on the bottom part of the figure) correspond to areas of lower temperature (blue regions in the upper part of the figure). The information is also complementary, with the temperature distribution giving a better indication of the location of the hot flame zone.

Turbulence by its nature is a three-dimensional phenomenon, so that with data in only two dimensions, some ambiguities remain. For example, Figure 4 shows another visualization of the gas concentration distribution from a turbulent jet. Now, however, the measurement sheet has been oriented normal to the jet axis, intersecting it six nozzle diameters downstream. It is clear from Figure 4 that even though the flow emerges from a round nozzle, it quickly

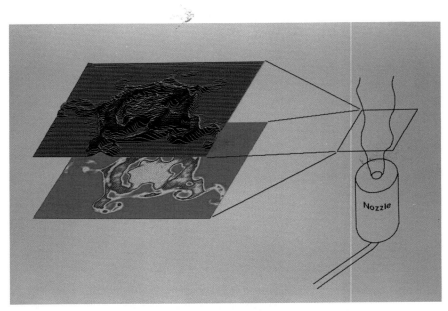

Figure 4. Alternative ways of representing the same two-dimensional gas concentration measurement in a turbulent nonreacting flow. The nozzle gas concentration was measured by imaging Lorenz-Mie scattering in a plane oriented normal to the axis of an axisymmetric jet of Reynolds number 4160. The illumination sheet intersected the centerline six nozzle diameters downstream, where the flow has become three dimensional.

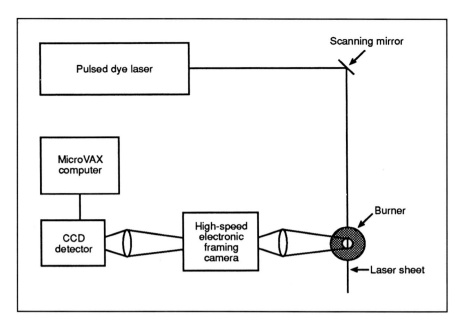

Figure 5. An experimental arrangement used for the time-resolved three-dimensional measurement of a scalar in a gas jet. A laser sheet is swept rapidly through the flow by a rotating mirror. Images of parallel vertical slices are produced on the phosphor screen of a high-speed electronic framing camera. The image is then recorded by a two-dimensional CCD (charge-coupled-device) array. The series of imaged planes constitutes a three-dimensional recording of the flow.

loses its axial symmetry, thereby becoming three dimensional. Depending on the orientation of the sheet, very different features of the flow become evident, and thus a single slice through the flow cannot contain all of the information required to fully describe the structures.

Progress has been made in developing techniques capable of providing three-dimensional flow measurements.[4-6] One way to obtain three-dimensional information from a flow is to simply record a large number of two-dimensional measurements from many closely spaced parallel sheets. The

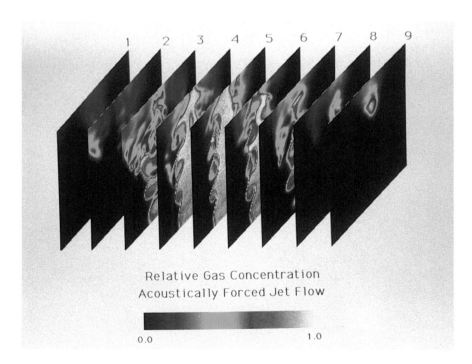

Figure 6. A series of flow planes in an acoustically forced jet, represented by false-color-mapped concentration contours. The concentration is determined from the intensity of Lorenz-Mie scattering. The region imaged is 1.8 centimeters in the streamwise direction and centered 2.4 cm downstream from a nozzle 0.3 cm in diameter. The frames correspond to planes spaced 0.8 millimeter apart.

most stringent requirement for this measurement is that data from all of the two-dimensional sheets must be recorded before the flow changes significantly. The detection system must have a high framing rate (that is, the rate at which images can be acquired) to record as many two-dimensional sheets as possible during this time. In addition, a laser source is desired that can provide sufficient energy during the measurement time to enable molecular light-scattering processes to be detected.

Figure 5 shows an experimental arrangement that has been used for making essentially instantaneous three-dimensional measurements in nonreacting and reacting flows.[5] A laser illumination sheet is swept rapidly through the flow, and the scattered light from the scanning sheet is recorded by a high-speed electronic framing camera capable of recording 10 to 20 images at framing rates up to 2×10^7 frames per second. The framing camera produces a series of images on a phosphor screen that correspond to different sheet locations. This intensity distribution can then be measured electronically with a CCD (charge-coupled-device) detector. In recent work[6] we showed that it is possible to get truly instantaneous (less than 1 microsecond) gas concentration measurements in turbulent jets and flames.

Figure 6 shows a false-color representation of a series of nozzle gas concentration distributions corresponding to different planes intersecting a flow. The contour characteristics are seen to change as the sheet intersects different locations in the flow. Although the concentration distributions shown in Figure 6 give a complete representation of the three-dimensional data, they do not provide much insight into the topology of the flow structures.

The approach we have used is to represent constant-concentration surfaces, which are analogous to lines of constant concentration in a two-dimensional plot. Figure 7 shows a constant gas concentration surface obtained from a set of

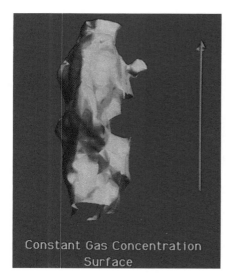

Constant Gas Concentration Surface

Figure 7. Instantaneous constant fuel-gas concentration surface in a turbulent Bunsen-burner flame. The surface corresponds to a concentration of 64 percent of the maximum in this region and has been generated from experimental data.   The flame was a stoichiometric methane-air mixture seeded with biacetyl vapor as a fluorescent marker, with a jet velocity of 19.5 meters per second. The imaged region is $2 \times 1 \times 0.5$ nozzle diameters (d = 6 millimeters) in size, centered five diameters downstream from the burner. The flow direction is from bottom to top.

slices similar to those shown in Figure 6. The data in the figure represent a constant fuel concentration surface in a turbulent premixed flame. Different concentration values would provide different surfaces, with higher concentration contours fitting inside lower ones. Figure 8 shows two different contours obtained from a single three-dimensional data set. Normally, these would lie one inside the other, but,

Figure 8. Constant-concentration surfaces in a photoacoustically perturbed Freon-air jet measured by Rayleigh scattering. The left- and right-hand structures correspond to Freon concentrations of 27 percent and 18 percent, respectively. The three-dimensional effect is heightened by the shadows cast.

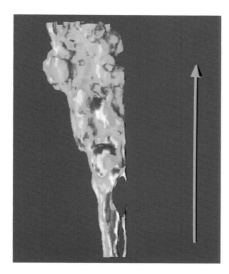

Figure 9. A three-dimensional isoconcentration surface reconstructed from a measurement of Mie scattering from a transitional aerosol-seeded jet of air. The surface corresponds to a region 6.8 × 2.1 × 0.7 nozzle diameters (*d* = 2 millimeters) in size, centered 10 diameters downstream from the orifice. The exit velocity of the jet was 8 meters per second. In this representation each point on the surface is color coded according to the magnitude of the concentration gradient vector.

for display, the higher contour value (left) has been removed from inside the lower (right) and light has been cast upon an imaginary plane to heighten the three-dimensional effect.

Figure 9 shows another means of relaying more of the three-dimensional information recorded in a single measurement. The figure shows a constant-concentration surface again, but now the color at each point on the surface has been coded by the magnitude of the concentration gradient vector at that location. The representation of the species data obtained in these measurements as constant-concentration surfaces coincides quite well with one of the current models of turbulent combustion.[7] According to the flame sheet model of combustion, chemical reactions in flames occur in thin sheets located in regions that have the proper mixture of fuel and oxidizer. In this model the data shown in Figure 9 correspond to the flame sheet in a turbulent flame. The availability of three-dimensional data allows the topology of the flame structures to be investigated.

The most difficult aspect of obtaining instantaneous three-dimensional data is the need for the measurement to be made when the flow is essentially stationary. To relax this constraint, measurements can be performed in forced flows. By causing the flow to evolve in a repeatable fashion, the constraint of having to make very rapid measurements is replaced with the need to make the measurement at the right phase of the repeatable flow.[4] Since the flow is repeatable, many instantaneous shots can be accumulated to integrate weak signals. Sequential measurements of several different quantities such as temperature, species, and velocity are also possible.

Another advantage of using forced flows is realized by varying the relative phase of the perturbation and the measurement. In this way the evolution of the three-dimensional structures can be recorded. It is then possible to construct an animated sequence to visualize the development of the three-dimensional surfaces of constant concentration. Figure 10 shows a sequence of surfaces obtained at different phase delays relative to an acoustic perturbation. The convection and evolution of the structures are evident.

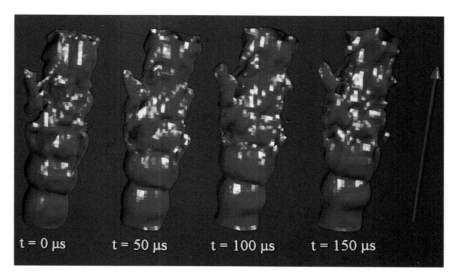

Figure 10. Three-dimensional time evolution of an acoustically forced jet. Shown are instantaneous three-dimensional surfaces obtained by delaying the phase of the measurement relative to the acoustic forcing. The phase is varied at 50-microsecond intervals to produce a "movie" sequence. The flow is from bottom to top at a velocity of 8 meters per second. The nozzle diameter is 3 millimeters.

Data Representation Issues

The preceding section gave a sampling of the type of experimental flow data currently available. For most quantitative research in this area, acquisition and display of single images are not sufficient. Ideally, many measurements are made for a given set of flow conditions, and statistical quantities of interest are calculated from the data. Therefore, the amount of data to be stored, analyzed, and displayed is large; effective and efficient means of displaying the data are needed.

The preceding figures showed several display approaches. However, none of these display techniques emerges as the single best approach for visualizing the data. In some cases the physics of the problem may dictate the type of display that most clearly illustrates the phenomenon under study. The data display techniques presented here by no means represent a complete survey of the methods proposed and used to examine flow data.[8] Other possibilities include a flexible scheme that can represent the concentration data as semitransparent clouds.[9] Another attractive approach, though computationally intensive and rather expensive, is to construct a hologram from this measured data.[10]

The constant-property surfaces presented here were generated using a modified version of the commercially available Movie.BYU graphics program. The hidden-surface calculations were performed on a MicroVAX II, and data display was done on a Macintosh II. Because of the complexity of surface rendering and the modest computational power used, calculation of some images took several hours. The surfaces are represented by a polygon mesh, and because of their complexity, many polygons are needed to fully match the resolution of the measurement. With our current hardware-software configuration, the number of polygons that can be represented is limited to approximately 8,000, whereas more than 30,000 polygons would be needed to fully display the resolution of our best measurements.

Another practical issue in displaying the data is cost. Using color provides an important extra dimension in displaying the complex data sets obtained. Currently, however, the cost of publishing two-color plates in some scientific journals represents more than half the cost of the laboratory computer that controls the experiment, stores the data, and displays the results. Therefore, the use of color figures (which can best present the results) might be hard to justify.

Even static color figures are far from the ultimate means of understanding the data. Because of the complexity of some constant-property surfaces, a good object hypothesis is difficult to obtain from a single view. Dynamic projection of three-dimensional data helps considerably. In our laboratory we calculate a sequence of single frames of different object orientations and subsequently animate the precalculated sequence. This animation capability is also extremely useful for time development data like that shown in Figure 10. Ideally, of course, these calculations and the display would be done in real time. Even with the rapid advances in computers, the cost of systems capable of such performance is significant.

Conclusion

Acquiring and displaying data from turbulent flows and flames presents a number of challenges for representing the information we can now obtain experimentally. While the emphasis here has been on experimental data, nearly identical problems face those working in computational fluid dynamics and combustion. Storage, analysis, and display of data represent a significant bottleneck. With the wealth of new data available from both experimental and computational work, there is hope that a more satisfactory means of visualizing data may lead to a significant new understanding of these very complex systems.

Acknowledgments

We gratefully acknowledge partial support of this research by the Air Force Office of Scientific Research (grant AFOSR-88-0100) and the National Science Foundation (grant MSM 83-51077).

References

1. M.B. Long, B.F. Webber, and R.K. Chang, "Instantaneous Two-Dimensional Concentration Measurements in a Jet Flow by Mie Scattering," *Applied Physics Letters,* Vol. 34, No. 1, 1979, pp. 22-24.

2. R.K. Hanson, "Combustion Diagnostics: Planar Imaging Techniques," *Proc. 21st Intl. Symp. Combustion,* The Combustion Institute, Pittsburgh, Penn., 1986, pp. 1,677-1,699.

3. M.B. Long, P.S. Levin, and D.C. Fourguette, "Simultaneous Two-Dimensional Mapping of Species Concentration and Temperature in Turbulent Flames," *Optics Letters,* Vol. 10, No. 6, 1985, pp. 267-269.

4. B. Yip, D.C. Fourguette, and M.B. Long, "Three-Dimensional Gas Concentration and Gradient Measurements in a Photo-Acoustically Perturbed Jet," *Applied Optics,* Vol. 25, No. 21, 1986, pp. 3,919-3,923.

5. B. Yip et al., "Time Resolved Three-Dimensional Concentration Measurements in a Gas Jet," *Science,* Vol. 235, Mar. 1987, pp. 1,209-1,211.

6. B. Yip, R.L. Schmitt, and M.B. Long, "Instantaneous Three-Dimensional Concentration Measurements in Turbulent Jets and Flames," *Optics Letters,* Vol. 13, No. 2, 1988, pp. 96-98.

7. N. Peters, "Laminar Flamelet Concepts in Turbulent Combustion," *Proc. 21st Intl. Symp. Combustion,* The

Combustion Institute, Pittsburgh, Penn., 1986, pp. 1,231-1,250.

8. R.A. Drebin, L. Carpenter, and P. Hanrahan, "Volume Rendering," *Computer Graphics* (Proc. SIGGraph 88), Vol. 22, No. 4, Aug. 1988, pp. 65- 74.

9. G. Russell and R.B. Miles, "Display and Perception of 3-D Space Filling Data," *Applied Optics,* Vol. 26, No. 6, 1987, pp. 973-982.

10. L. Hesselink, "Digital Image Processing in Flow Visualization," *Ann. Rev. Fluid Mechanics,* Vol. 20, 1988, pp. 421-485.

Kevin Lyons is a graduate student in mechanical engineering at Yale University. His research interests include turbulent-flow diagnostics and laser applications. He received a BE in mechanical engineering from Manhattan College in 1988.

Marshall B. Long is an associate professor of mechanical engineering at Yale University. His research concerns the development and application of multidimensional laser diagnostics of fluid flow and combustion phenomena. He received a BS in physics from the University of Montana in 1976 and a PhD in applied physics from Yale University in 1980.

Joseph K. Lam is a research and development technician in the Applied Physics Department at Yale University. His research interests include laser applications and computer imaging. Lam received a BS in physics from Southern Connecticut State University and laser training from San Jose City College.

Interactive Visualization of 3D Medical Data

Henry Fuchs, Marc Levoy, and Stephen M. Pizer
University of North Carolina

Introduction

Techniques for noninvasively imaging the interior of the human body have undergone a revolution in the last decade. New data acquisition modalities include computed tomography (CT), single photon emission computed tomography (SPECT), positron emission tomography (PET), magnetic resonance imaging (MRI), and ultrasound. All of these modalities have the potential for producing three-dimensional arrays of intensity values.

Unfortunately for the clinician, no fully satisfactory method for viewing this data yet exists. The currently dominant method consists of printing slices of the data onto transparent films for viewing on a backlit screen. This approach makes detection of small or faint structures difficult. It also hampers comprehension of complex three-dimensional structures such as branching arterial systems. Without such an understanding, the planning of surgery, radiation therapy, and other invasive procedures is difficult and error-prone.

Computer-generated imagery offers an effective means for presenting three-dimensional medical data to the clinician. Researchers have, over a period of 15 years, built up a large repertoire of techniques for visualizing multidimensional information. Applying these techniques in clinical settings has until recently been limited, partly because of low image quality and partly because of the large quantity of data involved. The recent advent of larger computer memories and faster processors has spawned a period of rapid growth in software and hardware techniques for data visualization. Widespread clinical use of these techniques can be expected to follow within the next five to 10 years.

Rendering Techniques

Three-dimensional medical data has, by itself, no visible manifestation. Implicit in the visualization process is the creation of an intermediate representation—some visible object or phenomenon—that can be rendered to produce an image. This intermediate representation can be almost anything: dots, lines, surfaces, clouds, gels, etc. Since the human perceptual system expects sensory input to arise from physically plausible phenomena and forms interpretations on that basis, the representation should be of a physically

plausible object. To promote easier interpretation, it should be of an intuitively familiar one. Most techniques for displaying three-dimensional medical data fall into the three broad categories of surface-based rendering, binary voxel rendering, and volume rendering. The characteristics of each category depend on the intermediate representation employed.

Surface-based techniques. The first category, surface-based techniques, applies a surface detector to the sample array, then fits geometric primitives to the detected surfaces, and finally renders the resulting geometric representation. The techniques differ from one another mainly in the choice of primitives and the scale at which they are defined. A common technique applies edge tracking on each data slice to yield a set of contours defining features of interest. A mesh of polygons can then be constructed connecting the contours on adjacent slices.[1] Figure 1 was generated using this technique. Alternatively, polygons can be fit to an approximation of the original anatomy within each voxel (a pixel in 3D), yielding a large set of voxel-sized polygons.[2]

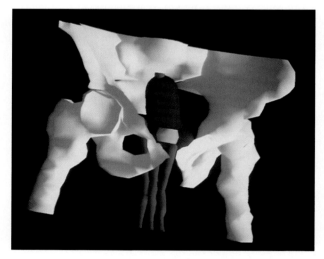

Figure 1. Interactive surface-based rendering on Pixel-Planes 4 of a female pelvis with vaginal inserts for radiation sources. The long bulbous object surrounding the tip of the three vertical shafts is a polygonally defined radiation isodose surface. (CT data courtesy of NC Memorial Hospital)

Reprinted from *Computer*, August 1989, pages 46-51. Copyright © 1989 by The Institute of Electrical and Electronics Engineers, Inc. All rights reserved.

These techniques have several desirable characteristics. Geometric primitives are compact, making storage and transmission inexpensive. They also exhibit a high degree of spatial coherence, making rendering efficient. Unfortunately, automatic fitting of geometric primitives to sample data is seldom entirely successful. Contour-following algorithms, for example, occasionally go astray when processing complicated scenes, forcing the user to intervene. These techniques also require binary classification of the incoming data; either a surface passes through the current voxel or it does not. In the presence of small or poorly defined features, error-free binary classification is often impossible. Errors in classification manifest themselves as visual artifacts in the generated image, specifically spurious surfaces (false positives) or erroneous holes in surfaces (false negatives).

Binary voxel techniques. These techniques begin by thresholding the volume data to produce a three-dimensional binary array. The cuberille algorithm renders this array by treating 1's as opaque cubes having six polygonal faces.[3] Alternatively, voxels can be painted directly onto the screen in back-to-front (or front-to-back) order,[4] or rays can be traced from an observer position through the data, stopping when an opaque object is encountered.[5]

Because voxels, unlike geometric primitives, have no defined extent, resampling becomes an important issue. To avoid a "sugar cube" appearance, some sort of interpolation is necessary. These techniques also require binary classification of the sample data, and thus suffer from many of the artifacts that plague surface-based techniques.

Volume-rendering techniques. These techniques are a variant of the binary voxel techniques in which a color and a partial opacity is assigned to each voxel. Images are formed from the resulting colored, semitransparent volume by blending together voxels projecting to the same pixel on the picture plane. Quantization and aliasing artifacts are reduced by avoiding thresholding during data classification and by carefully resampling the data during projection.

Volume rendering offers the important advantage over surface-based or binary voxel techniques of eliminating the need for making a binary classification of the data. This provides a mechanism for displaying small or poorly defined features. Researchers at Pixar of San Rafael, California, first demonstrated volume rendering in 1985. Their technique consists of estimating occupancy fractions for each of a set of materials (air, muscle, fat, bone) that might be present in a voxel, computing from these fractions a color and a partial opacity for each voxel, geometrically transforming each slice of voxels from object space to image space, projecting it onto the image plane, and blending it together with the projection formed by previous slices.[6] Figures 2-4 were generated using an algorithm developed at the University of North Carolina. Though similar in ap-

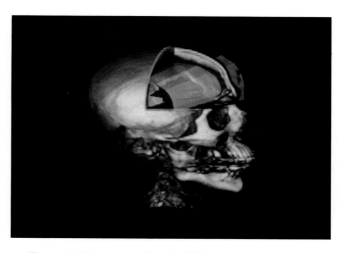

Figure 2. Volume rendering of 256 × 256 × 113-voxel computed tomography study of a human head. A polygonally defined tumor (in purple) and radiation treatment beam (in blue) have been added using our hybrid ray tracer. A portion of the CT data has been clipped away to show the 3D relationships between the various objects. (CT data courtesy of NC Memorial Hospital)

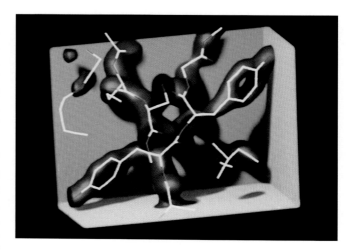

Figure 3. Volume rendering of isovalue contour surface from 24 × 20 × 11-voxel electron density map of staphylococcus aureus ribonuclease. 3D scan-converted backdrop planes, cast shadows, and a color-coded stick representation of the molecular structure have been added to enhance comprehension. Similar techniques can be used to render isodose contour surfaces for radiation treatment planning. (Electron density map courtesy of Chris Hill, University of York)

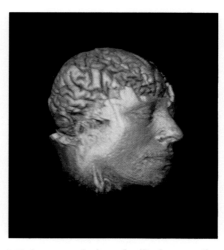

Figure 4. Volume rendering of edited magnetic resonance data set. The apparent mottling of the facial surface in the volume rendering is due to noise in the acquired data. Note that the user was not called upon to define surface geometry, but merely to isolate a region of interest. (MR data courtesy of Siemens AG, edited by Juiqi Tang)

proach to the Pixar technique, the algorithm computes colors and opacities directly from the scalar value of each voxel and renders the resulting volume by tracing viewing rays from an observer position through the data set.[7]

Despite its advantages, volume rendering suffers from a number of problems. High on this list is the technique's computational expense. Since all voxels participate in the generation of each image, rendering time grows linearly with the size of the data set. Published techniques take minutes or even hours to generate a single view of a large data set using currently available workstation technology. To reduce image generation time in our rendering algorithm, we employ several techniques that take advantage of spatial coherence present in the data and its projections. The first technique consists of constructing a pyramid of binary volumes to speed up the search for nonempty (nontransparent) voxels along viewing rays. The second technique uses an opacity threshold to adaptively terminate ray tracing. The third technique consists of casting a sparse grid of rays, less than one per pixel, and adaptively increasing the number of rays in regions of high image complexity. Combining all three optimizations, savings of more than two orders of magnitude over brute-force rendering methods have been obtained for many data sets.[8]

Another drawback of volume rendering is its lack of versatility. Many clinical problems require that sampled data and analytically defined geometry appear in a single visualization. Examples include superimposition of radiation treatment beams over patient anatomy for the oncolo-

gist and display of medical prostheses for the orthopedist. We have developed two techniques for rendering mixtures of volume data and polygonally defined objects. The first employs a hybrid ray tracer capable of handling both polygons and sample arrays. Figure 2 was generated using this algorithm. The second consists of a 3D scan conversion of the polygons into the sample array with antialiasing, then rendering the ensemble. Figure 3 includes polygons rendered using this algorithm.[8]

The computation of voxel opacity from voxel value in volume-rendering algorithms performs the dual tasks of classifying the data into objects and selecting a subset of these objects for display. The classification procedure commonly used to display medical data consists of a simple one-for-one mapping from voxel value to opacity. In many cases, it is impossible to obtain the desired visualization using such a mapping. For example, in the magnetic resonance study shown in Figure 4, the scalp and cortical surface have roughly the same voxel value. Any mapping that renders the scalp transparently will also render the cortical surface transparently.

How then to see the cortical surface? One possible strategy is to manually edit the data set to remove the scalp as shown in Figure 5. In this case, the boundary between erased and unerased voxels falls within regions that are rendered transparently. The boundary is therefore not seen in the volume rendering and need not be specified precisely. An alternative solution would be to combine volume rendering with high-level object definition methods in an interactive setting. Initial visualizations made without the benefit of object definition would be used to guide scene analysis and segmentation algorithms, which would in turn be used to isolate regions of interest, producing a better visualization. If the output of such segmentation algorithms included confidence levels or probabilities, they could be mapped to opacity and thus modulate the appearance of the image.

Display Hardware

Generating a two-dimensional image from a three-dimensional data set necessarily reduces information content. In particular, images do not use many faculties of the human visual system specifically adapted for perceiving depth: stereopsis, head motion parallax, and the kinetic depth effect. Such specialized display devices as stereo viewers, varifocal mirrors, cine sequences, real-time image-generation systems, and head-mounted displays have been developed to convey as much three-dimensional information as possible to the observer.

Stereo viewers. Relatively simple and inexpensive, stereo viewers offer a means for widening the pathway from the computer to the observer. Our current favorite is a polarizing liquid-crystal plate manufactured by Tektronix. The plate is

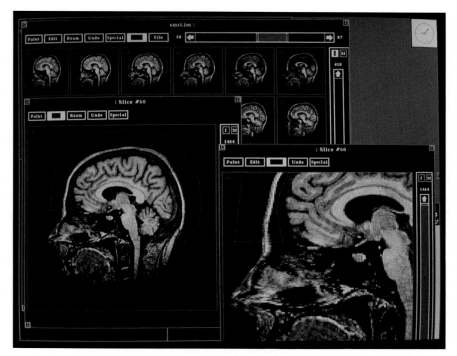

Figure 5. Slices from a 256 × 256 × 156-voxel magnetic resonance study of a human head being edited to remove the scalp and thereby reveal the underlying cortical surface. Depicted is a typical view of the workstation screen in our interactive Imex (image executive) medical-image-editing program, written by Peter Mills.

mounted on the front of a video display, left- and right-eye images are displayed on alternate video fields, and the plate's direction of polarization is electronically switched in synchrony with the alternation of images. The user wears inexpensive passive glasses with polarizing material of different direction in each lens. Using this system, multiple users can see the same stereo image, and each user can look at multiple stereo displays.

Varifocal mirrors. By combining a vibrating reflective surface with a point-plotting CRT, the varifocal mirror provides "true" three-dimensional perception of a distribution of glowing points of light. Our version consists of a vibrating aluminized mylar membrane stretched on a drumhead-like structure and acoustically vibrated from behind by a large conventional speaker driven by a low-frequency (30 Hz) sine wave. A user looking into this vibrating (and "varifocal") mirror sees the image of a simple point-plotting CRT on which a sequence of dots is rapidly displayed. The displayed list of dots is repeated at the 30 Hz rate, synchronized to the mirror vibration. Each dot is thus perceived at a particular depth, depending on the position of the mirror when the dot is displayed. As a user moves his head relative to the display, he sees different views of the data.

This display device provides both stereopsis and head-motion parallax. In addition, it can be viewed simulta-

neously by several users without their wearing any special apparatus. The limited size of the displayed volume, which is constrained by the size of the CRT and the deflection of the mirror membrane, presents a major drawback. Another disadvantage is the lack of obscuration by the displayed dots; features in the foreground do not hide features in the background.

Cine sequences. Sets of images that have been precalculated, stored in a frame buffer of sufficient memory capacity, and played back in real-time are called cine sequences. The most common type of sequence is one in which the light source and observer are fixed and the object rotates. The resulting play of reflections across surfaces in the data enhances comprehension of the scene. A type of sequence frequently used in volume rendering is one in which the object, the light source, and the observer are all fixed and only the opacities of voxels change. For example, our physician colleagues find it useful to interactively vary the position of a clipping plane, allowing them to study in detail the tiny complex structures of the middle and inner ear. We provide this capability by computing a sequence of images in which the opacities of all voxels lying between the observer and the clipping plane are attenuated to nearly zero, and each image in the sequence has the clipping plane in a slightly different position relative to the data.

When calculating a sequence of images, we usually vary only a single parameter such as observer position, light source position, cutting plane position, or opacity mapping. Users would often prefer to vary multiple parameters. Unfortunately, the number of images that must be precalculated to provide such multiaxis cine sequences is the product of the numbers of steps in the variation of each parameter; a modest 20 steps for each of two variables require the calculation and storage of 400 images. The largest frame buffer currently in our laboratory is the Pixar Image Computer, which has a capacity of 64 512 $\times$ 512-bit images. This seriously limits the extent to which we can independently vary multiple parameters during playback of cine sequences.

Real-time image-generation systems. Offering more flexibility than cine sequences for the presentation of moving imagery, real-time image-generation systems have found broad acceptance. For surface-based rendering techniques, high-performance graphics workstations are available from Ardent, Silicon Graphics, and Stellar. At the University of North Carolina, we have been using our locally developed Pixel-Planes 4 system to provide clinicians with real-time display of contour-based polygon renderings (see Figure 1).

For binary voxel representations, Phoenix Data Systems, Dimensional Medicine, and Dynamic Digital Displays have fielded systems capable of real-time or near real-time image generation. In addition, Kaufman is currently prototyping a system (and associated algorithms for 3D scan conversion of surfaces and polyhedra) that will be capable of displaying a 512 $\times$ 512 $\times$ 512 voxel binary volume in real time.[9]

At this writing, no system exists that can perform volume rendering in real time. The most widely used system is the Pixar Image Computer. Using a four-channel, single-instruction, multiple-data processor and Pixar's Chap-Volumes software package, the Image Computer can generate high-quality images of 256 $\times$ 256 $\times$ 256-voxel data sets in about one minute. At the University of North Carolina, we are currently developing Pixel-Planes 5, a massively parallel raster-graphics engine consisting of 16 40-Mflop graphics processors, 250,000 pixel processors, a 512 $\times$ 512 pixel color frame buffer, and a 640 megabits-per-second ring network.[10] In addition to enhancing our surface-based rendering capabilities, we intend to integrate Pixel-Planes 5 into a real-time volume-rendering workstation. The frame rate we expect from this workstation depends on what parameters change from frame to frame. Preliminary estimates suggest that for changes solely in observer position, we will be able to generate a sequence of slightly coarse images at between 10 and 20 frames per second. A sequence of images comparable in quality to Figure 4 will be generated at between one and two frames per second.

Head-mounted displays. Pioneered by Ivan Sutherland at the University of Utah in 1968, head-mounted displays incorporate stereopsis, head-motion parallax, and realistic images (including obscuration). These devices present stereo images to the user through displays mounted in front of each eye, track the motion of the user's head, and generate new images in real time in response to changes in the user's head position and direction of view. This provides the illusion of walking about a simulated object or even of walking inside a simulated environment. Most of the development in this area has been for military and aerospace applications at such places as Wright Patterson Air Force Base and NASA Ames Research Center. We have also been developing head-mounted displays for several years.

These systems demand very fast update rates and currently suffer from several technological weaknesses: poor resolution of the small video displays, high latency in the tracker-to-image feedback loop, and limited-range tracking systems. Nonetheless, they continue to hold great promise, and we hope to eventually incorporate a head-mounted display, Pixel-Planes 5, and our volume-rendering algorithms into an interactive radiotherapy treatment-planning system.

Topics for Future Research

A vital component of any computer-assisted medical image display system is a satisfactory user interface. In addition to the firms and research groups already mentioned, interactive medical image display systems have been developed by CEMAX, the Mayo Clinic, Sun Microsystems, and Lee Westover of our own department. User interfaces for many existing systems are constrained by the inability to generate images in real time. For volume-rendering systems in particular, feedback during selection of rendering parameters is usually provided by metavisualizations such as 2D plots of color and opacity versus input value and wire-frame representations of viewing frustums and motion paths. If future systems succeed in generating volume-rendered images in real time, these metavisualizations can be omitted or relegated to a supporting role. In such systems, sequences of rendered images would serve as feedback to the user of changes made in rendering parameters.

An important problem that has only begun to be addressed is how to visualize multiple data sets. Examples include superimposition of anatomic information from CT data and metabolic information from PET data, or simultaneous visualization of anatomy and radiation dose for cancer therapy planning. Realistic shading models have been used to visualize multiple 2D scalar fields by assigning one data set to surface relief and another to surface albedo or color. For three-dimensional data, the second data set can be used to modulate the color or opacity computed for voxels in the first data set. Alternatively, the second data set could be used to perturb the normals, shininess, or other properties of the surfaces displayed from the first data set. Recent investigations in this area by Hoehne et al.[11] and workers at the University of Chicago[12] show promise.

Current perspective suggests that the applicability of volume rendering to certain disciplines—diagnostic radiology in particular—hinges on answering the question: How correct is a volume rendering? Volume rendering, relative to surface-based techniques, has the disadvantage of rendering fuzzy surfaces represented by a band-limited sample array rather than sharply defined surfaces represented by geometric primitives. Since fuzzy surfaces do not occur in daily life, they are not intuitively familiar. Moreover, volume-rendered surfaces do not look fuzzy; they look precise. The danger therefore exists of interpreting these visualizations incorrectly. Since the radiologist is often required to make subtle judgments of feature size and shape, the potential exists for making erroneous diagnoses based on these visualizations. Clearly, volume rendering is useful for navigating through complex 3D data and for identifying gross anatomic abnormalities. It remains to be seen how useful it can be for perceiving fine features and to what extent it can replace slice-by-slice presentation of medical data in clinical practice.

Acknowledgments

We thank our collaborators in the Radiation Oncology Department at UNC School of Medicine and NC Memorial Hospital, especially Julian Roseman, Ed Chaney, and George Sherouse. We also thank Andrew Skinner and Richard David for assistance with clinical studies, Phil Stancil for hardware systems support, and Rick Pillsbury for observations about the utility of cine sequences. This research is partially supported by NIH Grant No. 1 PO1 CA47982-01, NSF Grant No. CDR-86-22201, DARPA ISTO Order No. 6090, ONR Contract No. N00014-86-K-0680, and IBM.

References

1. H. Fuchs, Z.M. Kedem, and S.P. Uselton, "Optimal Surface Reconstruction from Planar Contours," *Comm. ACM*, Vol. 20, No. 10, Oct. 1977, pp. 693-702.

2. W.E. Lorensen and H.E. Cline, "Marching Cubes: A High-Resolution 3D Surface Construction Algorithm," *Computer Graphics* (Proc. SIGGraph), Vol. 21, No. 4, July 1987, pp. 163-169.

3. G.T. Herman and H.K. Liu, "Three-Dimensional Display of Human Organs from Computer Tomograms," *Computer Graphics and Image Processing*, Vol. 9, No. 1, Jan. 1979, pp. 1-21.

4. G. Frieder, D. Gordon, and R.A. Reynolds, "Back-to-Front Display of Voxel-Based Objects," *IEEE Computer Graphics and Applications*, Vol. 5, No. 1, Jan. 1985, pp. 52-59.

5. D.S. Schlusselberg and W.K. Smith, "Three-Dimensional Display of Medical Image Volumes," *Proc. NCGA 86*, Nat'l. Computer Graphics Assn., Fairfax, Va., Vol. III, May 1986, pp. 114-123.

6. R.A. Drebin, L. Carpenter, and P. Hanrahan, "Volume Rendering," *Computer Graphics* (Proc. SIGGraph), Vol. 22, No. 4, Aug. 1988, pp. 65-74.

7. M. Levoy, "Display of Surfaces from Volume Data," *IEEE Computer Graphics and Applications*, Vol. 8, No. 3, May 1988, pp. 29-37.

8. M. Levoy, *Display of Surfaces from Volume Data*, doctoral dissertation, University of North Carolina at Chapel Hill, May 1989.

9. A. Kaufman and R. Bakalash, "Memory and Processing Architecture for 3D Voxel-Based Imagery," *IEEE Computer Graphics and Applications*, Vol. 8, No. 6, Nov. 1988, pp. 10-23.

10. H. Fuchs et al., "Pixel-Planes 5: A Heterogeneous Multiprocessor Graphics System Using Processor-Enhanced Memories," *Computer Graphics* (Proc. SIGGraph), Vol. 23, No. 4, July 1989.

11. K.H. Hoehne et al., "Display of Multiple 3D-Objects Using the Generalized Voxel-Model," *Proc. SPIE*, Vol. 914, 1988, pp. 850-854.

12. D.N. Levin et al., "Integrated 3D Display of MR, CT, and PET Images of the Brain," *Proc. NCGA 89*, Nat'l. Computer Graphics Assn., Fairfax, Va., Vol. I, pp. 179-186.

Henry Fuchs is Federico Gil Professor of Computer Science and an adjunct professor of radiation oncology at the University of North Carolina at Chapel Hill. His research interests include interactive 3D graphics, VLSI architectures, and 3D medical imaging. The principal investigator for several research projects funded by the Air Force, DARPA/ISTO, NIH, and NSF, he also served as chairman of the 1985 Chapel Hill Conference on VLSI and the 1986 Workshop on Interactive 3D Graphics held at UNC-Chapel Hill. He is on several advisory committees, including NSF Division of Microelectronics Information Processing Systems and Stellar Computer's Technical Board. He received a BA from the University of California at Santa Cruz in 1970 and a PhD from the University of Utah in 1975.

Marc Levoy is a research assistant professor of computer science and radiation oncology at the University of North Carolina at Chapel Hill. He is the principal developer of the Hanna-Barbera Computer Animation System and served as its director from 1980 through 1982. His research interests include scientific visualization, texture mapping, volume rendering, medical imaging, and molecular graphics. He received his bachelor's and master's degrees from Cornell University in 1976 and 1978 and his PhD in computer science from the University of North Carolina at Chapel Hill in 1989.

Stephen M. Pizer is a professor of computer science, radiation oncology, and radiology at the University of North Carolina at Chapel Hill, where he heads the multidepartmental Medical Image Display Research Group. His research covers human and computer vision, interactive 3D graphics, contrast enhancement, and workstation development. He conducts active collaborations with laboratories in the Netherlands, Germany, and the US, and is associate editor for display of *IEEE Transactions on Medical Imaging*. He received a PhD in computer science from Harvard in 1968.

Visualizing Large Data Sets in the Earth Sciences

William Hibbard and David Santek, University of Wisconsin-Madison

Introduction

With single data sets containing billions of points, meteorologists and other earth scientists face an avalanche of data received from their remote-sensing instruments and numerical simulation models.

The Space Science and Engineering Center (SSEC) at the University of Wisconsin-Madison led the evolution of weather visualization systems from paper to electronic displays with our Man-computer Interactive Data Access System (McIDAS). We have continued this evolution into animated three-dimensional images and recently into highly interactive displays. Our software can manage, analyze, and visualize large data sets that span many physical variables (such as temperature, pressure, humidity, and wind speed), as well as time and three spatial dimensions.[1,2]

McIDAS has produced three-dimensional animations of data sets from many diverse sources on videotape and on a special binocular stereo workstation. These animations are used in the classroom at the University of Wisconsin and other institutions, and by visiting scientists presenting case studies at conferences. Model developers are using McIDAS to produce highly interactive, real-time animations of the dynamics of their models.

Data Management

The McIDAS system manages data from at least 100 different sources, a diversity illustrating the flexibility of our data management tools. These tools consist of data structures for storing different data types in files, libraries of routines for accessing these data structures, system commands for performing housekeeping functions on the data files, and reformatting programs for converting external data to our data structures.

McIDAS includes data structures for grids, images, paths, and nonuniform data. Two- and three-dimensional grids are spatial arrays of numbers appropriate to numerical weather-model output and analyses of remote sensed data. Our grid structures permit grouping a range of times and multiple physical variables in a data set of billions of points, allow a variety of horizontal and vertical map projections, and indicate missing data points. Images are two-dimensional arrays of pixel intensities produced by satellites, radars, lidars (laser radars), and other sources. These images may include multiple spectral bands and may be grouped into time sequences, possibly containing billions of points. Paths are sequences of points through space or space-time, usually representing trajectories of air parcels derived from wind data. Nonuniform data consist of numbers without any spatial order that might be produced by surface observations, balloons, ships, and aircraft.

The McIDAS system provides numerous analysis functions for time and space interpolation of data, for deriving grids from nonuniform data, for deriving trajectories from wind grids, for converting data to a moving frame of reference, for making measurements from image data, and for applying a large variety of operators to grid and image data. (As part of the development of our three-dimensional visualization tools, we have inventoried four-dimensional data sets in meteorology and related earth sciences. A copy of this inventory is available at cost by writing to the librarian of SSEC.)

Three-Dimensional Visualization

The McIDAS tools for three-dimensional visualization of meteorological data run on an IBM mainframe and can load up to 128-frame animation sequences into workstations built at SSEC. The animations can be viewed directly (optionally, in binocular stereo) or recorded on videotape.

Our data are depicted in a rectangular box outline with height tick marks labeled in kilometers. A map, including topographical relief and boundary lines, can be drawn on the bottom of the box. The box visually defines the three-dimensional space, the map provides geographical context, and the topography is useful because it affects the weather.

We can depict gridded three-dimensional scalars using opaque or transparent contour surfaces (Figure 1) or a grid-mesh contour surface (Figure 2). A contour surface defines a constant value for a scalar variable. McIDAS can also depict a scalar as a transparent fog (Figure 3), where fog opacity is proportional to any scalar variable. The system generates contour lines (Figure 4) on a two-dimensional slice through a three-dimensional gridded scalar.

Wind vectors can be depicted using trajectory paths, which can be long and tapered (Figure 5), short with length proportional to speed (Figure 6), or faded to transparency

Reprinted from *Computer*, August 1989, pages 53-57. Copyright © 1989 by The Institute of Electrical and Electronics Engineers, Inc. All rights reserved.

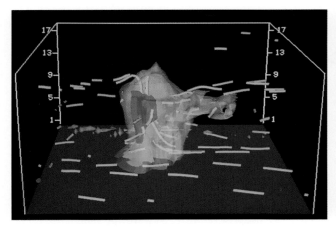

Figure 1. Regional Atmospheric Modeling System (RAMS) cloud model of a severe thunderstorm, showing a transparent 1.0-gram-per-cubic-meter condensate surface, a red 4.0-gram-per-cubic-meter hail surface, a blue 2.0-gram-per-cubic-meter rain surface, and wind trajectories. (With Gregory Tripoli, Univ. of Wisconsin Meteorology Dept.)

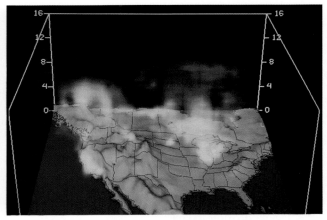

Figure 3. LAMPS model output for cloud water density over a topographical map. Volume is rendered as a transparent fog, with opacity proportional to cloud water density. (With Patricia Pauley, Univ. of Wisconsin Meteorology Dept.)

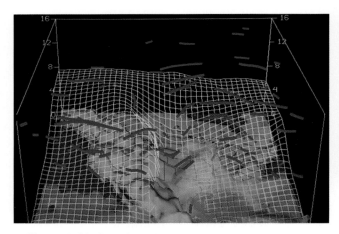

Figure 2. Limited-Area Mesoscale Prediction System (LAMPS) model output showing a grid-mesh 300-kelvin potential temperature surface, a transparent 8-gram-per-kilogram mixing-ratio moisture surface, and wind trajectories over a topographical map. (With Patricia Pauley, Univ. of Wisconsin Meteorology Dept.)

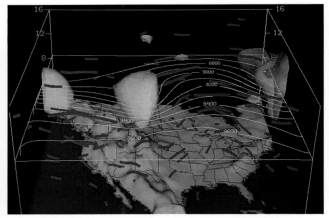

Figure 4. LAMPS model output showing a transparent 0.00016-per-second vorticity surface, trajectories, and 300-millibar height contour lines over a topographical map. (With Patricia Pauley, Univ. of Wisconsin Meteorology Dept.)

(Figure 7). McIDAS also represents winds with derived scalars, such as vorticity, contoured in Figure 4, or potential vorticity, contoured in Figure 5. Figure 8 shows depth-cued trajectory paths adapted to depict a network of underground caves.

McIDAS can texture map image data to surfaces in three-dimensional perspective, as shown in the two lidar images in Figure 9. In Figure 10, we have texture-mapped a visible satellite image to a surface defined by the corresponding infrared image. Pattern recognition discriminates clouds, and the visible pixels are blended with an artificial shade based on cloud-top geometry.

Our images also show the interactions between physical quantities. Figure 1 shows contour surfaces for condensate (transparent), hail (red), rain (blue), and wind trajectories from a thunderstorm simulation. Figure 2, taken from a model analysis of an extratropical cyclone, shows a grid-mesh potential-temperature contour, a transparent moisture-mixing ratio surface, and trajectories over a topographical map. Figure 11 depicts underground water tra-

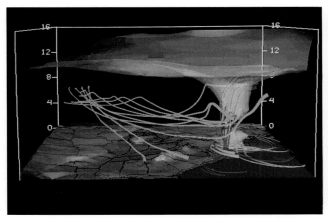

Figure 5. Mesoscale Analysis and Simulation System (MASS) model simulation of the Presidents' Day storm, showing a transparent 0.00002-kelvin per millibar per second potential vorticity surface and trajectories over a topographical map. (With Louis Uccellini, NASA Goddard Space Flight Center)

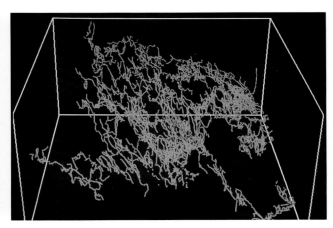

Figure 8. The Wind Cave network from data gathered by manual survey. (With Jem Nepstad, US Nat'l. Park Service)

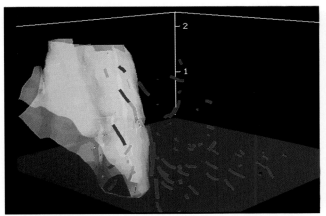

Figure 6. A microdownburst sensed by multiple doppler radars, with a transparent 30-DBZ radar reflectivity surface and wind trajectories. (With Robert Kropfli, NOAA Environmental Research Lab.)

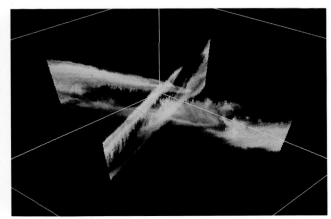

Figure 9. Cirrus cloud section by two vertical lidar (laser radar) slices. (With Ed Elorant, Univ. of Wisconsin Meteorology Dept.)

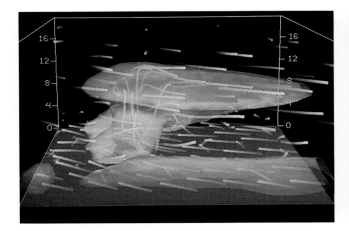

Figure 7. Thunderstorm simulation showing a transparent 0.5-gram-per-cubic- meter cloud water surface and trajectories. (With Robert Schlesinger, Univ. of Wisconsin Meteorology Dept.)

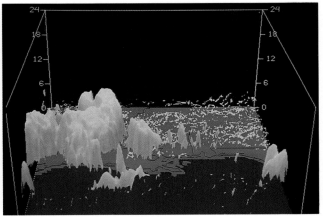

Figure 10. Perspective image of clouds over the Gulf of Mexico, generated from Geostationary Operational Environmental Satellite (GOES) infrared and visible data.

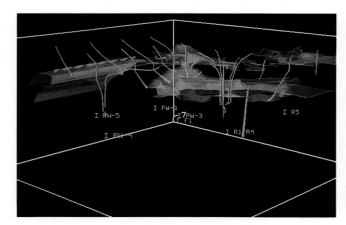

Figure 11. Hydrological model output showing transparent clay layers, ground-water trajectories, and labeled well positions. (With Kenneth Quinn, Warzyn Engineering)

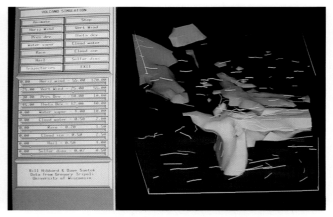

Figure 12. RAMS model of the atmospheric effects of a volcanic eruption, showing a green 0.07-gram-per-cubic-meter sulfur dioxide surface, a red 4.0-gram-per-cubic-meter water vapor surface, a blue 12.0-kelvin potential temperature deviation surface, and wind trajectories. The widgets to the left of the image control the display. (With Gregory Tripoli, Univ. of Wisconsin Meteorology Dept.)

jectories with transparent clay layers and text marking the locations of wells.

To enhance the depth information of our videotape animations, we usually combine time animation with a slight rocking of the three-dimensional scene.[3] The amplitude of this rocking is only one or two degrees and may be either vertical or horizontal, depending on the alignment of objects in the scene. This rocking is a very effective depth cue and is not ambiguous with most meteorological motions. We experimented with combining time animation with a steady rotation, but this created great ambiguity between the actual motion of objects and the apparent motion caused by rotation.

Transparency is an important part of our images, but it has presented some special problems. To render transparent surfaces efficiently, we developed a modified Z-buffer algorithm.[2] We analyzed and rendered each of the images in Figures 1-11 in about 30 seconds on our IBM 4381. Our workstation also poses a difficult problem for transparency: It does not separate red, green, and blue channels in its frame buffer. Rather, it was designed for false coloring of two-channel satellite data. We solved this problem by designing our images so that their pixels lie on two-dimensional planes through three-dimensional color space.

Interactive Visualization

Our experience with very large data sets has shown the importance of interactivity for their visualization. Thus, we are currently developing a highly interactive version of our system—using the Stellar GS-1000 graphics supercomputer—to produce three-dimensional animations in real time (i.e., drawing at the animation rate). This system can provide an interactive window into data sets containing tens

of millions of points produced by numerical models and remote sensing instruments.[4]

Figure 12 is an image produced by this system. It shows contour surfaces for sulfur dioxide (green), water vapor (red), potential temperature deviation (blue), and depth-cued wind trajectories. We can animate such images at five to 10 frames per second from a data set containing 10 different physical variables over 121 time steps in a $25 \times 35 \times 17$-point three-dimensional grid. This data set contains 20 million grid points in a five-dimensional array.

System features. The user controls the display with a mouse, and the system gives immediate response to commands to

- rotate, zoom, and pan in three dimensions;
- select any combination of the scalar variables and wind trajectories; and
- start/stop time animation and single-step time forward or backward.

The user can also select new defining levels for contour surfaces using the mouse. The computation of new surfaces occurs at a rate of about two per second and is asynchronous with the animation rendering. The new surfaces replace the old in the animation as they are computed.

Our system holds an entire data set in main memory, along with polygon and vector lists to represent the surfaces and lines generated from gridded data. We use compressed data structures to maximize the size of the data sets we can visualize. The 20-million-point data set is visualized on a

64-megabyte system; a 128-megabyte system could be used for a 50-million-point data set.

The animation involves decompressing the polygon and vector lists, transforming them to a two-dimensional projection, and shading the pixels. Because each frame of the animation is generated as it is displayed, the user can instantly rotate and zoom by changing the transform function. The user can also select the combination of viewed physical variables and control the time stepping by changing which polygon and vector lists are processed. The levels of contour surfaces are changed by computing new polygon sets from the gridded data, and this is done asynchronously with animation.

Scientific use. Interactive visualization is crucial to earth scientists, who must vary the way they look at a large data set according to its content. Controlling the combination of variables allows the user to examine specific cause-and-effect mechanisms. Coordinated hand-eye control of the view angle is a powerful way to understand three-dimensional geometries. Control of time stepping is needed to concentrate on particular events. Varying the defining levels of contour surfaces is important to quantitative understanding of data throughout a volume. We are working on an interactive mechanism allowing the user to move a plane through a three-dimensional volume, with contour lines of selected variables rendered on the plane. This mechanism will provide higher information density on the selected plane, so the user can concentrate on a specific spatial region.

A large data set often contains many interesting events and cause-and-effect links. Our system's interactivity lets scientists "play" with their data sets and pursue interesting physics at the pace of their own thoughts, without the distraction of waiting for the system to catch up.

Applications

Our visualizations are being used for teaching at the University of Wisconsin and other institutions. With Patricia Pauley of the University of Wisconsin Meteorology Department, we set up a series of animations on the binocular stereo workstation to help students in a weather laboratory better understand storm systems.[5] We are also making videotapes of weather visualizations available to other teaching institutions.

Scientists are using our visualizations to understand their data sets[6,7] and to present results at conferences. A videotape we produced with Louis Uccellini of the NASA Goddard Space Flight Center vividly depicts the development of the "Presidents' Day" storm that buried Washington, DC, in snow—when no snow was predicted.[8] This storm is being studied intensively by meteorologists trying to improve weather prediction. Our videotape clearly visualizes one simulation of this storm's dynamics and is being used for many conference and classroom presentations.

Scientists have begun using our interactive visualization system based on the Stellar GS-1000. Gregory Tripoli of the University of Wisconsin Meteorology Department used it for only a few hours, but that brief use helped him see and understand problems in his thunderstorm model that he had not seen during several years of viewing his data in two-dimensional plots. He has used this new understanding to correct problems in his model.

Clearly, interactive visualization is revolutionizing the ability of earth scientists to understand their enormous data sets.

Acknowledgments

We would like to thank Verner Suomi, Frances Bretherton, Robert Fox, J.T. Young, and Robert Krauss of SSEC; James Dodge, Gregory Wilson, James Arnold and Paul Meyer of NASA; and Ian Reid, Craig Upson, David Kamins, Jeff Vroom, and Brian Kowalski of Stellar for their help and support. We would also like to thank the guest editor, Gregory M. Nielson, and the *Computer* referees for their suggestions.

This work was supported by NASA Marshall Space Flight Center (NAS8-33799 and NAS8-36292).

References

1. E. Smith, "The McIDAS System," *IEEE Trans. Geosci. Electron*, Vol. GE-13, July 1975, pp. 123-136.

2. W. Hibbard, "4D Display of Meteorological Data," *Proc. Workshop Interactive 3D Graphics*, ACM, New York, 1986, pp. 26-33.

3. W. Hibbard and D. Santek, "Presidents' Day Storm, Visualization/State of the Art: Update," *SIGGraph Video Rev.*, No. 35, 1988.

4. W. Hibbard, "A Next Generation McIDAS Workstation," *Proc. Conf. Interactive Information and Processing Systems for Meteorology, Oceanography, and Hydrology*, Amer. Met. Soc., Boston, Mass., 1988, pp. 57-61.

5. P.M. Pauley, W. Hibbard, and D. Santek, "The Use of 4D Graphics in Teaching Synoptic Meteorology," *Proc. Conf. Interactive Information and Processing Systems for Meteorology, Oceanography, and Hydrology*, Amer. Met. Soc., Boston, Mass., 1988, pp. 33-36.

6. D. Santek et al., "4D Techniques for Evaluation of Atmospheric Model Forecasts," *Proc. Digital Image Processing and Visual Communications Technologies in Meteorology*, SPIE, Bellingham, Wash., 1987, pp. 75-77.

7. P.J. Meyer and M.S. Seablom, "Application of the Four-Dimensional McIDAS to LAMPS Model Output," *Proc. Conf. Interactive Information and Processing Systems for Meteorology, Oceanography, and Hydrology*, Amer. Met. Soc., Boston, Mass., 1988, pp. 33-36.

8. L. Uccellini, "Processes Contributing to the Rapid Development of Extratropical Cyclones," *Preprint Palmen Memorial Symp. on Extratropical Cyclones*, Amer. Met. Soc., Boston, Mass., 1988, pp. 110-115.

William L. Hibbard is a researcher at the Space Science and Engineering Center at the University of Wisconsin-Madison. His research interests are interactive computer graphics and image processing for earth sciences. He is a member of ACM, SIGGraph, SIGArt, and the IEEE Computer Society. Hibbard received a BA in mathematics and an MS in computer science from the University of Wisconsin-Madison in 1970 and 1974, respectively.

David A. Santek is a scientific applications programmer at the Space Science and Engineering Center at the University of Wisconsin-Madison. His interests include satellite data analysis, image analysis, and computer graphics. Santek received a BS in atmospheric and oceanic science from the University of Michigan in 1975 and an MS in meteorology from the University of Wisconsin in 1978.

The Role of Visualization in the Simulation of Quantum Electronic Transport in Semiconductors

Norman C. Kluksdahl, Alfred M. Kriman, and David K. Ferry
Arizona State University

Introduction

In simulating a semiconductor device, examining the raw numerical data rarely fosters an understanding of physical processes within the device. Visualization tools provide a useful method for interpreting this voluminous data and allow a better understanding of the semiconductor. Pictorial representation of data can reveal results not readily discerned from the data alone. Furthermore, animating a sequence of data frames permits visualization of time-evolving systems.

These advantages hold especially true when studying ultrasmall devices such as the resonant tunneling diode. The RTD is a gallium-arsenide semiconductor structure in which two thin layers (a few nanometers thick) of aluminum gallium arsenide (AlGaAs) form quantum tunneling barriers around a thin layer of gallium arsenide. The quantum tunneling probability in this structure possesses a sharp peak (Figure 1), corresponding to resonant tunneling.[1] Experimental devices incorporating this structure show negative differential conductivity in their current-voltage (I-V) characteristics,[2] as predicted by theory.[1,3]

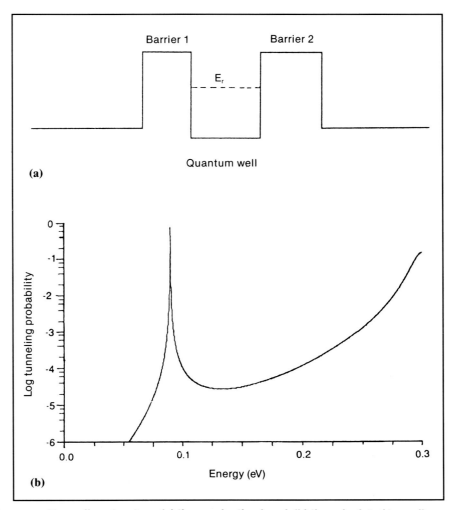

Figure 1. A resonant tunneling structure: (a) the conduction band; (b) the calculated tunneling probability for a typical resonant tunneling structure. In a device, the barriers are $Al_xGa_{1-x}As$, while the well and the contact regions consist of GaAs. E_r is the resonant energy level.

Efforts to model the RTD met with only limited success[3] until employment of the Wigner function formalism.[4-6] Coupled with increased graphics capability, this has led to a better understanding of the RTD and to the prediction of new physical phenomena within the RTD such as plasma oscillations during transient switching.

The Wigner Function

A classical system often employs a phase-space distribution function. This approach, the foundation of Monte Carlo simulations,[7] has found frequent use in modeling large semiconductor devices. It fails, however, when the feature sizes are such that the internal potential varies over a length shorter than a characteristic electron wavelength.[4]

An alternative approach, the Wigner function,[8] uses a formalism that correctly incorporates all the quantum mechanics inherent in a problem. The Wigner function is the Fourier transform of the density matrix, taken with respect to a difference variable:

$$f_w(x,p) = \frac{1}{2\pi\hbar} \int dy\, e^{ipy/\hbar} \varrho\left(x+\frac{y}{2}, x-\frac{y}{2}\right) \quad (1)$$

where $q(x,x')$ is the density matrix describing how the system is composed of a mixture of the system's eigenstates. This transformation, the Wigner-Weyl transform, when applied to the density matrix time-evolution equation, gives the equation for the Wigner function:

$$0 = \frac{\delta f}{\delta t} + v\frac{\delta f}{\delta x} + \frac{1}{\hbar} \int dP \int dy\, f(x,p+P) \sin(2Py) * [V(x+y) - V(x-y)] \quad (2)$$

The Wigner function has many advantages.[4,8] It is a real function, unlike the complex density matrix from which it is derived. The equation of motion is similar to the classical Boltzmann equation. And, finally, expectation values of operators such as the current operator are easily evaluated. This formalism does, however, have a few quirks.[4,8] The Wigner function is not a true probability distribution function in that it is not positively semidefinite—a direct consequence of the Heisenberg uncertainty principle. In areas where quantum mechanical effects dominate, the distribution may manifest negativity. This necessitates caution in evaluating expectation values to ensure meaningful results. More importantly, quantum mechanically exact boundary conditions must be specified to avoid excluding some orders of the quantum corrections.

The time-evolving Wigner function is found by numerically solving the equation of motion (Equation 2) with explicit finite differencing. Good convergence is obtained by retaining the second-order term in the Taylor series expansion. The final form of the equation of motion, after some algebra, is

$$f(t+\Delta t) = f(t) - \Delta t[v\frac{\delta f}{\delta x} + \theta(f)] + \frac{\Delta t^2}{2}[v^2\frac{\delta^2 f}{\delta x^2} + v\frac{\delta\theta(f)}{\delta x} - \frac{\delta\theta(f)}{\delta t}] \quad (3)$$

(In this notation, θ is the operator for the integral forcing function.) Also, measures must be taken to ensure that the nonlocal momentum operator in θ does not introduce artificial numerical reflections.[4,9]

The resulting discretized mesh can be thought of as a collection of equations, each of which occupies a "slice" of the mesh with a fixed momentum value p. These slices are coupled through the θ operator of Equation 3. Each slice then has a characteristic velocity ($v = p/m$) and direction of information propagation, and a corresponding boundary at which information enters. This is the specified boundary, then, for the slice.

Tunneling Problem

The simplest systems that can be studied are wave packets tunneling through a quantum barrier. Such examples, rife in elementary quantum mechanics textbooks,[1] provide a method of verifying the accuracy of the Wigner function equation of motion. Because the Wigner function shows both position and momentum, it offers new insights into the processes of tunneling and reflection, and not mere repetitions of already-solved problems. When graphically represented, the Wigner function displays a wealth of information about tunneling wave packets.

A Gaussian wave packet incident on a finite-thickness quantum barrier will split into two components: One fraction will tunnel through the barrier, and the remainder of the wave packet will be reflected. The Wigner representation of the wave packet has a Gaussian form in both position and momentum.

A quantum barrier potential is inserted into θ, an initial wave packet is placed on the mesh, and Equation 3 is iterated forward in time. As the iteration proceeds, the wave packet is plotted versus position and momentum, with amplitude represented by both height and color. Figure 2a shows the wave packet shortly after $t = 0$. Points with positive momentum move into the page; negative momentum corresponds to motion out of the page. In Figure 2b, the

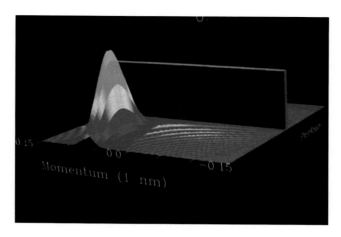

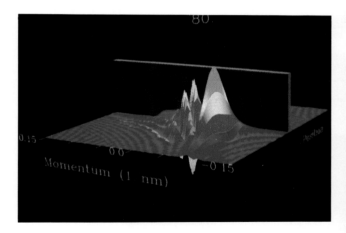

Figure 2. Wigner function of a Gaussian wave packet versus position and momentum against a vertical-wall barrier: (a) the incident wave packet; (b) the wave packet being reflected from the barrier. Most of the packet has reflected and is moving away from the barrier. A large correlation, centered about the zero-momentum axis peak, ties the incident and reflected components together until reflection is nearly completed (c). Almost no incident packet remains, and the correlation peak is appropriately reduced.

wave packet is in the late stages of reflecting; a Gaussian wave packet with negative momentum is forming. Some of the incident packet is visible at the barrier, and correlation between the incident and reflected wave packets is manifested as peaks in the distribution around the zero-momentum axis. In Figure 2c, the reflection is nearly completed: The incident wave packet has nearly vanished, the reflected wave packet has grown, and the correlation has been reduced. The negative peaks are a consequence of the uncertainty principle.

These plots, and the animated representation of the tunneling process, reveal that the effect of a barrier extends outward from its physical location and turns the wave packet slowly. Quantum reflection takes a finite time. In contrast, the classical view of this problem yields an impulse force and instantaneous reflection (for nondeformable bodies).

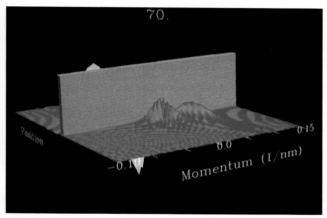

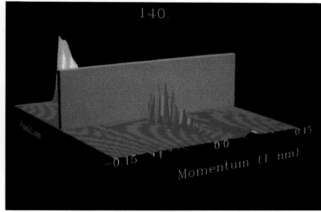

Figure 3. The tunneling wave packet, viewed from the opposite side of the barrier: (a) the transmitted wave packet is against the barrier, with two components-the actual wave packet on the right, and a correlation peak on the left; (b) the tunneling is completed, and most of the transmitted packet has left the domain. The correlation is a series of rapid oscillations at the zero-momentum axis.

The tunneling problem can be viewed from the other side of the barrier, as in Figures 3a and 3b. In Figure 3a, the transmitted wave packet shows as two parts: The rightmost wave packet at the barrier, and a correlation peak centered about the zero-momentum axis. Figure 3b shows the transmitted wave packet after the tunneling has completed. The transmitted wave packet is barely visible at the edge of the simulation domain. The most prominent feature of this figure is that the correlation appears as rapid oscillations along the zero-momentum axis. These oscillations do not contribute to density, but contain information about the correlation between the reflected and transmitted wave packets. When this correlation is retained, the system can be reversed to recover the initial wave packet. When it is removed, the system behaves as if two separate, uncorrelated wave packets were striking the tunnel barrier.

Device Simulations

The problem of the resonant tunneling diode is solved by first finding a density matrix and potential that are self-consistent.[4] The potential depends upon the densities of electrons and ionized donors in the device; the ionized donor concentration and the electron density depend on the potential. The structure of the device is shown in Figure 1a, with the barriers and well all 5 nanometers thick. Figure 4 shows the equilibrium self-consistent conduction band and the electron density.

The equilibrium density matrix, transformed into the Wigner function representation, becomes the initial condition for the time-evolution equation (Equation 3). Figure 5 shows the equilibrium Wigner function as density versus position and momentum. The white wire frames indicate the

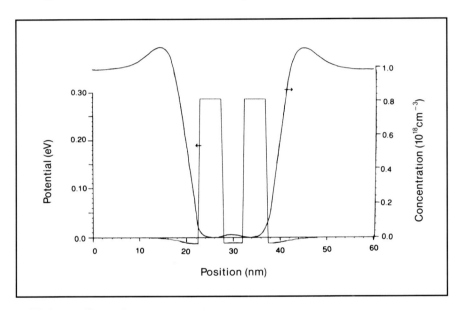

Figure 4. The equilibrium self-consistent conduction band and the electron density of the modeled resonant tunneling diode (RTD).

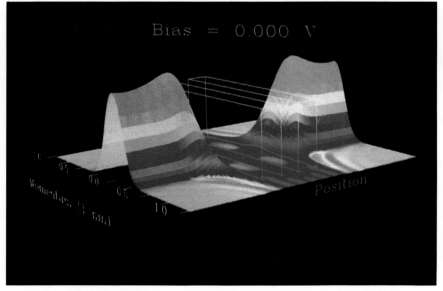

Figure 5. The equilibrium Wigner distribution for the RTD, versus position and momentum. The quantum barriers are indicated by the white wire frames.

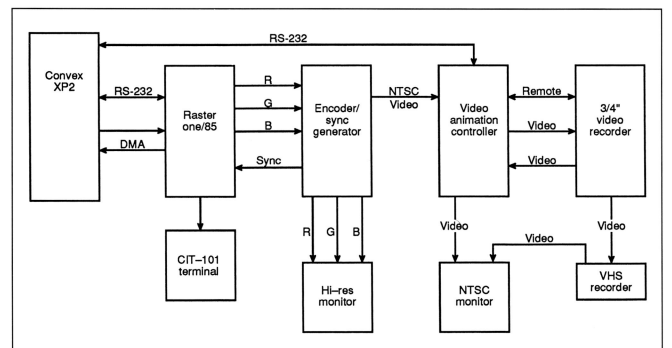

Block diagram of the animation equipment. Animation is totally automated under control of the user program on the Convex mainframe.

Animation studio

All computations are carried out on a Convex mainframe. Graphics are also generated on the Convex and then piped to a graphics workstation. An encoder/sync generator generates National Television System Committee video, providing source data for an animation controller. The controller is driven by the Convex and synchronizes video frames onto a ¾″ video tape recorder (see figure).

The application program generates the images through a graphics library, then hands control to an animation library. After the image is recorded, the animation library passes control back to the calling program, and the system is readied for another image. Using this approach, videotape generation is a hands-off automated process. Videotapes are finished by using an editing controller, a second ¾″ video tape recorder, and a title generator. The ¾″ master tape can then be copied onto VHS tape for distribution or presentation.

positions of the quantum barriers. This distribution shows two interesting features: quantum repulsion from the barriers leading to high momentum tails in the distribution near the barriers, and an accumulation near the barriers caused by the self-consistent potential.

A small potential is added to one end of the device, and the system is time-evolved by alternately stepping (Equation 3) in time and solving Poisson's equation until steady-state conditions are achieved. The current is calculated, and the process is repeated until the total I-V curve has been calculated (Figure 6).

Figure 7a shows the steady-state distribution for an applied potential of 0.22 volt, corresponding to the peak of the I-V curve. The base of the distribution is raised proportionally to the self-consistent potential $V(x)$ (but not on the same scale as the wire-frame barriers). The accumulation layer in the left contact region, the anode, has been swept out. The distribution in the right contact region, the cathode, is heavily depleted between the boundary and the barrier. At the cathode contact, the number of electrons leaving the device has been strongly reduced. Figure 7b shows the distribution for an applied bias of 0.44 volt, the valley of the I-V curve. Very few electrons are leaving the cathode contact. The cathode region has a triangular potential well between the boundary and the potential barrier, and the distribution at this point is a ring, the expected form of a quasibound state. Most notable is the strong tunneling the barriers between the contact regions. This tunneling is symmetric with respect to momentum and represents coupling between the anode and the quasibound state in the cathode well.

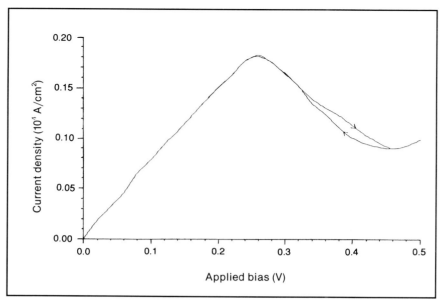

Figure 6. The calculated current-voltage curve of the modeled RTD.

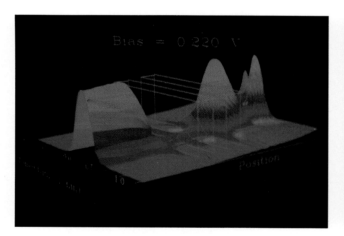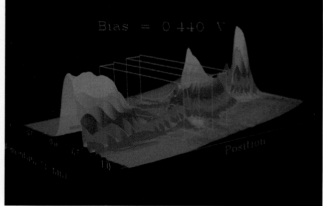

Figure 7. Two different RTD distribution profiles, varied through applied bias: (a) the RTD Wigner distribution for an applied bias of 0.22 volts shows depletion at the cathode contact, the anode accumulation swept out, and tunneling components of current; (b) the RTD distribution for an applied bias of 0.44 volts with the cathode end of the device dominated by a triangular potential well, resulting in a quantized state that is coupled to the anode end by tunneling through the barriers.

Transients have been studied by abruptly switching the bias from steady- state conditions at the peak of the I-V curve to the valley. A plot of each time step is synchronously edited onto videotape so that the resulting animation shows the transient distributions. As the device switches, the charge between the barriers is forced out, altering the potential. As the potential changes, the tunneling probability is changed, and the current changes correspondingly. A mechanism is thus established for oscillatory transient currents, and these have been observed.[5] One newly modeled result reveals these current oscillations to be sufficiently strong to cause large-scale collective oscillations within the entire device. Only with animation is this behavior observed in the model.

Conclusion

Graphical representation of wave packets during quantum tunneling shows explicitly the correlations between the transmitted and reflected components. When the time-evolving wave packet is animated, details of the reflection and transmission processes become strikingly evident.

In device simulation, a phase-space distribution is particularly advantageous, but such distributions require powerful visualization techniques in order to obtain a better understanding of the behavior predicted by models **and to** predict entirely new phenomena. Animated sequences show time-dependent phenomena which cannot be seen in single-image representations.

References

1. D. Bohm, *Quantum Theory*, Prentice Hall, Englewood Cliffs, N.J., 1951.

2. T.C.L.G. Sollner et al., "Resonant Tunneling through Quantum Wells at Frequencies up to 2.5 THz," *Appl. Phys. Lett.*, Vol. 43, Sept. 1983, pp. 588-590.

3. B. Ricco and M.Ya. Azbel, "Physics of Resonant Tunneling: The One-Dimensional Double Barrier Case," *Phys. Rev. B*, Vol. 29, Feb. 1984, pp. 1,970-1,981.

4. N.C. Kluksdahl, A.M. Kriman, and D.K. Ferry, "Wigner Function Simulation of Quantum Tunneling," *Superlattices and Microstructures*, Vol. 4, No. 2, 1988, pp. 127-131.

5. N.C. Kluksdahl et al., "Transient Switching Behavior of the Resonant Tunneling Diode," *IEEE Elec. Dev. Lett.*, Vol. 9, Sept. 1988, pp. 457-459.

6. W.R. Frensley, "Wigner Function Model of a Resonant Tunneling Semiconductor Device," *Phys. Rev. B*, Vol. 36, July 1987, pp. 1,570-1,580.

7. C. Jacoboni and L. Reggiani, "The Monte Carlo Method for the Solution of Charge Transport in Semiconductors with Application to Covalent Materials," *Rev. Mod. Phys.*, Vol. 55, July 1983, pp. 645-705.

8. P. Carruthers and F. Zachariason, "Quantum Collision Theory with Phase-Space Distributions," *Rev. Mod. Phys.*, Vol. 55, Jan. 1983, pp. 245-285.

9. B. Engquist and A. Majda, "Absorbing Boundary Conditions for the Numerical Simulation of Waves," *Math. Comp.*, Vol. 31, July 1977, pp. 629-651.

Norman C. Kluksdahl is a faculty associate in the Center for Solid-State Electronics Research at Arizona State University. He is currently studying quantum transport in semiconductors, although his interests also extend to VLSI and computer architecture. Kluksdahl served as technical consultant on the purchase of minisupercomputer and graphics equipment for the center and worked to establish a computer animation laboratory in the center.

Kluksdahl is a member of IEEE and Sigma Xi. He was a 1977 Presidential Scholar and a recipient of Motorola and Honeywell scholarships. Kluksdahl received his BS and MS in computer science from South Dakota School of Mines and Technology in 1981 and 1984, respectively, and his PhD in electrical engineering from Arizona State University in 1988.

Alfred M. Kriman is a senior research analyst in the Center for Solid-State Electronics Research at Arizona State University. From 1984 to 1986 he was a National Research Council postdoctoral fellow at the Naval Research Laboratory in Washington, DC. Kriman's research interests currently center on the analysis of the electronic structure and properties of microstructures.

Kriman is a member of the IEEE, the American Physical Society, Phi Beta Kappa, and Sigma Xi. He received an AB from Rutgers College in 1978, and AM and PhD degrees from Princeton University in 1980 and 1984, respectively, all in physics.

David K. Ferry assumed his current position as chair of the Electrical Engineering Department of Arizona State University this year. He had been director of the Center for Solid-State Electronics Research and professor of electrical and computer engineering at the university since 1983. Previously, he was with Colorado State University and the Office of Naval Research. He served on the NAS/NRC study on Thin-Film Microstructure Science and Technology, has codirected two NATO Advanced Study Institutes, and has served on program and organizing committees for several conferences. Since 1982, he has been a member of DARPA's Materials Research Council. He is author or coauthor of some 200 scientific works.

Ferry is a fellow of the American Physical Society. He received BS and MS degrees from Texas Tech University, Lubbock, in 1962 and 1963, respectively, and a PhD degree from the University of Texas, Austin, in 1966.

Graphical Analysis of Multi- and Microtasking Execution on Cray Multiprocessors*

Mark K. Seager, Nancy E. Werner, Mary E. Zosel
Lawrence Livermore National Laboratory
Robert E. Strout, II, Supercomputer Systems

Introduction

Writing and debugging explicit parallel codes can be difficult. In addition to specifying the program's fundamental algorithms, the successful parallel programmer must address a whole new set of problems. These include decisions about how to use the available processors to break up the computation (tasking), how the tasks are controlled and how they interact (synchronization), and how data is accessed or shared by the tasks (data scoping). If this set of problems is not enough, the programmer may be faced with nondeterministic processor scheduling that can make program correctness difficult to determine. The programmer also discovers increased interest in performance analysis because many new sources of overhead combine, with Amdahl's law, to produce far less than perfect speedup of the computation.

The Graphical Multiprocessing Analysis Tools (GMAT) described in this chapter provide visual insight into several of these problems. We do not, however, provide any advice about problems stemming from improper access to program data. Other tools are being developed to aid in that area.[1] Currently, the focus of GMAT is shared memory machines, but the ideas presented herein should extend to distributed memory machines. However many issues related to distributed memory machines are quite different.[2] The initial implementation at the Lawrence Livermore National Laboratory (LLNL) supports parallel applications on a four-processor Cray X-MP, an eight-processor Cray Y-MP, and an eight-processor Alliant FX/8.

Multiprocessing background. Today's Cray Research, Inc. supercomputers are shared-memory, multiple-instruction, multiple-data (MIMD) vector processors.[3] Each vector processor has scalar units and several vector (single-instruction, multiple-data, [SIMD]) units. These vector units include floating-point multiplication, addition, and reciprocal and integer units for shift, add, and logical operations. They can operate simultaneously, each issuing one result per each clock cycle. The Cray X-MP and Cray 2 both have four processors, but the new Cray Y-MP has eight. Cycle times on these machines range from 9.0 nanoseconds on early X-MPs to 4.1 nanoseconds on the Cray 2. Memory sizes range from 8 Mword (64 bit words) on the Cray X-MP-48 to 12 Mword on the late model Cray 2. Shared resources on the X-MP and Y-MP lines include all of main memory, a single clock (with its associated real-time clock register), one 32-bit semaphore register, eight address registers, and eight scalar registers. Shared resources on the Cray 2 are the main memory, clock, and four one-bit semaphore registers. Although the Cray X-MP and Y-MP memory sizes are much smaller than those of the Cray 2, these machines can be ordered with copious amounts (512 Mword) of slower secondary memory called solid-state disks. This shared device is really a "RAM-disk" for supercomputers.

Many Cray-class supercomputers are run in a time-sharing mode under the UNICOS (Cray Unix System V), NLTSS (Networking Livermore TimeSharing System), or LTSS/CTSS (Livermore/Cray TimeSharing System) operating systems. Some sites still run the batch-oriented COS (Cray operating system) operating system. In the UNICOS, NLTSS, and LTSS/CTSS environments, users submit work to the systems in units called jobs. User jobs utilize system resources on various levels known as tasks, processes, and processors. Processors are the physical CPUs. Processes are the operating system scheduled units of computation run on behalf of a user job. Tasks are portions of work within the user code. Tasks are implemented as separate threads of execution within a set of processes and are scheduled by the multiprocessing library.[3,4] For example, a job may have three processes running on two physical CPUs supporting five user tasks.

The multiprocessing library allows the programmer to create, control, and destroy tasks. It includes support for

*This work was supported in part by the Applied Mathematical Sciences subprogram of the Office of Energy Research, U.S. Department of Energy, by Lawrence Livermore National Laboratory under contract W-7405-ENG-48.

critical regions (portions of code where only one task can be active at a time) by locks, global synchronization (where all cooperating tasks must reach a single point before any can proceed), barriers, and events that provide primitive inter-task communication. Multiprocessing is typically used for large-grain parallelism (copious quantities of work) and has extent on the Fortran subroutine level.

Within the user's program, the multitasking library schedules tasks into (out of) system processes. This is known as binding (unbinding) tasks to (from) processes. Task scheduling within the user program takes place only if the task becomes blocked for some reason (e.g., waiting on a lock). If another task is ready to run but not bound to a process, the library does a task exchange. The operating system schedules processes to run, and this operation is known as "binding processes to processors." The NLTSS operating system performs preemptive process scheduling on a time-slice interval, based on priority, memory size, and time since last swap from disk. Family scheduling is a recent "improvement" in process scheduling. Under this algorithm, when any process of a user job is scheduled, then any remaining processes waiting to run are scheduled (over any other process in the run queue except for system processes) as physical CPUs become available.

In addition to (or instead of) explicit use of the multiprocessing library, programmers may also supply directives that instruct the processors to cooperate on specific sections of code called control structures (usually Fortran Do loops) without having specifically to create and control tasks. This mechanism is called microtasking, and it is quite useful for computationally intensive parallel outer loops. The overheads associated with microtasking are much less than those associated with multitasking, but its scope is more limited. Automatic detection of microtaskable loops is known as *autotasking*.[3]

Debugging multiprocessing codes is made difficult because the conventional debugging techniques (inserting **write** statements or using a symbolic debugger) tend to cause the runtime behavior of the code to change so much that time-dependent bugs vanish. And once the code is debugged the next issue is performance: why did this code not run as fast in parallel as was expected?

GMAT helps the applications developer find these types of "bugs" by tracing the interaction with the multi- and microtasking libraries. This is accomplished by instrumenting the libraries with the ability to log all calls. To keep the logging overhead to a minimum, this information is stored in a shared memory buffer. The resulting overhead is on the order 1000 clock periods per library interaction.

This logging capability within the library was originally exploited by a program called MAT (multiprocessing analysis tool.[5] From a trace file generated by the libraries, MAT produces a detailed, human-readable (ASCII text) file dis-

playing the execution of the multiprocessing code. The MAT output file contains a static trace of all multiprocessing events. The MAT trace dumps were very useful, but the combination of overwhelming amounts of data and inspiration provided by the Schedule trace facility gave rise to the GMAT project.[6]

Design goals of GMAT: The primary design goal of the GMAT family was to create a set of standard SunView tools that would graphically display, and help the user analyze, a library-generated execution trace file of a parallel application. Implicit in this is the ability to (1) turn tracing on and off (selective use); (2) have the multiprocessing library contain all the code required for tracing and still give users the ability to log their own events (ease of data generation); (3) watch the graphics interface as the application executes and be able to play back a previous execution trace over and over again to study portions very carefully (dynamic and static modes); and (4) use only what was available from Sun Microsystems in the way of creating a SunView application ("off-the-shelf parts"). Three fundamental aspects accomplish these goals: distributed computation, graphical display, and control. We need the distributed computation because the parallel application is running on a remote multiprocessing host, and the trace visualization tool runs on a Sun workstation.

In a multiprocessing environment, we would like to view two quite different types of information: task genealogy and synchronization. Since intertask synchronization is only really necessary as a result of concurrent execution, the notion of time is a fundamental aspect of the graphical display of synchronization data. But a timeline approach is not conducive for displaying task lineage, because the fork/join operations are generally separated by enough time so that getting all of it on a single screen is impossible. Hence, we developed two separate tools—called Stategraph and Timeline—and highlighted each aspect separately. Most of the control features between the tools are similar, and, hence, development work and user training is reduced.

Stategraph represents each task by a node in an ancestry tree and changes the node representation as events affecting the state of the task are processed. Lines are drawn connecting parent tasks to the children they spawn, thereby indicating the task's lineage. One limitation of the Stategraph is that only events affecting the state of each task are shown graphically. Other nonstate events (such as No Wait on Lock [NWL:], acquiring access to a critical region without having to wait) are only available from the pop-up information windows for each task.

Timeline represents each task by a line and posts nodes along the line as events occur. Thus, events are shown graphically and we can watch the execution of a task as the timeline grows downward. Timeline also provides a temporal sense, because the display is driven on a time-interval basis versus an event basis, as in Stategraph. One limitation of Timeline is that little history is kept. Since all events are posted (unless event filtering is chosen), the time line can grow rapidly, and we lose such past information as a task's parent or children. Because of space limitations, we will consider only Timeline in detail. (Interested readers may consult Seager et al. [1988] for more information on Stategraph.)

Timeline

Description and design consideration. Time is a fundamental aspect of synchronization, and hence the Timeline incorporates time as its central focus. As tasks are created, they begin to have a "timeline" (an existence, with state, in time). Timelines for each task are drawn adjacent to each other and downward (see Figure 1) as time passes for the task. The adjacency of the timelines helps interrelate the execution of the tasks during any time period. As the execution state of a task changes—for example, from "running" to "waiting"—so does the graphical representation of its timeline. Timeline shows significant events as icons superim-

posed on the timeline at the point of their occurrence (we will describe these representations later). Tasks are also connected by a horizontal line to tasks they spawn at the moment of spawning. Hence, at any given moment, the timelines show the history of the multiprocessing job.

Correlating the time between tasks is done by using time-stamp information associated with each event logged to the trace file. These time stamps are in units of machine cycles and represent real time as opposed to elapsed CPU time. As Timeline processes events, it looks at both the current and next event, finds the difference between the two time stamps, and then "waits" that amount of time before indicating the next event. Timeline "waits" by using the concept we refer to as *simulated waiting* or *warped time*. Since events are logged at intervals ranging from microseconds to minutes, during long intervals we are usually not interested in watching the timelines progress, unchanged, for that length of time. To avoid this, Timeline warps time after a few seconds of unchanging time lines by speeding up the "clock" rate by a factor of ten and then continuing to wait. Waiting, warping time, and waiting repeat until the interval between events passes. At that point, the clock is reset to normal. Because of

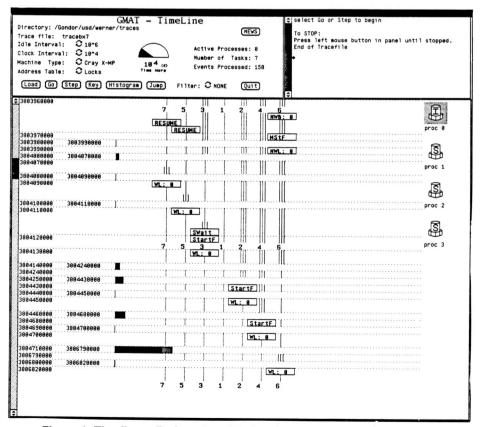

Figure 1. Timeline—display of a critical region bug leading to deadlock.

162

its geometric nature, time warp can dynamically compress very long compute-bound periods into tolerable segments of viewer time. But events separated by small intervals can come in such quick succession that the display cannot keep up. When this happens, the clock slows down by a factor of ten, and then continues to process events. If Timeline is still unable to keep up, the clock slows down again. When Timeline is once again able to keep up with the event rate, the clock is reset to normal. The user receives visual clues (discussed later) as time is warped so that it may be taken into account when interpreting the data.

Since Timeline shows the visual history of the tasks, we can interrelate significant events in the life of a task with those of the other tasks. This makes it easy to see the order of task spawning, synchronization between tasks, and execution state changes of tasks. Timeline also provides a level of consistency checking on the trace data. This allows us to identify and repeat the obvious flaws in the trace data—for example, the use of a lock before it had been initialized is detected and reported.

User interface layout. Although Timeline's window layout is relatively simple (see Figure 1), it can display an enormous amount of trace information at one time. In the window's upper-left corner (Figure 1), a panel controls file selection, processing speed, loading, running, and informative subwindows. At the center of Timeline's approach to trace-file visualization is time, and, hence, the center of the control panel contains the time-warp icon. It graphically displays the current time warp.

In addition to the time-warp icon, we added four other controls to the control panel to help reduce the amount of information produced in a graphical time line. Reduction of detail gives us insight into the parallel execution. These new controls are the address table, the filter option, the idle interval option, and the jump button.

The address table helps to abstract locks, barriers, and events. Since the user seldom needs to know the full address of every lock, barrier, or event that may be encountered, they are assigned a small integer value in the display (the first lock, say, is 0, and each lock-assignment event increments the counter by one). If at any time we need the correlation between these integer values and the actual addresses (e.g., debugging), we can bring up an address table with the mouse. The type of table that appears is controlled by the address table. An event table, lock table, or barrier table may be selected.

Options to filter the trace data are provided so that the user may screen out events of lesser interest. The filter item toggles between three filtering modes: (1) display all events (filter NONE); (2) display only multitasking events (filter micro); and (3) display only user events and events that change the state of the task (filter all).

Idle interval was added to help identify tasks that were runnable but not running in a physical processor.

The jump button allows the user to skip to interesting events in the trace. The user specifies whether to jump to an event count, to the next event originating from a specific task, or to the next event of a specific type. When selected, a pop-up window appears with a list of mnemonics (see Figure 2). A user can select a mnemonic with the mouse cursor. An action number may alternatively be entered directly in the jump window. When a jump is made, Timeline, will first clear the current time-line display. For a forward jump, the events are processed internally so that a consistent state is known internally to Timeline. For backward jumps, the new time lines will be drawn with ignorance of task states. This corresponds to throwing out the accumulated history of the tasks. From then on, as events are read for a task, Timeline derives and stores as much information as possible.

The Timeline version of the "histogram" button has a slightly different function from that of the corresponding button in Stategraph. Selecting this button toggles a pop-up window that plots the number of active processes as a function of time (as opposed to event) and hence may be interpreted as a graph of processor utilization. If the user changes the clock interval at any time during execution, the histogram will continue with the new clock interval. As a reference, Timeline displays periodically the number of clock cycles since the beginning of program execution in the bottom row of the histogram.

In the upper-right corner of Figure 2, a text subwindow prints all error messages and user prompts. A graphics subwindow displaying the time lines and process-state icons takes up the remainder of the screen. The time lines can be very long, and so there are scroll bars on the left side of the window for their static review. Icons indicating the number of processes associated with the job and their state are drawn along the right edge of the graphics subwindow. Although the process icons may change state, they remain stationary in the subwindow and are not affected by the subwindow's scrolling.

Graphical representation of tasks and processes. The representation of a task time line is divided into two graphical categories: posted events (both library and user defined) and run/wait states. For each task, posted events are entries in the trace file originating from the task that may affect the task's run/wait state. We represent posted events in Timeline as a box containing an identifying string. Often, the posted event will report another piece of auxiliary information. For example, the "waiting on a task" event will contain the number of the task on which it is waiting. This shows up in the box as an integer next to the characters. (See Figure 3 for a list of library-defined events.)

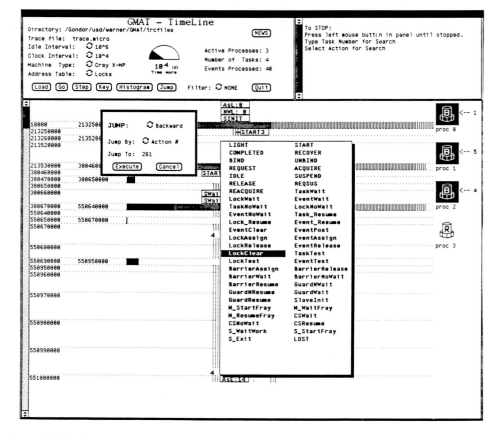

Figure 2. Timeline—display of "jump" and action number mnemonic pop-up subwindows.

Besides predefined library events, the user may define and log events to the trace file. User-defined events have many uses, but the primary one is to delimit specific computations of interest to the application developer. Library-defined events appear as square boxes; user-defined events appear as boxes with rounded corners. Timeline can be individually customized to associate a four-character label with each user-defined event.

Although a task will occasionally post an event, the task is always either waiting or ready to run. In either case, the task may also be bound to a process (actually running or "spin waiting"). Timeline represents these different run/wait states as vertical lines (see the top of Figure 3). It uses a single solid line if the task is ready to run but not bound to a process. A single dotted line is used if the task is waiting and not bound to a process. Three solid lines denote that a task is running (i.e., ready to run and bound to a process). And a single dotted line surrounded by two solid lines indicates that the task is waiting but still bound to a process (i.e., spin waiting). Between posted events, a task's time line is extended with its run/wait state. The visual effect is a column of indiscriminately spaced boxes connected either with dotted or solid lines.

We should note that since processes are scheduled by the operating system (which cannot make entries into the trace file), Timeline cannot determine if a task bound to a process is actually executing on a physical processor. But it should be clear that at the time a task is bound to a process, that process must be executing (otherwise the bind could not take place). To determine if the process is taken away from a physical processor by the operating system, Timeline monitors the task's event posting. If no trace entries for the task have occurred for some time interval, we assume that the process bound to this task is probably not executing. To indicate this, the parallel lines will become dotted. The idle interval item allows the user to control the size of this interval.

Another limitation of Timeline is the limited screen space for drawing the task time lines. If a task does not fit on the screen when created, it will never appear. But an internal task state will still be maintained to continue performing trace-data consistency checking.

Timeline displays the state of each process directly to the right of the time lines and shows processes as icons that change as the process state changes. A process can be either bound, idle, or suspended. The difference between the latter

Key to GHAT Symbols

||| Task is ready to run
||| Task is running
||| Task is waiting
||| Task is waiting and bound

LI☀HT	And Then There Was Light ...
START N	Task N has been started
COMPLETE	Task is completed
RECOVER	Task has been recovered
⎯N⎯	Task has posted action number N
STR: X	Identifier STR posted, with data X

AsB:	Assign Barrier	RlL:	Release Lock
AsE:	Assign Event	RESUME	Resume
AsL:	Assign Lock	SINIT	Initialize Slaves
ClE:	Clear Event	StartF	Slave Starts Fray
ExitS:	Slave Exits	SWait	Slave Waits for Work
MstF:	Master Starts Fray	TsE:	Test Event
MWaitF:	Master Waits on Fray	TsL:	Test Lock
NWB:	No Wait on Barrier	TsT:	Test Task
NWCS:	No Wait on CntrlStrctr	WE:	Wait on Event
NWE:	No Wait on Event	WB:	Wait on Barrier
PsE:	Post Event	WL:	Wait on Lock
ReqPro	Request Process	WG:	Wait on Guard
RlB:	Release Barrier	WGN:	Wait on Guard N
RlE:	Release Event	WaitCS	Wait on CntrlStrctr

[B] process is bound   [I] process is idle

[S] process is suspended   [R] process is reacquired

[U] process is unbound

Figure 3. Timeline symbols.

two is slight but important. A process suspended is no longer eligible to use a physical processor and therefore will not use CPU time. Yet an idle process is in a potentially expensive state; if it is using a processor, CPU time is still being used but no actual work is being done. For this reason, Timeline indicates idle processes with a characteristic gray process icon. An inverted process icon indicates bound processes actually performing program work.

Time warp. One of Timeline's major features is its ability to represent time when executing a multiprocessing job. Following the traditional view of a timeline, time should progress linearly, and events should be outlined at the time they occur. In deciding on the best way to show real time, we had to address several problems. First, supercomputers operate with a clock cycle in nanoseconds, and anything of interest takes multiple clock cycles to accomplish. So, naturally, the time line progresses by "blocks" of time rather than by individual clock cycles. Within each block, none, one, or many events possibly could occur. From experimentation, we found that a block size (clock interval as it is shown in Timeline's control panel; see Figure 2) of around

104 clock cycles yielded few intervals with multiple events in them. But the user may modify the clock interval to tune the granularity of inspection. If the viewer is very interested in exactly how time was spent during execution, a small clock interval could be set. Conversely, to get a rough idea of where large blocks of time are spent, a larger clock interval could be set.

Another timeline display problem is the wide disparity between the amount of time it takes the Sun workstation to update the screen (around 10^{-1} seconds) and the amount of real time represented in the supercomputer clock interval. The Cray X-MP-416 cycle time is 8.5×10^{-9} seconds, hence the default clock interval of 10^4 clock cycles represents 8.5×10^{-5} seconds in real time. Therefore, we must slow down representation of the application execution speed on the supercomputer by a factor of $0.1 / 8.5 \times 10^{-5} \approx 10^3$. This was our first step in breaking with the standard concept of time in this display environment.

We accomplish the timeline advancement with an update based on a combination of events and clock intervals. Starting at the first event in the trace, we set the timeline clock to zero. Timeline displays a time stamp (the number of clock cycles since the start of the trace) on the left edge of the subwindow and draws a horizontal line across the entire subwindow.

The subwindow is then updated, as we have described, for all the events occurring within the clock interval. After processing all the events in the clock interval, Timeline displays another time stamp and horizontal line, and draws the events for a new clock interval. In this way, each clock interval is automatically assigned as much timeline space as required.

The other piece of ergonomics that lead us to modify the time concept in Timeline was the need to present, in an efficient manner, intervals corresponding to long periods of computation or inactivity (because of being swapped out in a time-sharing environment). Simply updating the timeline every interval quickly becomes tedious, since hundreds or millions of inactive intervals are possible in a supercomputer environment. The viewer can quickly get lost wading through screen after screen of repeated graphical display. To avoid this, Timeline handles inactive intervals with a compact graphical representation. It displays a series of one or more inactive intervals in one horizontal row across the subwindow. For the first inactive interval, it draws a normal time stamp and a thin vertical bar at the left side of the row. For each successive inactive interval, Timeline displays the time next to the initial time stamp and draws an additional thin vertical bar to the right of the preceding bar. This causes a bar to grow from left to right as successive inactive intervals are processed.

The preceding strategy is an effective way to graphically compress the possibly quite large number of inactive intervals. But what about the viewer's time? Since we have slowed down the execution speed of the application by a factor of 10^3, one Cray X-MP second of compute (not uncommon in large parallel applications) corresponds to over 15 minutes of display time. To circumvent these possibly long displays of inactive intervals, we can dynamically modify the concept of time: time warp. After every 100 consecutive inactive intervals, the size of the interval is automatically increased by a factor of 10. This effectively warps the internal "clock" of the Timeline tool. A visual clue to the user is displayed graphically by changing the pattern of the left-right growing bar. If another 100 inactive intervals pass with the new update interval, the update interval is again automatically increased by a factor of ten and the bar pattern is changed again. Thus, by the change of the vertical bar pattern, the user can tell that a time-warp speedup is occurring. If necessary, the bars wrap around the row and continue drawing through the previous patterns. This continues until reaching the next event in the trace. With this logarithmic expansion, we can very quickly compress long intervals and still convey a sense of time progression. The time-warp technique also leaves behind a visual reminder of the long computation that is very compact and easy to integrate into the overall graphical display of the multiprocessing job execution.

Another time-warp visual clue is the control panel "speedometer," implemented to give the user a sense of the time warp as the subwindow is being updated. A logarithmic dial with a range from 10^7 (slowdown) to 10^{-7} (speedup) is displayed in the center of the control panel. The speedometer reading gives the current time-warp factor. For example, the default settings ("machine type" = Cray X-MP and "clock interval" = 10^4) yield a time-warp factor of 10^3, and hence the speedometer reading of 10^3 indicates that Timeline would take 10^3 seconds to display one second of program execution. When the number of inactive intervals grows and the clock interval is automatically increased, as described above then the speedometer decreases to 10^2 to 10 to 1 to 10^{-1} and so forth.

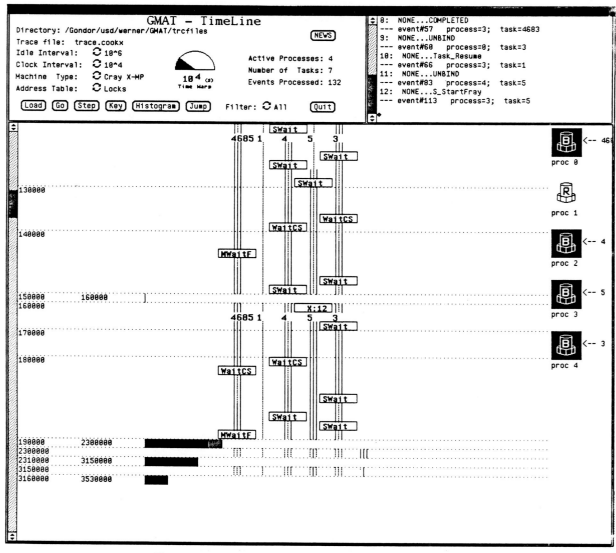

Figure 4. Timeline—multitasking with "filter all" in effect.

Trace consistency checking. Timeline can check trace files for consistency based on rules that dictate the order certain events should occur (e.g., a lock must be allocated before it is used). Posted events may affect the state of processes, tasks, microtasking, locks, barriers, or events. Whenever a state is updated, Timeline checks the previous states to be sure that the new state is reasonable. If the new state violates a rule, an error message appears in the text subwindow indicating the error number, the rule violation, and other related state information. In the absence of a regular icon, a rectangular icon containing an *X* (for eXception) followed by the appropriate error number is drawn at this location on the timeline (see Figure 4); otherwise the regular icon is drawn. Timeline corrects the state history to avoid unnecessary further indications of the same error (see Figure 5).

Intermittent logging. Another of Timeline's features is the ability to handle trace files that do not start at the beginning of a program's execution. This situation can arise when the application turns event logging off and then back on, or if the internal circular trace buffer wraps upon itself. Event data can also be lost when buffers are not flushed often enough. When this occurs, Timeline detects it and displays a message in the text subwindow to inform the user. In addi-

tion, a "LOST DATA" banner is superimposed on the time-warp bar produced by the data loss (see Figure 6).

Whenever data are missing, consistency errors can occur and are displayed in the text subwindow. As each error occurs, an effort is made to correct the state accordingly. When an event is read for a task, as much information as possible is derived and stored. Thus, after a few events are read, the structure is completely updated and task timelines appear correctly on the screen. The number of consistency errors rapidly diminishes as the trace history is correctly updated.

Extensions to timeline. The following is a list of possible additions we envisage for Timeline in the near future:

- Dynamic mode—complete the implementation of dynamic mode for GMAT Timeline, thereby enabling a user to view a graphical representation of a program during execution.

- Allowing users to specify consistency rules for their own events could be very useful in helping them find errors in the application automatically.

- Controlling update speed—currently, the screen is updated at a fixed rate, and there is no way to control

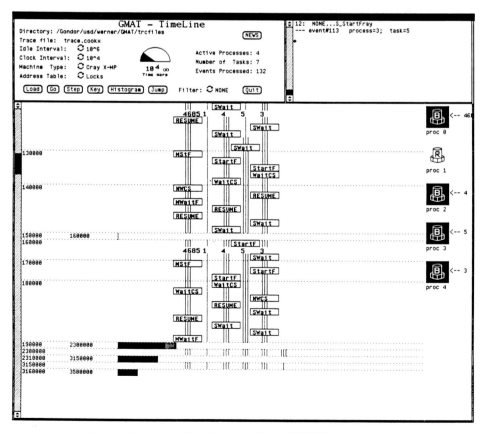

Figure 5. Timeline—multitasking with "filter NONE" in effect.

167

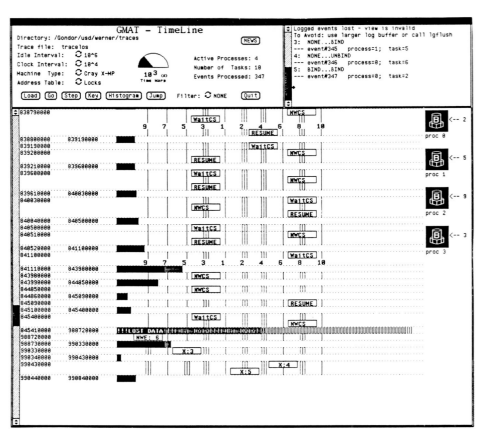

Figure 6. Timeline—consistency check.

how fast events are drawn. Thus, there are two speeds: one at a time or as fast as possible. Allowing the time before updates to be user controlled and allowing the user to proceed as fast or as slow as possible would be valuable additions.

- Printing the canvas—a print option could allow a permanent history of a trace file. This would allow the user to print a canvas before clearing it for the next series of events.

- It would be easy to add the user-specified names for user action numbers to the pop-up selection menu for Jumping on Action #.

Representative GMAT Sessions

The best way to explain typical uses of GMAT is by example. The following sections describe typical problems users in our NLTSS environment run across on a daily basis in working with parallel applications.

Locking locked locks: Classic deadlock. The first example is so common that almost everyone makes this mistake at one time or another in developing parallel codes.

Symptoms. The user got the following message from the system:

error 0401 processes deadlocked

while running the multi/microtasking job on the Cray X-MP. The symptom is very reproducible. Using the NLTSS debugger, we can find out what subroutine(s) the respective tasks are in, but no clue about who did what to whom and when. The fastest way to narrow down the problem is to generate an execution trace and "get a visual" of the problem.

Tracking down the problem. The tracing mechanism is turned on within the user program by adding three simple subroutine calls to the code (most users always have these lines in their code within an If statement that can be activated by setting a variable from within the debugger). The application is rerun to generate the trace file. The latter is then moved to the Sun workstation file system. Then Timeline views the trace file by selecting the appropriate directory and file in the control panel (upper left corner of Figure 1). Once Timeline chooses the correct file, load button is triggered and we are ready to view the trace. Next, Timeline selects the go control panel button to initiate the display, and we watch the computation until the end of the trace file is detected (this is the most likely source of the problem). At this point (see Figure 1), all active tasks should be waiting on lock 0, as indicated by the displayed action [WL: 0] on the task time lines. In this code, task 1 did not participate in the computations. Task 6 has the lock since it displayed a [NWL: 0] (NoWait on Lock 0) action (see the top of task 6's time line in Figure 1). But task 6 is again waiting on the lock that it already has (as can be seen at the end of its time line in Figure 1). Since the NLTSS multitasking library does not keep track of lock ownership, this task is unaware that it already has the lock. So it waits for the lock to be released which, of course, will never occur: a classic case of "deadlock."

A critical region too short. One of the early applications to be parallellized at the laboratory was the neutron-transport code IMP. Using a finite-element method closely related to the SN method, IMP solves the transport equation for neutrons. In modeling the neutron transport, there are seven independent variables (three positions, two directions of travel or angles, time and energy). In the SN technique, the space variables are discretized with the finite-difference or finite element technique, and we dispense with one of the angles by assuming longitudinal symmetry. The other angle is usually discretized with the finite-difference method in the direction cosine. We group energy into a small number of packets and integrate the whole system in time using some implicit technique (e.g., backward Euler).

A complete monotasking IMP job runs on the Cray X-MP for 150 to 500 minutes at an average rate of around 80 million Mflops. Many algorithmic dependencies exist in the IMP code, which make parallelization difficult. In addition, it would not be effective just to multitask this code, since there are significant load balancing issues. But we cannot microtask the outermost parallel loops, because some of the inner loops are recursive and this would not be feasible with today's microtasking technology. Therefore, we employ a strategy of mixed multi/microtasking. When processors become available, because the assigned multi-tasking work is accomplished, they can be put to work on the microtasked loops of other (longer running) tasks. Because of this complexity, IMF stumbled into several problems with the system support for parallel processing.

Symptoms. The user multi/microtasking job always crashes (in different places) while running on the Cray X-MP NLTSS and when requesting four processors; whereas it always runs successfully when using only three processors. The normal NLTSS debugger cannot contribute any further information: it claims that the registers have been "trashed" (overwritten with unrecognizable information).

Tracking down the problem. We generated and deposited a trace file on a Sun workstation using the steps deline-

ated in the previous example. After loading up the trace file and taking an initial look at the display, we determined that the library internal circular trace buffer had indeed wrapped upon itself. In this case, finding the problem will be harder (i.e., the events leading up to the crash are not at the end of the trace file). Finding the problem will be easier if we reduce the amount of information displayed on the canvas subwindow. So we choose the filter-all option in the control panel. We then allow the execution of the code to proceed, using the go button, until some very questionable events occur—at which time we hold down the right mouse button to stop processing the trace file. Figure 4 shows the state of the Timeline display after the mouse click. We should see that something is obviously wrong. Twelve error messages are displayed in the upper right text subwindow (Figure 4). After starting with the last message and looking backward in the text subwindow by scrolling, we determine that only the last error is not a spurious side effect of the buffer wrap around we noticed earlier. In fact, the last error message (12) is the *key* to the puzzle! It indicates that a slave (task 5) started a fray (S_StartFRAY) without the necessary preceding action (NONE). Note here that a rectangular icon containing an X followed by the error number (12; the middle of the canvas subwindow of Figure 4) is also drawn on the timeline to aid viewers in determining when the inconsistency occurred. Since the log is being filtered, other significant details are missing. We will have to back up from this point and restart the display without any filtering to get a better handle on the problem. We accomplish this by selecting the jump button with a click of the left mouse button. Timeline is now educated in the direction of travel desired by selecting "backward" with a mouse click on the JUMP cycle. (See the jump dialog box in Figure 2.) Next we tell Timeline how much to backtrack by typing an event number somewhat smaller than the event number at which error 12 was detected and selecting the execute button. The trace is then backed up to that event number and the filter is automatically reset to NONE. With the canvas subwindow now cleared, we begin the detailed analysis of the trace file by reselecting the go button. When we are once more in the trace-file problem area, we stop the display by holding the left mouse button down.

Figure 5 shows the status of the display at this point. We identify the problem by noticing the following. The StartF action (slave starts fray) is displayed on task 5's timeline. There should be a MstF action (master starts fray) preceding it, since a slave can only enter a fray after a master has initialized it. Looking backward in time, we should see that the last previous MstF action was followed by a MWaitF action (master waits for fray). When the master completes a fray, it must wait to be sure all activity is finished for that fray. Then it may begin a new fray. After the master completed the old fray and before it started a new fray, a slave (task 5) arrived thinking that the old fray was still active. Since no fray was in fact active, the slave went to some old address and counted itself in as actively working. Now the master waits for all active slaves to complete his latest fray. The errant slave, however, never completes the fray (as should be seen by the fact that task 5 runs from clock cycle 19,000 to 3,580,000). The job eventually blows up because of this misguided slave's activities. The only way this can occur is a bug in the critical section protection for shutting down completed frays within the microtasking support library!

An out-of-sync barrier. A research code was written to test new asynchronous iterative methods for solving large sparse linear systems of equations: $Ax = b$. Basically, each task updates a subset of the unknown variables based on the latest available solution estimate and residual $r^n = b - Ax^n$ without waiting for the other tasks to complete their updates. Thus, as one task is updating some subset of the iterate, other tasks are doing the same; and the values the first task is using as input data can change asynchronously during the update. This type of parallel computation is not repeatable on shared-memory machines but will converge if the underlying iterative method has the mathematical property of being a contraction mapping and if all the components of the iterate get updated from time to time.[8]

The parallel test code uses several asynchronous iterative methods with barrier synchronization points between methods. Within the methods, each processor also checks the error after a number of updates. And when the error is below a prescribed tolerance, it waits at a barrier for the others to finish their updates.

Symptoms: The execution times of the methods varied greatly from run to run, and the code tended to end with the system error:

***TASKING FATAL ERROR — Deadlock Achieved.
error 0203 at 00067655d error exit interrupt
a (000000) instruction has been issued

Tracking down the problem. The first obvious choice is to try the symbolic debugger. But in this case, running the code under the debugger changed the timing—and because of the asynchronous, nondeterministic nature of the computation, changed the course of the computation itself. The problem went away! Those with multiprocessing experience will be familiar with this frustrating situation. The next natural debugging step is to insert Fortran Write statements into the code to print out various quantities of interest (such as the error or number of iterations each task performs); but, again, this changed the timing of the run, and the problem went away! It should be clear that the classical monoprocessing debugging techniques are failing.

A trace of a run that ended in "deadlock" was generated and viewed on the Sun workstation. Though tracing does affect the execution timing, its affects are only a small perturbation and hence it is much easier to reproduce time-dependent bugs. We obtained no insight into the problem from this trace, because the same barrier was used everywhere—as we shall see. So the code was sprinkled liberally with user-defined events and another trace file of a deadlock run generated. We depict the resulting Timeline display in Figure 7. In the canvas subwindow, we can see that task 5 waited on barrier 0, as did tasks 2 and 3 (task 1 is not participating in the computation). Task 4 is the last to enter the barrier and does not have to wait. This is normal and explains why the first trace did not give us enough information to find the problem. The clue to the bug is the user-defined events: BR1e (barrier position 1 end) followed by BR3s (barrier position 3 start) on the timeline for task 4 and BR1e followed by BR2s (barrier position 2 start) on the timelines for tasks 2, 3 and 5 (task 1 is not participating). From that sequence we can deduce that task 4 did not call the barrier at position 2! By careful examination of the source for this asynchronous iterative method, the user was able to see that, indeed, task 4 was treated specially. The timeline of task 4 suggested where to look in the code. When task 4 was last through the computation, it performed cleanup activities and failed to call the barrier before returning, as did the other tasks. Hence, when task 4 got back to the driver and called the (same) barrier to sync up with the other tasks before beginning the next asynchronous iterative method test, the other tasks were released. All the tasks then remained one barrier point out of phase, and the deadlock message was generated at the end of the run when task 4 completed and the others hit the final barrier. From the source code, it was also apparent that if the computational sequence changed and task 4 was not the last one through, then the special code would not be executed and the processors would remain instep through the barriers. Timeline would have found this bug sooner if the user had opted for different barrier variables at each barrier point, rather than the same one throughout the code.

Conclusions

We have discussed tools for the graphical analysis of multitasking and microtasking applications. These tools allow the visualization of parallel execution profiles generated (with only minor user intervention) by applications running on the NLTSS and UNICOS Cray-class supercomputers (X-MP, Y-MP, and Cray 2). Two types of displays can be utilized for debugging, performance tuning, and general understanding of parallel applications: Stategraph (inheritance tree with nodes displaying the state of tasks) and Timeline (time based history of tasks).

It is our experience that tracking down synchronization and control bugs in multi/microtasking applications using Stategraph and Timeline is easier than conventional

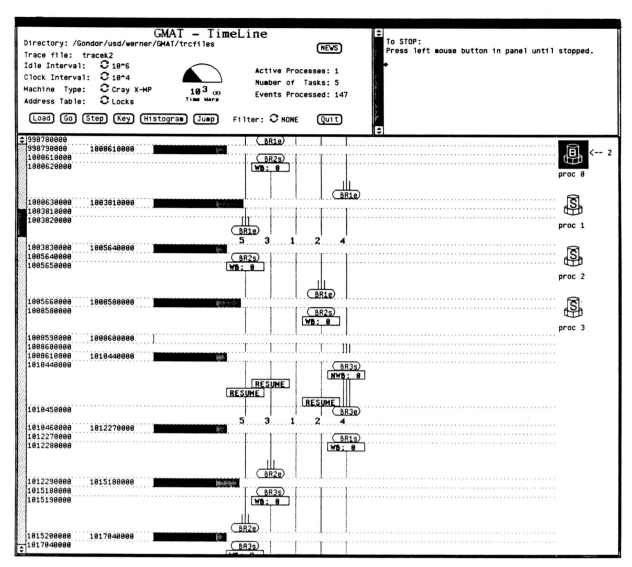

Figure 7. Timeline—multitasking barriers out of sync.

methods. Although GMAT is in its infancy, it should be clear that such an approach holds great promise for improving programmer productivity in the harsh multiprocessing LARRY environments. Cray Research also recognizes this and has acquired GMAT for distribution with the UNICOS 4.0 product set.

Acknowledgements

We would like to thank Jack Dongarra and Danny Sorenson of the Argonne National Laboratory for the sources of the Schedule display tool. It was from this tool that we began our development. Though only two routines from that tool remain in this source, we are very grateful to Dongarra and Sorenson for their support. This helped

greatly as an example in learning how to use the SunView windowing system and, in turn, greatly accelerated our development. Susan Campbell (Hewlett-Packard) and Scott Sikora (MIT) did the bulk of the actual Stategraph and Timeline coding during a summer at the LLNL Institute for Scientific Research.

References

1. G.M. Baudet, "Asynchronous Iterative Methods for Multiprocessors," *J. ACM,* Vol. 25, No. 2, 1978, pp. 226-244.

2. Cray Research, "Multitasking User Guide," *Tech. Report SN-0222,* Cray Research, Mendota Heights, Minn., 1984.

3. K. Crispin and R. Strout II, "NSYSLIB Library Reference Manual," *Tech. Report UCSD-912,* Lawrence Livermore National Library, Livermore, Calif., 1985.

4. J.J. Dongarra and D. Sorensen, "Schedule: Tools for Developing and Analyzing Parallel Fortran Programs," *Tech. Report ANL/MCS-TM-86,* Argonne National Library, Argonne, Ill., 1986.

5. L. Henderson et al., "On the Usefullness of Dependency Analysis Tools in Parallel Programming: Experiences Using Ptool," to be published in *J. Supercomputing,* 1989.

6. B. Kelly, "MAT Multitasking Analysis Tool," *Tech Report UCSD-342,* Lawrence Livermore National Laboratory, Livermore, Calif., 1986

7. T. Kerola and H. Schwetman, "Monit: A Performance Monitering Tool for Parallel and Pseudo-Parallel Programs," *1987 ACM SIGMetrics Conference on Measurement and Modeling of Computer Systems,* B.D. Gaither, ed., ACM, New York, 1987, pp. 163-174.

8. M. Seager et al., "Graphical Multitasking Analysis Tool (GMAT)," *Tech. Report UCID-21348,* Lawrence Livermore National Laboratory, Livermore, Calif., 1988.

Robert E. Strout II received the B.A. in computer science from the University of California at Berkeley (1981) and the M.S. in computer science from the University of California at Davis (1986). From 1983 to 1986, he was a computer scientist at the Lawrence Livermore National Laboratory. In 1988, he joined Supercomputer Systems as a senior engineer and is currently the programming environments project leader. His interests include parallel processing, parallel debugging, and performance evaluation. Strout is also a member of the Association for Computing Machinery.

Mark K. Seager is a staff mathematician in the Livermore Computing Center and a member of the Institute for Scientific Computing Research. His technical interests include parallel algorithm development and visualization, scheduling for parallel supercomputers, iterative methods for large sparse linear equations, and the finite-element method for solving PDEs. Seager has been with LLNL since 1983 and is a member of the Society of Applied Industrial Mathematicians. He received the Ph.D in numerical analysis from the University of Texas at Austin in 1984.

Mary E. Zosel has been group leader for the language group of the Lawrence Livermore National Laboratory since 1984. She is particularly interested in tools for parallel processing and program debugging. She has worked on archival storage systems and compiler development, is a member of ACM, and is vice-president of the Cray User Group. Zosel received the Ph.D in computer science from the University of Washington (1971) and was a member of the graduate group in computer science at the University of California at Davis from 1974 to 1988.

Nancy E. Werner is a computer scientist in the language group at the Lawrence Livermore National Laboratory where she has been working on parallel processing issues in a multiuser shared-memory supercomputing environment. Werner is working on the implementation and debugging of medium-grain (loop-level) parallelism. She received the B.S. from MIT (1961) and the M.S. from the University of New Mexico (1980).

Visualizing Wave Phenomenae with Seismic Rays

Victor Pereyra, Weidlinger Associates
Jose A. Rial, University of North Carolina

Introduction

Supercomputers have made possible a quantum leap in the size and sophistication of numerical simulations of engineering and physical systems. The large amount of input data necessary to drive such calculations, and the consequent massive output produced by them, challenges the practitioner's ingenuity. Interactive computer graphics and image processing have become important tools in solving this otherwise unwieldy data problem. Thus, both pre- and post-processing have benefited from visualization aids.

In this paper we illustrate some of these problems and current solutions from applied geophysics. We explore two fairly distinct types of applications from seismic prospecting and earthquake seismology. This is not a comprehensive look at the field but rather a sampler of some interesting problems and the effect that modern visualization techniques have had in their solution. Many more examples can be found in the current literature.[1-3]

Visualization in Seismic Prospecting

The purpose of geophysical prospecting is to construct images of the earth's interior from data collected on the surface or in wells to increase the efficiency of finding and exploiting oil and gas fields. Until recently, this imaging was limited by computer hardware to two-dimensional vertical slices. Thanks to increased availability of supercomputers both of vector and multiprocessor types, we can now acquire and analyze three-dimensional data sets. In turn, this has created the need for better visualization aids to help in the understanding and interactive manipulation of the results of such analyses.

We will present some examples of synthetic data sets and their visualizations for seismic prospecting. Seismic prospecting relies on man-made acoustic or elastic waves that propagate throughout the medium to be analyzed, much as in the case of medical imaging. Because of this similarity, some of the techniques are referred to as geotomography. The main differences with medical imaging are the scale of the problem and the fact that elastic waves in an inhomogeneous medium do not propagate along straight lines, as we assume in medical X-ray tomography.

In seismic prospecting, we activate a source of energy at or near the surface of the earth. This source generates elastic waves that propagate along the surface and through the body of the earth. Because of variations in the types of sediments and rocks found in its path, these elastic waves are refracted, reflected, and diffracted. Eventually, some of the energy returns to the surface, and it is recorded on a number of locations by an array of listening devices called geophones. This recording is nowadays done digitally and saved for further processing. For each source, the data contains time records of the ground motion at each geophone location during the period of observation. These time records encode information about the elastic properties of that part of the medium traversed by the propagating elastic wave in its travel from the source to the receiver. This wave energy propagates along curves called rays. One of the tasks of the exploration geophysicist is to decode the information contained in the seismic data and present it in a way that makes sense to the geologist, the interpreter, and eventually to the whole team that must make a decision on where to drill.

The type of reflection seismic prospecting just described will usually not be sufficient to generate all the information necessary to produce a complete model of the subsoil, including detailed and accurate stratigraphic and rock-type descriptions. But when coupled with other geophysical imaging methods—such as well-to-surface or well-to-well seismic sounding—and a variety of electric, electromagnetic, nuclear, and gravimetric measurements and any additional geological insight, we expect that a more complete picture will emerge.

Not all of these methods are in routine operation. On the contrary, most are at the research stage, especially in complex three-dimensional media. Only in the past few years have powerful supercomputers, coupled to versatile graphic workstations, made possible the practical implementation of some of these techniques. Integrating multiple data sets into a coherent picture of the subsurface is still in the future, although progress is being made steadily. In what follows, we present displays related to the simulation of wave propagation in elastic media.

In Figure 1 we show an example of finite-element output of an elastic wave-propagation simulation. This is a two-

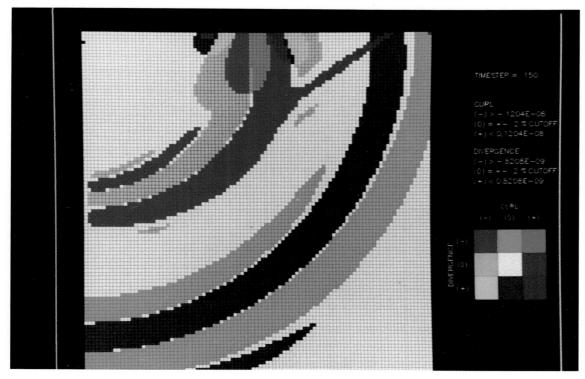

Figure 1. Finite-element solution of a two-dimensional vector wave equation. Two functions of the displacement field are plotted that make visible the pressure wave (in blues) and the transversal or shear wave (in reds).

dimensional symmetric calculation (vertical cross-section) on a simple model consisting of an homogeneous material layer. The wave energy is generated by a vertical point force activated on the upper left-hand corner at time $t = 0$, and the picture represents a "snapshot" of the displacement field at a later time, for half of the symmetric model. The resolution of this calculation is given by a 100×100 elements mesh in a 10×10 km physical square.

In an elastic isotropic continuum, various wave types are supported by the medium. To visualize these waves, we have pictured in this snapshot two different functions of the field: the dilatation or divergence and the rotation or curl components. By plotting them in different colors—blues for the divergence and reds for the curl—we can separate the faster dilatational (pressure) from the slower rotational (shear) wavefronts. We can also see ripples moving along the free surface (top of the picture) that correspond to Rayleigh surface waves. Finally, the red region connecting the pressure and shear circular wave fronts is produced by pressure-to-shear conversion at the free surface.

We have shown in this simple display how to visualize a considerable amount of numerical output data, capturing qualitatively most of the interesting phenomena evolving in the x, z, t space. Of course, animated sequences can be of help

here, and they are now frequently used if the appropriate hardware is available. For three-dimensional calculations, the amount of data and display difficulty grow considerably. In general, we will have a cube of data for each field variable, representing its value at points of the geologic region. This data cube may also evolve in time. We can employ color coding to display field values and animation for time sequences. One of the difficulties, akin to some problems in medical imaging, is that of visualizing interior features of a cube of material. A commonly used technique is to depict the data cube in perspective, as seen from some vantage point. Since the cube is considered as an opaque solid, we can see only some of its faces. By using animated sequences, now in space, we can inspect the interior of the cube by making a part of it transparent. This can be achieved in different ways—for instance, by sliding a cursor along one of the axes to indicate the depth at which we want the view. After choosing a proper depth, we should be able to switch the animation to time to see the evolution of a dynamic calculation. Other techniques now in development involve making the materials partially translucent to unveil inner features without losing sight of the overall structure. Of course, the amount of data to be manipulated in these displays is substantial. But this is the type of data currently produced in large-scale computations.

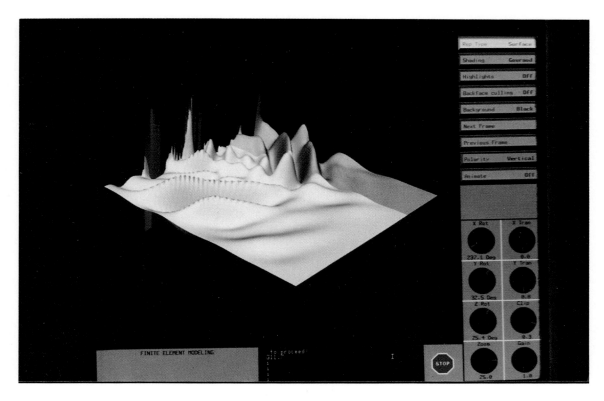

Figure 2. Finite-element solution of a two-dimensional vector wave equation. Displacement field is plotted as a surface. Color is used for material description.

In Figure 2, we show a different type of representation for a similar calculation. We use color now to indicate two different layers of material. The extreme left side of the rectangle corresponds to a vertical well. A source has been activated in the well, and this is a snapshot of the vertical displacement at a later time, plotted in a three-dimensional perspective.

A different, more economical computational technique takes advantage of the fact that elastic energy propagates along rays. Instead of trying to reproduce the complete received signal at each geophone, we try to model only some characteristics that can be recognized in the data. In particular, we concentrate our attention on body waves reflected by strong structural discontinuities, and we restrict our interest to the times of first arrival of such "echoes" at each geophone. Given a model description of the earth region under study, and the positions of sources and receivers, we can calculate approximately the energy paths (i.e., the rays), the travel times, and relative amplitudes. With this information, we construct synthetic seismograms by centering appropriate wavelets at the arrival times. These seismograms will not have, of course, the wealth of information of a full elastic wave simulation. But they can be obtained at a fraction of the cost by using a well-implemented seismic ray-tracing procedure.

Source-to-receiver seismic ray tracing has some similarities with the ray tracing used in computer graphics for high-quality rendering of three-dimensional scenes. But seismic ray tracing is in some respects simpler and in others more complicated. Seismic ray tracing is often performed in inhomogeneous media, the equivalent of a smoothly varying index of refraction in optics. This implies that the rays are curved or refracted and that a set of ordinary differential equations subject to multipoint boundary conditions must be solved for each ray. A further complication in elastic media results from the coexistence of (at least) two modes of propagation, namely pressure and shear or transversal waves. For instance, a compressional wave incident on a contact between different media will excite reflected and transmitted compressional waves—as well as corresponding shear waves—giving a total of four ray paths to follow. Although all possible rays generated at interfaces may be important, we usually trace only one kind from the source to the receiver at a time.

In any case, whereas this type of calculation is potentially expensive in a complicated three-dimensional scene, it requires only a fraction of the work necessary to calculate the evolution of the whole field for each shot of a survey. The ray-tracing calculation produces several kinds of outputs that need to be displayed in a meaningful and informative way. Just as important, the medium description needs to be such that models can be constructed, manipulated, updated, and, in general, operated on with reasonable ease.

Until very recently, the state of the art in geophysical prospecting allowed only the modeling of a "generalized layered earth." By this we mean that the material interfaces could only be one-to-one (x,y) surfaces covering the whole window of interest. Pinched-out layers and other unconformities could only be modeled by introducing artificially thin pseudolayers, thus extending the truncated layers to the boundaries of the geological cube. We imposed this limitation to facilitate the ray tracing, which is easier to do in layered media than in a more general type of media. By borrowing ideas from solid modeling, we have extended these concepts (see Millavec and Pereyra[4] and Pereyra[5]) to model complex structures of geological interest in a more natural fashion. The interfaces in our modeling system are made up of surface patches joined with a chosen degree of smoothness. These patches need not extend throughout the entire window of interest, and they can be one to one with

respect to any coordinate plane—thus allowing the easy representation of faults, vertical walls, multiple-valued folds, pinched-out layers, overhangs, isolated lenses, and other geological unconformities.

We show in Figures 3-5 several examples of such models and corresponding ray-traced shots from a source to a surficial array after reflection on a deep horizon. These displays can be produced today in medium-priced color workstations in a few seconds. (In our case, we used a Sun 3/260 workstation.) We chose the synthetic models to emphasize some of the new structures that can now be represented, and they exemplify the types of geological features we mentioned. All the surfaces in these models are represented by Coons patches.[6] Coons patches are quadrilateral surfaces, entirely defined by their boundary curves, by a process called blending or transfinite interpolation. The curves used here are planar, parametric cubic splines, although we can also employ general spatial curves.

For rendering, we introduce a mesh of uniformly spaced points in the surface parameters. By evaluating the surface

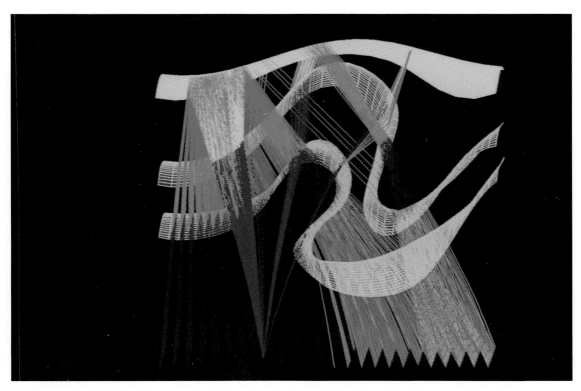

Figure 3. Model of a recumbent fold. Four material layers are separated by multivalued surfaces. A shot is set on the free surface, and we calculate and display the rays that join the source with an uniform array of receivers (also in the free surface) after reflecting on the bottom interface. Notice the diversity or ray paths that traverse different parts of the structure.

Figure 4. Model of a salt dome piercing a number of layers of harder material. We have made the interfaces transparent to see the interior detail, but the ray color changes indicate their presence.

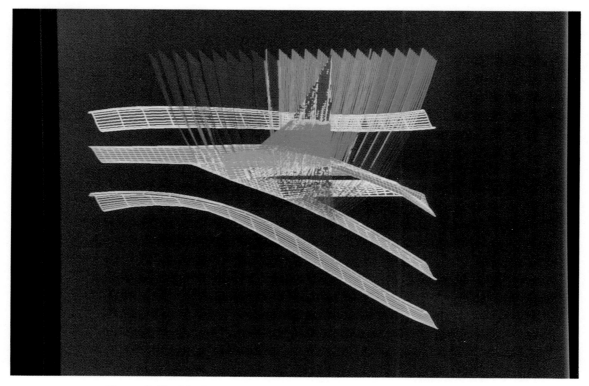

Figure 5. Model of a stratigraphic hydrocarbon trap, no hidden lines.

function on these points and joining them with straight lines, we create a lattice of discrete curves that determines the surface. We complete the rendering of the resulting connected quadrilateral grid by filling the quadrilaterals with a constant color. Color coding could emphasize depth cues or represent material velocities or other properties. In this representation we have used parallel projections with a hidden-surface algorithm to render the three-dimensional objects on the plane of the figure. Finally, we have superimposed the ray paths on the models, but to save some time we have not used hidden lines. We used color again to improve visualization. By using contrasting colors for each leg of the ray (segment between two interfaces), we can see more easily where they intersect the interfaces and can verify that the algorithm actually recognizes all the details of the structure. The color of ray bundles also gives some indication on the extent of the volumes of the different materials.

In Figures 6-9 we present views of similar models: but now the rendering algorithm is more sophisticated. In this depiction, hidden lines are used, as well as hidden surfaces, and the graphic system automatically smooths the surfaces and includes light sources with Gouraud shading.[7] This type of graphics still can be obtained in a few seconds with a high-end workstation—in this instance, an Ardent Computers' Titan II. In addition, this machine can rotate the pictures in real time, providing considerable flexiblility for rapidly inspecting the model from different view points.

Visualizing Seismic Rays in Earthquake Seismology

An important problem in earthquake seismology is the theoretical computation (prediction) of strong ground motions produced by seismic waves scattered by the uppermost crustal layers of the earth. The complex geometry of geological structures may readily induce focusing and amplification of the incoming waves; or it may effectively trap them, thus generating long-lasting, destructive oscillations. Among the most typical geological environments encountered at shallow depths are sedimentary basins and corrugated waveguides. The latter are rock formations disposed in layers of variable thickness and great lateral extension. The former are bowl-shaped topographic lows filled with sediments.

Since many cities and towns are built on the surface of sediment-filled valleys or sedimentary basins, seismologists must be able to predict local intensifications of ground shaking resulting from these site-dependent effects. But the mathematical complexities involved in representing realistic

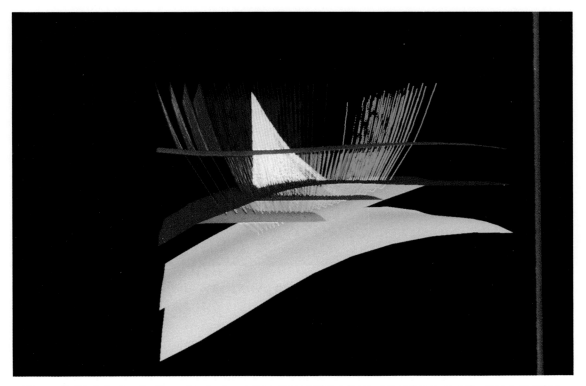

Figure 6. Model of a stratigraphic hydrocarbon trap; hidden lines, smoothing, and Gouraud shading.

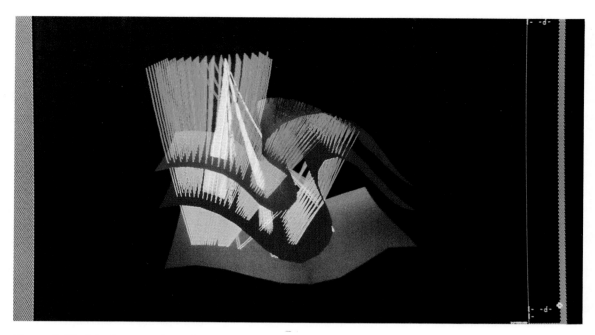

Figure 7. Model of a recumbent fold, as in Figure 3, but with a different point of view, different rendering algorithm, and workstation.

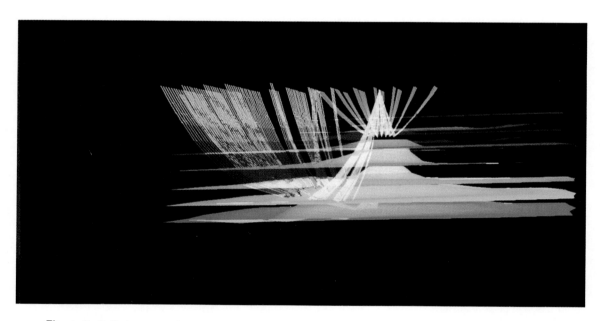

Figure 8. Salt-dome model, as in Figure 4, but with layers plotted with only partial transparency.

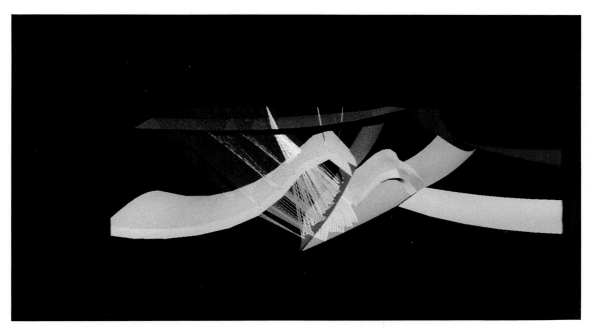

Figure 9. A complex double-faulted and folded model.

geological structures renders analytic—and many numerical—approaches useless. Effects such as focusing and excitation of free oscillations become unstable in arbitrarily shaped structures, mostly because of the inherent nonlinearities of the problem. Fortunately, we will show that ray theory can be used profitably in these cases, even when strong nonlinearities and instabilities occur.

Unstable oscillations (irregular, nonperiodic) occur frequently, especially in corrugated waveguides and in irregularly shaped basins. By an irregularly shaped basin we mean even those whose geometry—no matter how smooth and regular—cannot be described by the constant surface of a coordinate system in which the wave equation is separable. Within basins where geometries lead to nonseparable equations, seismic rays typically exhibit very complicated paths, which eventually touch every point throughout the entire volume of the basin. It is analytically and numerically impossible to predict the evolution of those complex paths even after a few reflections, since the ray trajectory becomes extremely sensitive to even minute changes in the initial direction and initial location of the ray. These unpredictable trajectories are called chaotic, or stochastic, and the mathematical problem is defined as nonintegrable.

Stable and predictable modes of oscillation, however, are confined by modal caustics (see Figure 10); the ray trajectories are regular and periodic. The problem is separable, and, consequently, caustic surfaces exist that will confine a given ray trajectory within a fraction of the basin's volume for all times. The problem is integrable, because a solution that describes exactly the ray trajectories and the modes of oscillation can be found analytically.

Regular and irregular motions can coexist within the same basin. This may happen for instance if, as in Figure 11, the small subbasins surrounding the central valley have locally a geometry that leads to separable equations. In such a case, local normal modes will be excited, and we will observe periodical oscillations. Inside the small basins depicted in Figure 11, the stable modes can be of two basic shapes indicated in Figure 10. Rial[8] has shown that these are the typical modes of basins with separable topography. In Figure 10a, the rays—seen in perspective view—are confined by the model caustics, in this case hyperboloids of one and two sheets. These "bouncing-ball" modes are solutions to the scalar wave equation in triaxial ellipsoidal coordinates. In Figures 10b and 10c, the basin is radially symmetric and so are the confining caustics, which become hyperboloids of one sheet. The mode depicted in Figure 10b is stable. In Figure 10c, the same mode is unstable, because the basin is a Gaussian surface, not a separable ellipsoid as in Figures 10a and 10b. Visualizing the ray paths in this way reveals the mode shapes and helps to determine the limits of stability.

It should be intuitively obvious that regular motions produce amplification and time-lengthening of the incident seismic waves and irregular, chaotic motions will induce attenuation or diffusion (defocusing). From a seismologist's point of view, it is then important to know whether and where the incoming earthquake waves will be reinforced or attentuated by the basin's geometry. If the model of the

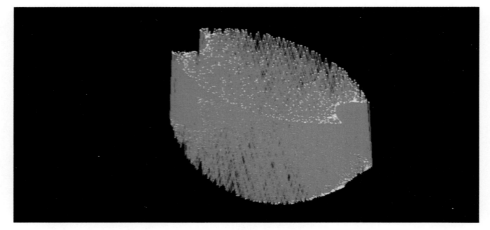

10a

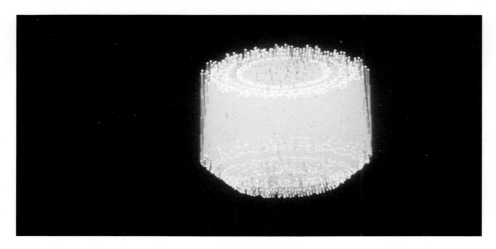

10b

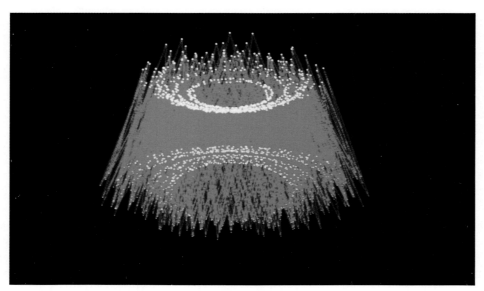

10c

Figure 10. (a) Rays confined by modal caustics; (b) radially symmetric, basin, stable mode; (c) Gaussian-shaped basin, unstable mode. A, b, and c were generated by a single, multiple bouncing ray. The bounces at the earth's surface are marked by white points and those at the basin's bottom by orange points. The ray is confined to a finite volume limited by the modal caustics (see p. 181 for details).

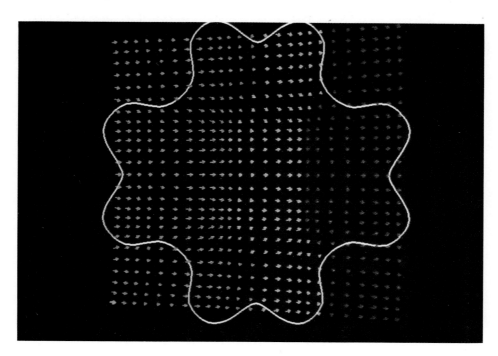

11a

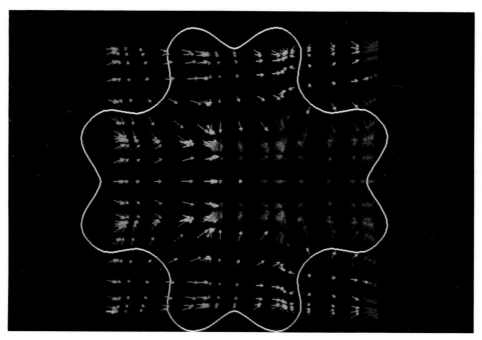

11b

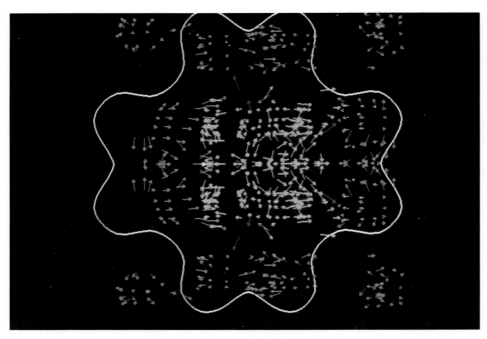

11c

Figure 11. Map view of a seismic *P* wave as it interacts with a three-dimensional model of a sedimentary basin. The wave is simulated by a bundle of rays issuing from a point source located deep in the earth and to the left of the figure. The topography of the basin's bottom is generated by adding cosine corrugations to a Gaussian surface whose maximum depth is at the center of the figure. The white curve is a contour line of the basin at a depth equal to one-third of the maximum. Each ray emerging at the earth's surface after refraction through the bottom of the basin is identified by a small arrow. The arrow is the horizontal projection of a unit vector along the approaching ray as it intersects the earth's surface. The length of each arrow is proportional to the incidence angle of the ray, a shorter arrow indicating a steeper ray. The relative times of arrival are indicated by color coding—early arrivals in blue and late arrivals in red. One ray at the lower-left corner is colored white for reference. Figures 11B and 11C depict the same rays as in the previous figure after one and after three successive internal reflections, respectively. In Figure 11B, we can observe the grouping of rays in the areas where stable resonances will emerge. In Figure 11C, it should already be clear that the small basins surrounding the central one have trapped the rays that will excite local stable resonant modes there. Lower eiger frequencies will, of course, be excited in the central basin.

basin in Figure 11 represented some actual urban center, such as the Los Angeles central basin and surrounding valleys, experimentation using color displays, such as those in Figure 11, could help reveal potentially dangerous areas where shaking is intensified or lengthened by the basin effect.

A more quantitative approach is also possible. For many years, physicists have studied complex, dynamical systems using idealized models. One such model, generically named "billiards," studies the paths of massless billiard balls (point particles) bouncing repeatedly inside a frictionless, smoothly bounded domain.[9,10] Physicists have extensively studied two- and three-dimensional billiards because they closely imitate the behavior of important physical phenomena.[2] Regular (integrable) and irregular (chaotic, nonintegrable)

trajectories of the billiard balls are observed; their presence or absence depends essentially on the geometry of the boundary.[9] It is not difficult to show that two- and three-dimensional billiards are kinematically identical to our models of seismic rays in basins or in corrugated waveguides—and thus that the wealth of techniques and results on the subject of nonlinear, multidimensional mappings and chaos are available for application to seismological problems. One important technique, the phase-space representation, helps to visualize the complicated long-term evolution of a multiply reflected seismic ray inside a layer with a corrugated boundary, as we shall see.

We can describe three-dimensional billiards and seismic rays bouncing inside geologic structures by nonlinear iterative mappings of the form

$$\mathbf{X}_{n+1} = \mathbf{F}(\mathbf{X}_n) \qquad (1)$$

where $\mathbf{X}$ is the position vector of a ray or the set of its direction cosines (in three-dimensions, $\mathbf{X}$ may be six-dimensional; i.e., three coordinates and three angles), $\mathbf{F}$ are nonlinear functions, and n is the number of reflections. After a few reflections, the explicit mathematical relationship between the current and the initial position and direction of the ray is hopelessly complicated algebraically and highly nonlinear. The equivalent of Equation 1 for a two-dimensional corrugated waveguide can be approximated by the expressions:

$$X_{n+1} = X_n + 2\,\mathbf{H}\,\tan(\alpha_{n+1}) \qquad (2a)$$

$$\alpha_{n+1} = \alpha_n - 2wk\,\sin(kX_n) \qquad (2b)$$

where X is the position of the ray at the bounce point on the corrugation of amplitude w and wavelength $2\pi/k$, and α is the angle the ray makes with the vertical at that point. The corrugation's amplitude is given by the function $\cos(kX)$. The objective of the study is to investigate the behavior of bounce point X and angle α as the number of bounces n grows large and the amplitude of the corrugations and/or their wavelength are changed. When w is zero, the angle α does not change; the ray simply moves away from the initial location at intervals of constant length, and the problem becomes trivial. But even a small perturbation generated by a nonzero value of w will induce chaotic ray paths.

In Equations 2a and 2b, the ordered pairs X, α form a set of points in two-dimensional space that, when plotted, describes all possible "states" of the system, that is, all the possible locations of the ray and its vertical angle for all times. The resulting plot is the phase-space plot or Poincaré section of the ray system. Figure 12 shows an example of such a phase plot as applied to the behavior of rays trapped in a cosine-corrugated waveguide of wavelength L and mean thickness H.

For initial angles less than about 42 degrees, the pairs of points X, α form closed elliptical orbits around the center of the figure, indicating that the ray trajectories are regular and invariant. For any given closed orbit, the largest and smallest values of X give the locations of the model caustics. Between the caustics, the rays visit every point along the x direction as long as enough number of bounces are computed. As the vertical initial angle increases, "resonant" islands appear, corresponding to trajectories that touch only a few points along the x direction. These are still stable paths. The phase plot shows where the instability begins. Beyond the resonant "islands," a chaotic "sea" is generated by points that seem to fall at random over that area of phase space; no individual trajectories can be predicted. Physically, the rays in the waveguide are bouncing from point to point at very shallow angles. This analysis reveals the coexistence of deterministic and random regimes of wave propagation, as well as the ray path's limits of stability. We should note that the stochastic behavior has in fact a deterministic origin, given by Equations 2a and 2b. Thus, the phase-space representation indeed offers a powerful, condensed, and useful way of visualizing the global states of nonlinear dynamical systems, a promising prospect indeed, since analytic and numerical approaches are of such limited use here.

But how and why does stability end and chaos begin?

The length and scope of this chapter only allow us a brief discussion. Figures 13a-13d show a slightly different use of phase-space plotting. The geometry is identical to that of Figure 12, that is, a cosine-corrugated, two-dimensional waveguide. Figures 13a-13d, however, show the effect of increasing the amplitude of the corrugation on the general behavior of the ray system. And instead of a few, we use 10,000 initial conditions, an almost continuous set of take-off angles at intervals of about one-hundreth of a degree. Instead of a large number of reflections, we calculate only the first eight.

Since the plot surface is a 2-torus, as the curves reach the right or the left edge they are continued on the left and right edges, respectively. As the initial angle increases, the state of the system "turns around" the torus at increasingly higher rates until it is impossible to follow its evolution.

The effect of increasing the amplitude of the corrugation should be clear. The stochastic area of the plot increases rapidly toward the center. As the slopes and curvatures of the reflector increase, the nonlinearity of the problem increases as well, and so does the area in phase space occupied by chaos. The "chaotic sea" appears just as a collection of random points. Closer examination demonstrates that as a function of initial angle, the final angle or position of any of the reflections is a smooth, continuous function of the initial angle. But as the initial angle increases, the function begins to show strong oscillations of ever-increasing frequency. As the frequency increases, the sampling rate becomes insufficient to record the rapid changes, and the continuous curve becomes a seemingly random set of points. If, however, we increase the sampling rate and enlarge the scale, we recover a smooth function similar to the original, which may still show some high-frequency oscillations. A higher sampling rate and a new enlargement will again produce a smooth function similar to the one we started with. We find an identical situation if we increase the number of reflections and keep the interval of initial angles constant.

It is this self-similar character of the phenomenon that makes the overall appearance of the phase plots so complex. Indeed, it is well known that the repeated iteration of a

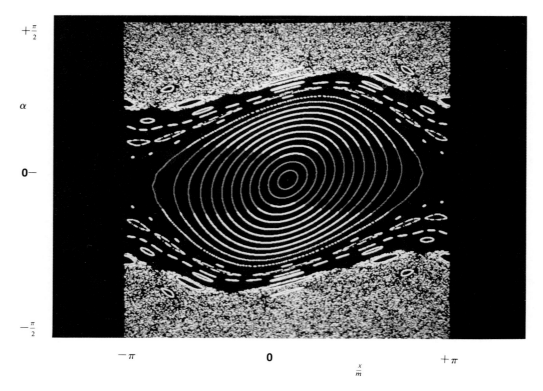

Figure 12. The phase-space plot (or Poincaré section) of a ray system. The abscissa represents distance along the x-direction modulo 2π. The ordinate is the angle of the ray with the vertical, modulo π. Twenty initial conditions at $x + 0$ for the vertical angle varying between 0 and $\pm 90°$ are plotted. For each initial condition 1000 reflection points (iterations) are calculated and plotted. The blue shading includes rays that hit the bottom of the guide at precritical angles. The refractive index across the corrugated lower boundary is 0.5. The dimensions of the waveguide are such that L, H and w are in the ratio 100:10:2. The thick stochastic area is the strong indicator of ray-path instability and chaotic behavior and begins when the initial angles are greater than about 42°.

nonlinear deterministic mapping such as described by Equation 2 can generate an outcome as random looking as if generated by flipping a coin.

Summary

We have presented some applications of modern visualization techniques to wave propagation problems arising in geophysics. We have considered problems in energy resource exploration by seismic methods and in earthquake seismology. In both types of applications, visualization techniques have been crucial in conveying the information contained in an otherwise unwieldy amount of output data. And the choice of appropriate display formats makes this information more easily understandable, increasing considerably its value.

It is important to understand that often the analyst requires only qualitative information to make a quick decision on the correctness of the work done so far and on how to proceed from there. This situation arises in our applications when constructing a model, at various stages of the ray-tracing process, and in more complex tasks (not discussed here) such as inverse modeling, that is, determining a parametrized model from seismic data. It is here where this type of display proves invaluable by efficiently conveying qualitative information, and by making obvious details that otherwise would be very hard to detect, if we only look at numerical information.

Acknowledgments

We would like to thank D. Vaughan and G. Wojcik of Weidlinger Associates for the application corresponding to Figure 1, and P. Samec of Stanford University for Figure 2. We also thank Sun Microsystems and Ardent Computers for the use of their equipment.

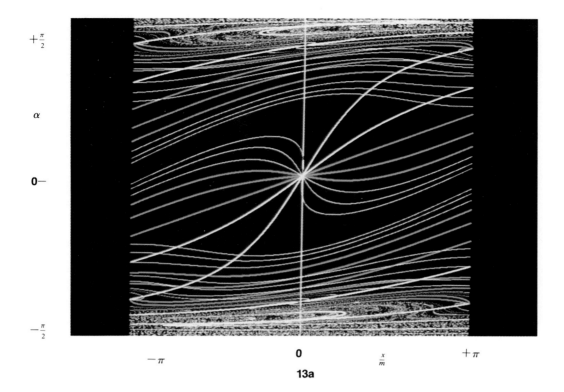

13a

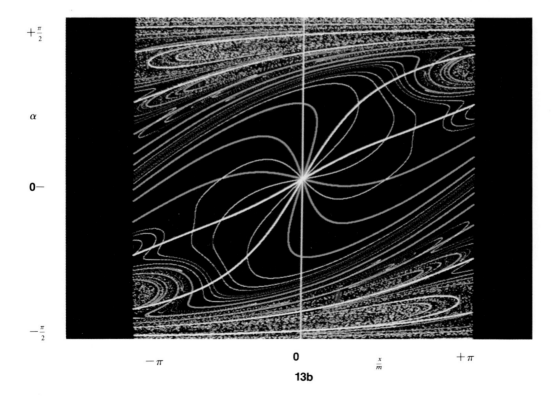

13b

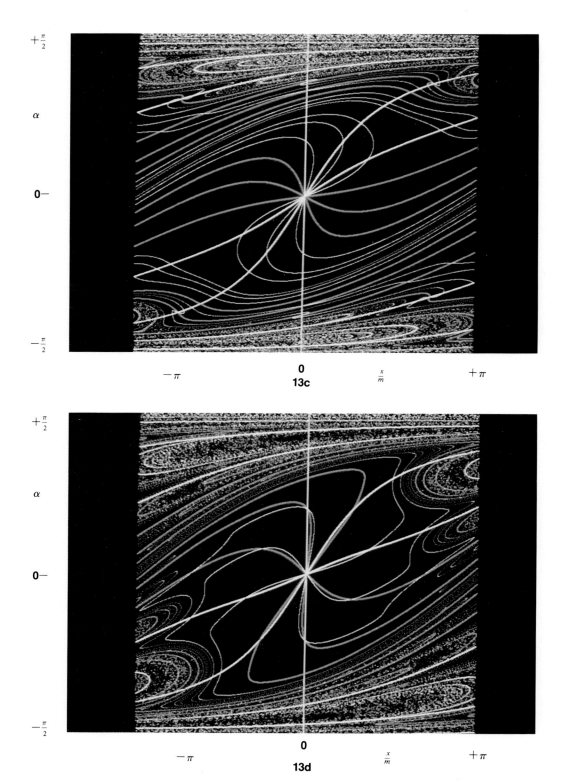

Figure 13. A slightly different phase plot (see text for details) for the same waveguide as in Figure 12. The ratio *L:H* is as before, 100:10, but the amplitude *w* changes from 1 in Figure 13a to 4 in Figure 13d. In Figures 13a-13d, the eight reflections are color coded such that the first two are white, the next three blue, and the last three red. Each colored curve starts at the center and evolves as the initial take-off angle increases from zero. The curves coming out of the center and extending to the right correspond to positive values of the initial take-off angle, and to the left to negative values. The plot is an odd function of *x*. The vertical white line is the set of all initial conditions.

References

1. J.F. Claerbout, *Imaging the Earth's Interior,* Blackwell, Oxford, England, 1985.

2. O. Yilmaz, "Seismic Data Processing," in *Investigations in Geophysics,* Vol. 2, Society of Geophysicists, Tulsa, Okla., 1987.

3. H.R. Nelson, New Technologies in Exploration Geophysics, Gulf, Houston, Tex., 1983.

4. W. Millavec and V. Pereyra, "GEOBLD: An *Interactive 3D Geometrical Modeling System," Inversion Project Report 88-05,* Weidlinger Assoc., Los Altos, Calif., 1988.

5. V. Pereyra, "Two-Point Ray Tracing in General 3D Media," *Inversion Project Report 88-03,* Weidlinger Assoc., Los Altos, Calif.

6. R.H. Bartels, J.C. Beatty, and B.A. Barsky, *An Introduction to the Use of Splines in Computer Graphics,* Morgan Kaufmann, Los Altos, Calif., 1987.

7. J.D. Foley and A. Van Dam, *Fundamentals of Interactive Computer Graphics,* Addison-Wesley, Menlo Park, Calif., 1983.

8. J.A. Rial, "Seismic Wave Resonances in 3D Sedimentary Basins," *Geophysical J.,* Int'l., Vol. 99, 1989, pp. 81-90.

9. M.V. Berry, "Regularity and Chaos in Classical Mechanics, Illustrated by Three Deformations of a Circular 'Billiard' " *European J. Phys.,* Vol. 2, 1981, pp. 91-102.

10. M.V. Berry, "Semiclassical Mechanics of Regular and Irregular Motion," in *Chaotic Behavior of Deterministic Systems,* G. Ioos, R. Helleman, and R. Stora, eds., North-Holland, Amsterdam, Netherlands, 1983, pp. 171-272.

Victor Pereyra was born in Buenos Aires, Argentina, and was a professor of computer sciences at the Universidad Central de Venezuela in Caracas from 1967 to 1984. He is currently an associate at Weidlinger Associates, Los Altos, California, where he has worked since 1984 on basic research and applications of scientific computing to problems of wave propagation in geophysics. Pereyra is also a consulting professor in the Computer Science Department at Stanford University, where he has often been a visiting faculty member in the past 25 years. He has also held visiting positions at the California Institute of Technology, University of Southern California, University of Wisconsin, Université de Montréal, Oxford University, and University of California-Lawrence Berkeley Laboratory, among others.

Pereyra is a member of SIAM, is an associate editor of several numerical analysis journals, and has published more than 60 papers in various areas of numerical analysis and its applications. He received his PhD in computer sciences from the University of Wisconsin, Madison in 1967.

Jose A. Rial is an associate professor of geophysics and associate director of the MacCarthy Geophysical Observatory at the Geology Department, University of North Carolina at Chapel Hill. From 1979 to 1981, he served as head of the Geophysics Department, Central University, in Caracas, Venezuela. From 1981 to 1982, he was research associate at Caltech, and until 1984 adjunct professor at the University of California, Santa Cruz. He joined the UNC faculty in 1985.

Rial is member of the American Geophysical Union and the AAAS. Born in Tenerife, Spain he received his BS from the Central University in Caracas, MSc from the University of Michigan, and PhD from Caltech. For the last three years Dr. Rial has been engaged in research involving the nonlinear dynamics of rays in realistic earth models.

A Holistic Method for
Visualizing Computer Performance Measurements

Neale Hirsh, Cray Research
Bruce L. Brown, Echo Solutions

Introduction

Periodically, an article written by a highly reputed computer scientist encourages fellow scientists to use the scientific method when making computer performance measurements and analyzing the results.[1,2] We have no doubt about the wisdom of this approach.

We can define the scientific method in many ways.[3] In this chapter, by scientific method we mean

- Measuring computer system performance in a controlled environment under a variety of experimental manipulations.

- Determining which experimental factors and factor interactions are statistically significant, using traditional linear models hypothesis testing.

- Conducting an exhaustive multivariate graphical analysis of the data.

We found that the multivariate graphical analysis captured the total pattern of complex results from the experiment. It also displayed subtle and complex interactions that were operationally useful to know and that had eluded a multivariate analysis of variance.

Following the scientific method was fairly inconvenient because of the necessary controls in gathering data and doing reality checks. Had we not done a controlled experiment, however, we probably would have been satisfied with a more traditional method of analysis and would have missed the insights from multivariate graphics.

Original Measurements and Experimental Design

The test system consisted of a dedicated IBM 4381 mainframe connected to a Cray X-MP/416 system through a dedicated, high-speed network (Figure 1). The IBM system had 16 Mbytes of memory and 16 3380 disk drives on two channels. The IBM mainframe operating system was the MVS/XA (release 2.1.2) with JES2, communicating with a network and a Cray system through an MVS-resident Cray software product called the Cray Station.* The interconnecting network was a Cray data-streaming interface on a single, dedicated 4381 channel. The physical medium was a Cray FOL-3 fiber-optic link.

The Cray X-MP/416 system is a four-processor machine with 16 Mwords of memory, four DD-49 disk drives, and a 512 Mword solid-state disk drive. It ran either of two operating systems, referred to simply as OS#1 and OS#2 to help us protect confidential aspects of system performance. (It is a struggle to maintain proper confidentiality, and we suspect that is one of the reasons for the rarity of controlled studies of computer system performance. Another reason is surely the difficulty of collecting the data.)**

The test data sets were MVS files containing uppercase characters with no blank spaces. The data sets were fixed blocked at 22,300 bytes (half of a 3380 disk track), a typical file size for MVS-to-Cray transfers. During the test, the data sets were fetched or disposed (received or sent) across the system, while simultaneous measurements were made of the data-transfer rate and the end-to-end elapsed time of the transfer.

We varied six factors in the test, as shown in Table 1. The right-hand column refers to the number of discrete states allowed for each factor. Table 1 lists seven factors, but since we did not test all possible combinations of data-set size and data-set organization, we combined the two into a single factor for analysis.

The operating system had two states, OS#1 and OS#2. The data-transfer format had three states, called character blocked, binary blocked, and transparent. (Character- and binary-blocked formats represent transformed data; transparent format represents raw data.)

The data-transfer direction was either to the Cray mainframe (fetch) or away from it (dispose). Blank compression

---

*The Cray Station has been replaced by a more comprehensive product called SUPERLINK.

**The test system cost over $15 million, and was available to us on a semireliable schedule. Even when we had the system, it sometimes behaved erratically, although not enough to bring it down. (This is very common in developmental environments.) We also encountered undocumented changes in system software and peripheral configurations. Accordingly, we repeated many measurements, taking about 65 hours of dedicated test time to do 240 measurements. If we had been paying for system time at a commercial rate. it would have been prohibitively expensive.

190

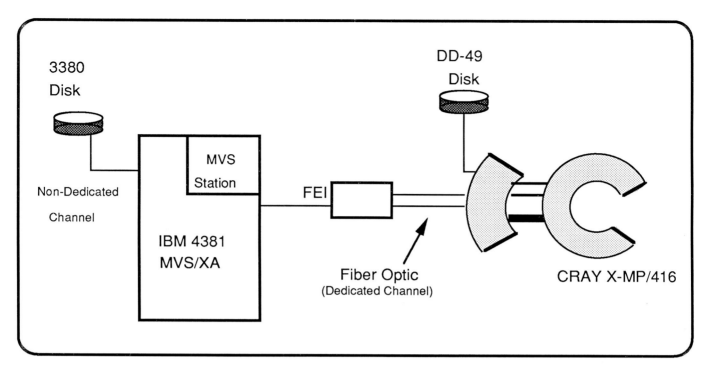

Figure 1. Block diagram of test system.

Table 1. Measurement factors and levels.

Factor	Levels
Operating system	2
Data-transfer format	3
Data-transfer direction	2
Blank compression	2
Segment size	2
Data-set size	3
Data-set organization	3

Table 2. Organization and size of medium data sets.

Organization	Logical record length	Records
1	80	435,000
2	2900	12,000
3	23,200	1500

was either "on" or "off" at the IBM system. Segment size, the number of bytes transferred from the IBM system to the network in one logical unit, was either 4 or 28 Kbytes.

Data-set size had three states, corresponding to data sets of size 0.1, 34.8, and 100 Mbytes. Data-set organization also had three states—a small, a medium, and a large logical record length—but they were all nested within the medium data-set size (34.8 Mbytes). Actually, the three data-set organization states were combinations of two MVS parameters: logical record length and the number of logical records, as shown in Table 2. Since we did not have all combinations of data-set size and data-set organization, they were combined into one factor, "data-set size and organization," with five levels.

While measuring data-transfer rate, we measured end-to-end elapsed time of each transfer because it was easy to do without disturbing the main experiment. The variables are related by the following equation:

$$\text{Data transfer rate} = \frac{\text{Number of bytes transferred}}{\text{End-to-end elapsed time}}$$

During the measurements, we allowed the normal IBM utilities, network software, and teleprocessing monitors to run freely—as we did the normal Cray daemons, utilities, and software monitors. They helped to keep the system somewhat representative of its normal, uncontrolled self. The disadvantage was the variability added to the measurements by the added polling traffic on the network and loading of the CPUs by SMF/RMF, and so on. The statistical analyses of the data model take account of this experimental error. The larger the error component is, the more difficult it is to obtain statistically significant results. In a controlled experiment, we make every effort to reduce experimental error variability, thus increasing the power of the statistical tests.

We implemented a number of controls to reduce error variance in the experiment:

- We disconnected or varied off-line the extraneous devices normally connected to the system.
- We cleared the disk drives at the start of each trial to avoid fragmentation.
- We repeated a measurement when it was very far from its expected value (i.e., suspicious). If we lacked the time needed to repeat the measurement, we held it over to the next session. If the measurement was still suspicious, we would inquire about the possibility of the system's hardware or software having been changed since the last measurement session. Sometimes it had been changed. We would then undo the change, which was a significant effort.
- We monitored the Cray and IBM CPU utilizations during the measurements.
- We sent short dummy files across the system to verify that it was operating correctly.

We also saved the log files on the IBM and Cray systems, and inspected them for anomalies and other unpleasant surprises. The step-by-step procedure to vary the factors, measure the performance, and analyze the results constituted the experimental design. This is a common definition,[4] but others have equal validity.[5]

From Raw Measurements to a Statistical Model

For supercomputer performance measurement, benchmarks are the most common measurement tools. The measurements are gathered and interpreted in raw units (e.g., CPU seconds). Only rarely does an analyst abstract the measurements into other units of measurement or test them under a variety of experimental conditions. Consequently, the benchmark literature is almost entirely composed of descriptive statistics of raw data.

Statistical analysis is a combination of mathematics and philosophy. In statistical theory, we grapple with the very difficult and exciting problem of inferring "what is" from "what is observed." The raw measurements are not only interpreted directly but for what they represent as an example of all possible comparable measurements. In this chapter, we interpret the measurements in terms of the components that, in theory, comprise them: treatment effects,* interactions, and error components.

To use any such method, we first assume that the raw data are only a subset, a sample of a larger population of data that could potentially be, but were not obtained. We visualize all of the potential raw measurements as locations in a "sample space," which is a coordinate system containing all the data. Any observed subset of the measurements is also in this geometrical coordinate system and so is any transformation of the measurements. The measurements are thought of as "random variables" instead of "variables."**

Each random variable has an inferred or assumed distribution, a definable topographical region within the sample space. The assumed distribution is an integral part of the "model" for the data. This is such a basic assumption that the fundamental problem in engineering statistics can be phrased as: "start with observed data and find a model that describes it."[7]

Analysis of variance (ANOVA) is the statistical model adopted for this study.[8] ANOVA is undoubtedly the premier statistical mode for analyzing data gathered under well-controlled experimental conditions. It is a powerful way of partitioning and summarizing the information in an experiment.

In this chapter, we will introduce another quantitative method for dealing with computer performance data that is in some ways even more powerful. We will demonstrate the use of the principal components (PC) Multigraf, one of a group of newly developed multivariate graphical visualization methods.[9] The PC Multigrafs parallel and complement the ANOVA approach to data analysis by actually allowing the investigator to view geometrically the various ways of partitioning and modeling the data. They are a crucial component of interpretation.

This study uses six experimentally manipulated variables (Table 1). We test for significant differences in all possible combinations of the variables: two at a time, three at a time, and so forth. A six-way ANOVA, which consists of 63 significance tests, is appropriate for the data reported here. Reading these complex ANOVA results will require the use of abbreviations for each of the six experimental variables, as shown in Table 3.

In the following section, we interpret the results of significance tests by looking at the "alpha level," where alpha is the probability that the hypothesis of "no difference between the means" should be rejected. Although we can use alpha like a simple index, it is not simple. It is based on a sophisticated statistical decision model.[8] When applied to an ANOVA analysis, it depends on three primary assumptions: (1) normality of within-cell distributions,* (2) homogeneity of vari-

---

*A treatment effect can be defined as the difference between the mean for a particular treatment and the grand mean.

**A random variable, or stochastic variable, is one whose different values occur with probabilities that are, at least theoretically, specifiable.[6]

Table 3. Variable names and abbreviations.

Name	Abbreviation
Operating system	SYST
Data-transfer format	TRFO
Data-transfer direction	DIRC
Blank compression	BLCO
Segment size	SEGS
Data-set size	DSAO

ance across the cells (homoscedasticity), and (3) the assumption that treatment effects are independent of error effects.

Fortunately, ANOVA is robust with respect to violation of the first two of these, normality and homoscedasticity.[10] The third assumption, independence of treatment and error effects, is by far the most important. If this assumption does not hold, as it often does not in practice, the estimates of alpha will not be precise and may be nothing more than rough approximations. The only real assurance we can have that this assumption holds is to assign experimental units randomly to treatment groups—that is, a true experimental design.[11] For computer performance data, this means randomly assigning the measurements (as they vary by serial order, hour or day of observation, etc.) to the various experimental manipulations. Fortunately, this is usually possible.

Preliminary Results of a Six-Way Analysis of Variance

Two questions arise: "Why bother with the ANOVA in the first place? Why not explain the difficulty that arises when using it and then go on to a more suitable method of analysis?" The answer, as we have explained, is that ANOVA is a reliable starting point and a good "reality check" during multivariate graphical analysis. There are at least three reasons for using ANOVA: (1) it is hard to find major effects and patterns in multivariate space, (2) "noise" and good data are often graphically indistinguishable, and (3) translation or rotation can obscure the identity of important patterns.[13] The ANOVA methods and the multivariate graphical methods are best used as complements to one another.

---

*Normality within a cell (of measurements) refers, of course, to the Gaussian distribution. Box[10] demonstrated that the sampling distribution of the F ratio (the test statistic used in ANOVA) is relatively insensitive to moderate departures from the normality assumption. In that same reference he also showed that the F ratio is little affected by inequalities in the variances if there are equal numbers of observations in the cells.

Since we have six independent variables to analyze, the proper analysis is a six-way ANOVA for data-transfer rate and a similar analysis for end-to-end timings. Table 4 shows the analysis and high-level results.

Table 4. Analysis and high-level results.

Method of analysis	ANOVA
Dependent variables	Data-transfer rate
	End-to-end timing
Independent Variables	Operating system
	Data-transfer format
	Data-transfer direction
	Blank compression
	Segment size
	Data-set size and organization
Holistic plot	Scatterplot of data-transfer rate versus end-to-end timings
Results	Efficient operating systems are at top of scatterplot.

Table 5 shows a section of the matrix of input data. This section is only for disposed data-transfer rates on OS#1, thus showing the data recordings for only one-fourth of the 240 measurements in the full design. This one-fourth of the full data matrix has 15 rows (for the five levels of data-set size and organization times the three data-transfer formats), and four columns: 60 data entries out of the 240 that make up the complete experiment as far as data-transfer rates are concerned.

The input to the six-way ANOVA is complex, but the results of the ANOVA are even more complex, with 63 significance tests to be explained. Our strategy is to examine just one test, a two-way interaction between data-transfer format and data-set size and organization, and then to broaden our argument to the other 62 significance tests.** Figures 2 and 3 show the major results.

**The table of means for this two-way interaction has 15 means—all combinations of five levels of data-set size and organization with three levels of transfer format. We also have three-way, four-way, five-way, and six-way tables of means, but of course these tables are much larger. For example, the five-way interaction tables have between 48 and 120 means, and the six-way table contains all 240 of the original measurements. When we consider all of these tables for displaying interactions, we are dealing with a very large number of means. In all, there are 1,944 means distributed over 63 tables for data-transfer rate, and another 1,944 means in 63 tables for end-to-end timings.

Table 5. Matrix of Measurements: Data Transfer Rate as a function of Data Transfer Format*

Dataset Size	LRECL	Blank Comp.		No Blank Comp.	
		4K	28K	4K	28K
small	small				
medium	small				
medium	medium		char. blocked (5 rows)		
medium	large				
large	small				
			bin. blocked (5 rows)		
			transparent (5 rows)		

*Table is only for OS#1 and *Dispose*

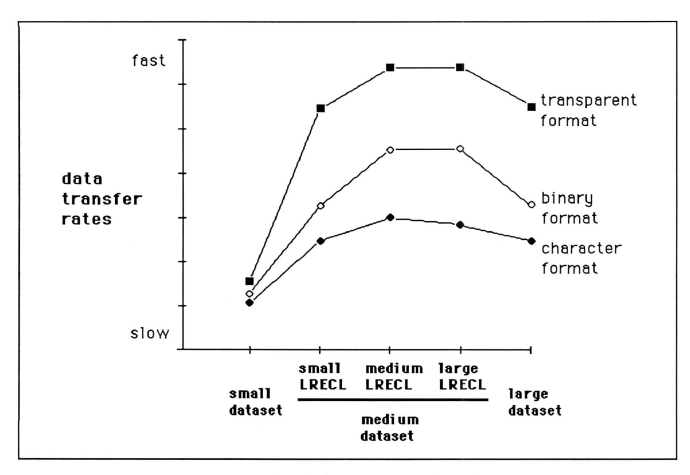

Figure 2. Effects of two-way interaction of transfer format and data-set size and organization on data-transfer rate. ( ), transparent format; (o), binary format; ( ), character format.

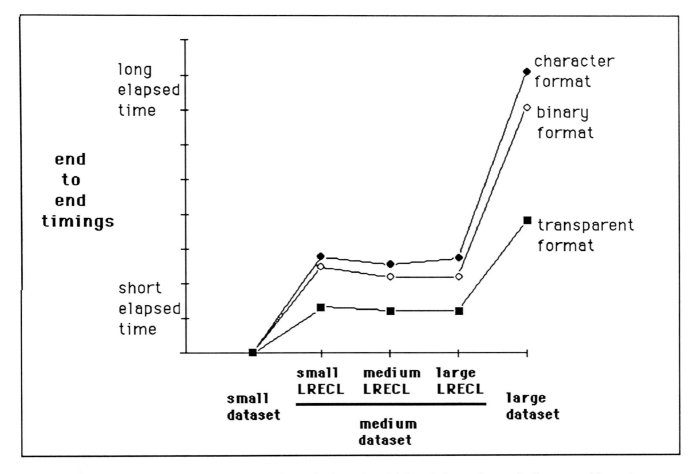

Figure 3. Effects of two-way interaction of transfer format and data-set size and organization on end-to-end timings. (   ), character format; (   ), binary format; (   ), transparent format.

We first consider data-transfer rate. Figure 2 shows that the fastest rates are for the transparent format, then binary-blocked, and finally character-blocked formats. The rates are inversely proportional to the complexity of the formats themselves, not a surprising result. We notice that the performance curves for data-set size and organization are convex, with the highest data-transfer rates being in the mid-range (medium-sized data set with a medium logical record length). Small data sets are the slowest.

At first look, large data sets are apparently slower than medium data sets. But we must remember that both small and large data sets have a small logical record length, which is the slowest of the three medium data sets. The large data sets are about equal in data-transfer rates to the medium sized data sets that also have small logical record length. In other words, medium and large data sets are about equal in data-transfer rate.

We now consider end-to-end timings (Figure 3). As predicted, the longest end-to-end times are for character-blocked format, then binary, and then transparent formats. But the curves in Figure 3 are virtually flat across the mid-range, which is not predicted. It is especially surprising

when we remember that data-transfer rate is nothing more than data-set size divided by end-to-end timings.

When we now examine the significance tests of the six-way ANOVA, sixty-three significance tests for each of the two measured variables, the results are even more disturbing.* The pattern of significance as reflected in the alpha levels (Figures 4 and 5) is very different for the two. Using an alpha level of 0.05 as the upper limit of significance, most of the significant results for data-transfer rates are for segment size and its interaction with other factors. But for end-to-end timings, the significant results are for data-set size and organization and its interaction with other factors.

---

* The particular ANOVA model used is a six-way mixed effects model, with operating system, data-transfer format, data-transfer direction, and blank compression as fixed-effects factors, and segment size, and data-set size and data-set organization as random-effects factors. Even though 63 significance tests are possible (six one-way tests, 15 two-way, 20 three-way, 15 four-way, 6 five-way, and one six-way), only 47 appear in Figure 3. That is because 16 of the tests could not be performed without replicating the study.

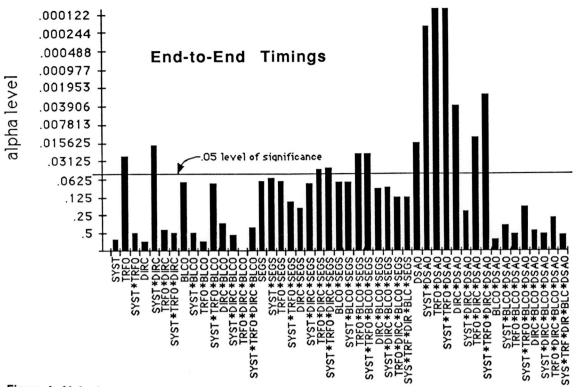

Figure 4. Alpha levels for six-way analysis of end-to-end timings. Horizontal line indicates 0.05 level of significance.

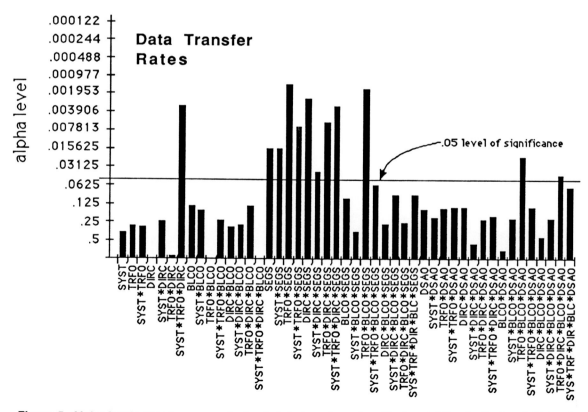

Figure 5. Alpha levels for six-way analysis of data-transfer rates. Horizontal line indicates 0.05 level of significance

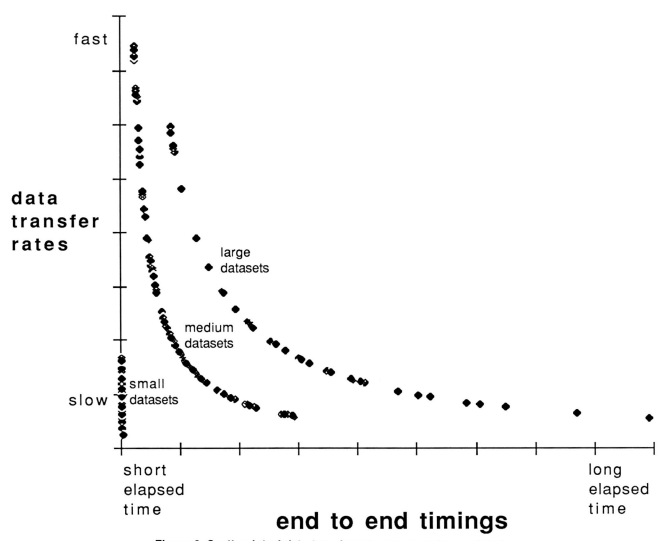

fast

data
transfer
rates

large
datasets

medium
datasets

small
datasets

slow

short
elapsed
time

long
elapsed
time

end to end timings

Figure 6. Scatterplot of data-transfer rate versus end-to-end timing.

These divergences can be understood by looking at a bivariate scatterplot of data-transfer rate versus end-to-end timings for all 240 measurements (Figure 6). Notice that the plotted points for large data sets and medium data sets each fit a hyperbola (actually, half of a hyperbola). A hyperbola is the geometric shape formed by a reciprocal relationship between x and y. This is, of course, the defining relationship between data-transfer rate and end-to-end timings. The points for the small data sets also lie along a hyperbola, but it is one that is tight into the corner, with most of its defining points being "missing" (because they never occur). In the geometry of these three hyperbolas, we can find the answer to the observed discrepancies, both in the plots of the two-way interactions and also in the results of the significance tests.

Consider first the contrast between efficient and inefficient operating system configurations, both in data-transfer rates and also in end-to-end timings. The most efficient configurations are those with short end-to-end timings and fast data-transfer rates: hence, the points that fall in the upper left area of Figure 6 for each of the three hyperbolas. Likewise, the inefficient configurations are represented by the data points in the lower right. Notice that the most efficient configurations for each data-set size (each of the three hyperbolas) do not differ much in end-to-end timings. All are short. But they differ substantially in data-transfer rate, with small data sets having by far the slowest rates. Conversely, the least-efficient configurations do not differ much from large to medium to small data sets in data-transfer rates (all are slow), but they do differ substantially in end-to-end timings. That is curious, because data-transfer rate is nothing more than a reciprocal transformation of end-to-end timings controlled for data-set size.

To understand this curious effect, consider the nature of a reciprocal transformation. In a series of numbers such as 1, 2, 4, 8, 16, and so forth, the successive intervals become larger as we ascend. But for the reciprocals of these numbers $1/2$, $1/4$, $1/8$, $1/16$, and so on, the intervals become successively smaller. (The denominator represents end-to-end timings.) It follows that end-to-end timings magnify differences for the inefficient configurations, relatively, and data-transfer rates magnify differences for efficient configurations (see Figure 6). It should be obvious that this can shift the ANOVA results considerably, as well as shifting relative positions of means in plots such as those in Figures 2 and 3. In other words, a reciprocal transformation of data is nonlinear, and, in ANOVA, it can cause a statistically significant interaction to disappear or cause one to appear where it was not before.*

The apparent conflict between Figures 2 and 3 could now be explicated in every detail, although it would be tedious. For brevity, it is sufficient to say that these two figures have exactly the relationship expected from a reciprocal transformation. Figure 3 should be a metrically adjusted mirror image of Figure 2 (were it not for the data-set size differences), and it is if we examine the three logical-record-length points where data-set size is constant. In the area of small, medium, and large logical record lengths (in medium data sets), the conflict between figures results from the relative insensitivity of end-to-end timings for efficient configurations, where logical record length has its major effects.**

The lesson is that we should not be too hasty in reporting the results of the first ANOVA performed on a set of data. A metric transformation of the data can substantially alter the conclusions. Fortunately, a holistic plot of the data such as in Figure 6 can help by providing a context for interpretation. In what follows, we shall see that a more sophisticated kind of holistic plot can be even more helpful in understanding the data.

Further Results of a Multivariate Analysis

We saw in the previous section that the ANOVA was hard to interpret in the face of a nonlinear (metric) transformation. But a holistic scatterplot was very helpful in identifying the characteristics of operating system efficiency. In this section, we will show that a multivariate graph facilitates this process and withstands even structural transformations.

We attempt to make a smooth transition from univariate ANOVA to multivariate ANOVA ("MANOVA") by "experimenting with" (that is, reorganizing) the observations. During the experimentation, we keep in mind that many results of the ANOVA were reliable, and should be identifiable in the MANOVA.

We will first find additional dependent variables (the M in MANOVA). We could obtain them by repeating the experiment, of course, with fewer factors and more dependent variables. Alternatively, we could obtain them converting (say) data-transfer direction into two dependent variables. This requires a minor rearrangement of Table 4 and similar tables, where observations that differ only in the fetch and dispose dimensions are folded in with other observations. This reduces the total number of observations, of course.*** Table 6 shows the analysis and high-level results.

---

*The null hypothesis for testing interactions in ANOVA holds that we can account for the pattern of means for two or more joint factors by the additive combination of effects on the separate factors. The resulting statistical test for an interaction is just a test of whether the means depart significantly from additivity. It should be obvious that a nonlinear transformation of the data can change an additive relationship into a nonadditive one, or vice versa. A logarithmic transformation, for example, will turn a multiplicative relationship into an additive one. In the multidimensional scaling literature, Kruskal,[12-14] and others developed methods for testing whether an interaction could survive every possible monotonic transformation. But these methods lack the flexibility and power of ANOVA and have never enjoyed broad acceptance. When we have a defensible metric (such as data-transfer rate or end-to-end times), ANOVA is the preferred method of analysis. The experimental question being asked has an implied metric. For example, when we inquire about elapsed time, we are interested in turnarounds of minutes or hours, not log minutes or log hours. And it should be clear from Figures 4 and 5 that any given ANOVA results apply only to the actual metric used in the ANOVA. That is, we would certainly not be justified in doing a logarithmic or other nonlinear transformation on the data before running an ANOVA just to make the data consistent with normality or homoscedasticity assumptions—as was once common practice[15]—since the transformation could radically change our conclusion about interactions away from those that would hold for the implied metric of our study.

**We drew upon information in Figure 11, which has not yet been presented, to know that LRECL has its greatest effect upon the most efficient configurations.

***It is appropriate for the measurement design in this chapter but might not be appropriate for other designs (see Winer,[11] p. 162).

Table 6. Analysis and high-level results.

Method of analysis	MANOVA
Dependent variables	Data-transfer rate
	End-to-end timing
	Data-transfer direction (2 variables)
	Data-set size & organization (5 variables)
Independent variables	Operating system
	Data-transfer format
	Blank compression
	Segment size
Holistic plot	Multigraf
Results	OS#1 is more efficient.
	Within OS#1, neither data-transfer format nor blank compression are major effects.
	Within OS#2, 28-K segment size is most efficient, depending on a four-way interaction.

In Table 6, the analysis has become multivariate by making data-set size and organization and data-transfer direction into dependent variables. In essence, we have a four-way multivariate analysis with 20 dependent variables ($2 \times 2 \times 5$) and 24 observations.

The results are shown in a PC Multigraf (Figures 7 and 8). The Multigraf is a specialized graph for viewing simple effects, interactions, and higher-order interactions from a factorial data set within a reduced multivariate space. It is based on the mathematics of principal components analysis, coupled with error-reducing algorithms for tightening the dimensionality of the visual representation. The PC Multigraf is a part of the DataMax multivariate graphical data analysis system,[9,16] which also includes discriminant Multigrafs, canonical correlation Multigrafs, regression Multigrafs, and so forth.

In Figures 7 and 8, we represent the 20 dependent variables as vectors, with only the labeled end points of each vector shown around the perimeter of the circle.*

**A fundamental feature of Multigrafs is the use of non-perpendicular vectors to represent many dimensional data in a reduced space. For an explanation of the rationale of this approach see Brown, Williams and Barlow.[17]

Table 7. Abbreviations for Multigrafs in Figures 7 and 8.

Abbreviation	Explanation
fetSsEET	Fetch for small databases (with small LRECL), measure of end-to-end times
disSsEET	Dispose for small data sets (with small LRECL), measure of end-to-end times
fetSsDTR	Fetch for small data sets (with small LRECL), measure of data-transfer rates
disSsDTR	Dispose for small data sets (with small LRECL), measure of data-transfer rates
fetMsEET	Fetch for medium data sets (with small LRECL), measure of end-to-end times
disMsEET	Dispose for medium data sets (with small LRECL), measure of end-to-end times
fetMsDTR	Fetch for medium data sets (with small LRECL), measure of data-transfer rates
disMsDTR	Dispose for medium data sets (with small LRECL), measure of data-transfer rates
fetMmEET	Fetch for medium data sets (with medium LRECL), measure of end-to-end times
disMmEET	Dispose for medium data sets (with medium LRECL), measure of end-to-end times
fetMmDTR	Fetch for medium data sets (with medium LRECL), measure of data-transfer rates
disMmDTR	Dispose for medium data sets (with medium LRECL), measure of data-transfer rates
fetMlEET	Fetch for medium data sets (with large LRECL), measure of end-to-end times
disMlEET	Dispose for medium data sets (with large LRECL), measure of end-to-end times
fetMlDTR	Fetch for medium data sets (with large LRECL), measure of data-transfer rates
disMlDTR	Dispose for medium data sets (with large LRECL), measure of data-transfer rates
fetLsEET	Fetch for large data sets (with small LRECL), measure of end-to-end times.
disLsEET	Dispose for large data sets (with small LRECL), measure of data-transfer rate
fetLsDTR	Fetch for large data sets (with small LRECL), measure of data-transfer rate
disLsDTR	Dispose for large sets (with small LRECL), measure of data-transfer rates

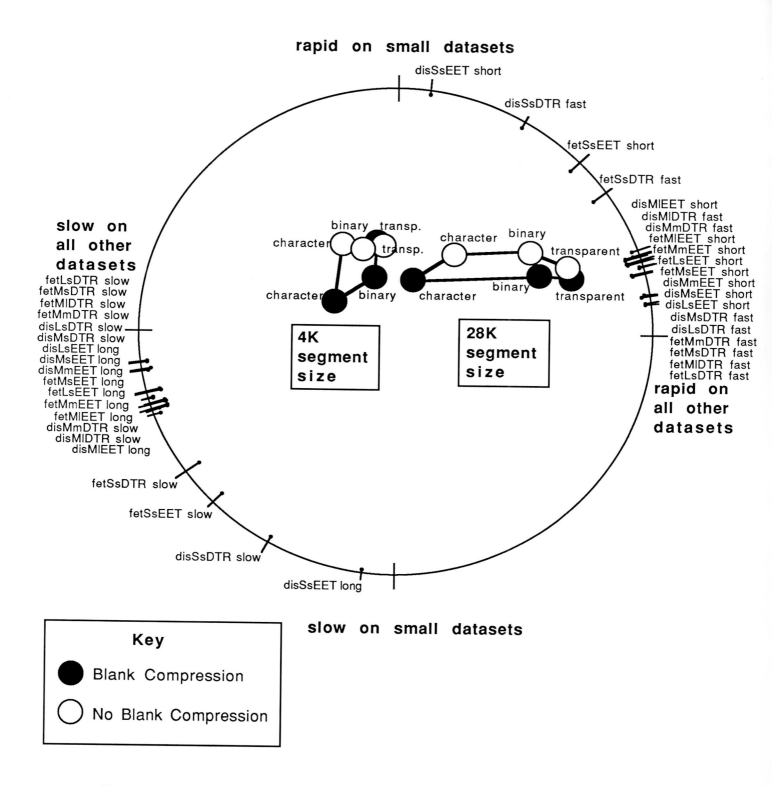

Figure 7. Principal Components Multigraf for OS#1. Black points indicate blank compression; white points indicate no blank compression.

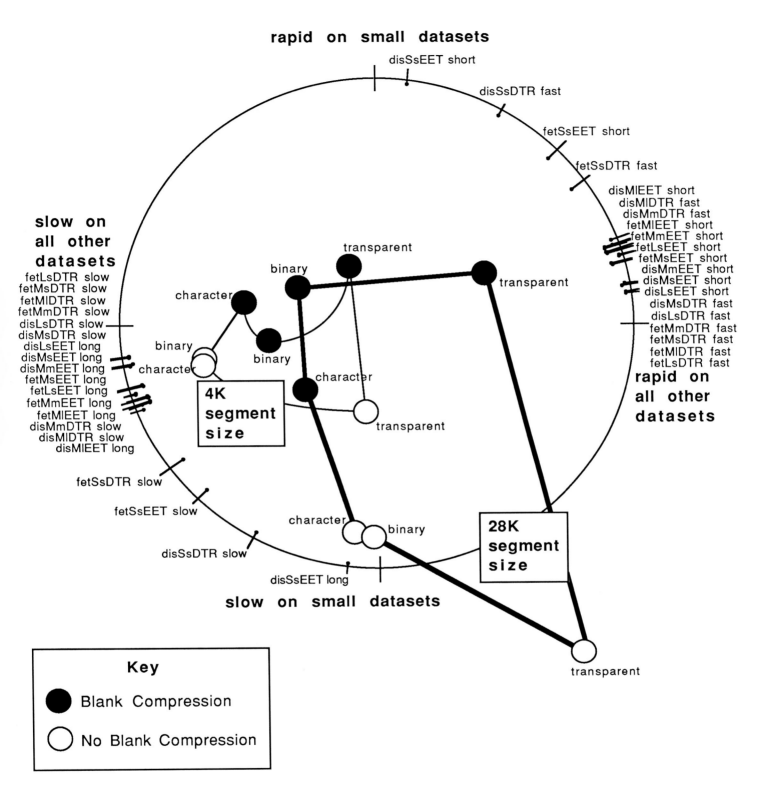

Figure 8. Principal Components Multigraf for OS#2. Black points indicate blank compression; white points indicate no blank compression.

The vectors around the perimeter essentially define the meaning of the topographical locations within the Multigraf. Table 7 provides a key to the abbreviations.

In the Multigrafs, the vertical axis shows the continuum from rapid to slow on small data sets. Data points at the top of Figures 7 and 8 have relatively rapid processing for small data sets, and those at the bottom of the figure have relatively slow processing for small data sets. We show 16 of the 20 vectors for the dependent variables, the ones corresponding to performance on medium and large data sets, as axes inclined slightly off the horizontal. The axes are grouped together rather tightly, indicating that they are highly correlated. Data points at the right of the figures have relatively rapid processing for large and medium data sets, and those on the left have slow processing.

The 24 data points within the two figures (connected in groups of six) make up the four-way interaction. Actually, Figures 7 and 8 are a single Multigraf separated for easier viewing. Figure 7 corresponds to OS#1 and Figure 8 to OS#2.

For ease in perceiving the four-way interaction between operating system, data-transfer format, blank compression, and segment size, we use lines to group the points. The lines make up two polygons of six points each. In Figure 7, the two polygons are for the 4-K and 28-K segment sizes for OS#1, and in Figure 8, they are for 4-K and 28-K segment sizes for OS#2. Within each of the polygons, we can see the effects of the three data-transfer formats (transparent, binary blocked, and character blocked), with blank compression turned on (black points) or off (white points).

The statistically significant effect for segment size (found in the six-way analysis of Figures 3 and 4) should be obvious in these two figures: the six-point polygons for 28-K segment size are to the right of those for 4-K segment size in both Multigrafs. This means that in both operating systems, the 28-K segment size is more rapid than 4K for medium and large data sets. The two segment sizes are about equal vertically, because they do not differ much in end-to-end timings or data-transfer rate on small data sets. We can also see the topological basis for the statistically significant effect for operating system. The six-point polygons for OS#1 tend to be higher in the figure and slightly more to the right, indicating that OS#1 is more efficient both for small data sets and for medium and large data sets.

Notice that the Multigraf provides considerably more information about the relative performance of OS#1 and OS#2 than can be found within the pattern of significance for various main effects or interactions. For example, when we consider only OS#1, data-transfer format and blank compression do not have a very large effect. The six points in each of those polygons are not very far apart. Their effects are also relatively small for the 4-K segment size with OS#2. But they have a very large effect on OS#2 with the 28-K

segment size—that is, the six points in that polygon are quite far apart. What we are witnessing is the four-way interaction of operating system, data-transfer format, blank compression, and segment size displayed in a two-dimensional projection of the 20-dimensional dependent variable space. The outcome of the experiment is captured in a single figure! (We presented it in two parts to facilitate visualization.)

We note that, for both operating systems, the effect of data-transfer format is for transparent to be faster than binary blocked, which is in turn faster than character blocked. But the pattern is slightly different for OS#1 than for OS#2. For OS#1, the character blocked to binary blocked is the major difference; whereas for OS#2, the binary blocked to transparent is the major difference. These are the significant interactions, found in the ANOVA, between operating system and data-transfer format.

Examining each main effect and interaction in this way can be tedious in a complex design. Notice that it is also somewhat unnecessary: when we have sufficiently assimilated the graphical pattern of a high-order interaction (in this case, the four-way one), all lesser interactions are completely derivable from it. (We base our discussion of main effects and two-way interactions on the four-way Multigraf.) This is the opposite of traditional univariate graphical methods, wherein higher-order interactions are notably difficult to display and conceptualize. Typically, we use traditional graphing methods only to display simple effects and two-way interactions—not higher-order interactions. It is somewhat of a surprise to find that when we move from univariate graphing to multivariate graphing in a multidimensional space, it makes higher-order interactions much easier to visualize. We would expect that going to a multivariate space would make things harder.

Multigrafs, by displaying the data's gestalt, help us to reconcile and understand disparities in univariate analyses. Multigrafs are especially adept at displaying the high-order interactions so difficult to conceptualize in a univariate framework.

We next explore operating system efficiencies further by going to a five-way MANOVA, decreasing the number of dependent variables and increasing the number of data points. The resulting Multigraf is richer and tells a more comprehensive story.

Highest-Level Analysis

Earlier, seeing the data's structure was difficult because of so many significance tests. We were encouraged, however, by the holistic scatterplot (Figure 6) to look for efficient operating systems and the interactions affecting them. We saw that differences in data-transfer rates were magnified in efficient systems but that the opposite occurred for end-to-end timings. Multigrafs showed that OS#1 was more efficient, and had different sensitivities, than OS#2. We still

Table 8. Analysis and high-level results.

Method of analysis	MANOVA
Dependent variables	Data-transfer rate
	End-to-end timing
	Data-transfer direction (2 variables)
Independent variables	Operating system
	Data-transfer format
	Blank compression
	Segment size
	Data-set size and org.
Holistic plot	Multigraf
Results	Efficient configurations (OS#1 & OS#2) have high data-transfer rates & much variance; short end-to-end times have little variance; very sensitive to logical record lengths.
	Inefficient configurations (OS#1 & OS#2) have low data-transfer rates & little variance; high end-to-end times with high variance.

needed a more complete story about the appropriateness of data-transfer rates versus end-to-end timings as a measure of computer system performance.

To answer these questions using Multigrafs, we begin by transforming the data into a five-way MANOVA, restoring data-set size and organization to its former status as an independent variable. Table 8 shows the analysis and high-level results.

Four dependent variables (2 $\times$ 2) and 120 observations occur in Table 8, leading to a Multigraf in four-dimensional dependent-variable space. The geometric interpretation should be relatively easy, since there are only four axes (Figure 9).

The 120 data points fall naturally into 24 clusters, representing each of the 24 four-way configurations of operating system $\times$ data-transfer format $\times$ blank compression $\times$ segment size. The most efficient configuration is OS#1 with transparent data-transfer format, blank compression off, and 28-K segment size; white circles highlight the corresponding groups of observations. The least-efficient configuration is OS#2 with character-blocked data-transfer format, blank compression off, and 4-K segment size; black circles highlight the corresponding groups of observations.

We see how the data points fall into hyperbolas for large and medium data sets and into a truncated hyperbola for small data sets. (The same hyperbolas appeared in Figure 6 but were rotated 90 degrees clockwise.) Comparing the operating system configurations is still hard, though, because the data points and lines are fairly tangled. It is much easier to visualize on a video display monitor, using color to highlight and separate each configuration.*

Another way to look at Figure 9 is to leave all the data points unshaded and the same size and to disconnect the lines between points (Figure 10).

On the horizontal axis (data-transfer rates), the most efficient operating system configurations have a great variance, with medium and large data sets having the highest rates. It is as if the transfer rates were adjusted to the needs of the task. The most inefficient configurations have very little variance in data-transfer rates; small, medium, and large data sets are uniformly slow.

On the vertical axis (end-to-end timings), the most-efficient operating system configurations vary little in elapsed times. All jobs go through in a short time. The least-efficient configurations vary greatly, with small jobs taking a short time, medium jobs taking a medium time, and large jobs taking a long time. The comparisons are annotated on Figure 10.

In the DataMax system, lower orders of Multigrafs are available from the five-way MANOVA. One of these Multigrafs will be generated to demonstrate the effect of logical record lengths on operating system efficiency.

Figure 11 is a Multigraf of the three-way interaction of data-transfer format $\times$ segment size $\times$ data-set size and organization. We obtained the graph by averaging over operating system and over blank compression.

On the left side of Figure 11, the small, medium, and large logical record lengths do not vary much in the 4-K segment size configurations, but they vary quite a bit in the 28-K segment sizes (on the right side). In other words, logical record length has its greatest differential effect on the most efficient configurations. This information was valuable to us in making sense of the contrast on Figures 2 and 3, that logical record length effects showed up more in data-transfer rates than in end-to-end timings. The primary effect of logical record length was on efficient configurations, which were magnified by measurements of data-transfer rates.

---

*In the DataMax system, Multigrafs appear on the screen in three dimensions, using linked rotation of points and vectors and "draftsman's views" (front, side, and top) to create this three-dimensional representation. The user can also select a variety of ways to connect the points with lines and from a variety of colors to highlight important interactions and groupings.

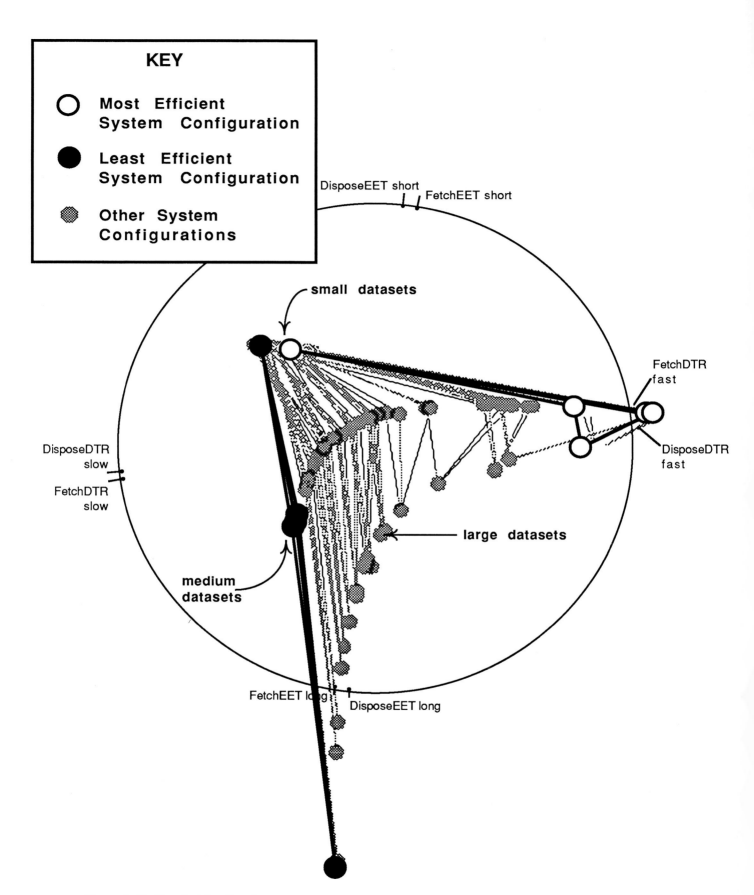

Figure 9. Multigraf of the five data-set size and organization points (connected) for each of 24 operating system configurations.

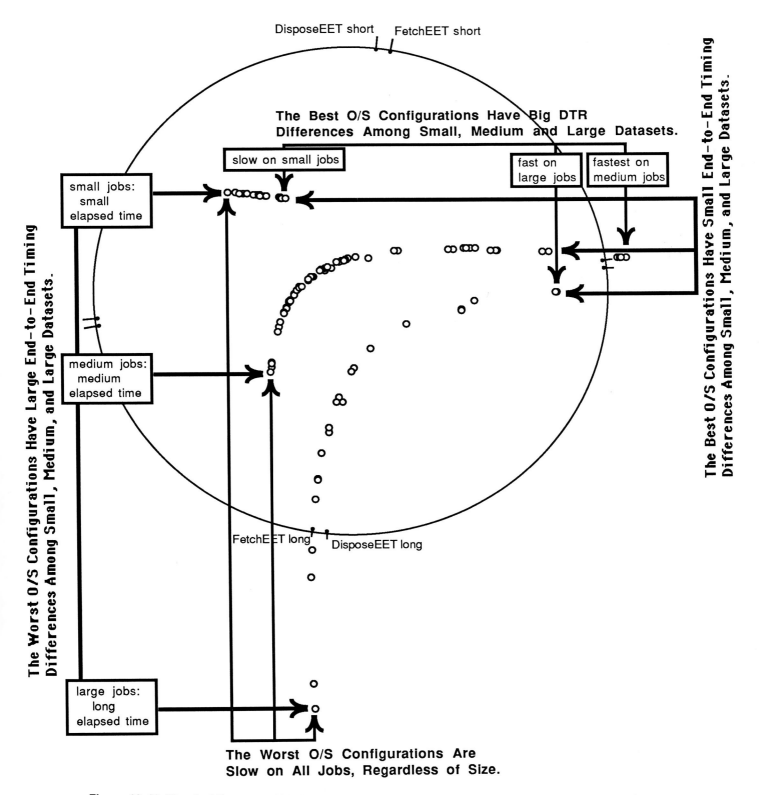

Figure 10. Multigraf of the same 120 data points shown in Figure 9, unconnected and with topological explanations.

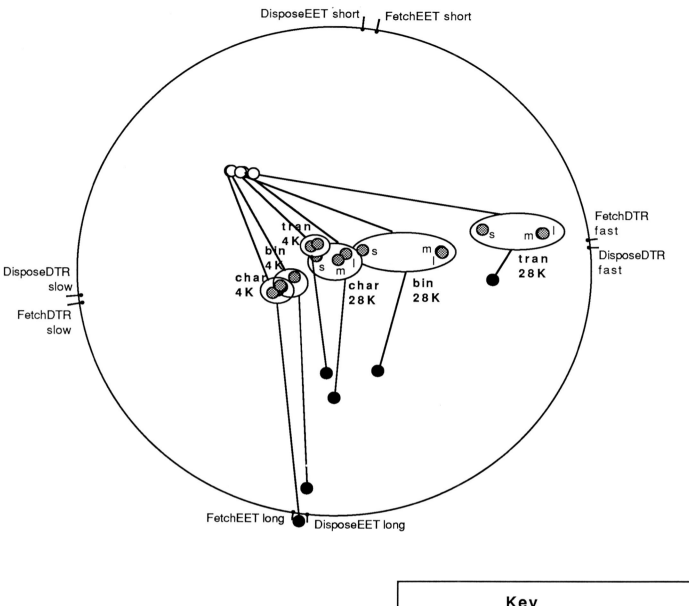

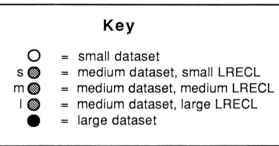

Figure 11. Multigraf of the three-way interaction among transfer format, segment size, and data-set size and organization.

Likewise, in Figure 11 (or even in Figures 6, 9, or 10), the data points representing large data sets have the same horizontal distribution as medium data sets but differ substantially in the vertical dimension. This is the topological basis for data-set size and organization having significant effects on end-to-end timings (the vertical axis) but not on data-transfer rates (the horizontal axis).

Conclusions

We have demonstrated the value of multivariate visualization methods and have learned at least four major things about the experimental analysis of computer performance:

1. Conclusions and decisions from ANOVA may not survive reasonable and defensible transformations of the data. The results from any particular ANOVA configuration may therefore be misleading if they are not considered within a broader context.

2. Multivariate graphical visualization methods are conceptually closer to the data and facilitate an integration of the complementary information from the various transformations.

3. Univariate plots of interactions can become hopelessly complex when we go beyond two- or three-way interactions. Multivariate plots of interactions, on the other hand, are most illuminating when we examine the highest-order interaction in the experiment and work down. The lower-order interactions are all implicit within the higher.

4. Even statistically nonsignificant interactions can be informative when plotted multivariately. The corollary to this is that graphically specifiable, precise, and useful interactive effects can escape detection in traditional analysis of variance methods.

Our evidence suggests the utility of aggressively using graphical analysis in analyzing data and formulating conclusions, particularly when the data are multivariate with complex interrelationships. We would argue that multivariate graphics are absolutely essential to a clear understanding of the data in complex computer system performance applications.

Acknowledgments

We thank Echo Solutions of Orem, Utah, for providing us with a version of DataMax used for the graphical analysis in this chapter. We also thank Joe Glenski and Keith Fredericks of Cray Research, Inc. for collecting the data.

References

1. P.J. Denning, "What Is Experimental Computer Science?" *Comm. ACM,* Vol. 23, No. 10, 1980, pp. 543-544.

2. D. Ferrari, "Considerations on the Insularity of Performance Evaluation," *IEEE Trans. Software Engineering,* Vol. SE-12, No. 6, June 1986, pp. 678-683.

3. G.E.P. Box, "The Scientific Context of Quality Improvement," *Quality Progress,* June 1987, pp. 54-61.

4. J.C. Kelly, "The Statistical Nature of Computer Performance Evaluation," *Proc. Computer Performance Evaluation Users Group,* Sept. 1975, pp. 5-18.

5. *Technometrics,* Vol. 2, No. 26, May 1984 [special issue on experimental design].

6. R. Yaremko et al., *Handbook of Research and Quantitative Methods in Psychology: For Students and Professionals,* Lawrence Erlbaum, Hillsdale, N.J., 1986.

7. G. Hahn and S. Shapiro, *Statistical Models in Engineering,* John Wiley, New York, 1967.

8. G.E.P. Box, W.G. Hunter, and J.S. Hunter, *Statistics for Experimenters: An Introduction to Design, Data Analysis, and Model Building,* John Wiley, New York, 1978.

9. B.L. Brown and A.C. Rencher, *The DataMax General Data Analytic System: Multivariate Graphical Methods,* Vol. 1, Echo Solutions, Orem, Ut., 1990.

10. G.E.P. Box, "Non-Normality and Tests on Variance," *Biometrika,* Vol. 40, 1953, pp. 318-335.

11. B.J. Winer, *Statistical Principals in Experimental Design,* McGraw-Hill, New York, 1971.

12. J.B. Kruskal and M. Wish, *Multidimensional Scaling,* Sage, Beverly Hills, Calif., 1978

13. R.N. Shepard, A.K. Romney, and S.B. Nerlove, eds., *Multidimensional Scaling: Theory and Applications in Behavioral Sciences,* Vol. 1, Seminar Press, New York, 1972.

14. J.B. Kruskal, "Analysis of Factorial Experiments by Estimating Monotone Transformations of the Data," *J. Royal Statistical Soc.,* Ser. B, Vol. 27, 1965, pp. 251-263.

15. J.W. Tukey, "The Comparative Anatomy of Transformations," *Ann. Mathematical Statistics,* Vol. 33, 1957, pp. 602-632.

16. A.C. Rencher and B.L. Brown, *The DataMax General Data Analytic System: Statistical Methods,* Vol. 2, Echo Solutions, Orem, Ut., 1990.

17. B.L. Brown, R.N. Williams, and C.D. Barlow, "PRIFAC: A Pascal Factor Analysis Program," *J. Pascal Ada Modula-2,* Vol. 3, No. 2, 1984, pp. 18-24.

Neale Hirsh is the founder and manager of the Capacity Planning Group at Cray Research, a consulting group whose clients represent most areas of supercomputing. Neale's research interest is workload characterization. He has published in the American Statistical Association and the Cray Users Group. He is a member of IEEE and Sigma Xi. Neale has an M.E.E. in Electrical Engineering and a Ph.D. in Experimental Psychology (S.U.N.Y. Stony Brook, 1980).

Bruce L. Brown is Professor of Psychology, Brigham Young University, Provo, Utah. He also serves as a consultant for ECHO Solutions, Orem, Utah, and is the primary author of the visualization component of DataMax.

His published works include two books on quantitative methods: *Statistics for Behavioral Sciences* (with F. Fallik, 1983), and *Statistical Analysis, A Simplest Case Approach* (with R. Williams, in press). He received his Ph.D. in psychology from McGill University, Montreal, Canada in 1969.

Section 4: Scientific Visualization at Research Laboratories

Lawrence J. Rosenblum, Naval Research Laboratory

Large scientific research centers are developing visualization methodologies and tools. This special section examines work under way at Los Alamos, Lawrence Livermore, the National Center for Supercomputing Applications, NASA Ames, and the Naval Research Laboratory.

Introduction

The concept of *scientific visualization* reaches back into prehistoric times when a caveman drew a map of his local environment on his cave wall. In antiquity, legend tells us that Archimedes was slain by a Roman soldier while visualizing figures sketched in the sand. In this century, chemists began to understand the structure of matter and satisfied the need to visualize molecules with wooden and plastic models. Visualizing data and concepts is not new, nor is it computer dependent.

In the computer age, we have progressed through line-printer output, contour plots, etc., to more sophisticated techniques. Yet, scientific visualization has only emerged as a technology in the last two or three years.

Visualization is no longer a useful supplement to scientific and engineering progress; it is now essential for many disciplines. Complex computational models, executing on supercomputers, produce simulated data in quantities that require geometrically based algorithms for interpretation. From multibeam echosounders mapping the ocean bottom to radio telescopes studying the heavens, sensors provide more numerical data than can ever be examined point by point. Large scientific research centers have responded by establishing and/or expanding groups devoted to the development of visualization methodologies and tools for an integrated understanding of very large data sets.

There are three levels of visualizing data for numerical simulations: *postprocessing, tracking,* and *steering.* Postprocessing refers to portraying the data after the numerical simulation is complete. Tracking provides real-time displays, allowing termination of a faulty simulation. Steering permits interaction with the computation; simulation parameter values can be altered midstream and the computation continued.

To date, most efforts deal with techniques for effective postprocessing: methods for transferring simulation data to the user and then displaying and interactively manipulating it. Steering offers great potential benefits, but both hardware and toolset problems must be solved. Steering is not new, but the complexity of many of today's simulations enhances its value. While emphasis is being placed on supercomputer steering, perhaps the "graphics minisupercomputers," with their tightly integrated computational and graphical power, are the platform for learning how to effectively steer complex simulations.

Current Visualization Activities

The surveys in this section examine aspects of scientific visualization work at five major laboratories and centers in the United States. With a half dozen or so supercomputers each—the numbers change as older models are replaced—Lawrence Livermore National Laboratory (LLNL) and Los Alamos National Laboratory (LANL) each have among the largest concentrations of supercomputing power in the world. "Distributed Visualization at Los Alamos National Laboratory" by Richard L. Phillips describes several approaches to visualizing simulated data. The video animation facility of Karl-Heinz Winkler and associates at LANL represents the state of the art in scientific visualization, but is too expensive to replicate widely. Philips also presents methods used at LANL for connecting supercomputers with display units, ranging from dumb terminals to powerful workstations. Of particular interest is the Scientific Visualization Workbench, an inexpensive and effective way of using "televisualization" to move data from supercomputer to user and to modify the user's display.

"Visualization Tools at Lawrence Livermore National Laboratory" by Brian Cabral and Carol L. Hunter describes three projects at LLNL. The Magic Project is developing techniques to move data from a Cray and effectively display it on high-resolution color terminals in the scientist's office. Laser disk technology provides a real-time animation capability. The Graphics Workstation Project has examined visualization applications of workstations with graphics accelerators and is currently extending this work to "graphics minisupercomputers." The Advanced Visualization Research Project uses high-end graphics devices to perform algorithm development, especially in the implementation of volumetric methods.

The National Center for Supercomputing Applications (NCSA), one of five National Science Foundation-sponsored supercomputer centers, serves a national user base rather than on-site users. In "Scientific Visualization and the Rivers Project at the National Center for Supercomputing Applications," Robert B. Haber describes NCSA's approach to the development of visualization tools for scientists who may be hundreds or thousands of miles away, as well as meeting the needs of researchers with special, complex requirements. Haber's Rivers (Research on Interactive Visual Environments) Project is an interesting and potentially important attempt to extend high-end visualization to the interactive steering of supercomputer simulations. Other groups at NCSA deal with "routine" graphics, with custom high-quality animations for scientists, and with the development of toolsets ranging from generating color palettes to volume visualization (see below).

At the Ames Research Center of the National Aeronautics and Space Administration, scientific visualization is more focused. "Scientific Visualization in Computational Aerodynamics at NASA Ames Research Center" by Gordon Bancroft et al. describes tools specifically oriented toward flow analysis problems. This approach is oriented toward performing graphics calculations on the supercomputer and using high-end workstations as rendering engines to display flow fields generated by aircraft flight. A suite of software provides both display and interactive analysis capability. The authors also describe animation hardware featuring Winchester disk technology, which allows the storage of more than one gigabyte of data and supports editing, special effects, and video output.

In addition to in-house computational science, the Naval Research Laboratory (NRL) supports a varied experimental research program. NRL scientists travel worldwide to perform experiments using platforms that include satellites, aircraft, ships, and submarines. "Visualization of Experimental Data at the Naval Research Laboratory" by Lawrence J. Rosenblum deals with the role of scientific visualization in understanding experimental data sets. The difficulty in extracting parameters of interest from the measurements is described for five diverse application areas, and the role of visualization in developing understanding of these data is illustrated. The role digital imaging and signal processing play should be noted. These areas are perhaps more difficult to generalize into toolsets than computer graphics, but they are an important part of the suite of visualization technologies.

Trends and Directions

These surveys make it clear that the postprocessing problem is well on the way to solution. Higher bandwidth networks are needed, as are more capable workstations, higher resolution, better interaction, etc., but these will arrive. The scientist will sit at his desk and see simulation results quickly and effectively. Effective steering tools are further away, and efforts such as the Rivers Project are important because successful steering tools will change the very nature of computational science.

One much-discussed issue in the scientific visualization community is "How much graphics processing should be done on the supercomputer and how much should be moved to the workstation?" A variety of approaches is seen. At NASA/Ames, the workstation is used primarily for rendering the aircraft in flight. At NCSA, data is downloaded from the supercomputer onto a minisupercomputer devoted to visualization processing. Meanwhile, LANL and LLNL are experimenting with a variety of techniques for moving data in unprocessed, partially processed, and graphical formats between supercomputer and display units that range from dumb terminals to high-end graphics workstations. Perhaps this issue is unresolvable because, in addition to the technical arguments, many factors in such a decision relate to organizational structure. The questions include: "Is time available on the supercomputer and at what cost?" and "How is the visualization developer's time paid?" The distinction should be drawn, however, between the need to develop general visualization tools, which require minimal interaction with the scientist, and the need for interdisciplinary teams of scientists and visualization specialists working closely together to attack front-line scientific issues. Examples of both can be found in these articles, and both are essential.

An illustration of this distinction can be seen in an important methodology called volume visualization (or volume rendering), mentioned in several of these articles. Because volume visualization portrays structure with information at each voxel (volume element), information about the interior of an object is known. This differs from traditional surface ("polygon") rendering methods and turns out to be invaluable for many analysis problems. Integrated with transparency, interactive display, and motion, volume visualization is capable of providing new understanding. It also integrates well with image processing. For many empirical data sets, the future processing paradigm will be for signal processing algorithms to extract the parameters of interest, image processing algorithms to smooth and enhance the "signal," and interactive analysis of the resulting data space using volumetric methods to gain understanding of complex structures. Primarily a methodology today and the subject of much research both to develop better and faster algorithms and to integrate it into the scientific analysis process, volume visualization is one of tomorrow's tools.

Where scientific visualization tools have been successfully implemented, attention has been paid to assuring ease of use and continuity. Software, system, and devices are made to appear transparent to the user. This requires the use of standards and pseudostandards for graphics, systems, language, and communication. Examples include PHIGS+, CGM, X Windows, Unix, and Postscript. With such tools the visualization specialist assures that hardware and software modifications, upgrades, and additions are implemented without constantly forcing scientists to interrupt their research to learn new sets of commands.

Finally, the need for visualization paradigms and formalisms stands out. Even for simple tasks such as color palette selection for an animation, there are few guidelines save experience (although the work of Donna Cox et al. at NCSA provides a good starting point). Guidelines for proceeding through the analysis process for experimental data sets are similarly lacking. In the excitement over the obvious benefits of scientific visualization, few questions have been asked about the nature of perceived information and how well the human visual system actually performs. Because visualization is a new, emerging discipline, the lack of structures is not surprising, but their development is necessary and offers significant research opportunities.

These surveys represent the cutting edge of an important, emerging field. They are examples of the exciting work springing up worldwide. As the development of new scientific visualization tools makes these methodologies available to more researchers, the knowledge produced by the integration of visualization into the scientific process will further benefit mankind. Taken together, these surveys provide a foundation for others to build on.

Lawrence J. Rosenblum is a computer scientist in the Marine Systems Branch at the Naval Research Laboratory, where he has worked since 1977. His current research interests include visualization of oceanographic data and vision for underwater autonomous vehicles. He has also developed real-time data acquisition systems for oceanographic experiments aboard ships and aircraft.

Rosenblum received a BA in mathematics from Queens College, City University of New York, in 1964. He received an MS in 1966 and a PhD in 1971, both from the Ohio State University in mathematics. He is past chairperson of the IEEE Computer Society Technical Committee on Computer Graphics and is currently vice chairperson of the Computer Society's Technical Activities Board and co-chairperson of Compusat 89, the "Interdisciplinary World of Computing" satellite symposium. He is a member of the Computer Society, ACM SIGGraph, and the American Geophysical Union.

Distributed Visualization at Los Alamos National Laboratory

Richard L. Phillips, Los Alamos National Laboratory

Introduction

The Los Alamos National Laboratory is operated by the University of California for the US Department of Energy. Among other activities, LANL performs research and development in support of the nation's nuclear weapons programs. This requires large computer simulations of hydrodynamic phenomena. Because of the volume and complexity of resultant data, methods for visualization of information are essential. This article discusses several approaches to scientific visualization at LANL.

Even the editors of the *Visualization in Scientific Computing*[1] report would agree that scientific visualization is not a new concept; only the term is new. Figure 1 presents a brief history of visualization capability, tied primarily to the evolution of graphics hardware. Looking at the prehistory part of the diagram, many of us can recall doing what we thought was scientific visualization using crude printer-plots. Later, when film recorders became available, researchers like Prueitt at Los Alamos led the way in producing sophisticated slides and animated films of scientific computations.[2] But, while the ViSC concept is not new, a recent confluence of technologies, both hardware and software, is revolutionizing the way we do scientific visualization. These developments appear on the timeline beginning in the early 1980s.

In that same time frame, much of the software for producing highly realistic rendering of scientific data began to show up as resident firmware in workstations. Then, in 1988, a series of papers on volume rendering appeared[3,4] that improved on similar methods described earlier.[5] While earlier approaches to rendering (such as Gouraud shading[6] or ray tracing[6] required the data to have some geometric structure, volume visualization techniques can directly render scattered observations in three-space by determining the optical depth from the opacity of the volume elements along the viewing path. The resulting image, when displayed on a high-resolution color monitor, shows the characteristics of the entire data set—interior and exterior—at a glance.

In the late 1980s, specialized graphics accelerators for industry standard workstations as well as graphics supercomputers were announced. As a single-user system, the graphics supercomputers are quite expensive, but they do offer unprecedented interactive visualization power. Further along the timeline, 800-megabit-per-second networks will begin to appear. The driving force in that development is the proposed ANSI standard (X3T9.3 Committee) high-speed channel (HSC) specification that Los Alamos is spearheading. Soon to become a standard, HSC hardware is already being developed by leading computer and workstation vendors. Workstations equipped with graphics accelerator

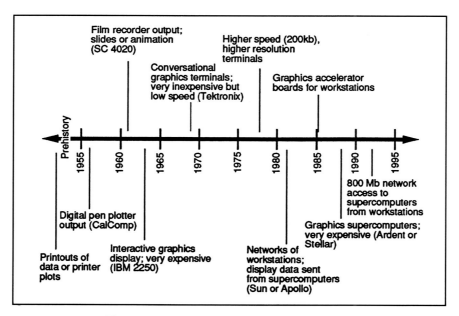

Figure 1. Evolution of visualization capability.

EH0307-9/90/0000/0212$01.00 © 1989 IEEE

212

boards, coupled with HSC network access to supercomputers, offer exciting opportunities for visualization, particularly in the computing environment of Los Alamos.

The Los Alamos computing environment can be characterized as widely distributed and massively interconnected. Workstations, terminals, and mainframes can all communicate with one another with relative ease. The dominant type of computing is large-scale scientific simulation using the seven Cray computers in the Central Computing Facility. To deal with the huge amount of data produced by this environment, a variety of tools and approaches have been developed for visualizing scientific information. I will describe several of these techniques, emphasizing distributed approaches to visualization.

Centralized Visualization:
The Ultra-Speed Graphics Project

Karl-Heinz Winkler and his associates[7] have developed a video animation facility based on a Gould PN9080 system and a Gould IP8500 image-array processor. While not a distributed visualization facility, this system's capabilities have whetted the appetites of Los Alamos users for an equivalent tool. With it, complex finite difference simulations produced on a supercomputer can be viewed as 8-bit-per-pixel pseudocolor images at a resolution of 1,024 + 1,024 at 8 frames per second or 512 + 512 at 30 frames per second. Arbitrary color lookup tables can be specified to induce desired features to emerge. This facility forms the basis for Winkler's Los Alamos Numerical Laboratory, which is used not only by Los Alamos researchers but by scientists from throughout the world. The facility allows investigators to explore huge collections of simulation data in a relatively short period and occasionally has led to the discovery of unexpected phenomena.

The system is organized so that data sets computed on the Crays are transferred to the display system over a 27-megabit-per-second parallel interface. While this data rate is high enough to allow continuous monitoring of typical numerical experiments, the image support processor is used primarily to receive large sets of compressed solution numbers from several Crays, turn them into individual images at a rate of up to 100,000 images per day, and display them as movies on digital display devices. Storing the images in digital form completely decoupled from a particular color representation allows tremendous flexibility in digging out features hidden in the numbers. Figure 2 graphically shows the computer simulation of a high-speed jet entering a quiescent ambient gas.

While the Winkler work is ground breaking and important, it represents an approach to visualization that only a few can afford; such a facility is clearly expensive to replicate.

Other approaches to visualization at Los Alamos seek to bring the visualization environment into the scientist's office, using relatively low-cost workstations and network connections to the Crays. There are several ways to accomplish such a connection; some are discussed below. Many of these approaches have been inspired by, or are an outgrowth of, the Ultra-Speed Graphics Project.

General Approaches to Distributed Visualization

Figure 3 depicts several approaches to connecting graphics displays to supercomputers. They are all in use or under development at Los Alamos.

The connection shown in the upper left is typical of one still in use at Los Alamos. In particular, the terminal would be one of the Tektronix family, a 4014 or 4125. A special high-speed interface provides 300-kilobit-per-second access to a Cray and, because of the efficient data format used by Tektronix terminals, complex images can be produced quickly. There is no opportunity, however, to perform any local processing with these systems. All data is produced and sent by a supercomputer.

Simple workstations connected to a supercomputer (upper right diagram in Figure 3) offer many advantages over a simple terminal. Since there is local processing power, the user can save data sets produced by the supercomputer and manipulate them further off-line. However, the graphics performance of many low-end workstations is inferior to the terminal arrangement discussed above. Although the local area network connection (Ethernet) to the Cray has a bandwidth of 10 megabits per second, the actual throughput is much less, typically 0.5-1 megabit per second. This is partly due to protocol overhead, but also because what is referred to in the figure as a "dumb" workstation typically has poor drawing performance. Examples of these are Motorola 68000-based workstations with no graphics acceleration hardware.

But there are workstations with superior graphics performance; the silicon-enhanced systems from Silicon Graphics are but one example. You can also equip a workstation with a graphics accelerator board. Workstation manufacturers provide these, as do third-party hardware suppliers. Recently, Alliant Computer Systems and Trancept Systems (now a subsidiary of Sun Microsystems) introduced accelerators that promise to have a strong impact on visualization efforts. Alliant offers the GX4000, a board set that plugs in to a standard Sun Microsystems workstation. This board implements the proposed PHIGS+ standard in microcode and thus provides a 3D graphics capability for the host workstation. This means that full 3D data can be sent from a supercomputer and transformed locally. Thus, an object can be animated just by transforming it and

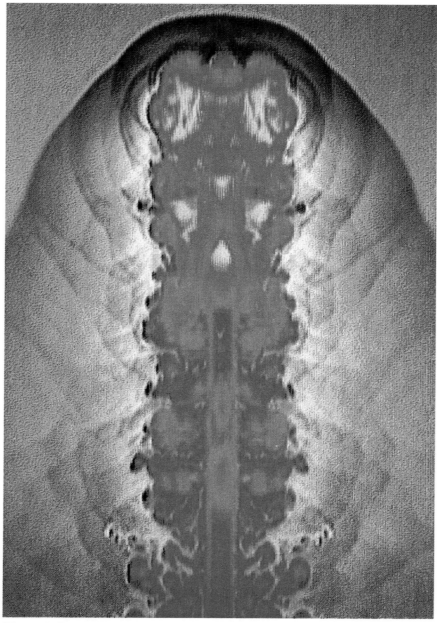

Figure 2. Numerical simulation of a gas jet penetrating a quiescent medium.

redisplaying it in a new orientation. Depending on the complexity of the object, good to excellent animation rates can be achieved, that is, 4 to 24 frames per second.

The Trancept board is called the TAAC-1, an acronym for Trancept Application Accelerator. As the name suggests, this board can be used to speed up all kinds of local computing tasks. When used for graphics applications, it can perform sophisticated rendering operations at very high speeds. While the board is an add-on to a Sun Microsystems workstation, it has its own frame buffer and is capable of producing high-resolution 24-bit-per-pixel images. The board also has the potential of accepting data directly (bypassing the Sun processor) at 600 megabytes per second. Work under way at Los Alamos to exploit this feature will be described later.

While the graphics performance of both of these accelerators outstrips conventional workstation hardware, the data delivery rate to them is, in general, still limited by Ethernet throughput. This may not be a problem for investigations where a relatively small amount of object data is sent from the supercomputer and is expanded locally to produce high-quality images, animated sequences, or both.

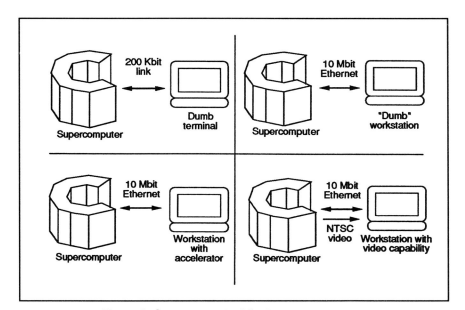

Figure 3. Supercomputer/display connections.

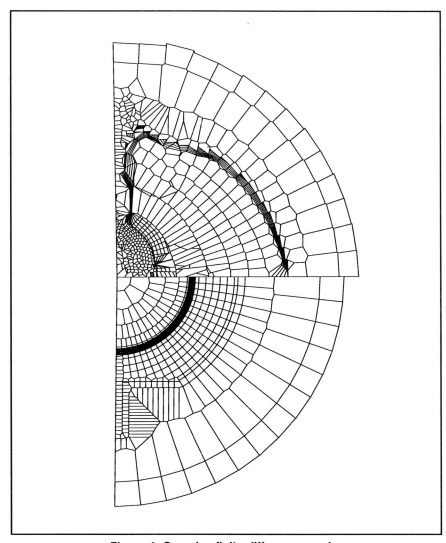

Figure 4. Complex finite difference mesh.

There is a large class of problems, however, where this is not an especially useful approach. These are typically simulations involving finite difference calculations where complex meshes are used to describe the spatial aspects of the problem. An example of such a mesh is shown in Figure 4.

This represents one instant in time in a sequence of many thousands of such images. As the problem evolves, some part of the mesh changes from one time step to another. Each image comprises several thousand data points and, due to Ethernet limitations, you cannot expect to achieve very good graphics display rates. Accelerator boards are no help here because there is no local algorithmic processing they can usefully perform. An exception would be the case where only those parts of the image that change in a time interval are sent to the workstation. The accelerator would maintain the graphics database and apply the changes locally. This is not a simple task, however, and has not been done in practice.

Another approach to remote data visualization is to perform some, if not all, of the graphics processing on the supercomputer and send the complete representation to the workstation as an image, that is, pixels. But, if the image resolution is say, $512 \times 512 \times 8$, one-quarter megabyte of data must be sent for each display. Such a volume of data would seem to preclude this approach, at least in the Ethernet environment described above. There are ways to circumvent the brute force approach, however. One is to buffer several images in the workstation's virtual memory and then enter a local animation loop. The other is to convert the images to video at the supercomputer and provide an alternate display link to the workstation. Both approaches are being pursued at Los Alamos.

Specific Distributed Visualization Projects

This section describes two distributed visualization projects—Simple Interface and the Scientific Visualization Workbench—under way at LANL and discusses implications for the future.

SI: An interface between a supercomputer and a workstation. Saltzman[8] has developed a system for viewing pixel images produced on a supercomputer on a standard Sun workstation; no special hardware is required. SunView, the standard Sun window system, runs on the workstation. Communication with a Cray is via Ethernet.

SI (for Simple Interface) is based on a client/server model. The Cray runs an SI server that listens for requests from the client side running on a Sun. When the Sun requests image data, the server opens a communication path (via sockets) and sends the requested information. Once done, the server breaks the path and goes about listening for additional requests. At this point, the program on the workstation can peruse the frames of data it has

received, either a frame at a time or in an animation loop. Figure 5 shows SI in use.

SI has the advantage of requiring only standard hardware and software and, thus, can be widely used. At Los Alamos, the nearly 700 Sun workstations make the ubiquity of use important. SI allows only 128 colors to appear in an image, however, and only 10 frames may be cached locally. If these limitations are not significant, SI represents a very effective distributed visualization tool.

Visualization using video images. The lower right panel in Figure 3 shows a workstation connected to a supercomputer by both Ethernet and a National Television System Committee video link. Of course, the workstation must have a device that can handle video data. This is a type of accelerator, a board that accepts an image directly and displays it on the workstation screen. Parallax Graphics makes such a board. It can digitize an NTSC video signal in real time, that is, 30 frames per second. The Scientific Visualization Workbench[9] developed at Los Alamos makes use of the Parallax board capabilities, in conjunction with an already-developed supercomputer frame buffer system[10] and the News window system.

Fowler and McGowen developed the supercomputer frame buffer system. The frame buffer attaches directly to a Cray channel capable of delivering data at 48 megabits per second. The developers visualized the system being used by communicating with the Cray via a dumb terminal at 9,600 bits per second. Supporting software then converts graphics metafiles to raster images and sends them to the frame buffer channel. Images are viewed on an RGB (red, green, and blue) monitor at up to 26 frames per second. The RGB signal can be displayed remotely by extending it to a user's office by fiber optics. The Scientific Visualization Workbench takes this one step further by bringing the video signal into a window on a workstation screen.

This image-based approach to visualization overcomes the speed limitations of other approaches, but at a price. Image quality is lost by rasterization for the frame buffer and certainly by NTSC encoding of the video signal. Thus, you trade image fidelity for bandwidth.

On the other hand, the user can see images as fast as they can be produced by the supercomputer—as high as 26 frames per second—and temporal fidelity is often more important than image quality. The flexibility to experiment with new visualization algorithms, rather than relying solely on rendering methods provided by the workstation vendor, is another advantage to be gained from processing graphics data on a supercomputer.

The structure of the Scientific Visualization Workbench is depicted in Figure 6.

The workbench comprises a Sun Microsystems 3/160C workstation equipped with a Parallax 1280 Series Video-

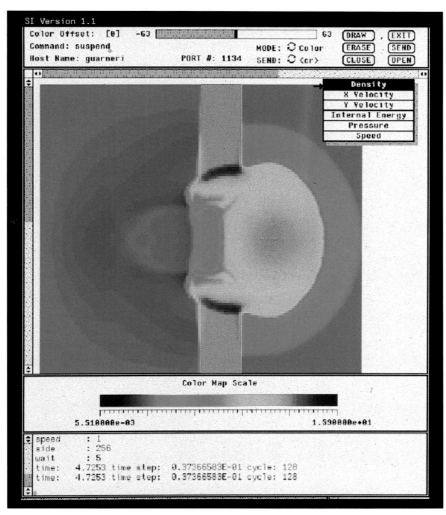

Figure 5. Simple Interface in use.

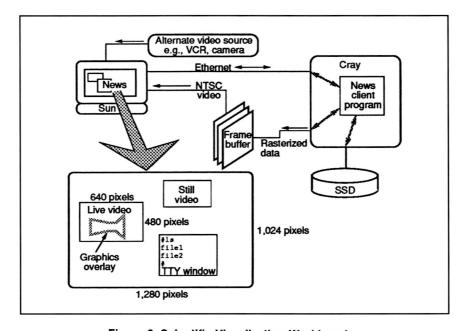

Figure 6. Scientific Visualization Workbench.

graphics Processor, a Sony high-resolution color monitor, a Cray Research supercomputer equipped with a solid-state drive (SSD), and a 512h × 512v × 8 bits-per-pixel frame-buffer attached to the Cray by a 48-megabit-per-second channel. Communication between the Sun and the Cray is via Ethernet using TCP/IP protocol. The Cray runs Unicos 3.0 (System V-based Unix), and a special Parallax-enhanced version of the News 1.1 window system (Pnews) runs on the Sun. A News client program on the Cray controls the transmission of rasterized data to the frame buffer and ultimately to the workstation over an NTSC video link. Because of the Postscript underpinnings of News, it is possible to produce color or black-and-white hard copy of the video images of anything on the screen. The magnified workstation screen in the lower left of the figure suggests the presence of several types of windows, in which independent processes run simultaneously. Figure 7 is an actual screen dump of the workbench in use.

Higher speed networks: Implications for the future. Los Alamos is leading the specification and development of an 800-megabit-per-second channel, the HSC (high-speed channel)[11] for use in a fiber-based, point-to-point crossbar network. DEC, IBM, Sun, Tektronix, and others have already committed to building HSC hardware, while DEC is playing a key role in the development of the network, called CP*. Figure 8 shows a diagram of the future Los Alamos Integrated Computer Network (ICN), based upon the HSC and CP* technology.

With the availability of such high network bandwidth, many distributed visualization schemes become possible. For example, one need no longer be content with NTSC video or require a separate video link. CP* will easily accommodate CCIR 601 digital video or even the emerging high-definition television (HDTV) standard of 1,100 lines. The Scientific Visualization Workbench would be upgraded to account for that capability.

Another approach being explored involves a Sun workstation equipped with a Sun TAAC board modified to operate at HSC speeds. With this system, you can transfer full floating-point, 3D graphics data sets from the supercomputers at very high speed and use the local processing power of the TAAC board for fast rendering of the data. This configuration is being tested over a direct fiber link between a workstation and an IBM 3090/200 equipped with an HSC interface.

Many changes are under way within the Los Alamos computing infrastructure to improve capabilities for distributed visualization. As the CP* network is put in place, gateways to Ethernet and FDDI (Fiber Distribution Data Interface) fiber networks will also be provided. The CP* backbone will provide the bandwidth for transmission of 24-bit color images with a resolution of 1,024 × 1,024 at a rate close to 30 frames per second. This will permit local office viewing of images generated on a supercomputer, using a high-resolution successor to the Scientific Visualization Workbench. Alternatively, users will be able to trans-

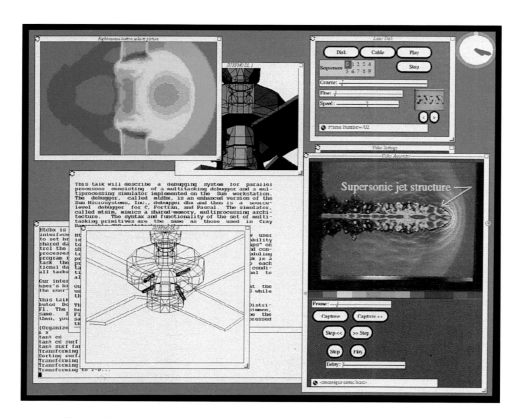

Figure 7. Screen dump of Scientific Visualization Workbench display.

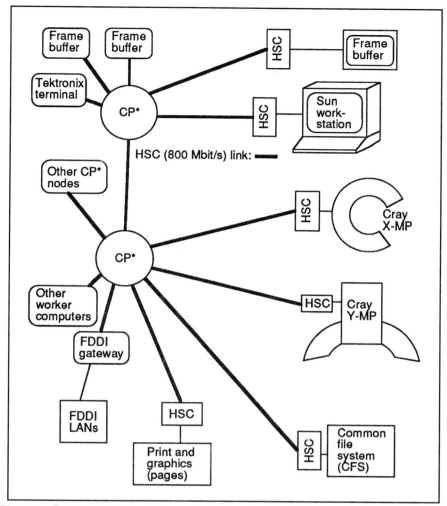

Figure 8. Future Integrated Computer Network with high-speed channel and CP*.

fer data sets of 3D, floating-point information at a rate of 100 megabytes per second to accelerator-equipped workstations or to 3D workstations like the Silicon Graphics Iris for local rendering.

As in many organizations, security is an important issue, and the attendant necessary firewalls are often a barrier to effective interactive use of computing facilities. At Los Alamos, this issue will be resolved in early 1990 by the introduction of a secure IP (Internetwork Protocol) router. Then, users in all parts of the computing environment will enjoy high-speed distributed visualization.

Exploratory work on the use of massively parallel computer architectures for scientific visualization is just beginning. The recent installation of a Thinking Machines CM2 with 65,536 processors will accelerate this effort. One of the CM2 frame buffers has already been installed on the cable video network mentioned earlier, making its output available for use with the Scientific Visualization Workbench.

Finally, most of the techniques and systems described here are portable to other installations. The Scientific Visualization Workbench can be easily duplicated or implemented on different hardware, using different software. The Simple Interface can be installed wherever SunView is available on workstations and RPC (remote procedure call) is supported on the network. Even HSC, being an ANSI standard, and CP*, which will be publicly available, can be implemented elsewhere.

References

1. "Visualization in Scientific Computing," *Computer Graphics*, B.H. McCormick et al., eds., Vol. 21, No. 6, Nov. 1987.

2. M.L. Prueitt, "A Window on Science," *IEEE Computer Graphics and Applications*, Vol. 7, No. 9, Sept. 1987, pp. 4-8.

3. C. Upson and M. Keeler, "V-Buffer: Visible Volume Rendering," *Computer Graphics,* Vol. 22, No. 4, Aug. 1988, pp. 59-64.

4. R.A. Drebin, L. Carpenter, and P. Hanrahan, "Volume Rendering," *Computer Graphics,* Vol. 22, No. 4, Aug. 1988, pp. 65-74.

5. G.T. Herman and J.K. Udupa, "Display of 3D Digital Images: Computational Foundations and Medical Applications," *IEEE Computer Graphics and Applications,* Vol. 3, No. 5, Aug. 1983, pp. 39-46.

6. J.D. Foley and A. Van Dam, *Fundamentals of Interactive Computer Graphics,* Addison-Wesley, Reading, Mass., 1982. See Chapter 16.

7. K.-H. Winkler et al., "A Numerical Laboratory," *Physics Today,* Vol. 40, No. 10, Oct., 1987, pp. 28-37.

8. J. Saltzman, "Simple Interface (SI): An Interface Between a Cray Supercomputer and Sun Workstation," LA-UR-88-2171, Los Alamos National Laboratory, June 1988.

9. R.L. Phillips, "A Scientific Visualization Workbench," *Proc. Supercomputing 88,* Nov. 14-18, 1988, Orlando, Fla., pp. 148-155, CS Press, Los Alamitos, Calif., order No. 882.

10. J.D. Fowler and M. McGowen, "Design and Implementation of a Supercomputer Frame Buffer System," *Proc. Supercomputing 88,* Nov. 14-18, 1988, Orlando, Fla., pp. 140-147, CS Press, Los Alamitos, Calif., order No. 882.

11. B. Morris and D. Tolmie, "High-Speed Channel (HSC): Mechanical, Electrical, and Signalling Protocol Requirements," *Draft Proposed American National Standard, X3 T9.3/88-023,* Aug. 1988.

Richard L. Phillips is a staff member in the Computer Graphics Group of the Computing and Communications Division of the Los Alamos National Laboratory. His current research interests are scientific visualization, multimedia workstations, distributed computing, window systems, and electronic publication.

Phillips received a BSE in mathematics in 1956, an MSE in aerospace engineering in 1957, and a PhD in aerospace engineering in 1964, all from the University of Michigan. He is treasurer of ACM SIGGraph and played major roles in the 1978, 1986, 1987, and 1988 SIGGraph conferences. He is a member of the IEEE, the IEEE Computer Society, and ACM.

Visualization Tools at Lawrence Livermore National Laboratory

Brian Cabral and Carol L. Hunter, Lawrence Livermore National Laboratory

Introduction

Lawrence Livermore National Laboratory (LLNL), operated by the University of California for the US Department of Energy, supports research programs in nuclear weapons, magnetic fusion energy, laser fusion, laser isotope separation, biomedical and environmental sciences, and applied energy technology. These programs require research in basic scientific disciplines, including chemistry and materials sciences, computer science and technology, engineering, and physics.

Scientists have at their disposal seemingly limitless data and computing power, and they are always seeking enhancements of their ability to access, explore, represent, and manipulate data. Scientific visualization is an emerging interdisciplinary field that is responding to the need for insight into data representations through the creation of visualization tools.[1] There is no "right" way to provide insight, and the user directly benefits from different efforts at scientific visualization. In this article, we describe two efforts to develop visualization tools at Livermore, one within the Computation and Defense Sciences Departments and the other within the Engineering Department.

Graphics in the Supercomputer Environment

For 40 years, scientists have produced numerical simulations with computers and derived insight from calculations. During this time, increases in computing capability have accompanied increases in calculation complexity and computer graphics sophistication. However, many graphics methods from the 1950s are still adequate for decision-making today and are vital tools to the scientist. Visualization tools range from x,y plots to animated three-dimensional renderings. Visualization tools should include any and all data representations and allow a researcher to choose between a simple plot and a complex image based on deadlines and detail constraints.

In the quest for faster, more powerful, and more responsive computation, Livermore developed a complex supercomputer environment over the years, managed by the Livermore Computer Center (LCC). The environment includes seven Crays, hundreds of workstations, and the interconnecting network structures. Graphics for the 2,000 supercomputer users is provided by the Television Monitor Display System, an 18-year old DeAnza central-frame buffer system. TMDS provides black and white, low-resolution

(512×512) service throughout the one-mile-square facility, at up to 30 frames per second. It is not feasible to upgrade to high resolution and color or extend the network with the existing hardware. In 1988, an LCC-chartered committee made recommendations for the functionality required to replace the TMDS.[2] We will describe our prototype efforts to provide information on the performance of the TMDS, using high-resolution color systems that add functionality and interactivity.

Most LLNL research involves considerable computational effort. Massive amounts of data are consulted repeatedly in various transformations and representations. This work involves frequent comparisons—comparing new calculations to old calculations, to previous time steps, to experiments, to calculations on different software, and to analytic solutions. An essential component of scientific visualization is on-line browsing into multiple windows to allow comparison of data and the ability to follow a train of thought on the screen. Scientific visualization must address quantitative as well as qualitative information. At any point in browsing through graphics images, the scientist needs to be able to query the graphics system as to the specific values of data being displayed. Many different easy-to-use tools must be available to improve the scientist's everyday, analysis graphics capabilities.

Magic. Magic, or Machine Graphics in Color, is designed to bring high-resolution, color images to the offices of researchers over a high-speed network. The Magic network (Figure 1) transfers Cray graphics data up to one kilometer at a throughput rate of 2.5 megabits per second. When we started the project, we wanted to deliver Cray supercomputer graphics to advanced graphics terminals in researchers' offices at a high speed using low-cost, off-the-shelf products.[3] We chose Tektronix 412x graphics terminals because they offered high plotting speeds, high resolution, a wide range of color, picture segmentation, flexible graphics-input tools (cursor, mouse), fill-area, raster-plotting functions, and three-dimensional capabilities. The terminals were a known and reliable medium. The network solution was an unknown.

Magic provides a platform for high-level data representation and algorithm experimentation. Users understand their problem domain; our local graphics experts understand graphics. The experts developed a variety of data representations and worked with the users to identify the most informative representations. Interest was most often sparked

Reprinted from *Computer*, August 1989, pages 77-84. Copyright © 1989 by The Institute of Electrical and Electronics Engineers, Inc. All rights reserved.

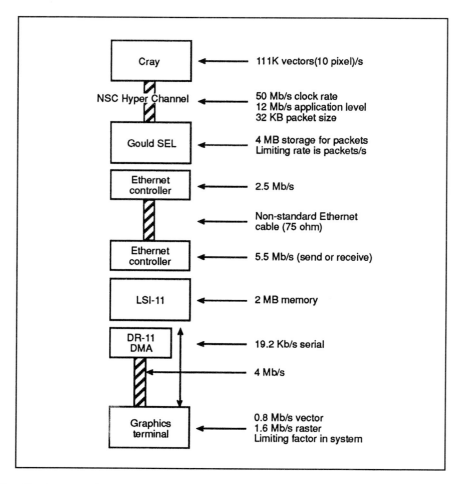

Figure 1. The Magic network transports data from any Cray in the LCC, over HyperChannel to a Gould SEL computer being used as a graphics concentrator, over a combination of existing 75 ohm coax and 50 ohm coax to remote buildings where an LSI-11 buffers the data to a Tektronix graphics terminal.

when the graphics showed an unusual feature that looked like a "bug in the graphics," but 95 percent of the time they turned out to be a bug in the user's application. Variations of color tables proved to be extremely informative; the use of a rainbow color table and a gray-tone color table were most productive. Color presents the opportunity of displaying multiple parameters of the user's data (Figure 2).

A follow-on effort with the Magic network has provided real-time animation with the use of a Super VHS laser video disc recorder. Frames are captured from the Tektronix and replayed on the video disc player. A second follow-on effort, MacMagic, involves sending raster images from the Cray environment to a Mac II over the Magic network. Image-Tool,[4] developed by the National Center for Supercomputing Applications, proved to be an extremely powerful public-domain product; this package provides the ability to manipulate the palette, view multiple images, and animate sets of image frames. ImageTool was modified to accept a

message stream from the Magic network and display raster images sent from the Cray.

The Graphics Workstation Project. The Graphics Workstation (GWS) Project moves the user's graphics environment from the supercomputer to a workstation and provides interactivity, a friendly user interface, and additional functionality.[5] In our initial project, we used four Sun-3/160 graphics workstations with floating-point and graphics accelerators and a color and monochrome monitor for each workstation.

The most important tool developed to date is a postprocessing program for two-dimensional data on a rectangular mesh. The screen displays panels with push buttons, sliders, pop-up windows, and a zoom and pan feature. Typical plots are line and pseudocolor plots of various physical data (temperature, pressure, density, etc.), mesh plots, velocity-vector plots, and material-boundary plots, all of which can be superimposed.

Figure 2. Two different physics variables are represented on a two-dimensional grid (a) by using a two-dimensional color table (b) where the horizontal axis of the color table represents one variable, and the vertical axis represents the other variable. The upper right corner of the color table represents high values of both physics variables.

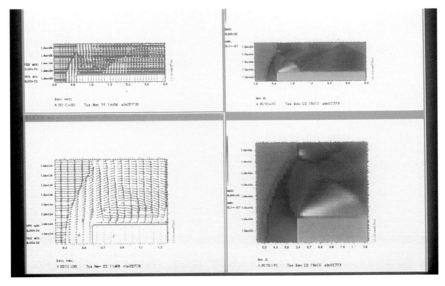

Figure 3. Multiple images display a wind tunnel with different data representations, allowing the user to follow a train of thought and compare images; (b) is a zoomed image of the (a) material, contour, and vector plot, and (b) is a zoomed image from the pseudocolor plot.

As many as four different frames can be displayed at one time (see Figure 3) for comparison and follow-train-of-thought capabilities. A pick-and-query capability (Figures 4 and 5) is designed to determine the exact value of coordinates and physical data (quantitative information) at any point on the screen. Other GWS tools include a metafile viewer to display previously stored graphics images; a three-dimensional surface plotting routine (Figure 6); and a Cray-to-Sun system that allows a Cray application to send graphics from a Cray graphics library over the network to a remote Sun workstation window.

The GWS project is a success because it demonstrates the feasibility of workstation graphics for supercomputer data and provides essential capabilities—comparison, train-of-thought capabilities, and both qualitative and quantitative information. However, the performance of GWS was inadequate: a faster CPU, more memory, and higher performance graphics were required. The main goal of the current phase of GWS is to obtain high-performance graphics from portable graphics software based on standards.[6] In 1988, the GWS project ordered two Stellar GS1000 graphics workstations because they integrated a powerful floating-point capability with very high speed graphics. Our high-performance graphics and workstation tools will be based on a standard software platform that includes Unix, C, PHIGS, and X Windows.

The Advanced Visualization Research Project

The Advanced Visualization Research Project at LLNL addresses changing technological constraints, while allowing for rapid research, development, and the delivery of new visualization algorithms to engineers and scientists. AVRP is currently involved with ongoing work in the areas of parallel graphics algorithms and visualization system integration. Through vigorous research and the development of new visualization algorithms, AVRP strives to influence the direction of scientific visualization.

In this section, we describe an existing software system that allows scientists to experiment with state-of-the-art visualization algorithms. The considerations that drive the system's architecture include the varied data structures used in computational models; the need for interactivity; the

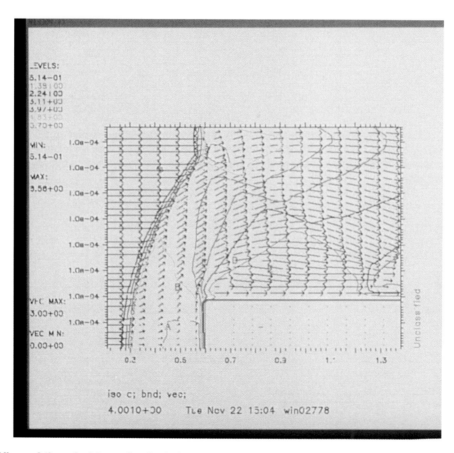

Figure 4. View of the wind tunnel calculation in which velocity vectors are superimposed over material interfaces and density contours. B, C, D, E, F are pick-and-query characters, which relate to the text window in Figure 5.

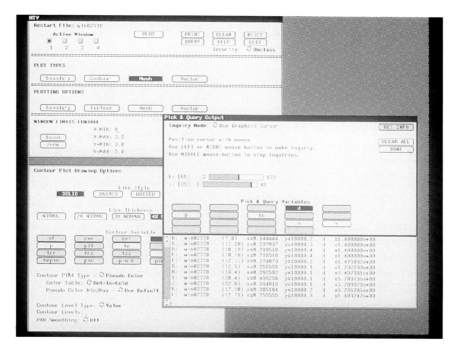

Figure 5. Screen dump of the monochrome screen showing control panel, contour selection panel, and pick-and-query results of the user's quantitative search of the data.

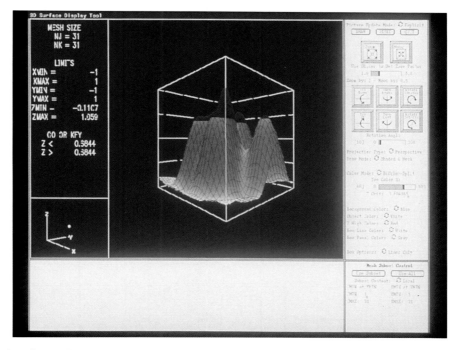

Figure 6. An alternative tool provides 3D rendering of the wind tunnel calculation. The tool provides quantitative as well as qualitative information via the bicolor split feature, allowing the user to select the z-value to be used for the split.

speed, capabilities, and diversity of the laboratory's graphics hardware; and the need to rapidly prototype new visualization algorithms.

A function-based taxonomy. We are developing new methods to transform symbolic and numerical data into a visual form. By abstracting the symbolic and numerical data into a general taxonomy, we define an interface between scientific applications and visualization tools. Much of the analysis done by scientists compares results of experiments and/or simulations. These results can be described as a function of m-independent variables.

Usually, an independent variable is one of three spatial variables, x, y, and z and the temporal variable, t. Our taxonomy characterizes scientific data as a set of functions with an arbitrary number of independent variables. It further characterizes these functions based on the geometric spacing (Eulerian geometries are a rectangular fixed lattice; Lagrangian geometries are an arbitrarily spaced moveable lattice) of the independent variables.

The AVRP software architecture is composed of four major components (see Figure 7). At the user level, a set of tools and algorithms graphically render scientific data sets. The user interface and graphics device abstraction are provided for all AVRP tools by Gab (Graphics Abstraction) and Glib (Graphics Library). Cell IO provides the scientific data abstraction that allows us to build a general interface to the AVRP tools.

By characterizing scientific data with the described taxonomy, we have decoupled scientific applications from specific visualization techniques. This abstraction allows us to build a general interface to many scientific applications. The Cell IO software supports a file format that accepts multiple functions represented as two-dimensional and three-dimensional Eulerian grids of data. The engineer may

specify an arbitrary number of dependent variables per cell, multiple time steps, and multiple grids (that is, functions) of any discrete resolution. Dependent variables may be used in any combination within a single grid, and the number and type of dependent variables may vary from grid to grid.

The Cell IO data abstraction defines the structure of the data and the syntax of the file, rather than the semantics of the grid data. Thus, it is possible for one tool to expect a two-dimensional grid and another to expect a three-dimensional grid. Most tool/application interface problems occur because of the nonuniformity of syntax and data structures required by various tools or subroutines. This software makes it easier for an application to interface to our visualization tools than with methods based on graphics libraries. Our architecture provides the scientific programmer a high-level, easy-to-use, generalized interface to visualization tools.

Glib is a three-dimensional graphics package based on a low-level graphics system (such as X Windows or Silicon Graphics GL graphics package). Our philosophy is to provide, via Glib, the graphics functionality needed by our tools and to avoid the excess software of the high-level graphics libraries. Gab is a set of high-level windowing abstractions built upon Glib. By basing all our tools on Gab and Glib, we can guarantee the performance and behavior characteristics of the underlying system. As the X Windows user interface tool kits and three-dimensional extensions mature, the need for Gab and Glib may disappear.

Tools and algorithms. The purpose of the AVRP tools is to provide our scientists with new visualization algorithms. All of the tools are based on the Cell IO, Gab, and Glib software detailed above. Next, we describe four of the tools from the AVRP system. Our tools can display two-dimensional time sequences, time sequences of contours of three-

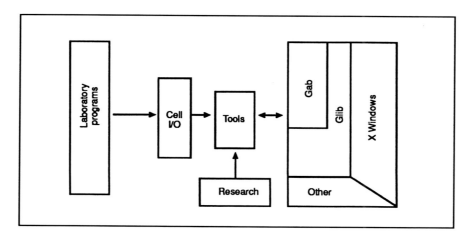

Figure 7. The AVRP software architecture.

226

dimensional grids, and various components of three-dimensional finite difference meshes, and can volumetrically render three-dimensional grids. Most tools provide interactive rotation, zooming, panning, and other geometric manipulations.

We can interactively display two-dimensional meshes of data with an arbitrary number of dependent variables using Surface. Any two of these dependent variables can be displayed at one time, one spatially and the other with color. Since any two independent variables define a mesh, we can display any tensor product surface. Users interactively choose the dependent variables for display and select orientations at specific times in the data set. Using this tool, it is simple to make an animation of a time sequence of two-dimensional surface data (see Figure 8).

Interactive displays of contour surfaces carved from or constructed out of a three-dimensional volume are possible with an isosurface tool. The isosurface algorithm is based on the marching cubes algorithm.[7] We support multiple grids with differing x, y, and z resolutions and multiple time steps. The user interactively selects the dependent variable to be contoured, the dependent variable to be displayed using color on the isosurface, and the threshold value of the isosurface. We can optionally render the surface semitransparently and allow multiple contours to be displayed at once (see Figure 9).

Finite difference grids traditionally have been developed piece by piece using mesh generators in a very tedious and error-prone process. The accuracy of the mesh is of critical importance. We have developed Image, an interactive mesh analysis tool for verifying finite difference grids. These meshes drive electromagnetic simulations that take hours of supercomputer time. The user manipulates the meshes interactively, choosing slice planes and various components of the mesh for display, and querying for the location of a cell in the three-dimensional mesh using a mouse.

We developed a technique similar to the one described in Upson and Keeler[8] to render semitransparent volumes of three-dimensional data using our volume visualization tool, Cell-Tracer. Ray tracing is used to approximate the rendering integral equation[9] that must be solved for each cell in the grid to "see through" a volume. This powerful technique allows the engineer to browse through the interior of the

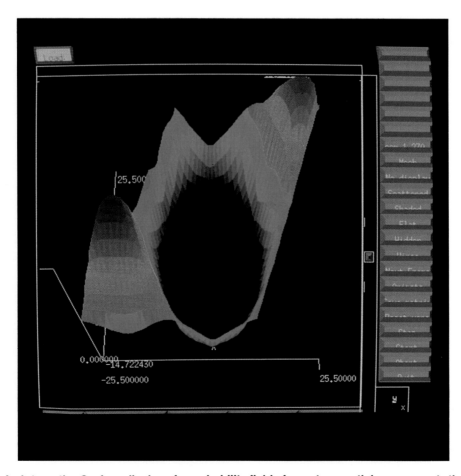

Figure 8. An interactive Surface display of a probability field of quantum particles represents the area of the box covered by the crystal.

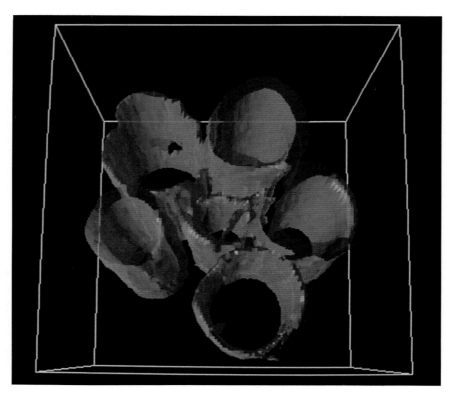

Figure 9. Isosurface rendering of a three-dimensional reconstructed image of data from a nondestructive evaluation using a neutron transport.

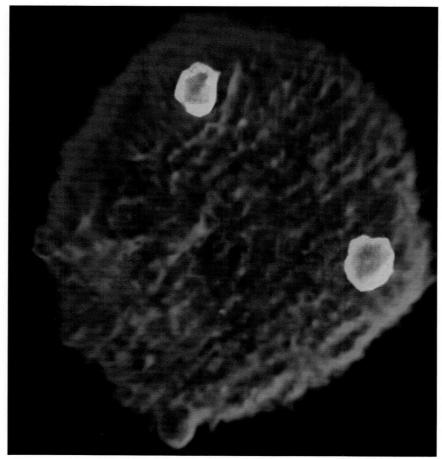

Figure 10. Semitransparent volumetric rendering of the nucleus of a human cell. The red clumps are chromosome groupings within the cell nucleus.

three-dimensional object and to view the surface of the object.

The AVRP software system is supported on a wide variety of vendor hardware used by the Engineering Department at LLNL. Currently, AVRP tools are available on Silicon Graphics, DEC, Sun, and Stellar platforms. Our philosophy is to port to the low-level graphics library on each system, thereby providing the greatest performance at the lowest software cost.

Conclusion

The scientific visualization challenge is to develop a set of visualization tools that are interactive, provide qualitative and quantitative information, are easy to use, offer new ways of visualizing data, allow the scientist to be more productive, and are available on any workstation. We have described two different attempts at providing these tools. The GWS philosophy is to base everything on standards and to require high-performance equipment. The AVRP philosophy is to research and develop new visualization techniques and deliver them to engineers and scientists.

In the future computing environment of LLNL, a scientist will expect to access graphics capabilities in three different modes: graphics created on supercomputers and displayed in the office, graphics created on workstations, and graphics distributed between supercomputers and workstations. To provide these capabilities to each scientist, advances in network technology and workstation performance are essential to maintain the required high throughput rates. In the research areas, we intend to integrate all the AVRP tools so that we have a common environment through a language-based interpreter. We plan to research massively parallel visualization algorithms based on unique and specialized LLNL-developed hardware.

All of our efforts could be enhanced by scientists and vendors standardizing on a multivariate data representation, to include geometry, topology, and other data objects as NCSA has suggested.[10] Visualization tools built on this standard could be integrated into any environment that makes use of the standards. Visualization tools can aid scientists in gaining insight and productivity and, thus, improve the quality of their science.

Acknowledgments

The Magic project was funded and supported by the Defense Sciences Department, A Division, and the Livermore Computer Center at LLNL. The Magic project team consisted of Joe Requa, Jeff Rowe, Bob Lockhart, Dale Nielsen, Pete Keller, Lance Sloan, Dave Wiltzius, Keith Johnson, Dave Handeli, and Pat Gray. Neale Smith provided MacMagic support. The GWS project was funded and supported by the Defense Sciences Department, B Division, and the Livermore Computer Center. The GWS project team consisted of Jeff Long, Gene Cronshagen, Nancy Johnston, Carol Hunter, Linnea Cook, Mike Anastasio, and Bruce Goodwin. The Engineering Department AVRP team consisted of Brian Cabral, Mike Allison, Chuck Grant, Bob Schectman, Mark Wagner, and Bryan Lawver. Jeff Rowe created Figure 1; Pete Keller created Figure 2; Jeff Long created Figures 3, 4, 5, and 6; Brian Cabral created Figures 7, 8, 9, and 10. We appreciate the efforts of Derek Hendry, Gary Laguna, and Rebecca Springmeyer in reviewing this article.

References

1. B. McCormick, T. DeFanti, and M. Brown, "Visualization in Scientific Computing," *Proc. ACM SIGGraph,* Vol. 21, No. 6, Nov. 1987, p. 3.

2. C. Hunter et al., "Requirements for Octopus Display Replacement," Lawrence Livermore National Laboratory, Livermore, Calif., UCRL-53886, Sept. 12, 1988.

3. J. Rowe, "Magic," *Tentacle,* Vol. VII, No. 5, Computation Dept., Lawrence Livermore National Laboratory, May 1987, pp. 1-7.

4. J. Hardin, A. Stowell, and F. Bond, "Creating Tools for Science," *NCSA Access,* Vol. 3, No. 1, Jan.-Feb. 1989, pp. 8-10.

5. C. Hunter, "New Graphics for Cray Users," *Proc. Cray User Group,* Spring 1987, pp. 168-171.

6. L. Cook, "Visualization, Prototyping, and Scientific Togetherness," *Unix Review,* Mar. 1989, pp. 48-50.

7. W. Lorenson and H. Cline, "Marching Cubes: A High-Resolution 3D Surface Construction Algorithm," *Proc. SIGGraph 87,* 1987, pp. 163-169.

8. C. Upson and M. Keeler, "V-Buffer: Visible Volume Rendering," *Proc. SIGGraph 88,* 1988, pp. 59-64.

9. J. Kajiya, "The Rendering Equation," *Proc. SIGGraph 86,* 1986, pp. 143-150.

10. M. Folk, "HDF: A File Format for Sharing," Data Link, Nat'l. Center for Supercomputer Applications, Univ. of Illinois at Urbana-Champaign, Jan.-Feb. 1989, pp. 1-9.

Brian Cabral is a computer scientist in the Engineering Department at Lawrence Livermore National Laboratory and is project leader of the Advanced Visualization Research Project. His interests include computer graphics algorithms and systems, computational geometry, operating systems, computer architectures, and computer languages. Cabral received a BS from California State University, Stanislaus, in 1983 and an MS from the University of California at Davis in 1988, both in computer science.

Carol L. Hunter is the graphics coordinator and the mainframe graphics group leader for the User Systems Division of the Livermore Computer Center at Lawrence Livermore National Laboratory. She is responsible for the long-term planning, implementation, and integration of graphics hardware and software to support the 2,000 supercomputer and workstation users of the center. Previously, she was the graphics workstation project leader, a team leader, and a computer scientist for the Nuclear Software Systems Division at Livermore. She is a member of SIG-Graph and ACM.

Scientific Visualization and the Rivers Project at the National Center for Supercomputing Applications

Robert B. Haber, National Center for Supercomputing Applications

Introduction

The rapid growth of large-scale computing in the basic sciences and the steady accumulation of high-bandwidth data sources (radio telescopes, medical scanners, etc.) are largely responsible for the recent interest in scientific visualization as a computational technology. This article reviews activities in scientific visualization at the National Center for Supercomputing Applications at the University of Illinois at Urbana-Champaign.

NCSA is one of five National Science Foundation-sponsored supercomputing centers that serve the national research community in computational science and engineering. The center began operations in 1985 and now serves a national user base of more than 2,500 academic researchers in virtually all areas of science and engineering. NCSA has also established an industrial partners program, which involves five major US corporations. These companies house individual researchers at the center and have network access to the supercomputers at their home offices. From its inception, NCSA has promoted the development and use of scientific visualization as a necessary ingredient for computational science and engineering.

NCSA's primary computing resources are a Cray X-MP/48 with a 128-megaword solid-state storage device and a Cray-2S/4-128. The larger systems are supplemented by an Alliant VFX-80, an Alliant FX-8, and a large number of workstations and personal computers. In addition to delivering reliable service to its users, NCSA includes in its mission the education and training of new supercomputer users, expansion of the role of computational science and engineering in academic and industrial research, and development of advanced computational technologies to support research.

Overview of NCSA Activities in Scientific Visualization

NCSA's user community is multidisciplinary and contains a wide spectrum of expertise in computational technology and visualization techniques. As a result, NCSA has developed a variety of services and initiatives to provide visualization capabilities to its users. The following sections contain a brief review of visualization-related activities at the center, and the research and development activities of the Rivers Project.

Visualization and Media Services Group. The Visualization and Media Services Group contains two recently merged parts: Scientific Media Services and the Scientific Visualization Project. SMS produces film and video output of graphics generated during scientific research by NCSA researchers and computer users. Automated procedures have been implemented to produce hard copy from user-generated image files stored in standard formats. These files might be created directly by users (perhaps with guidance from consultants) with available graphics applications packages—such as NCAR (National Center for Atmospheric Research) graphics, Movie.BYU, and NCSA Image—or by NCSA's visualization staff.

The images are first displayed on a high-resolution Raster Technologies frame buffer attached to the Alliant VFX-80, converted to standard television signal NTSC (National Television System Committee) format, and then transferred to videotape. The problem of producing smooth video animation from images, which might take minutes per frame to generate, is solved using an Abekas digital video recorder, a device commonly used in entertainment, special effects, and commercial animation applications. Recently, real-time scan converters were added to transform high-resolution RGB (red, green, blue) video signals from the frame buffers to NTSC format. Another recent equipment upgrade includes an Abekas A60, supporting direct-image file transfer from Ethernet and digital component video recording (this eliminates the need to convert to the lower-quality composite NTSC video format).

The Scientific Visualization Project is staffed by computer graphics and visualization experts who produce custom, high-quality visualization animations for scientists selected through a peer review process. This service is not automatically available to all NCSA users. SVP typically generates images on the Alliant VFX-80 (or a graphics workstation) using a rendering package from Wavefront Technologies (or custom software developed at NCSA).

In a typical production cycle, the scientist confers with the SVP staff to discuss alternative methods to visualize the simulation data. SVP then develops an animation storyboard to plan the appearance, motion control, and sequence of the animation. The thousands of frames needed to create a typical animation are produced under the control of an

Reprinted from *Computer*, August 1989, pages 84-89. Copyright © 1989 by The Institute of Electrical and Electronics Engineers, Inc. All rights reserved.

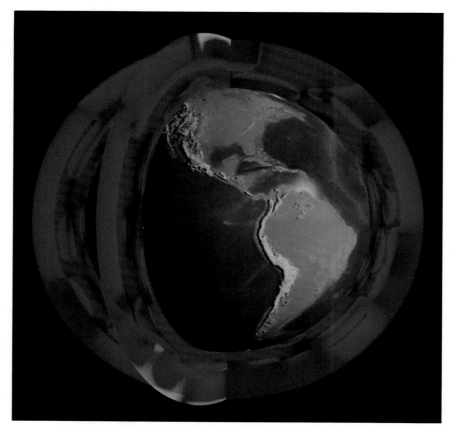

Figure 1. Visualization of global climatic effects of increased greenhouse gases. (W.M. Washington and T.W. Bettge of NCAR performed the simulation; J.B. Yost of NCSA performed the visualization.)

automated batch rendering control system. SMS then transfers the images to videotape or slides. A typical image frame produced by this method appears in Figure 1.

Software Development Group. The Software Development Group (SDG) generates original software packages for computational science. In many cases, prototype software systems, developed in other parts of NCSA, are converted into useful products with reliable software engineering, full documentation, and enhanced features. The software is developed to run on equipment from several vendors (such as Apple Computer, IBM, and Sun Microsystems).

To date, much of this effort has been targeted at low-cost hardware platforms to provide improved computing environments for NCSA's many users. SDG software may be obtained free of charge via anonymous FTP (file-transfer protocol) across the network, or for the cost of distribution media and handling via catalog order.

SDG software is a key element in NCSA's efforts to deliver visualization capabilities to remote users. NCSA

Telnet, the first SDG product to emerge (with more than 20,000 users in the US, at last count), provides multiple simultaneous session connection over TCP/IP networks, a built-in FTP server for file transport, and VT102 and Tektronix 4014 graphics emulation on IBM and Apple Macintosh personal computers.

There is also a growing suite of visualization software tools designed to work together to provide a comprehensive solution. NCSA Image and NCSA ImageTool provide color raster image display and manipulation capabilities to users with Macintosh and Sun workstations (see Figure 2). NCSA DataScope enables the scientist to simultaneously display floating-point arrays and images generated from those arrays. NCSA PalEdit supports interactive construction, editing, and manipulation of color lookup tables for raster displays, and is designed to work with the other color display programs. NCSA CompositeTool allows the scientist to composite, overlay, annotate, and prepare presentation quality images for slides and prints. Current work in SDG is aimed at developing X Window System support

Figure 2. Visualization using NCSA Image of an astrophysics study of supernova-induced shock waves accelerating clouds in the interstellar medium. (M.L. Norman, J.R. Dickel, M. Livio, and Y.-H. Chu of NCSA and the Department of Astronomy of the University of Illinois.)

for the entire software suite to significantly expand the base of supported hardware. Work is also beginning on software tools for 3D and volumetric rendering.

User training, consulting, and education. NCSA places a high priority on training and education in its mission to expand the use of supercomputing and visualization. NCSA hosts frequent workshops and seminars throughout the year, some targeted specifically at scientific visualization. Intensive training is provided to consultants who serve as local resources at the 60 colleges and universities participating in the center's Academic Affiliates Program. A visitors' program supports individual researchers who wish to visit NCSA for direct interaction with consultants and the visualization staff.

Recently, NCSA established the Renaissance Experimental Laboratory, a classroom for supercomputing and visualization education equipped with 20 personal IRIS workstations donated by Silicon Graphics. Classes in visualization in the REL are offered through the University of Illinois Computer Science Department. Other courses emphasize applications of visualization in mathematics, computational chemistry, biophysics, art, and design.

The NCSA Rivers Project

During the fall of 1987, NCSA initiated a research project to explore several emerging computational technologies that promise to have a significant impact on the scientific computing environment. This program became known as the Rivers (Research on Interactive Visual Environments) Project. Specifically, Rivers is developing hardware and software systems for extending high-end 3D visualization from a batch process to an interactive process, and for visualization-based interactive steering of supercomputing simulations in a high-performance distributed environment.

The process of visualization. A structured view of the process of visualization motivates the Rivers hardware and software architectures. Visualization can be viewed as a series of transformations that convert raw simulation data into a displayable image. The goal of these transformations is to convert the information to a format amenable to understanding by the human perceptual system while maintaining the integrity of the information. Three major transformations occur in most visualization procedures:

- The *data enrichment and enhancement* step operates on the raw data provided by the simulation and modifies it in one or more ways to derive data for subsequent visualization operations. Examples include data filtering to remove noise (numerical or observational), calculation of gradients in field solutions, and interpolation to a regular grid.

- *Visualization mapping* can be viewed as an operation that constructs an imaginary object, here called an abstract visualization object or AVO, from the derived data produced by the enhancement and enrichment operations. Typically, this involves a series of mappings of the simulation data into the attribute fields that describe the AVO (geometry, time, color, transparency, luminosity, reflectance, surface texture, etc.). A common example is the mapping of scalar field data into height or color.

- *Rendering* is the last transformation in the visualization process. The rendering mapping operates on the AVO to produce a displayable image. Rendering can involve familiar operations from computer graphics and image processing, but might also involve new algorithms that respond to new requirements of scientific and engineering visualization, such as volumetric rendering.

Important conclusions can be drawn from this model of visualization:

(1) The process can be conveniently segmented into modular operations.

(2) In many cases the modules can be made generic and shared across several science disciplines.

(3) A specific visualization process can be defined as a dataflow graph with mapping modules as nodes (the graph can be reconfigured to define alternative visualization methods, and the system can be extended by adding new modules).

(4) Interactive control over mapping parameters is desirable to fine-tune a given idiom.

(5) Visualization has a pipeline structure that can be exploited in hardware and software design to obtain improved performance.

The Rivers software design. A modular software system is under development with the above model in mind. Key principles of the Rivers software design are

- software modules should support distributed execution across multiple, heterogeneous hosts;

- appropriate user interfaces should be available for defining configurations and for adjusting parameters;

- low-level issues such as graphics languages and communications protocols should be hidden from the user (a layered design);

- software standards (X.11, PHIGS+, Unix, etc.) should be used to the greatest extent possible; and

- software components should be designed for compatibility with high-performance systems for interactivity.

The Rivers hardware architecture. The pipelined structure of the visualization process requires careful attention to balance in hardware system design. In addition to raw graphics performance, a balanced visualization system must provide commensurate sustained bandwidth between distributed hosts (that is, the network); between mass storage systems and host memory; and between host memory and special-purpose graphics accelerators. Multiprocessor, shared memory architectures are also attractive since they map well onto the pipelined structure of visualization. Since visualization includes a considerable amount of computation-intensive calculation in the early stages of the pipeline, powerful general-purpose processors are needed in addition to powerful rendering engines. At present, the general-purpose computation is often the main bottleneck.

Figure 3 diagrams the distributed hardware system for visualization now under development within Rivers and other segments of NCSA. A key theme is the use of dual, three-tier schemes for both the computing and network strategies. Middle-tier systems, such as the Alliant VFX-80, provide higher performance capabilities that can be shared by a group of users without the compromises necessary with national resources like the true supercomputers. For example, the VFX-80—with a closely coupled visualization system, a connection to the Ultra network, and a disk array mass storage system (planned)—provides a shareable, high-performance visualization capability that is too expensive to reproduce on every desk top.

All high-level machines, including the supercomputers and middle-tier processors, are connected by the highest speed network available (NCSA installed an UltraNet system in December 1988, with a peak bandwidth of 100 megabytes per second). This network will be reserved and optimized for massive data transfer using large packet sizes (for real-time visualization, distributed processing, and accessing the shared high-performance mass storage system).

A middle-tier network forms the backbone for handling messages, smaller data packets, and conventional network traffic between the large machines and the bottom tier networks connecting the workstations. At present, a 50-megabit-per-second HyperChannel network and an 80-megabit-per-second ProNet-80 network fulfill this function. (The FDDI, or Fiber Digital Data Interface, standard is expected to take on the middle-tier function when it becomes available). The objective here is to segregate the

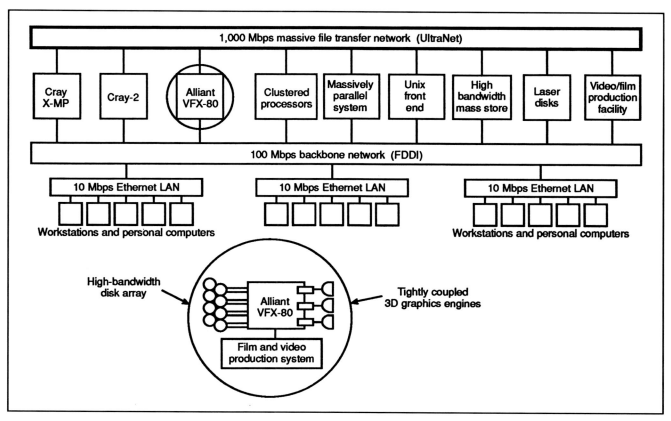

Figure 3. Hardware architecture for distributed simulation and visualization specifies the NCSA three-tier computing strategy.

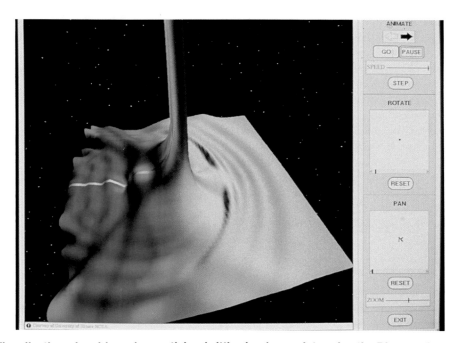

Figure 4. Visualization of rapid crack growth in a brittle aluminum plate using the Rivers polygon animation tool. (H.M. Koh, H.S. Lee, and R.B. Haber, NCSA and Departments of Theoretical and Applied Mechanics and Civil Engineering, University of Illinois (simulation); S. Chall, R. Idaszak, and P. Baker, NCSA (visualization).)

massive data transfers from terminal keystrokes and smaller messages to provide the best efficiency and performance.

Hardware engines for accelerating the rendering operations are a key part of the plan. At present, the Rivers Project includes a variety of graphics accelerators for polygon rendering (Raster Technologies GX4000 boards on Sun-4 platforms, the Alliant VFX-80, SGI workstations) and for volumetric rendering (the Sun TAAC-1 application accelerator).

Figure 4 shows a prototype three-dimensional, interactive animation tool that the Rivers group developed. The tool is capable of animating complex polygon data sets in real time on the workstation or VFX-80 screen. Although relatively simple, the tool has been used to view data from a variety of disciplines—solid mechanics, atmospheric sciences, and astrophysics.

Conclusion

The visualization approaches described above vary considerably in cost and applicability to the requirements of various computer users. The SDG software suite runs on inexpensive platforms and exemplifies visualization technology immediately practical at almost any computer site. The SMS production facility requires staffing and capital expenditures that imply a reasonably large user base. Lower cost visualization facilities can be assembled by trading off performance, quality, and flexibility. Also, several computer vendors are working on new products that provide integrated visualization systems at lower price levels. Thus, this technology should become accessible to a larger user group with time.

High-quality visualization production by graphics experts using flexible software rendering systems continues to produce impressive results. The expense of this approach remains high, due to the labor-intensive nature of the process and the relative scarcity of visualization experts. High-performance, interactive visualization as in the Rivers project is also currently expensive due to equipment costs. While the necessary graphics performance is now available in some high-end graphics workstations, it will take several years for the cost of balanced mass storage and network systems to become affordable for single users. Until then, the techniques used in Rivers will be suitable for shared, department-level facilities. Therefore, the Rivers visualization system can be viewed as a development prototype for affordable, workstation-based systems that might appear in three to five years.

Recent experience in the Rivers project has demonstrated that very-high-performance systems can be built using hardware and software standards. Standards are particularly important in helping to amortize the significant software development effort needed to make high-level visualization tools available to applications users.

The emerging HSC (high-speed channel) standard interface will facilitate the integration of the high-performance, distributed systems needed for real-time interactive visualization. National gigabaud networks (proposed for the mid to late 1990s) will allow remote access to interactive supercomputing and visualization.

Acknowledgments

Many talented individuals have contributed to the success of the visualization program at NCSA. It is impossible to identify all of the individual contributors here. However, I want to credit Matt Arrott, Polly Baker, Dan Brady, Steve Chall, Donna Cox, Stefen Fangmeier, Joe Hardin, Ray Idaszak, Tim Krauskopf, Dave McNabb, Nancy St. John, and Craig Upson for their leadership and contributions to visualization development at NCSA.

Various aspects of the visualization work at NCSA are supported by the National Science Foundation, the state of Illinois, Alliant Computer Systems, Apple Computer, Cray Research, Silicon Graphics, Sun Microsystems, Ultra Network Technologies, and NCSA's corporate partners.

Robert B. Haber is an associate professor of theoretical and applied mechanics and civil engineering at the University of Illinois at Urbana-Champaign. He is also a research scientist at the National Center for Supercomputing Applications, where he directs the Rivers Project. His research interests include finite element methods in computational solid mechanics, computer-assisted design and optimization, and applications of computer graphics visualization to computational science and engineering.

Haber received a bachelor of architecture degree in 1977 and a PhD in civil engineering in 1980, both from Cornell University. He is a member of the American Society of Civil Engineers, the American Academy of Mechanics, the International Association for Computational Mechanics, ACM (SIGGraph), the American Association for the Advancement of Science, and Sigma Xi. He is a Cray Research Affiliate, and president of Allus, the Alliant Users' Society.

Scientific Visualization in Computational Aerodynamics at NASA Ames Research Center

Gordon V. Bancroft, Todd Plessel, Fergus Merritt, and Pamela P. Walatka, Sterling Software
Val Watson, NASA Ames

Introduction

At NASA Ames Research Center, scientists are using the Numerical Aerodynamic Simulation (NAS) facility to perform experiments in computational aerodynamics.[1] Scientists model complex fluid mechanics problems using supercomputers and new numerical algorithms. The computer-generated models show vehicles and the air space surrounding them. Physics formulas are used to simulate the flow of air about the vehicle. Scientists use high-performance computer graphics workstations to view and, in some cases, animate these simulations.

The high-performance graphics workstation is connected to a supercomputer with a high-speed channel. Postprocessing (processing performed after the simulation is complete) is by far the most commonly used method for visualization of computational aerodynamics. A flow simulation is executed on a supercomputer, and then the results of the simulation are processed for viewing.

Tracking and steering involve interaction. Tracking allows the scientist to track his or her flow solution so it can be stopped and, perhaps, restarted should undesirable results be obtained. Steering goes one step further and allows the scientist to change parameters of the flow solver as it executes. Examples of this might be increasing the angle of attack of an aerodynamic body, stretching a grid to move points, or perhaps increasing the Mach number. These are more desirable methods than postprocessing, yet much less common given the current state of supercomputer and workstation evolution and performance. Distributed processing is the term used when the process of visualizing the solutions is distributed between the workstation and the supercomputer.

The software cycle for fluid dynamics simulation begins with the creation of a grid that describes the walls of a vehicle and the surrounding space. Flow-solver programs (that is, algorithms derived from physics formulas for the flow of air) are then executed (typically on supercomputers) to generate flow-field solutions. The raw data from these solutions consists of density, momentum vector, and total energy per unit volume specified at each grid point in the computational domain. A typical computational domain may contain one million grid points. This raw data must be converted to a scene depicting the physics in a manner the scientist can easily interpret. Color and visual cues (shading, animation, etc.) are used to demonstrate the physics of the particular result.

Visualization Requirements

The views of the simulation portrayed by the computer graphic workstations must be 3D because visualization of the interrelated flows of all three dimensions simultaneously is important. The scenes must be dynamic for the time-variant features of the flow fields to be understood. Although the motion need not be real time, the motions must be rapid enough to give a proper understanding of the dynamic features of the flow.

The flow fields typically have a large range of scales. Therefore, the scientist must be able to zoom into a region of small-scale features and zoom back out to view the overall flow field. Furthermore, the scenes should be high definition to contain adequate detail at all scales.

The scenes should simultaneously contain solid body objects, such as an aircraft (with hidden surfaces removed), and points or lines (such as lines representing the paths of tracer particles inserted into the flow field). As the scenes evolve in time, illustrating the flow dynamics (for example, the movement of tracer particles), the viewing position must be simultaneously changeable in real time (as the flow evolves) to maintain the best view or to get a different perspective.

Dynamic change of the viewing position is one of the best cues for enhancing the 3D aspects of the scene. In addition, new visualization effects, such as ribbon traces, smoke, shading of function-mapped parts, antialiasing, variable transparency, volume visualization, and stereo, are being requested by scientists to further enhance their ability to analyze flow fields.

Hardware

The hardware currently in use for computational fluid dynamics at NASA Ames includes supercomputers, workstations, digital video recording equipment, film recorders,

Reprinted from *Computer*, August 1989, pages 89-95. Copyright © 1989 by The Institute of Electrical and Electronics Engineers, Inc. All rights reserved.

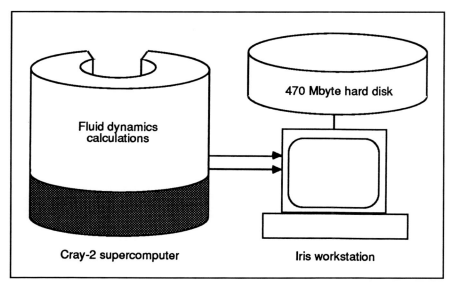

Figure 1. Scientists use the supercomputer to generate solutions to aerodynamic problems, with five variables (density, x-, y-, and z-momentum, and energy) for each of a million or more grid points. The HyperChannel link is used to move the data to the workstation, where the numbers are turned into graphics. Many functions, such as pressure, shock wave, or particle trace, can be plotted from the solutions. The interactive visualization greatly enhances the understanding of the solutions.

still cameras, color printers, digital scanners, and color copiers.

The calculations to generate the flowfield solutions are done on the supercomputer (see Figure 1). The visualizations—animations and scenes—can be created in three ways:

(1) Transfer the whole solution file (containing the solution at each grid point) to the large disk on the workstation and generate the scene on the workstation.

(2) Produce graphics files on the supercomputer and transfer these graphics files to the workstation.

(3) Create the scene using the supercomputer interactively while viewing the scene on the workstation.

The key features of a workstation are its rapid 3D transformation speed (for changing the viewing position), its high-definition display, and its rapid display creation speed. On the current workstation, a Silicon Graphics 3130, 3D coordinates can be transformed at a rate of 80,000 coordinates per second. The display has high spatial resolution (1,024 pixels horizontally by 768 pixels vertically) and high color resolution (24 color planes giving more than 16 million simultaneous colors). Scenes with a very simple solid object and thousands of lines or points can be generated at a rate of more than 10 per second—a rate that provides satisfactory motion for understanding dynamics.

The workstation contains a z-buffer[2] for hardware implementation of hidden-surface removal. However, many

seconds are required to create scenes of typical aerodynamic vehicles if the z-buffer and Gouraud shading[5] are used. Therefore, these scenes must be recorded on videotape or 16-mm movie film to allow satisfactory viewing of the dynamics.

The next generation of workstations, to be available to NASA scientists before the end of 1989,[3] is expected to meet the requirements for dynamic viewing, as indicated in Table 1. Benchmark software has been developed at NASA Ames to test what kind of graphics performance can be expected from these next-generation workstations (this software is available at no charge through the authors from NASA Ames as part of our graphics development effort).

Currently, animations of the scenes are recorded to videodisc or videotape with the hardware shown in Figure 2. The high-definition scene is digitally sampled by a scan converter to a lower resolution RS170a format. This format can be encoded from separate red, green, and blue components into the standard single composite NTSC (National Television Standards Committee) signal used by standard video recorders and players. As each frame is displayed, control information tells the Abekas to record. It then stores the frame as digital NTSC.

This process occurs at real-time rates, so the time required to record a computer workstation frame is limited by the time it takes to render it. The workstation then continues on with the next frame and repeats the process until the animation is complete. The Abekas uses Winchester disk technology (1.3 gigabytes per 100 seconds of

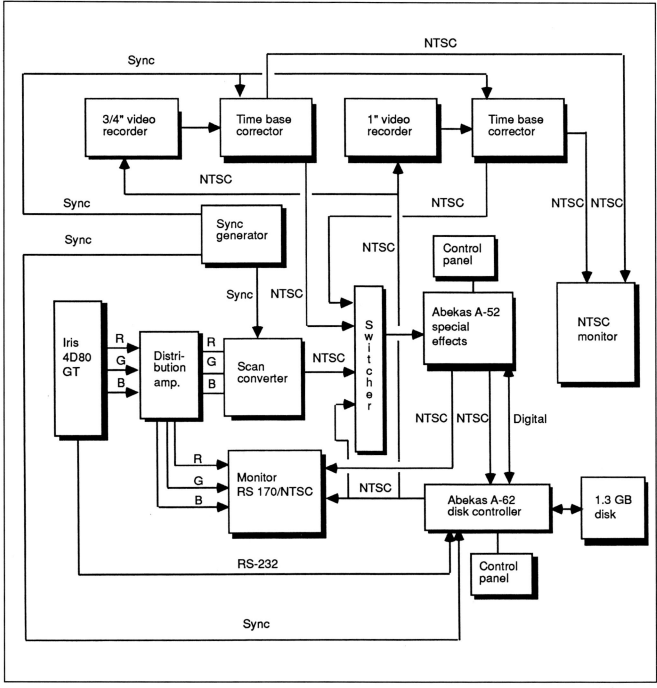

Figure 2. This Abekas video recording system diagram is used to animate the aerodynamic scenes. Animation enhances understanding of the flow dynamics by showing the scenes from different viewpoints or for different times. Simple animations can be done on the workstations, but group presentations or complex scenes require video or film recording.

Table 1. Features of current and next-generation workstations.

Feature	Iris	Future W/S
CPU	2,600 Dhrystones	20,000 Dhrystones
	0.1 Mflops	2.0 Mflops
Memory	4 MB	16 MB
Bus	Multi (2 MB/sec)	VME (>20 MB/sec)
Disk	474 MB	1,000 MB
3D trans.	80 K/sec	800 K/sec
Filled polys	16 K/sec	200 K/sec
Z-buffered	0.5 K/sec	100 K/sec
Dsply mem.	$32 \times 1 K \times 1 K$	$76 \times 1 K \times 1 K$

(Polygons 400 pixels; z-buff polygons are shaded)

video), allowing stored video to be edited (using the A52 special effects) or the disks to be rerecorded. There are no generation losses within the system due to the digital formatting.

The hardware for recording the scenes on 16-mm film is shown in Figure 3. The Dunn camera is controlled from the workstation using an RS-232 hardware connection and the Graphics Animation System (GAS) software described later in this article. Other Dunn cameras and color printers are used for making stills.

Software

The following are examples of postprocessing software packages in use at the NASA Ames Research Center:

Plot3 D accepts as input the flow-field solutions from the supercomputer and creates as output a variety of scenes that can be viewed dynamically with the workstations.[4] The software makes extensive use of color and 3D cues (such as shading and perspective as on p. 269 of Foley and Van Dam[2]). A very popular scene is path lines of particles released at selected points inside the flow field (Figure 4). Another example is color mapping on a vehicle surface representing the magnitude of some scalar property on the surface, such as pressure. Plot3D software is available for properly configured Silicon Graphics, Apollo, and Sun workstations; Cray2/Unicos, Alliant/Unix, and Convex supercomputers; and VAX 11/780 minicomputers. Output can be saved to files for use with the GAS animation program.

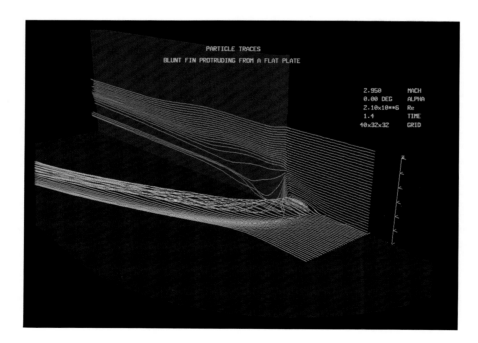

Figure 3. This is an example of a scene created with Plot3D, one of the postprocessing software packages used for visualizing computed aerodynamic solutions. The object is a blunt fin (simplified abstraction of a wing protruding from a wall); the rake-like lines are particle traces, indicating the streamlines of the flow of air.

Visualization of Experimental Data at the Naval Research Laboratory

Lawrence J. Rosenblum, Naval Research Laboratory

Introduction

The Naval Research Laboratory began operations in 1923 when it was created in response to Thomas Edison's suggestion that "The government should maintain a great research laboratory . . . In this could be developed . . . all the techniques of military and naval progression without any vast expense."

The original two NRL divisions, Radio and Sound, pioneered in the fields of high-frequency radio and underwater sound propagation, producing communications equipment, direction-finding devices, sonar sets, and the first practical radar equipment built in the United States.

New divisions were created, and today NRL's mission is to conduct a broadly based multidisciplinary program of scientific research and advanced technological development directed towards new and improved materials, equipment, techniques, and related operational procedures for the US Navy. Fulfilling this mission has resulted in research programs covering a wide spectrum of scientific areas from astronomy and satellites to the deep ocean; from studies of the structure of materials to radar, electronics, and computer science. The ability to visualize scientific data, that is, produce data products in graphical formats that enable the human eye/brain to perceive and infer patterns, is playing an increasingly important role in helping NRL achieve its goal of developing and transitioning technological innovation to the fleet and to society as a whole.

NRL provides its researchers with a Cray and a Connection Machine for large-scale computation, as well as numerous midsize computer facilities and desktop computers. The problems associated with providing appropriate graphics for numerical simulations on supercomputers at NRL are similar to those discussed elsewhere in this issue of *Computer* for other large laboratories. However, much of the science at NRL (and elsewhere) is experimental and, with measuring devices producing ever higher data rates, the need to visualize experimental data is now inherent to the data analysis process for many disciplines.

In computational science, the problem is to create appropriate models. Once this is achieved, visualization can typically be directly performed on the numerical simulation data. On the other hand, for experimental data, the parameters of interest must be extracted from the data sets. For example, in physical oceanography, temperature is measured, but a quantity called *activity* (see the section entitled "Physical oceanography") is calculated and visualized. Similarly, in molecular modeling, diffraction intensities are measured and electron densities are calculated and used to model the structure. This article will focus on applications of visualization to experimental data, discuss the methods used to derive parameters of interest, and show the role of visualization in interpreting the data.

Physical Oceanography

Much of the earth's surface is covered by water. The need to model the global climate places increased importance on understanding ocean processes because of their strong coupling to the atmosphere. Similarly, naval systems for surface operations and antisubmarine warfare require detailed knowledge of the ocean environment. The ocean is a particularly difficult medium to study; it is a 3D space that varies temporally and is filled with inhomogeneities of all scales (from microbubbles to whales) while being subject to a wide variety of forcing functions, including thermodynamic, seismic, atmospheric, inertial, and tidal.

To study ocean processes that range in length scales from meters to kilometers, NRL scientists tow two primary devices through the ocean. A vertical array of closely spaced thermistors provides temperature measurements of the upper ocean, while a Doppler shear profiler uses sonar to measure the magnitude and direction of subsurface vertical shear of the current (i.e., differences in the currents at different depths). After processing, these data provide important clues about physical processes in the ocean.

Figure 1, which shows measured shear magnitude and direction as obtained from Doppler profiler data, demonstrates the role of visualization. Both magnitude and direction are seen to be horizontally layered. The strong shear magnitude near the surface (red bands in the upper panel) suggest forcing by variations in the trade winds. In the lower panel, the direction can be seen to cycle five times, indicating five cycles of a "near-inertial" internal wave. The sense of color (i.e., direction) progression implies that the energy in these waves is moving downward. This is consistent with the input of energy at the surface by the wind. The ability to visualize field-collected data in this manner not only provides knowledge directly, but also assists the oceanographer in prescreening data for further analysis. Figure 1, shown

Reprinted from *Computer*, August 1989, pages 95-101. Copyright © 1989 by The Institute of Electrical and Electronics Engineers, Inc. All rights reserved.

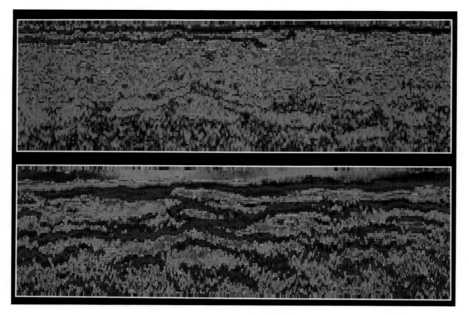

Figure 1. Ocean currents: a vertical slice through the upper 300 meters of ocean east of Barbados, for 130 kilometers of horizontal tow. Panel (a) shows the magnitude of the vertical shear with intensity increasing across the color scale from blue to red and violet. Panel (b) shows shear direction, color coded from 0 to 2 π radians. This figure is typical of visualization tools used for a "quick look" at oceanographic data sets.

without axes and with certain processing anomalies visible, also illustrates the concept of "peer graphics." Like most scientific graphics, this figure was not made for publication but rather for previewing the data and for discussion with colleagues. The figure was created with software that allows the quick display of any pair of 2D data sets and gives the user several choices of color selection for each set.

The use of temperature data is more complex, because our primary interest lies in activity; that is, the local variability of temperature. A fast Fourier transform-based algorithm[1] is used to extract activity values from thermistor "chain" measurements. The resulting activity data are interpolated, color coded, median filtered, and displayed (see the top panel of Figure 2). To compare fine-structure activity with other parameters, the activity field is edge detected. The resulting outlines of high activity "patches" are overlaid on fields of physical parameters conjectured to relate to the generation of enhanced activity (see the three lower panels of Figure 2). This visualization technique makes obvious the strong correlation of enhanced activity with high shear and low Richardson number (a theoretical predictor of turbulence), suggesting that shear instabilities are creating the enhanced fine-structure activity.[2]

Electronic Warfare

Neutralizing an incoming missile is fundamental to the survival of the fleet in any modern-day naval encounter. The Central Target Simulator facility, a laboratory containing computer-controlled simulators, was created to develop protective countermeasures for ships and aircraft from radio frequency guided missiles. Figure 3a shows a simulator that allows both the missile hardware RF section and the computer section to be simulated as if the missile were actually flying against a target. Using the simulator, dozens of simulations can be performed quickly to test the vulnerability of the fleet to missile attack.

The yellow circles on the wall of the simulator's anechoic chamber are the conical sections of microwave antennas driven from an RF switching network. The network is digitally controlled to allow transmission of RF signals that create a tactical environment simulating the radar and guidance systems of a missile. A multiprocessor architecture is used to move the targets over this antenna array, creating an illusion of motion. Various engagement scenarios are created to test the missile, the target's defense, or a missile's susceptibility to electronic countermeasures (ECM).

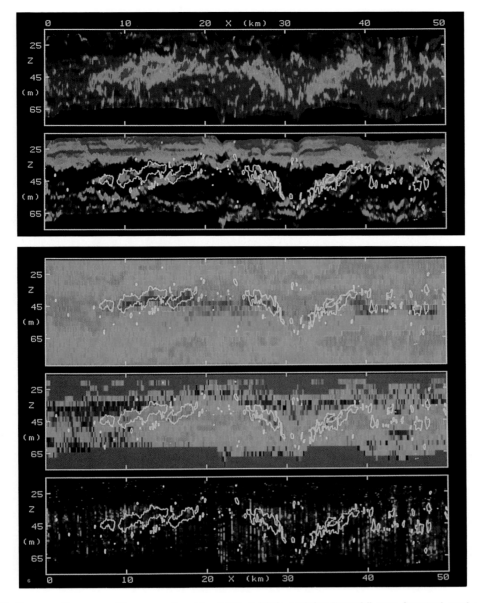

Figure 2. From a Sargasso Sea experiment where a high activity "patch" was located and repeatedly transected. Panel (a) shows activity, with yellow to red indicating high activity regions. The remaining panels show high activity contours overlaid on (from the top) (b) vertical temperature gradient, (c) shear, (d) Richardson number, and (e) internal wave potential energy. Yellow to red indicates low or inverted temperature gradient, high shear, low Richardson number, and high IWPE.

Visualization tools are necessary to portray the complex data contained in a simulation in real time. Patterns not readily observable in simulation data become apparent when viewed pictorially. Animations of simulation test results are also used to confirm that the correct real-world environment is being simulated and that the hardware is being properly exercised, as well as to aid in analysis of missile and ECM effects.

Figure 3b is a frame from a computer-generated animation of a missile/ship engagement. The generation of the ship, the chaff cloud, the missile, and the missile beam use classical polygon rendering/animation techniques. The moving background of sea and clouds are generated using an implementation of fractal mathematics.[3] The realistic ocean and clouds give a sense of motion to the visualization, increasing the viewer's comprehension of the spatial dy-

Figure 3. Electronic countermeasures: The ECM laboratory is shown in (a). The size can be seen by comparison with the person standing at center rear. A frame from an ECM animation is shown in (b). The chaff cloud to the right of the ship is an attempt to mislead the missile.

namics. In addition to creating a more realistic looking scene, fractal methods are computationally less costly than polygon techniques.

Molecular Modeling

The accurate determination of the atomic arrangements of substances in various states allows the scientist to understand the relationship between the structural and the physi-

cal, chemical, and biological properties of a substance. Products of molecular modeling range from new, improved antibiotics to safer, more powerful propellants for solid-fuel rockets. The need to visualize molecules predates computer graphics; chemists have long "visualized" by using a Tinkertoy-like construction set. Molecular modeling is one of the oldest areas of computer-based scientific visualization, and one where, hand-in-hand, both fields have helped the other progress further.

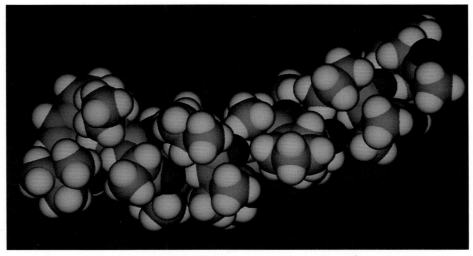

Figure 4. Space-filling model of a molecular structure used in the study of synthetic antibiotics. It represents a synthetic apolar analog of the membrane-active fungal peptide antibiotic zervamycin IIA. Atoms are color coded: hydrogen, white; carbon, violet; oxygen, red; and nitrogen, blue.

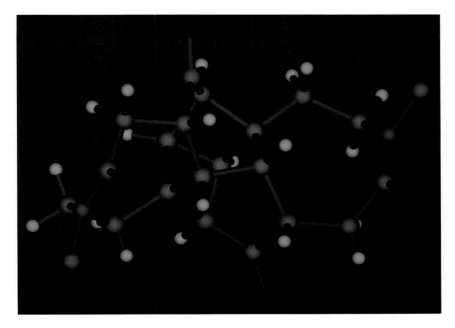

Figure 5. Ball-and-stick model of a product of a photochemical reaction, referred to as a photodimer from N-Chloroacetyltyramine. Atoms are color coded: hydrogen, white; carbon, violet; oxygen, red; and nitrogen, blue.

The mathematics used to help solve molecular structures were developed at NRL. Jerome Karle, head of NRL's Laboratory for the Structure of Matter, and Herbert Hauptman, a former LSM member, received the 1985 Nobel Prize in Chemistry for their use of the mathematics of diffraction physics to show that enough information could be deduced from diffraction patterns to permit the direct solution of crystal structures—the "direct method" for molecular determination via x-ray crystallography. Isabella Karle of the LSM has also made major contributions

to the development of the methods and procedures for structure determination, including the molecular structures illustrated in Figures 4 and 5.

The output of a molecular structure determination by x-ray crystallography is a numerical set of atomic positions. Visualization enables the mind to grasp the structure and its implications. Two common visual representations are the space-filling model and the ball-and-stick model. The space-filling model is useful for analyzing potential sites for molecular interactions. With such knowledge, scientists can create new, useful molecules. Figure 4, from a study of synthetic antibiotics, illustrates the space-filling model.[4]

The ball-and-stick model is superior for visualizing the overall structural configuration of a molecule. It shows the bonds between atoms and enables visualization of the angles between the bonds and of the distances between the atomic centers. By imagining the breaking of given bonds, the formation of new bonds, and a flexing of the structure, the mechanisms of chemical reactions can be understood. Figure 5 is one of a stereo pair that represents the product of a photochemical reaction with the two components of the molecule joined together with a central cage structure.[5] With practice, scientists can view a stereo pair (without stereo viewing devices) and "see" the molecule in three dimensions. Computer-based molecular modeling offers the user many advantages, including color selection, zooming in on features of interest, user-controlled interactive movement, easy generation of molecules with a very large number of atoms, and matching of multiple molecules for determining possible sites for molecular interactions. The molecules were generated on a VAX 8650 using custom software developed in-house.

Underwater Acoustics

Matched-field processing[6] is a new technique for processing ocean acoustic data measured by an array of hydrophones to produce an estimate of the location of sources of acoustic energy, including whales, volcanoes, and submarines. This method differs from source localization techniques used in other disciplines, for example, radar and astronomy, in that it attempts to exploit the complicated underwater acoustic environment to improve the accuracy of the source location estimate.

Central to the idea of matched-field processing is the premise that an ocean acoustic propagation model can reliably be used to compute a replica of the acoustic field measured by the hydrophone array. Using one of a number of proposed algorithms,[7] the computed replica field is matched with the measured acoustic field to produce a 3D ambiguity measure as a function of the unknown source location variables, for example, range, bearing, and depth. The best estimate of the source location is then obtained from the location of the peak of the ambiguity function. To succeed, both the specific ocean environment and the array configuration must generate an acoustic field sufficiently unique to produce an ambiguity function where the peak can be identified against the background. In addition, uncertainties in the locations of the hydrophone elements and the environment as well as modeling errors must not significantly degrade the identification.

Visualization plays an important role in the analysis of the ambiguity function. To develop understanding of the matched-field process, not only must the peak be identified, but the structure inherent within the 3D ambiguity function needs to be understood. In Figure 6a, the ambiguity surface volume has been generated using an isosurface method. The plane facing the reader represents a range-bearing slice for fixed depth; the top plane, range-depth for fixed bearing; and the side plane, depth-bearing for fixed range. In this example, the acoustic source is located in the center and two false target "sidelobes" can be seen at the left and right ends of the volume. The scientist develops understanding of the acoustic effects by interactively moving through the volume (for example, Figure 6b) in real time, using dials on a knob-box to control direction. Efforts are under way to apply volume rendering techniques[8] to this problem, both to provide even better visualization of data such as in Figure 6 and, in the future, to develop methods to understand dynamic (i.e., time varying) ambiguity functions.

Radar

Synthetic aperture radar (SAR) is a type of radar that constructs a detailed 2D image by utilizing the motion of the platform to synthesize the effect of a large antenna aperture.[9,10] The properties of the electromagnetic radiation for the 3-to-30-centimeter wavelengths used for SAR make it very useful for surveillance and remote sensing of the earth's surface. Day or night, SAR penetrates clouds, rain, and, to some degree, foliage, yielding a clear picture of the surface under most weather and ground-cover conditions. Used over the ocean, SAR can provide indications of sea state, subsurface ocean processes, and even some bathymetric (ocean floor) features.

Typically, SAR is flown on an aircraft or satellite and a scene is illuminated by short frequency-modulated radar pulses at rates of 1,000 to 2,000 pulses per second. Typical data recording rates are between 10 and 90 megabits per second. The antenna beamwidth defines the illuminated area. Complex processing is required to reconstruct the SAR image from the received signals.

To obtain range resolution, a reference matched FM filter compresses the return pulses after they have scattered from the surface. The azimuth (along track) resolution is formed synthetically as the SAR system moves past a scene. Echo amplitude is sampled and phase history reconstructed during the time period between consecutive pulses. This forms the synthetic aperture that can contain several thousand points along the azimuth direction. A matched Doppler filter is correlated with the reconstructed phase delay to compress the signal in azimuth. Each pixel is then

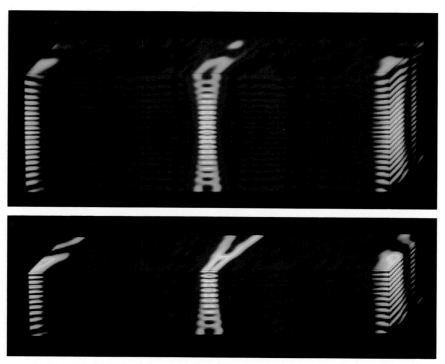

Figure 6. Isocontour rendering of an acoustic ambiguity function. Axes are range (horizontal), bearing (vertical), and depth (into the screen). The acoustic source is at the center of the volume (green-to-red). Focused acoustic energy can be seen at the left and right portions of the volume as well. The full ambiguity function is shown in (a), while (b) shows part of the volume after interactively slicing into it.

formed, until a complete image emerges. Corrections are made for effects such as the earth's rotation beneath the SAR platform that would otherwise distort the image.

Visualization is essential to interpret the large quantities of SAR data; rich details can easily be seen in the images. Figure 7, acquired from a 1984 experiment on NASA's Challenger space shuttle (Shuttle Imaging Radar, SIR-B), shows a portion of the Atlantic Ocean, 45 kilometers in azimuth by 34 kilometers in range, some 135 kilometers south of Long Island.

Although SAR penetrates the ocean's surface only to a depth of about one inch, many features of the ocean can be seen.[9] One feature is the continental shelf (upper right quadrant) in which the image brightens over the rapid drop-off to the deep ocean floor (lower half) as depth changes abruptly from 100 meters for the continental shelf to over 700 meters in the Hudson Canyon.

SAR images can be used to identify oceanographic effects caused by wind, wave, and current interactions. Periodic waves can be seen in the image, especially in the center right portion. These are subsurface internal gravity waves, triggered by currents flowing across the edge of the continental shelf.

Conclusion

The above examples illustrate how visualization is helping NRL investigators understand experimental data obtained from complex measurements, taken in the laboratory, in the air, and at sea. The techniques—signal processing, image processing, animation, polygon-rendering, fractals, and volumetric methods—and results shown illustrate the diverse methods required for experimental data from different disciplines. The multidisciplinary examples provide a sampling of how visualization is enhancing scientific knowledge. The diversity also demonstrates the difficulty in developing generalized visualization tools for experimental data.

However, it is reasonable to expect that mergers of certain techniques will become common. In particular, volumetric methods, used primarily to display "real" objects (e.g., medical and stress analysis applications), are increasingly being used to display spaces consisting of arbitrary, but related, parameters. Thus, signal processing, image processing, and volume visualization will combine to permit effective interpretation of the structure of multidimensional spaces. The need to perform time-varying volume rendering is becoming important.

Figure 7. Synthetic aperture radar image of the Atlantic Ocean south of Long Island. The 1984 image was taken at 4:03 a.m. EST from the Challenger space shuttle at a height of 218 kilometers. The image is color-coded, with dark representing low intensity; blue, middle intensity; and white, high intensity regions of backscattered radiation. Both ocean floor features and subsurface wave interactions can be seen.

Primitive forms of computer-based visualization have been with us since the earliest computers, but the focus on visualization as a discipline is new. As computers and measurement devices become increasingly powerful, the role of visualization in the discovery process will become even more essential. New visualization techniques will be required, as will structures for their effective application. As these develop, visualization will provide even deeper insight and understanding into the real world around us.

Acknowledgments

The work discussed in this article represents the efforts of many people: physical oceanography, George Marmorino, Cliff Trump, and the author; electronic warfare, Bob Normoyle (Quest Corp.) and Tony Ricci; molecular modeling, Ronald M. Brown from data developed by I.L. Karle and others; matched-field visualization, Dick Heitmeyer and the author; and SAR radar, NRL's Digital Image Processing Laboratory. I thank all the above for their assistance in developing this article as well as Jim Lucas et al. in NRL's Technical Information Division for their assistance in producing the supplemental video.

References

1. L.J. Rosenblum, "Visualizing Oceanographic Data," *IEEE Computer Graphics and Applications,* May 1989, pp. 14-19.

2. G.O. Marmorino, L.J. Rosenblum, and C.L. Trump, "Fine-Scale Temperature Variability: The Influence of Near-Inertial Waves," *J. Geophysical Research,* Vol. 92, No. C12, Nov. 1987, pp. 13,049-13,061 and 13,215-13,219.

3. *The Science of Fractal Images,* H.O. Peitgen and D. Saupe, eds., Springer-Verlag, New York, 1988.

4. I.L. Karle et al., "Conformation of a 16-Residue Zervamicin IIA Analog Peptide Containing Three Different Structured Features: z10-helix, a-helix and b-blend ribbon," *Proc. Nat'l Academy of Science,* Vol. 84, Aug. 1987, pp. 5,087-5,091.

5. D.S. Jones and I.L. Karle, "The Crystal and Molecular Structures of Two Photodimers from N-Chloroacetyltyramine," *Acta Crystallographica,* Vol. B30, part 3, Mar. 1974, pp. 617-623.

6. A.B. Baggeroer, W.A. Kuperman, and H. Schmidt, "Matched-Field Processing: Source Localization in Correlated Noise as an Optimum Parameter Estimation Problem," *J. Acoustic Society America,* Vol. 83(2), 1988, pp. 571-587.

7. M.B. Porter, R.L. Dicus, and R.G. Fizell, "Simulation of Matched-Field Processing in a Deep-Water Pacific Environment," *IEEE J. Oceanic Engineering,* Vol. OE-12, No. 1, 1987, pp. 173-181.

8. K.A. Frenkel, "Volume Rendering," *Comm ACM,* Vol. 32, No. 4, Apr. 1989, pp. 426-435.

9. R.O. Harger, *Synthetic Aperture Radar Systems,* Academic Press, N.Y., 1970.

10. B.L. Huneycutt, "Spaceborne Imaging Radar-C Instrument," *IEEE Trans. Geoscientific and Remote Sensing,* Vol. 27, No. 2, Mar. 1989, pp. 164-169.

Section 5: Video

Introduction

Stop! Don't put this tape in your machine and start to watch it from beginning to end. It is not intended to be used this way. It is a learning tool that accompanies this book and, as such, it is to be used as you are studying the text.

Many of the ideas discussed in the papers need to have the benefit of animation so that they may be fully understood. Still photos just don't convey the right kind of information; even if you have a lot of them. Animation is one of these phenomena where the sum of the parts is greater than the whole.

The video itself does not stand alone. It was not designed to stand alone. It supplements the written material of the book. The ideas are first presented here and then supplemented by the video. This book and the video are intended to be used together. For the most part, the articles of this book are not to be read straight through from beginning to end. They are research papers and they must be studied; and the video segments can aid in this process. Portions of a paper are studied and then the corresponding portions of the video are viewed. Then back to the book for more information and then possibly a replay of some of the video and so forth.

Enjoy!

Video Contents

The following is the table of contents for the video, *Scientific Visualization*, compiled by Gregory M. Nielson. Each entry has two numbers listed with it. The first is the time through the tape where this entry can be found. This is to aid one in locating a particular entry on the video. We could have used sequence numbers but were not sure how consistent these would be from one VCR to the next. The second number is the approximate total running time of the entry.

Transcription

The following is a transcription of some of the material of the video. It includes the preface, by Bruce Shriver, the overall introduction by Gregory M. Nielson and the introductions to each of the segments.

Visualization in Engineering and Scientific Computation

Hello, my name is Bruce Shriver. It's my pleasure to introduce this videotape to you. This video tape is the companion to both the August 1989 special issue of *Computer* Magazine on Scientific Visualization and to the Computer Society Press book *Visualization in Scientific Computation*, based, in part on that special issue. The special issue of *Computer* was the result of a well-crafted, detailed, technical proposal that the IEEE Computer Society Technical Committee on Computer Graphics, then under the chairmanship of Larry Rosenblum, submitted to me as editor-in-chief of *Computer* in 1988.

Greg Nielson, who was guest editor of the special issue of *Computer* and primary editor of the book, moderates this tape. Without his technical expertise and his incredible energy, diligence and drive, none of these projects–the special issue, the book, and this tape–would have come about.

Visualization in Engineering and Scientific Computation is, as you undoubtedly suspect, concerned with the emerging set of techniques that help us "see"–that is, "visualize" or "represent"–the results of complex computations. Indeed, the very way we represent facts, data, information, concepts or ideas often limits what we can say and understand about them. If we describe a particular physical phenomena, such as the temperature distributions in an unevenly heated slab, using sentences in a natural language, we cannot necessarily prove anything about the phenomena itself because of the way in which we have described it. That is, sentences in a natural language are not terribly conducive to developing rigorous proofs about the physical phenomena. Yet, if we have a differential equation formulation that accurately models the situation, we might be able to describe things that have happened, are happening, or will happen with respect to the temperature distribution based on the analysis of the equations describing the phenomena. However–and this is indeed the key to understanding when one can proceed in this particular way–the particular mathematical representation that was selected to describe the physical situation MUST directly aid us in understanding the phenomena involved or we simply discard it as not being helpful to us at all. It is unlikely that we can model the same physical situation by difference equations, ordinary differential equations, partial differential equations, complex variables, differential-difference equations, an abstract algebra, in vector or tensor notation by Horne clauses, and on and on and expect to gain the same insight into the physics involved. The representations we choose limit the questions we can ask as well as the answers that can be given. Choosing the RIGHT representation is one of the keys to INSIGHT. Sometimes the right representation is pointed out because the road in which analysis is done is well worn by those who have trod down it before us. Other times, finding the right representation is at the very root of the intellectual activity termed "discovery." Ever since primitive electronic digital computers began to be used in the early-to-mid 1940s for ballistic missile trajectory computations, we have been performing increasingly complex engineering and scientific computations and simulations. We often program the computer to aid us in "approximating" the mathematics involved. These approximate mathematical solutions, because of their size and complexity, produce millions and millions of pieces of data as output, during a typical computer run. Engineers and scientists are faced with attempting to get information out of this extremely large amount of data–data that often deals with multi-dimensional models over time.

"Scientific visualization" embodies an emerging set of tools and techniques which aids one in finding information in large multi-dimensional data sets and then displaying it graphically–often using color, intensity, and animation. The information might have to do with when and where isometric curves or surfaces intersect, or when and where patterns begin appearing in the data, or when and where "critical" points are reached in the data. This information, when displayed graphically, often leads to insights that are buried within the reams of data, because we can interactively modify the displays to find new representations for the information–representations that help us understand the phenomena under consideration. Visualization tools and techniques allow us to explore both the local and the global nature of the data over time. The need to discover and understand the information in the large multi-dimensional data sets does not arise from approximating the mathematics employed in engineering and scientific computation alone. Huge amounts of data are also generated from satellite transmissions, from imaging systems, such as magnetic resonance medical scanners, and from large, geographically dispersed land-based sensor systems–each of which produce voluminous data. "Visualization" techniques build on the wealth of results from the two reasonably well-developed fields of computer science "computer graphics" and "image processing." As DeFanti, Brown, and McCormick state in their paper in the special issue of *Computer*, "The information conveyed to the researcher undergoes a qualitative change because it brings the eye-brain system, with its great pattern-recognition capabilities, into play in a way that is impossible with purely numeric data."

I certainly hope that you enjoy this videotape which is a companion to the special issue and the Computer Society Press book and that it proves useful in engaging your eye-brain system into understanding the material in both. Thank you.

00:11:03   INTRODUCTION, by Gregory M. Nielson

Hello and welcome to our video on Scientific Visualization. Over a year ago we began our work on the August 1989 issue of *Computer*. This special issue of *Computer* is devoted to the topic of Visualization in Scientific Computing. Since we were interested in extremely high-quality papers, we went through a rather rigorous refereeing process involving as many as a dozen referees in some cases. During this process of refereeing the manuscripts, it became clear that the science contained in these papers could be enhanced tremendously by some type of visual demonstration. It was at this time that Bruce Shriver suggested the idea of a companion video.

In order to get material for our video, we went back to each of the authors and asked them to provide a segment of approximately five minutes. What we have compiled here is what we received. As a consequence of the varying resources available to each of the scientists, the physical quality of the segments varies considerably; but I don't believe this detracts much from our main goals which are learning and understanding, rather that realism or art. Also, we do not have an exact one-to-one match. For some of the papers, a video would not have been appropriate or would not have added a great deal.

These video segments are truly companions to their papers. They do not stand alone and they are not intended to stand alone. They assume a context established by the material in the paper and so one needs to have read the paper prior to viewing a particular segment. In addition to having a copy of the paper around when you are viewing the video, you might also find it handy to have access to the reverse, pause, and fast forward controls of the VCR you are using. This will allow you to re-read portions of the paper and to replay the corresponding video segments Also, I suggest that you read the overview paper by DeFanti, Brown, and McCormick before viewing any of the segments.

The organization of this video tape is pretty much the same as the book, taking into consideration that some papers do not have companion videos. At the beginning of each segment, I give a short discussion about the video and how it relates to the paper, and in some cases, point out particularly interesting aspects. I hope you enjoy viewing these video segments and better yet I hope they help you to learn and understand more about Scientific Visualization.

00:13:20   Representation and display of vector field topology in fluid
            flow data sets
                by James Helman and Lambertus Hesselink

James Helman and Lambertus Hesselink of Stanford University describe techniques for automatically analyzing and extracting information from fluid flow data sets. Rather than try to simply display the data the idea is to extract certain topological information and to display this. As the authors point out, a jillion little arrows displayed in a cube would not reveal much about a three dimensional flow. But detecting vortices and other interesting places and displaying these in an integrated manner is potentially very useful. This general idea is very important in Scientific Visualization. By this I mean the idea of having some algorithm find interesting things in the data and then concentrating the viewer's attention and the display efforts on these interesting aspects. Helman and Hesselink determine critical points, which are points at which the magnitude of the tangent vector is zero, and then classify them according to the eigenvalues of the Jacobian. These points are attractors, deflectors, saddle points, or what have you. The complete list is in Figure 5. These critical points are then joined by tangent curves which are instantaneous streamlines. Figure 7 shows an example, but this particular one is unstable and an instant latter will look like that of Figure 8. Flows evolve through time and so therefore their graphical representations will also. Animating something like Figure 8 can reveal a lot of information about a flow, but Helman and Hesselink do something a little different. Since they are studying two dimensional flows, they can use the third dimension for time and so tangent curves become surfaces as can be seen in Figure 10. This gives the added advantage that the history and future of streamlines are visible all in one image. Later in the video, you will see these surfaces animated. A challenging research problem is to extend the techniques presented here to three-dimensional flows.

00:21:38   Visualization idioms: A conceptual model for scientific visualization systems
by Robert B. Haber and David A. McNabb

Hello, I'm Bob Haber at the National Center for Supercomputing Applications. The term "visualization idiom" refers to the overall process of transforming scientific information into displayable images. The following segment illustrates the application of that concept to the problem of understanding the physics of dynamic fracture mechanics. This is a very complicated problem and therefore it is necessary to use multiple visualization idioms to fully understand the behavior. In addition, it is useful to have interactive control; that is, to be able to tune those idioms, in real time. To gain the compute performance we need for that interactivity, we are going to be using an Alliant VFX 80 mini supercomputer. This machine has a shared memory architecture with eight vector processors. In addition, we have a parallel graphics engine for doing rendering at very high rates. We'll be using the space ball for three-dimensional view control and menu with sliders and buttons controlled through the mouse for other interactive input. Let's now take a look at what this visualization system looks like.

00:28:57   Projection pursuit techniques for the visualization of high dimensional data sets
by Stuart L. Crawford and Thomas C. Fall

Our next segment is by Stuart Crawford and Thomas Fall of Advanced Decision Systems of Mountain View, California. The title of their paper is "Projection pursuit techniques for the visualization of high-dimensional data sets." The emphasis here is on multidimensional data sets. The paper surveys the relatively new topic of projection pursuit as a tool for exploratory data analysis and because of the nature of this topic, the paper is somewhat technical, but the video is not. In a nutshell, they are interested in detecting patterns in multidimensional data sets. The human mind does the detecting and the graphics workstation through the use of the techniques of this paper tries to present the data in a form conducive to this. Since the user is busy trying to find interesting things in the data, it is important that he not be distracted by having to think a lot about running the controls of the program. Therefore it is important to have an interface that is easy for the user to use and the authors have tried to accomplish this.

00:35:59   Computation and manipulation of 3D surfaces from image sequences
by H. Harlyn Baker

This next video segment is from Harlyn Baker of SRI and supplements his paper "Computation and manipulation of 3D surfaces from image sequences." The main goal of this research is to develop techniques that will capture 3D structure from sequences of 2D images. As with the paper, the video is divided into two parts. The first dealing with the case where the sequence of images are obtained from a camera moving around in a fixed scene and the second concerned with sequences which are slices of 3D medical data. While Baker's terminology is a little different, the problem addressed here is the same as the surface based methods of Fuchs, Levoy, and Pizer in that contour surfaces for 3D volumetric data is being computed. Not only are the contour surfaces computed, but they are also modeled in the sense that the interconnection topology between the surface facets is determined. This is extremely important for any application beyond just viewing the surfaces. Several examples which rely on this type of model surface are illustrated in the video. The sequence showing the potential for simulated surgery is particularly interesting. Baker's approach to surface modeling is based on a process he calls the "weaving wall" which takes contours on 2D images and assembles them into a 3D surface. Similar to the paper, the video is a survey of the techniques and their applications. For more details and to learn exactly how the "weaving wall" works, one should consult Baker's recent paper in Computer Vision.

00:46:29   Acquisition and representation of two- and three-dimension data from turbulent flows and flames
by Marshall B. Long, Kevin Lyons, and Joseph K. Lam

This next segment comes from Marshall Long, Kevin Lyon, and Joseph Lam of the Department of Mechanical Engineering and the Center for Laser Diagnostics at Yale University. The title of their paper is "Acquisition and representation of two- and three-dimension data from turbulent flows and flames." As the title indicates, there are two parts to the paper and also the video: the data acquisition and the data display. I think it helps quite a bit to know how the data is acquired Even though this is briefly discussed in the video, it is much easier to understand how this is done from the description given in the paper and so one should probably review this prior to taking a look at the video. The second portion of the video is devoted to the techniques used to display the data. Two-dimensional data sets obtained on a slice through the flow can be displayed by an image where intensity or color is varying with the quantity that has been measured. With this type of image, it is usually quite easy for the eye to detect contours. Contours for volumetric data are surfaces rather than planar curves and are therefore much more difficult to detect. Usually these surfaces are precomputed and then displayed. We have in this video segment, in addition to some still shots of the figures of the paper, four animation sequences of which one should take note. A constant fuel concentration surface, like that of Figure 7 is viewed by rotating it about in space. A second animation sequence shows some precomputed contour surfaces being scanned. This is probably a good way to view this type of volumetric data, especially if the user can interactively vary the contour constant, but it does takes considerable computation power to compute these contour surfaces. A third animation sequence shows the temporal evolution of a image like that of Figure 2 of the paper. And a final animation sequence illustrates the temporal evolution of a particular fuel concentration surface.

00:53:28   Interactive visualization of 3D medical data
          by Henry Fuchs, Marc Levoy, and Stephen M. Pizer

The next segment relates to the paper by Henry Fuchs, Marc Levoy, and Stephen Pizer from the University of North Carolina. The paper surveys their research activities in the area of interactive visualization of 3D medical data and the video pretty much parallels the paper. In conjunction with other researchers from radiology and biochemistry, they are working on two approaches to rendering 3D volumetric data. The first is what is called surface-based techniques and requires the polygonal approximation to a constant contour surface. As we see in the video, their approach is based upon first getting the curve contours for each slice and then assembling this into a triangulated surface. Once the contour surface is known present workstations will have no problem with the interactive display of the surface. One drawback to the particular approach shown in the video is that user assistance is required for getting the contours and providing bifurcation information during the 3D assembly stage. Other methods, such as the marching cubes technique, work in a somewhat different fashion.

The second area of 3D visualization that is being attacked by this group is volume visualization. Here the idea is to take the entire cubical array of voxel data and produce a single 2D image. This approach to visualizing 3D medical data was pioneered at PIXAR a few years back. Most techniques are based upon some type of assignment of opacity to each voxel and then casting rays from the view point through the cube of data and integrating along the rays. While this type of visualization of 3D medical data shows great promise, there are still several drawbacks: It is compute intensive and this severely limits interaction and interaction is pretty much mandatory for clinical use. The first method shown in the video is that of Lee Westover and produces about one image per second on a fairly low resolution image. The next section of the video is a prepared loop, (i.e., a cine loop of the Levoy algorithm) which they say takes about a minute per image.

00:59:36   Visualizing large meteorological data sets
by William Hibbard and David Santek

This next segment is associated with the paper "Visualization of Large Data Sets in the Earth Sciences" by Bill Hibbard and David Santek of the University of Wisconsin at Madison. They describe the functionality of their McIDAS system. This is an acronym for Man Computer Interactive Data Access System. As with several of the application papers, here we have three-dimensional data over a cubical grid. What is different here is that at each 3D position, there are both scalar values and vector values. For example, a meteorologist may want to display both temperature and wind vector fields in order to learn something about their interplay. Through a very judicious choice of photographs in the paper, we can see the variety of techniques they have used to display this type of three-dimensional data. Two techniques are used for displaying scalar values: contour surfaces and transparent opacity clouds. A contour surface is simply the collection of points in three space when the scalar function is constant; i.e., for example, all the locations where the temperature is say 75 degrees. This surface is then rendered in traditional computer graphics style as an opaque object with light shinning on it. A transparent opacity cloud can be used to display clouds or other density fields. The way these guys show 3D vector fields is to display little arrows of one type or another. Of course, the number of these arrows has to be rather small or the picture is a real mess. At the time the paper was written, the authors were in the process of porting their software to a Stellar. The goal here is to get animation and interaction.

01:05:54   The role of visualization in the simulation of quantum
           electronic transport in semiconductors
                 by N. C. Kluksdahl, A. M. Kriman, and D. K. Ferry

At Arizona State University, researchers Norman Kluksdahl, Alfred Kriman, and David Ferry are using visualization and animation of simulation data to augment their understanding of the behavior of Quantum Electron Transport in Semiconductors. Although the paper is quite technical, the visualization processes employed give a very graphic portrayal of the electron tunneling behavior on the quantum mechanical model and, therefore, of the underlying real semiconductor device. In a sense, some preprocessing of the simulation data occurs by employing the so-called Wigner function. This formulation reduces the multidimensional phase space solution of these systems to one that involves the axes of position, momentum, and probability amplitudes of the electron Gaussian wave packets. These three axes are readily graphed using colored contours with hidden surface elimination. By animating a series of images in the time sequenced simulation the authors maintain that the real semiconductor device characteristics, such as the observed collective oscillations in the resonant tunneling diode, can be better understood.

01:11:23   Graphical analysis of multi/micro-tasking on Cray
           multiprocessor
                 by Mark K. Seager, Nancy E. Werner, Mary E. Zosel and
                 Robert E. Strout, II

This next segment comes form Mark Seager, Nancy Werner, and Mary Zosel of Lawrence Livermore National Laboratory, and Robert Strout of Supercomputer Systems. The paper is titled "Graphical Analysis of Multi/Micro Tasking on Cray Multiprocessors." Their application is somewhat different than those of the other application papers. The goal is to provide visual information to a programmer so as to aid in the design and debugging of parallel programs. The video is a demonstration of GMAT which stands for Graphical Multiprocessing Analysis Tool. That portion of GMAT which they call "timeline" is demonstrated. Another portion called "stategroup" is discussed in the paper but not covered in the video.

01:18:22   Visualizing wave phenomena with seismic rays
            by V. Pereyra and J. A. Rial

     This segment is from Victor Pereyra and J. A. Rial and is a demonstration of some of their techniques covered in their paper "Visualizing Wave Phenomena with Seismic Rays." They are using conventional techniques from graphics to show the results of tracking the path of a wave that is generated at the surface and travels down through several layers and is eventually reflected back to the surface. The wavy surfaces in the video represent the boundaries between the layers and are modeled with parametric Coons patches. This is an improvement over previous methods in that folds and other quite natural formations can be modeled.

01:21:44   A holistic method for visualizing computer performance
            measurements
            by Neale Hirsch and Bruce L. Brown

     The next video segment is from Neale Hirsch of Cray Research and Bruce Brown of BYU. One thing this video illustrates is that graphics do not have to be super fancy or spectacular in order to be useful. The clever use of graphics and geometry can reveal interesting and useful insights into multifaceted phenomena as it does for Hirsch and Brown in their analysis of computer performance measurements. While the particular experiment they discuss is quite interesting, it is not the most important message for those interested in Scientific Visualization. The way they analyzed their results of their experiment using Principle Component multigrafs is what is of interest. The most interesting scientific visualization portion of the video is at the end where one sees the multigrafs of Brown being manipulated until something quite interesting is discerned.

01:27:13   Distributed visualization at Los Alamos National Laboratory
            by Richard L. Phillips

     This next video segment was provided by Dick Phillips. His paper, "Distributed Visualization at Los Alamos National Laboratory" gives a good overview of what is going on in the hardware area at Los Alamos. Their problem is to take the results of numerical simulations or the analysis of experimental data from the supercomputer and get these results to the scientist's workstation in a usable form. How to divide the duties between the workstation and the supercomputer is a challenging problem. While several approaches are covered in the paper, including Fowler and McGowen's frame buffer for the Cray, the video concentrates on the functionality of Phillip's Scientific Visualization Workbench. This collection of software and hardware, which is schematically shown in Figure 6, allows a scientist to sit at his workstation and simultaneously have windows open to a variety of sources of graphical information; including, for example, a video signal from a camera that is monitoring some experiment, a video signal from a frame buffer on the Cray, or a window open showing standard graphics generated at the workstation.

01:31:27   Visualization Tools at Lawrence Livermore National
            Laboratory
                by Brian Cabral and Carol Hunter

This next segment comes from Brian Cabral and Carol Hunter of Lawrence Livermore National Laboratory. Their paper is an overview of two projects aimed at providing visualization tools for the scientists at the laboratory: the Graphics Workstation Project and the Advanced Visualization Research Project.

01:38:46   Scientific visualization and the Rivers project at the National
            Center for Supercomputing Applications
                by Robert B. Haber

Hello, I am Bob Haber at the University of Illinois' National Center for Supercomputing Applications. The NCSA is one of five National Science Foundation sponsored centers providing supercomputer cycles to close to 3000 users across the nation. This group of scientists and engineers are involved in diverse research, but they share a common need to visualize the results of their supercomputing calculations. To meet this need, the NCSA offers a diversity of visualization services. The following sequences will illustrate three modes of visualization that we support.

The first is high-quality software-rendered visualization backed by a team of visualization experts that work with the scientists. The second mode involves interactive desktop visualization tools designed to be used directly by the scientists in their own office. The third approach is real-time 3D interactive visualization under development in the NCSA Rivers project. The scientific media services group at NCSA provides slide and video production services in support of all these activities. In addition, the renaissance experimental lab is a facility with visualization facilities that supports teaching and research at the University. Bob Wilhelmson, a research scientist in atmospheric sciences at NCSA, will use his data to illustrate the three modes of visualization. The first is the high-end software rendered approach where Bob worked with the scientific visualization staff at NCSA.

<Study of a Numerically Modeled Severe Storm>

The next segment illustrates the use of interactive desktop visualization tools developed by NCSA Software Development Group. These are designed to run on common hardware platforms, such as the Apple Macintosh and Sun workstations. These tools have been distributed free of charge to thousands of scientists across the country.

<Storm Visualization II: Interactive desktop tools>

The last segment will illustrate the use of real-time 3D interactive visualization techniques. Bob Wilhelmson will be using an Alliant VFX 80 and software developed in the NCSA Rivers project to probe in a variety of ways the 3D data set generated by his thunderstorm simulation.

<Storm Visualization III: Interactive 3D Visualization>

01:49:21   Scientific visualization in computational aerodynamics at NASA Ames Research Center
                    by Gordon Bancroft, Todd Plessel, Fergus Merritt, Pamela P. Walatka, and Val Watson

This next video was provided by Gordon Bancroft and his colleagues at NASA Ames Research Center. Their paper on Scientific Visualization in Computational Aerodynamics discusses current and future workstation requirements in this area. Also discussed are five software packages which have been developed at NASA Ames. Particularly noteworthy is RIP or Real-Time Interactive Particle tracer. It is an example of a distributed graphics tool communicating at the instance of interaction over a high-speed network as opposed to most other systems which precompute and postprocess for display.

01:53:25   Visualization of experimental data at the Naval Research Laboratory
                by Larry Rosenblum

This next segment comes from Larry Rosenblum. As with the paper, the video is a sampling of scientific visualization activities at the Naval Research Laboratory. The video has four examples. The first segment on matched-field acoustics is interesting in that it shows the usefulness of being able to interactively scan through slices of 3D data. Max's, min's, and other characteristics are easily detected with this technique which is really quite easy to implement. The third segment on the numerical simulation of salt fingers is important in that it illustrates the usefulness of some rather straight-forward scientific visualization techniques Interesting aspects of this mixing process can be detected which ultimately leads to a better understanding of the entire physical phenomenon.

02:00:00   Acknowledgments
Thanks to the

Technical Committee
on
Computer Graphics
of the
IEEE Computer Society

for sponsoring this project. The members of the Executive Committee are:

Maxine Brown
Micheal Danchak
Tom Foley
Arie Kaufman
Gary Laguna
Steve Levine
Greg Nielson
Arthur Olson
Larry Rosenblum
John Sibert
and
Mark Skall

The introduction to each of the segments was
Directed
by
Ken Sweat

and

Produced
by
Wayne Woodland

Thanks to

Chris Allain
VIDOX Productions
for producing the preface segment.

Thanks to all the staff of the Computer Society Press, especially

Michael Haggerty and Wally Hutchins
who edited this video.

Thanks to the workstation vendors:
Ardent Computing
and
Silicon Graphics

Thanks to:

College of Engineering and Applied Sciences, ASU
Clovis R. Haden, Dean
Engineering Computing Services, ASU
William E. Lewis, Director
Engineering Lab. Services, ASU
George Moeller, Director

The programs running on the workstations in the background during the introductions to the segments represent research in progress at ASU. Thanks to the CAGD and graphics students:

David Lane
Brett Blomquist
Bernd Hamann
for the use of their work.

Thanks to all the members of the
CAGD Group, ASU
for their cooperation and support;

Joe Reuter
was particularly helpful.

Special thanks to

Tom Foley

for help and support on a myriad of tasks.

Special thanks to

Keith Voegele

for a tremendous amount of help and good ideas.

Special thanks to

Bruce Shriver

for the idea of this video and his many good suggestions
that have gone into it.

Special thanks to

Eugene Falken

for seeing the potential of this project and his
encouragement to carry it through.

Index

About the Authors

Gregory M. Nielson is a professor of computer science and adjunct professor of mathematics at Arizona State University, where he teaches and does research in computer graphics, computer-aided geometric design, and scientific visualization. He has lectured and published widely on the topics of curve and surface representation and design, interactive computer graphics, scattered data interpolation, and the analysis and visualization of multivariate data. He has collaborated with several institutions, including NASA, Xerox, and General Motors. He is a participatory guest scientist at Lawrence Livermore National Laboratory.

Professor Nielson is on the editorial board of *ACM Transactions on Graphics,* the *Rocky Mountain Journal of Mathematics, Computer-Aided Geometric Design, Visualization, and Computer Animation Journal,* and *IEEE Computer Graphics and Applications* magazine. He is one of the founders and a member of the steering committee of the IEEE-sponsored conference series on *Visualization,* and currently chairs the IEEE Computer Society Technical Committee on Computer Graphics. He is also a member of ACM and SIAM.

Professor Nielson received his PhD from the University of Utah in 1970.

Bruce D. Shriver is currently the Vice-President for Research at the University of Southwestern Louisiana and a professor in the Center for Advanced Computer Studies. Prior to coming to USL in July 1989, he was Director of the Pacific Research Institute of Information Systems and Management (PRIISM) and the Henry Walker Distinguished Professor chairholder at the University of Hawaii. Before that, he was a research staff member at IBM's Thomas J. Watson Research Center in Yorktown Heights, New York, where he was also Department Group Manager of Software Technology. From 1973 to 1984, Dr. Shriver was at USL, where he was the Alfred Lamson Research Professor in Computer Science.

Dr. Shriver has published over 70 technical papers and reports, chaired 18 dissertation committees, and has been General Chairman or Program Chairman of over 25 conferences. He has lectured extensively in the United States and abroad, was the founding Editor-in-Chief of *IEEE Software,* has served three terms as a member of the Board of Governors of the IEEE Computer Society, was Chairman of the IEEE Technical Committee on Computational Medicine, and Vice-Chairman of ACM's Special Interest Group on Microprogramming. He is currently the Chairman of the International Federation of Information Processing (IFIP) Working Group 10.1 on Architectural Systems Concepts and Characteristics and the Editor-in-Chief of *Computer.* He received his PhD in computer science from the State University of New York at Buffalo in 1971. He is a member of the ACM and a Fellow of the IEEE.

 **IEEE Computer Society**

IEEE Computer Society Press Publications

Monographs: A monograph is an authored book consisting of 100-percent original material.

Tutorials: A tutorial is a collection of original materials prepared by the editors, and reprints of the best articles published in a subject area. Tutorials must contain at least five percent of original material (although we recommend 15 to 20 percent of original material).

Reprint collections: A reprint collection contains reprints (divided into sections) with a preface, table of contents, and section introductions discussing the reprints and why they were selected. Collections contain less than five percent of original material.

Technology series: Each technology series is a brief reprint collection — approximately 126-136 pages and containing 12 to 13 papers, each paper focusing on a subset of a specific discipline, such as networks, architecture, software, or robotics.

Submission of proposals: For guidelines on preparing CS Press books, write the Editorial Director, IEEE Computer Society Press, PO Box 3014, 10662 Los Vaqueros Circle, Los Alamitos, CA 90720-1264, or telephone (714) 821-8380.

Purpose

The IEEE Computer Society advances the theory and practice of computer science and engineering, promotes the exchange of technical information among 100,000 members worldwide, and provides a wide range of services to members and nonmembers.

Membership

All members receive the acclaimed monthly magazine *Computer*, discounts, and opportunities to serve (all activities are led by volunteer members). Membership is open to all IEEE members, affiliate society members, and others seriously interested in the computer field.

Publications and Activities

Computer **magazine:** An authoritative, easy-to-read magazine containing tutorials and in-depth articles on topics across the computer field, plus news, conference reports, book reviews, calendars, calls for papers, interviews, and new products.

Periodicals: The society publishes six magazines and five research transactions. For more details, refer to our membership application or request information as noted above.

Conference proceedings, tutorial texts, and standards documents: The IEEE Computer Society Press publishes more than 100 titles every year.

Standards working groups: Over 100 of these groups produce IEEE standards used throughout the industrial world.

Technical committees: Over 30 TCs publish newsletters, provide interaction with peers in specialty areas, and directly influence standards, conferences, and education.

Conferences/Education: The society holds about 100 conferences each year and sponsors many educational activities, including computing science accreditation.

Chapters: Regular and student chapters worldwide provide the opportunity to interact with colleagues, hear technical experts, and serve the local professional community.

IEEE Computer Society Press

Other IEEE Computer Society Press Titles

MONOGRAPHS

Analyzing Computer Architectures
Written by Jerome C. Huck and Michael J. Flynn
(ISBN 0-8186-8857-2); 206 pages

Branch Strategy Taxonomy and Performance Models
Written by Harvey G. Cragon
(ISBN 0-8186-9111-5); 150 pages

Desktop Publishing for the Writer:
Designing, Writing, and Developing
Written by Richard Ziegfeld and John Tarp
(ISBN 0-8186-8840-8); 380 pages

Digital Image Warping
Written by George Wolberg
(ISBN 0-8186-8944-7); 340 pages

Integrating Design and Test —
CAE Tools for ATE Programming
Written by Kenneth P. Parker
(ISBN 0-8186-8788-6); 160 pages

JSP and JSD —
The Jackson Approach to Software Development
(Second Edition)
Written by John R. Cameron
(ISBN 0-8186-8858-0); 560 pages

National Computer Policies
Written by Ben G. Matley and Thomas A. McDannold
(ISBN 0-8186-8784-3); 192 pages

Physical Level Interfaces and Protocols
Written by Uyless Black
(ISBN 0-8186-8824-2); 240 pages

Protecting Your Proprietary Rights in Computer
and High-Technology Industries
Written by Tobey B. Marzouk, Esq.
(ISBN 0-8186-8754-1); 224 pages

X.25 and Related Protocols
Written by Uyless Black
(ISBN 0-8186-8976-5); 304 pages

TUTORIALS

Advanced Computer Architecture
Edited by Dharma P. Agrawal
(ISBN 0-8186-0667-3); 400 pages

Advances in Distributed System Reliability
Edited by Suresh Rai and Dharma P. Agrawal
(ISBN 0-8186-8907-2); 352 pages

Autonomous Mobile Robots:
Perception, Mapping and Navigation — Volume 1
Edited by S. S. Iyengar and A. Elfes
(ISBN 0-8186-9018-6); 425 pages

Autonomous Mobile Robots:
Control, Planning, and Architecture — Volume 2
Edited by S. S. Iyengar and A. Elfes
(ISBN 0-8186-9116-6); 425 pages

Broadband Switching:
Architectures, Protocols, Design, and Analysis
Edited by C. Dhas, V. K. Konangi, and M. Sreetharan
(ISBN 0-8186-8926-9); 528 pages

Computer and Network Security
Edited by M. D. Abrams and H. J. Podell
(ISBN 0-8186-0756-4); 448 pages

Computer Architecture
Edited by D. D. Gajski, V. M. Milutinovic, H. J. Siegel, and B. P. Furht
(ISBN 0-8186-0704-1); 602 pages

Computer Arithmetic I
Edited by Earl E. Swartzlander, Jr.
(ISBN 0-8186-8931-5); 398 pages

Computer Arithmetic II
Edited by Earl E. Swartzlander, Jr.
(ISBN 0-8186-8945-5); 412 pages

Computer Communications:
Architectures, Protocols, and Standards (Second Edition)
Edited by William Stallings
(ISBN 0-8186-0790-4); 448 pages

Computer Graphics Hardware: Image Generation and Display
Edited by H. K. Reghbati and A. Y. C. Lee
(ISBN 0-8186-0753-X); 384 pages

Computer Graphics: Image Synthesis
Edited by Kenneth Joy, Nelson Max, Charles Grant,
and Lansing Hatfield
(ISBN 0-8186-8854-8); 380 pages

Computer Vision: Principles
Edited by Rangachar Kasturi and Ramesh Jain
(ISBN 0-8186-9102-6); 700 pages

Computer Vision: Advances and Applications
Edited by Rangachar Kasturi and Ramesh Jain
(ISBN 0-8186-9103-4); 720 pages

Digital Image Processing (Second Edition)
Edited by Rama Chellappa
(ISBN 0-8186-2362-4); 400 pages

Digital Private Branch Exchanges (PBXs)
Edited by Edwin Coover
(ISBN 0-8186-0829-3); 394 pages

Distributed Computing Network Reliability
Edited by Suresh Rai and Dharma P. Agrawal
(ISBN 0-8186-8908-0); 357 pages

Distributed–Software Engineering
Edited by Sol Shatz and Jia-Ping Wang
(ISBN 0-8186-8856-4); 294 pages

Domain Analysis and Software Systems Modeling
Edited by Ruben-Prieto Diaz and Guillermo Arango
(ISBN 0-8186-8996-X); 312 pages

DSP–Based Testing of Analog and
Mixed Signal Circuits
Edited by Matthew Mahoney
(ISBN 0-8186-0785-8); 272 pages

Fault Tolerant Computing
Edited by V. Nelson and B. Carroll
(ISBN 0-8186-8677-4); 428 pages

Formal Verification of Hardware Design
Edited by Michael Yoeli
(ISBN 0-8186-9017-8); 340 pages

Hard Real-Time Systems
Edited by J. A. Stankovic and K. Ramamritham
(ISBN 0-8186-0819-6); 624 pages

Integrated Services Digital Networks (ISDN)
(Second Edition)
Edited by William Stallings
(ISBN 0-8186-0823-4); 406 pages

For further information call 1-800-CS-BOOKS or write:

IEEE Computer Society Press, 10662 Los Vaqueros Circle, PO Box 3014,
Los Alamitos, California 90720-1264, USA

IEEE Computer Society, 13, avenue de l'Aquilon,
B-1200 Brussels, BELGIUM

IEEE Computer Society, Ooshima Building, 2-19-1 Minami-Aoyama,
Minato-ku, Tokyo 107, JAPAN